英美社会文化概论

Introduction to Society and Culture of Britain and America

主　编　峻　岭
编　者　雪　兰　霄　荣

安徽大学出版社

图书在版编目(CIP)数据

英美社会文化概论/峻岭主编. —2 版. —合肥:安徽大学出版社,
2005.6 (2008.3 重印)
ISBN 978-7-81052-160-4

Ⅰ.英… Ⅱ.峻… Ⅲ.①英语-高等教育-自学考试-自学
参考资料②文化-英国-高等教育-自学考试-自学参考资料
③文化-美国-高等教学-自学考试-自学参考资料
Ⅳ.H319.4:G

中国版本图书馆 CIP 数据核字(2005)第 052338 号

本书已经安徽省高等教育自学考试委员会办公室组织审定，作为全省自学考试统一教材使用。

英美社会文化概论　　　峻　岭　主编

出版发行	安徽大学出版社 (合肥市肥西路 3 号 邮编 230039)	印　刷	中国科学技术大学印刷厂
联系电话	编辑室 0551-5108498 发行部 0551-5107716	开　本	787×1092 1/16
		印　张	21.5
		字　数	550 千
责任编辑	李　梅	版　次	2005 年 6 月第 2 版
封面设计	孟献辉	印　次	2008 年 3 月第 4 次印刷
经　销	新华书店		

ISBN 978-7-81052-160-4　　　定价　32.00 元

前　言

本书是为高等教育自学考试师范本科英语专业选编的教材。

全书分四个部分。第一部分介绍英国社会与文化;第二部分介绍美国社会与文化;第三部分为语言文化选读,覆盖几个主要话题,帮助读者从语言和文化的关系来分析英美社会文化在语言交际和语言学习中的作用;第四部分为各章练习的参考答案(客观题部分)。

为了方便读者,第一、二部分各章配有词汇表、注释和练习题。

本书以扩展知识面为宗旨,建议读者通读各章节内容,把握重点,形成自己的见解,而不是追求语言形式。

编者水平有限,成书较仓促,不足之处,恳请读者指正。

编　者

2005 年 5 月

Contents

Part I The United Kingdom of Great Britain and Northern Ireland

Part II The United States of America

Part Ⅲ Language and Culture

Part IV Key to the Exercises

Part Ⅰ

The United Kingdom of Great Britain and Northern Ireland

Chapter 1 The Land and People

England and English

England is a highly urbanized country, with 80% of its population living in cities, and only 2% of the population working in agriculture. It's largest city is the capital, London, which is dominant in the UK in all fields: government, finance, and culture. England is physically the largest of the four nations, and it has by far the largest population. This dominance in size is reflected in a cultural and economic dominance too, which has the result that people in foreign countries sometimes make the mistake of talking about England when they mean the UK significantly, people in England sometimes make that mistake too, but people in the other three nations would not: they might call themselves British (as might the English) or they might call themselves Scottish or Welsh or Irish, but they certainly wouldn't call themselves (or like to be called) English. So oddly, of the four nations, the English feel most British, and therefore have the weakest sense of themselves as a separate "English" culture within Britain.

British history has been a history of invasions. Before the first century A. D. Britain was made up of many tribal kingdoms of Celtic people: a powerful culture or iginating in central Europe. Then in 43AD Britain was invaded by the Roman empire[1], and England and Wales (though not Scotland or Ireland) became a part of the Roman empire for nearly 400 years. As the Roman empire came under threat from the east, the Roman armies and Roman protection were withdrawn from Britain, and Britain was again divided into small kingdoms, and again it came under threat from outside this time from Germanic peoples: the Angles, and the Saxons.

One of the best-known English legends derives from this time. In the fifth century AD it is said that a great leader appeared, united the British, and with his magical sword, Excalibur, drove the Saxons back. This is the story of King Arthur-2, and has been embellished by singers, poets, novelists and even filmmakers ever since.

Although King Arthur's existence is in doubt, you can visit places associated with his legend, such as the cliff-edge castle at Tintagel in Cornwall. According to legend Arthur gathered a company of knights to him, who sat together at Arthur's castle at Camelot (possibly the real hilltop fort at Cadbury Hill in Somerset). Conflict between his knights led to Arthur creating the famous "round table" at which all would have equal precedence[3]. Perhaps this could be seen as an indicator of the way in which the English have wished to see their monarch as something other than a remote dictator, and have in fact managed to gradually bind the monarchy into a more democratic system, rather than completely rejecting it[4].

Whatever Arthur's success, legend or not, it did not last, for the Anglo-Saxons did succeed in invading Britain, and either absorbed the Celtic people, or pushed them to the western and northern edges of Britain. Despite the fact that contemporary English people think of King Arthur as their hero, really he was fighting against them, for these Anglo-Saxon invaders were the forefathers of the English, the founders of "Angle-land" or "England" as it has become known.

Two more groups of invaders were to come after the English: from the late 8th century on, raiders from Scandinavia, the ferocious Vikings[5], threatened Britain's shores. Their settlements in England grew until large areas of northern and eastern England were under their control. By then the English heroes were truly English (Anglo-Saxon), such as King Alfred the Great[6], who turned the tide in the south against the Vikings. There remains to this day a certain cultural divide between northerners and southerners in England, which, while not consciously "Saxon" versus "Dane", may have its origins in this time[7]. The richer southerners tend to think of northerners as less sophisticated than themselves, while northerners think southerners arrogant and unfriendly. They are also marked by having distinctly different accents.

The next invaders were the Normans, from northern France, who were descendants of Vikings. Under William of Normandy (known as "William the Conqueror"[8]) they crossed the English Channel in 1066, and in the Battle of Hastings, defeated an English army under King Harold[9]. This marks the last time that an army from outside the British Isles succeeded in invading. William took the English throne, and became William the First of England. The Tower of London[10], a castle in thc centre of London which he built, still stands today.

The Normans did not settle England to any great extent: rather they imported a ruling class. The next three hundred years may be thought of as a Norman (and French-speaking) aristocracy ruling a largely Saxon and English-speaking population. It is this situation which produced another of England's heroic legends. This is the legend of Robin Hood[11], a Saxon nobleman oppressed by the Normans, who became an outlaw, and with his band of "merry men" hid in the forest of Sherwood in the north midlands of England. From this secret place, armed with their longbows, they then went out to rob from the rich to give to the poor. This early English socialist[12] (!) has featured in many television series and films, both British and American. Some writers have seen in the popularity of this legend of a rebellion hidden in the green wood a clue to the English character: a richly unconventional interior life hidden by an external conformity[13]. But, like all stereotypes, this one has its weaknesses, as many English people, especially young people, like to display their unconventionality externally—for example English punk rockers with their vividly dyed spiky hair[14]. But it is certainly true that the lifeless fronts of many English houses conceal beautiful back gardens. Gardening is one of the most popular pastimes in England, and the back garden provides a place where people's outdoor life at home can go on out of the public gaze. This may contrast with people from other countries whose outdoor life might be more social—sitting on the front porch watching passers-by.

The next few hundred years following the Norman invasion can be seen as a process of joining together the various parts of the British Isles under English rule, so that and English identity eventually became swamped by the necessity of adopting a wider British identity, both to unite the kingdom internally, and to present a single identity externally as Britain became an imperial power. At the same time power was gradually transferred from the monarch to the parliament. Charles the First's attempt to overrule parliament in the 1640s led to a civil war in which parliamentary forces were victorious, and the king was executed. After a gap of eleven years in which England was ruled by parliament's leader, Oliver Cromwell[15], the monarchy was restored. Further conflict between parliament and the king led to the removal of the Scottish house of Stuart[16] from the throne, and William and Mary[17] were imported from Holland to take the throne, thus finally establishing parliament's dominance over the throne.

Scotland and Scots

Scotland is the second largest of the four nations, both in population and in geographical area. It is also the most confident of its own identity because alone amongst the non-English components of the UK it has previously spent a substantial period of history as a unified state independent of the UK. Thus it is not a big leap for the Scottish to imagine themselves independent again.

Physically, Scotland is the most rugged part of the UK, with areas of sparsely populated mountains and lakes in the north (The Highlands), and in the south (The Southern Uplands). Three-quarters of the population lives in the lowland zone which spans the country between these two highland areas. The largest city is Glasgow, in the west of this zone. Scotland's capital city is Edinburgh, on the east coast forty miles away from Glasgow. It is renowned for its beauty, and dominated by its great castle on a high rock in the centre of the city. Both cities have ancient and internationally respected universities dating from the 15th century.

Scotland was not conquered by the Romans, though they did try to, and for a while occupied as far as the edge of the northern highland zone. But the difficulty of maintaining their rule there caused them to retreat to a line roughly equivalent to the contemporary boundary between England and Scotland. Along this line, from sea to sea, they, like the Chinese, built a wall to mark the northern edge of their domain, and to help defend it. It is called "Hadrian's Wall"[18] after the Emperor of Rome at the time of its building, and although ruined, lengths of it can still be seen and walked along.

Nor was most of Scotland conquered by the Anglo-Saxons, although an Angle Kingdom was established in the southeast—hence Edinburgh's Germanic name. British Celts displaced from the south by Saxon invasion occupied the area around what is now Glasgow, and in this same period (around the sixth century AD) people from northern Ireland invaded the south-west. They were called the Scots, and it is they that gave the modern country of Scotland its name. The original Scottish Celts, called the Picts, were left with the extensive but unproductive Highland Zone. The division between highland and lowland Scotland remains a cultural divide today, in much the same way as north and south England see themselves as different from each other. There are even areas in the highlands where (in addition to English) people speak the old Celtic language, called "Gaelic".

Like England, Scotland began to experience Viking raids in the ninth century, and it was the pressure from this outside threat that led Scottish kings to unify, forming an independent singular Scottish state at just about the same time that Anglo-saxon England was also unifying. The presence of this larger powerful kingdom on its southern doorstep was the key factor in Scottish politics from that time on, with frequent wars between the two. William Shakespeare's play "Macbeth[19]" is set in the Scotland of this period. The town of Berwick upon Tweed near the Scottish border in present day England is said to have changed hands thirteen times as a result of Anglo-Scottish conflict. Despite the conflict, there were close ties between the two countries with extensive intermarriage between the two aristocracies, and even between the royal families. A recent Hollywood movie, *Braveheart*, told the story of William Wallace's[20] uprising in 1298, which was quelled by the English. But only a few years late the Scots, under the leadership of Robert the Bruce[21], were victorious at the Battle of Bannockburn[22], leading to 300 years of full independence.

In 1603, however, Queen Elizabeth[23] the First of England died childless, and the next in line to the throne was James the sixth of Scotland[24], so he also became James the First of England, uniting the two thrones. But for another hundred years Scotland maintained its separate political identity. However, in 1707 by agreement of the English and Scottish parliaments, Scotland joined the Union. There followed two rebellions in 1715 and 1745 in which the heir to the Stuart claim (deposed in 1688 by the English parliament) to the British throne attempted to reassert his right to rule Britain, gathering support in Scotland then marching with an army into England. In 1745 this led to a brutal military revolt from the British army. The rebel army was destroyed at the Battle of Culloden[25] (the last battle on British soil) in northern Scotland. Scottish highland clan (extended family group) culture was effectively destroyed at this time, and today exists largely as a way of parting tourists from their money by selling them "tartan" souvenirs or histories of "their" clan. For following Culloden, and even more importantly, the agricultural changes of the 18th century which led to depopulation of the highlands, many Scots sought their fortune outside

Scotland—in England, America, Canada, or Australia. So that there are more people of Scottish descent outside Scotland than in it, and many of those come back to find their "roots", forming a good target for the sellers of such souvenirs.

The dream of an independent Scotland has not vanished, but it does not seem to be one shared by most Scots. Scotland elects its members of parliament to the London parliament in just the same way as the English do. It sends 72 representatives to London, but at the last election (in 1992), of those 72 only 3 were elected from the Scottish Nationalist Party—a political party which wants an independent Scotland. However, the largest group of MPs(49) was from the Labour party, which has said that if they are elected as the UK government at the next election they will set up a regional parliament for Scotland to manage its own internal affairs within the UK.

Scotland has a great tradition of innovation in the arts, philosophy and science. The inventor of the telephone was a Scot, and the first man to transmit a television picture was another. Its writers have given the world such well-known work as Walter Scott's[26] romances of highland Scotland, and "*Auld Lang Syne*"[27] (by Robert Burns, who wrote in the Scots dialect). But the work which many consider to best sum up Scotland's position is the famous novel *Dr Jekyll and Mr Hyde*, by Robert Louis Stevenson[28], which describes how the civilized scientist Dr Jekyll transforms periodically into the crude and violent Mr Hyde. This description of the dual nature of man if perhaps a good way to think of Scotland: superficially fully integrated into the UK, but concealed beneath this is a still-strong Scottish identity[29].

Wales and Welsh

The capital of Wales is Cardiff, a small city of about 300 000 people on the south coast. This southern area was an important element in Britain's industrial revolution, as it had rich coal deposits. Coal-mining became a key industry for the Welsh, employing tens of thousands at its height. So its recent disappearance has been a major economic and cultural blow. But South Wales has been very successful in attracting investment from abroad—particularly Japan and the United States, which has helped to create new industries to replace coal and steel.

Wales is the smallest among the three nations on the British mainland, though larger than Northern Ireland. It is very close to the most densely populated parts of central England. Though it is hillier and more rugged than adjacent parts of England there is no natural boundary. So Wales has been dominated by England for longer than the other nations of the union. Nevertheless, what is remarkable is that despite this near-ness and long-standing political integration Wales retains a powerful sense of its difference from England. It also retains its own language, Welsh. This is a Celtic tongue completely different from English, spoken by 19% of the population, a much higher proportion of the population than speak Gaelic in Scotland. Again, all those Welsh-speakers are also fluent in English.

Like the rest of Britain, before the arrival of the Roman empire, Wales was a land of Celtic peoples, living in a number of small tribal kingdoms. Wales was conquered by the Romans eventually, though with difficulty. The Welsh chieftain Caradoc fought a long guerrilla campaign from the Welsh hills against the invader. When the Romans left Britain Wales was again a Celtic land, though again divided into separate kingdoms, but unlike England it did not fall to the Anglo-Saxon invaders of the fifth century.

But Wales was always under pressure from its English neighbours, particularly arter the Norman conquest, when Norman barons set up castles and estates in Wales under the authority of the English Crown. Thus there was a need to unify Wales to successfully resist the English. This did not happen until Liywelyn ap Gruffudd[30] brought a large portion of Wales under his rule, and by a military campaign forced the English to acknowledge him as Prince of Wales in 1267. But when he died, the English king, Edward the First, set about conquering Wales, building a series of great stone castles there from which to control the population. These castles stand today as one of Wales' greatest tourist attractions (along with its beaches, cliffs and mountains), and tourism is now an important industry.

Edward the First named his son the Prince of Wales, and the first son of the monarch has held that title ever since (including the present day Prince Charles) to try to bring Wales into the British nation. The last real attempt to resist that process was in the early 15th century when Owain Glyndwr[31] led an unsuccessful rising against the English. Today Glyndwr and Llywelyn are more than simple historical figures for the Welsh, they are the almost legendary heroes of Welsh nationalism. Their brief campaigns are the only times in history when Wales has existed as a unified independent nation.

A hundred years after Glyndwr, in 1536, Wales was brought legally, administratively, and politically into the UK by an act of the British parliament. This close long-standing relationship means that modern Wales lacks some of the outward signs of difference which Scotland possesses—its legal system and its education system are exactly the same as in England. Often official statistics are given for

"England and Wales". However, Wales is different, and one of the key markers of that difference is the Welsh language—the old British Celtic tongue which is still in daily use. But as a source of the Welsh identity this is sometimes divisive, because 80% of the Welsh don't speak the language, and yet feel Welsh. Since most of the Welsh speakers are in the north, this deepens a cultural division between the more populated, industrial south, and the rural north of Wales.

As in Scotland the Welsh people elect their MPs to the London parliament. The Welsh too have nationalist party, "Plaid Cymru"[32] (The Party of Wales), which campaigns for an independent Wales. Of the 38 Welsh MPs, 4 are members of this party. Under a Labour government Wales will probably gain its own parliament to manage its own internal affairs.

Words & Expressions

urbanized/ˈɔːbənaizd/*a.* 都市化的

Welsh/welʃ/*a.* 威尔士人的;威尔士语

Celtic/ˈækeltik/*a.* 凯尔特大的;凯尔特语

Angles/ˈæŋglz/*n.* 盎格鲁人(5世纪由德国北部移居英国)

Saxon/ˈsæksn/*n.* 撒克逊人(原住德国,一部分于5世纪中叶至6世纪上半叶移居英国)

Excalibur/eksˈkælibə/*n.* 亚瑟王之魔剑

embellish/imˈbeliʃ/*vt.* 传颂;歌颂

Tintagel/tinˈtædʒəl/*n.* 廷塔哲岬(在英格兰西南部,传说中的King Arthur 诞生处)

Cornwall/ˈkɔːnwəl/*n.* 康瓦尔(英国西南部之一郡,首府 Bodmin)

Camelot/ˈkæmilɔt/*n.* 传说中 Arthur 王之宫殿朝廷所在地

Somerset/ˈsʌməsit/*n.* 索美塞得郡(英格兰西南部一郡)

precedence/priˈsiːdənz/*n.* 上席;较高位置

monarch/ˈmɔnək/*n.* 君主;帝王

contemporary/kənˈtempərəri/*a.* 当代的

Scandinavia/skændiˈneivjə/*n.* 斯勘的纳维亚(北欧国家的原称,指:瑞典、挪威、丹麦、芬兰、冰岛)

ferocious/fəˈrəuʃəs/*a.* 凶残的;野蛮的

versus/vəːsəs/*prep.* 对(多用于诉讼或竞技等之中,缩写作 *v.* 或 *vs.*)

sophisticated/səˈfistikeitid/*a.* 世故的;城府深的

aristocracy/ˌærisˈtɔkrəsi/*n.* 贵族;贵族阶层

outlaw/ˈoutlɔː/*n.* 被流放者;罪犯

interior/inˈtiəriə/*a.* 内部的

punk/pʌŋk/*n.* 朋克,小阿飞,小流氓

spiky/ˈspaiki/*a.* 竖起的;直立的

conceal/kənˈsiːl/*vt.* 隐瞒

porch/pɔːtʃ/*n.* 门廊

execute/ˈeksikjuːt/*vt.* 处决

overrule/ˌəuvəˈruːl/*vt.* 推翻

substantial/sʌbˈstænʃəl/*a.* 相当(长)的

rugged/ˈrʌgid/*a.* 崎岖的;不平坦的

sparsely/ˈspɑːsli/*ad.* 稀少地

span/spæn/*vt.* 跨越

retreat/riˈtriːt/*vi.* 撤回

domain/dəˈmein/*n.* 领土;领地

change hands (财产等)转换所有者;易手

intermarriage/intəˈmæridʒ/*n.* 异族通婚;近亲通婚

quell/kwel/*vt.* 镇压

depose/diˈpəuz/*vt.* 废黜(国王等)

reassert/riːə'səːt/*vt*. 再申明

tartan/tɑːtn/*a*. 用格子呢制的

souvenir/'suːvəniə/*n*. 纪念品

adjacent/ə'dʒeisənt/*a*. 邻近的

long-standing *a*. 长期的;长年累月的

Gaelic/'geilik/*n*. 盖尔语

baron/'bærən/*n*. 男爵

Notes

1. the Roman Empire:罗马帝国。始于公元前31年,公元192年进入全盛时期,政治、经济和文化都得到充分发展。进入3世纪之后,罗马奴隶制社会陷于全面危机,经济衰败,政治混乱,基督教逐渐流行和传播。至帝王后期(284~476)戴克里先建立君主统治,各地爆发了广泛的人民起义,给帝国的统治以严重打击。395年,帝国分裂为西罗马帝国和东罗马帝国。

2. King Arthur: 亚瑟国王,6世纪时英格兰统治者,圆桌武士的领袖。有关他的传说很多。

3. ...creating the famous "round table"... equal precedence:亚瑟的骑士们经常为开会时的座位问题而争吵,致使亚瑟采用圆桌,这样,骑士们就无法分出地位的高低主次了。

4. Perhaps this... completely rejecting it: 或许这可以被看做是象征着英国人如何看待其君主的一种愿望,他们不希望把他们的君主看做一位可望而不可及的统治者。事实上,英国人已逐渐将君主制融入一个更为民主的体制之中,而不是完全的拒绝。

5. the ferocious Vikings:指第8世纪至第10世纪残暴地掠夺欧洲西海岸的北欧海盗。

6. King Alfred the Great:阿尔弗雷德国王(849~899),英格兰撒克逊民族的一位国王。

7. There remains... origins in this time:直到今天英格兰的北方人和南方人之间还存在着一定的文化差异,这种差异虽不像撒克逊与丹麦人之间的差异那样明显,但是到现在来看还是有其根源的。

8. William the Conqueror:威廉一世征服者(约1028~1087),法国诺曼底公爵,英格兰第一位诺曼人国王(1066~1087在位)。1066年9月27日引兵渡海对英格兰开战,获全胜。同年圣诞节,威廉在威斯敏斯特大教堂加冕为英格兰国王。

9. King Harold:哈罗德国王,英格兰最后一位撒克逊民族的国王,1066年诺曼底法国入侵英格兰时,在关键的Hastings战斗中被杀。从此英格兰被征服,诺曼底统治者当了英国国王,即威廉一世。

10. the Tower of London:伦敦塔,位于泰晤士河北岸,伦敦塔桥附近,是伦敦著名古迹之一。威廉一世于11世纪为保卫和控制整个伦敦城而建造了该塔,占地18英亩。经过历代君主的扩建和修整,整个建筑反映了英国不同朝代的建筑风格。9个世纪以来,曾作过堡垒、王宫、监狱、皇家铸币厂和伦敦档案馆。现在是王冠、王袍、兵器和盔甲陈列馆。

11. Robin Hood:罗宾汉,英国传说中的一位著名的绿林好汉,在森林里盘踞,以劫富济贫杀害贪官污吏为宗旨。

12. this early English socialist:这位早期的英格兰社会主义者。此处作者把劫富济贫,宣传平等思想的农民起义者及绿林好汉称为"社会主义者"。

13. Some writers... by an external conformity:在这个广为流传的绿林反叛神话中,一些作家看到了体现英国人个性的迹象:表面上似乎一致,但实际上保持着一种强烈的独特的生活方式。

14. for example English punk rockers... dyed spiky hair: 例如英国的一些朋克把头发理成鸡冠状,并染成很鲜艳的颜色,以此来表达他们的反叛心理。

15. Oliver Cromwell:奥利弗·克伦威尔(1599.4.25 ~ 1658.9.3)。英格兰军人和政治家,生于英格兰东部的亨廷顿,曾两次当选国会议员,由于反对国王,捍卫公民自由和宗教自由,他很快成为英国资产阶级革命的领袖。1649 年国王查理一世被处死后,议会宣布英伦三岛成立共和国,克伦威尔成为共和国首领,称为"护国公"。1649 年,他又征服了爱尔兰。

16. the Scottish house of Stuart:苏格兰斯图亚特王室。1371,年罗伯特二世成为第一代斯图亚特国王,为苏格兰王室。1603 年,詹姆斯六世继承英格兰王位,斯图亚特从此成为英格兰王室。

17. William and Mary:威廉和玛丽。英国资产阶级革命王朝复辟时期的第二个国王是詹姆斯二世。他和他的妻子都是天主教徒,他的统治遭到议会中资产阶级势力和新教徒的强烈反对。因此,英国议会于 1687 年底邀请詹姆斯二世的女儿、新教徒玛丽和她的丈夫、荷兰国王威廉(新教徒)到英国联合执政。威廉的军队在英国登陆时未遇任何反抗,詹姆斯二世逃跑,这就是英国历史上 1688 年的"光荣革命",又称"不流血革命"。1689 年,议会通过"权利法案",限制国王权力,从而开始了延续至今的君主立宪制。

18. Hadrian's Wall:哈德良长城。罗马人保卫不列颠北疆的屏障,长 118 公里,不列颠总督尼波斯监造,公元 136 年竣工。

19. Macbeth:《麦克白》,莎士比亚创作的四大悲剧之一。现实生活中的麦克白在 1040 年杀死堂兄,自立为苏格兰国王。1057 年在一场战争中被英格兰支持的一方人杀死。他大起大落的生平构成了莎翁创作的基本情节。

20. William Wallace 威廉·华莱士(约 1270 ~ 1305),苏格兰最伟大的民族英雄之一。1298 年 7 月 3 日爱德华一世的军队入侵苏格兰。华莱士率领苏格兰人民奋起反抗,在斯特灵的福尔柯克战役中被爱德华的军队打败。华莱士继续带领游击队在苏格兰各地进行斗争,1305 年被捕,后在伦敦被处决。

21. Robert the Bruce:罗伯特·布鲁斯(1274.7.11 ~ 1329.6.7)。14 世纪苏格兰争取国家独立的斗士,1306 年成为苏格兰国王。1314 年,他率领苏格兰军队在班诺克本大败英格兰军队,迫使英格兰政府承认他的地位。根据北安普敦条约(1328),英王承认他为苏格兰国王并完全放弃英格兰对苏格兰宗主权的要求。

22. the battle of Bannockburn:班诺克本战役(1314.6.23 ~ 1314.6.24)。苏格兰历史上的一次大决战。在这次决战中,由罗伯特·布鲁斯统帅的苏格兰军队打败了爱德华二世统帅的英格兰军。苏格兰军在敌强我弱的情况下,巧妙利用地形,粉碎了敌人的优势兵力。通过这次战争,苏格兰重新获得独立。

23. Queen Elizabeth:伊丽莎白一世(1533.9.7 ~ 1603.5.24)。英格兰历代最伟大的君主之一。在位 45 年中,她不愿发动战争,因而保证国家稳步走向繁荣。伊丽莎白时代是英国最辉煌的年代,以莎士比亚文学为标志的英国文学达到鼎盛。此外,英国航海业在这一时期开始发展,繁荣了对外通商。伊丽莎白实行了一系列强国政策,使英国成了海上霸王,走上了殖民主义道路。

24. James the Sixth of Scotland:苏格兰詹姆斯六世(1566.6.19~1625.3)。1567年起统治苏格兰,称詹姆斯六世。生于爱丁堡,1岁继承苏格兰王位。成年后,竭力与英格兰女王伊丽莎白保持良好关系,因为伊丽莎白无嗣,他可继承英格兰王位。1603年,伊丽莎白逝世后,立即继位。

25. the battle of Culloden: Culloden 战役。1745年苏格兰王子查尔斯·爱德华斯图亚特带领他的部下与英格兰军队发生的一场战斗,最后以苏格兰的失败而告终。

26. Walter Scott:沃尔特·司各特(1771.8.15~1832.9.21)。英国小说家,历史小说的首创者。他著名的作品都是写苏格兰和英格兰的历史,许多材料取自民间传说。其中有《苏格兰编剧歌谣集》、《爱丁堡评论》、《威弗利》等。

27. Auld Lang Syne:著名苏格兰民歌《友谊地久天长》。

28. Robert Louis Stevenson:罗伯特·路易斯·斯蒡文森(1850.11.13~1894.12.3)。英国著名冒险故事和散文作家。他的作品种类繁多,构思精巧。他著名的有:《新天方夜谭》故事集、《金银岛》、《黑箭》、《绑架》、《卡特琳娜》等。

29. superficially... Scottish identity: 表面上(苏格兰)已完全与英国融入一体,但实际上仍然保持了强烈的苏格兰特征。

30. Llywelyn ap Gruffudd: 卢埃林·阿普·格鲁菲德(? ~1282.12.11)。威尔士北部圭内斯的诸侯。1262年他曾以武力反对威尔士南部英格兰贵族。1272年,他再次公开反抗英格兰人。1282年,卢埃林和他的兄弟戴维又发动一次争取民族独立的起义,以卢埃林被杀,起义被英格兰军队镇压而告瓦解。

31. Owain Glyndwr:欧文·格林道瓦尔(1354~1416)。自称为"威尔士王子"。率威尔士人反抗英格兰人的统治,但未成功。人们称他为"威尔士的民族英雄"。1400年9月,他在威尔士北部发动起义,起义很快就发展成为威尔士的民族斗争。1404年,格林道瓦尔控制了威尔士大部分地区,建立了独立的威尔士议会,并开始制订自己的外交及基督教会政策。1405年,他遭到亨利王子的围剿,不久起义即告失败。

32. "Plaid Cymru":威尔士党,1925年8月成立。要求威尔士有更大的自治权,同时希望与英格兰保持紧密的关系。

Exercises

Ⅰ. Explain each of the following

1. the British Isles
2. Robin Hood
3. the Anglo-Saxons
4. the Vikings

Ⅱ. Fill in the blanks

1. Britain Consists of ________ nations, including England, ________, ________ and ________.

2. Britain is a country with a history of invasions. In 43 AD Britain was invaded by ________, in the late 8th century they experienced ________ raids from Scandinavia and in the 11th century they suffered invasions from ________.

3. The Anglo-Saxons began to settle in Britain in ________ century.

4. The capital of Britain is ________, which has great influence on the UK in all fields including________,________ and ________.

5. Charles the First, king of Britain, was executed, because he attempted to ________ in the English Revolution.

6. Name two Scottish cities which have ancient and internationally respected universities: ________ and ________.

7. The battle of Bannockburn led by Robert the Bruce succeeded in winning the full independence of ________.

8. Both the Scottish and Welsh people elect their members of parliaments to the London Parliament and each holds ________ and ________ seats respectively.

9. The capital of Scotland is ________, which is well-known for its natural ________.

10. Although Wales is the smallest of the three nations on the ________ mainland, it's good at getting ________ from abroad, particularly Japan and ________.

Ⅲ. Choose the correct answer in each of the following

1. Three of the following are characteristics of London. Which of the four is the exception?

   A. London is a political, economic and cultural centre of the country.

   B. London has a larger population than all other cities in England.

   C. London is not only the largest city in Britain, but also the largest in the world.

   D. London has played a significant role in the economic construction of the country.

2. The Tower of London, a historical sight, located in the centre of London, was built by ________.

   A. King Harold

   B. Robin Hood

   C. Oliver Cromwell

   D. William the Conqueror

3. Who were the ancestors of the English and the founders of England?

   A. The Anglo-Saxons.

   B. The Normans.

   C. The Vikings.

   D. The Romans.

4. Which city is the largest in Scotland?

   A. Cardiff.

   B. Edinburgh.

   C. Glasgow.

   D. Manchester.

5. Why did the Scottish Kings decide to from an independent singular Scottish state in the ninth century?
   A. They needed a unified independent nation to fight against Viking raids.
   B. They felt it necessary to develop their own industry.
   C. They were threatened by the Anglo-Saxons' invasion.
   D. They had to do it in order to resist the English.
6. Where do the majority of people in Scotland live?
   A. In the Highlands.
   B. In the Lowlands.
   C. In the Uplands.
   D. In the west of Scotland.
7. Which of the following statements is NOT true?
   A. Wales was invaded by the Romans.
   B. Wales was occupied by the Anglo-Saxons.
   C. Wales was conquered by the Normans.
   D. Wales was threatened by the English.
8. Which of the following parties in Scotland still wants an independent Scotland?
   A. The Labour Party.
   B. The Liberal Party.
   C. The Scottish Nationalist Party.
   D. The Conservative Party.
9. When did Scotland join the Union by agreement of the English and Scottish parliaments?
   A. In 1715.
   B. In 1688.
   C. In 1745.
   D. In 1707.
10. Llywelgn ap Gruffudd is more than a simple historical figure for the Welsh. He is almost considered the legendary hero of Welsh nationalism because ________.
   A. he became the first Prince of Wales in 1267
   B. he brought the English under his control
   C. he led a historic uprising against the English
   D. he unified Wales as an independent nation

Ⅳ. Answer the following questions brietly

1. "British history has been a history of invasion". Please illustrate this point with the examples from the text. How did each of the invasions influence English culture?
2. What are some general characteristics of Scotland? How did Scotland become part of the union of Great Britain?
3. Are there any differences between England, Scotland and Wales in terms of cultural tradition?

Chapter 2 The History of the Nation

We cannot hope to learn the history of Britain in such limited space, but certain episodes and certain people from British history form a necessary part of our general knowledge. As far as reading is concerned, many of the most exciting novels have a historical background, and may actually include real historical events, enlivened by the author's imagination[1].

The Middle Ages

The clearest historical item in the general knowledge of most British people, so clear that it has become a sort of joke[2], is the year 1066, when the French-speaking Normans under William the Conqueror invaded England from France, defeating the Saxon king Harold[3] at the Battle of Hastings (a town in Sussex on the south coast). Harold himself was killed, pierced through the eye with an arrow. Of the time before that the average person knows little[4]. He knows about the Romans, of course, and he is sure to know the story of the fine Saxon king, Alfred the Great, who was so busy thinking of ways of defeating the invading Danes that he let the cakes burn in the farmhouse where he was sheltering unrecognised[5]. Alfred's statue can still be seen in Winchester (Hampshire), his old capital. Of the still earlier king Arthur, and his Knights of the Round Table, even the experts know almost nothing, except that he is associated with Cornwall and is the central figure of many legends[6].

After the year 1066, the next episode most people remember is the Crusades[7]. These were a series of wars in which armies from all oyer Europe tried to snatch the "Holy Land" (i. e. Palestine, where Jesus Christ once lived) from the "Infidels" (i. e. the Muslims)[8]. The most famous of the English Crusaders was the Norman king, Richard Lion-Heart, about whom and about whose enemy Saladin many stories have been told[9].

The Crusades remind us that Britain even at that time was a Christian country. Each village had its church, and many of these Norman-style churches are still standing. Indeed, the Church (using the word collectively) was extremely powerful in those days, and the Pope in Rome, who could always inspire the fear of eternal damnation[10] by "excommunicating" (i. e. expelling from the Church) a king or even a whole nation, wielded great political power over the whole of Western Europe.

The other great rivals, besides the Church, of the king's authorith were the powerful local chiefs, called barons, who were always causing trouble. At one stage they made King John, younger brother of Richard Lion-Heart, sign a document called the Magna Carta ("Great Charter")[11] by which he promised to recognise their rights, and it was only with the Pope's help that John was able to prevail against them. The Magna Carta is now in the British Museum, London.

All the kings of this period spoke French as their mother tongue, and had close family connections and in some cases extensive territories in France itself. Disputes between England and France were common. Hence came the next outstanding episode in English history, a war with France which lasted, on and off, for a hundred years[12]. It was fought entirely in France, where English bowmen defeated the heavily armend French knights in the famous battles of Crecy and Agincourt, and the whole of France very nearly fell into English hands. Eventually, however, partly through the inspiration of the brave girl Joan of Arc,[13] and partly through the effective use of guns, which had only just been invented, the French drove the English from their country for good. England became completely severed from France, and the English language finally took the place of French in all classes of society.

The Sixteenth Century

Passing quickly over a long period of civil wars, the Wars of the Roses,[14] fought between two branches of the English royal family who each claimed the throne, we approach the end of the Middle Ages and the beginning of the modern period[15], though we are still nearly five hundred years away from our own day. About this time, Europe as a whole was changing rapidly. The invention of printing made books much easier to produce and therefore much cheaper, so that ideas could spread quickly. It was the age of the great voyages of discovery by men like Columbus and Vasco da Gama[16], and the beginning of the imperialist expansion which resulted in Europeans establishing themselves throughout the American continent. It was also the beginning of freedom of thought in the Christian religion, when the decline in the Pope's political power was followed by a decline in his religious authority. As a result, "Protestant" churches sprang up in Northern Europe in opposition to the established Roman Catholic Church, and Protestant-Catholic hatred became a constant theme in European history—a hatred which is still far from dead in places like Ireland even today.

In England, the first great blow to the Roman Catholic Church was delivered by

Henry VIII, the terrible king who is popularly remembered for having had six wives, one after the other, two of whom be beheaded. The religious trouble arose in connection with the first of these wives, who after many years had still failed to produce a malc heir. Henry wanted to divorce her. This could only be arranged by the Pope, and the Pope would not agree. The result was a long quarrel which ended in Henry's declaring that he and not the Pope was the head of the Church in England: in other words the English Church had broken away from the central organisation of Christianity. It was not until *after* this great event that Protestant doctrines questioning some of the actual beliefs and practices of the Catholic Church began to spread in England, and people began to take sides, not for or against the King, but for or against Catholicism.

The dispute was embittered by the belief among Catholics that any revolt against the traditional Christian faith was "heresy", the work of the devil, to be resisted by the most violent means. Henry VIII's elder daughter Mary[17], a devout Catholic, had so many Protestants burnt to death that she is remembered less by her official title Mary I than by her nickname Bloody Mary. No wonder, then, that when she was succeeded by her half-sister Elizabeth[18], whose main interest lay in creating a strong united country in which there should be no more religious persecution, Protestantism gradually became the dominant faith.

Everybody remembers the reign of Elizabeth I. She gave her name to an age, the Elizabethan Age, which remains in English minds as an age of glory. Most people associate it whth two things. The first is literature, especially the literature of Shakespeare, for this was the age when Shakespeare lived and when English literature blossomed. The second is adventure on the sea. For the first time English ships began to explore the world and trade with distant countries. They soon came into conflict with the might of Spain, whose huge ships had been sailing the seas for a hundred years and who had established a rich empire in the Americas. Moreover, the Spaniards were Catholics and hated Protestantism. Sea fights between Spanish and English ships were frequent, and astonishingly, the English were the more aggressive and the more successful. Their greatest sailor was Sir Francis Drake[19], a Devon man, and there is a famous story of how when the great Spanish fleet, the "Armada", came sailing up the English Channel to attack the heart of England, Drake calmly finished his game of bowls at Plymouth before leading the English fleet to victory. It was a lucky victory in many ways[20], but it marked the beginning of an English naval tradition which has never been forgotten.

During the second half of Elizabeth's reign it was the Protestants who were persecuting the Catholics, but for political rather than religious reasons. For Catholics were constantly suspected of undermining Elizabeth's authority and trying to overthrow her Protestant government. The most famous of a number of Catholic conspiracies (many of them imaginary) in English history occurred in the reign of Elizabeth's successor James I. This was the "Gunpowder Plot" to blow up King and Parliament, in which a man called Guy Fawkes was caught in the cellars of the House of Commons in the very act of preparing the explosives. "Guy Fawkes" Night" is still celebrated on November 5th each year, when effigies of Guy Fawkes are burnt amid brilliant fireworks.

The Seventeenth Century

The century following Elizabeth is dominated by one of the most important events in the whole of British history[21], the temporary overthrow of the monarchy, when the country became for more than ten years a sort of republic founded by Oliver Cromwell. The trouble arose with King Charles I. Charles believed he had a "Divine Right" to govern[22]. Parliament believed he was a human being answerable to the people. For a time, Charles actually ruled without Parliament, and levied taxes without Parliament's approval. In this he was opposed particularly by the "Puritan" elements[23], those with very strict Protestant principles, nicknamed the "Roundheads" because of the bare look of their shorn heads contrasted with the long, curly wigs of the King's more fashionable supporters, the "Cavaliers"[24]. And so the great Civil War broke out.[25] Many terrible battles were fought, but in the end, through the genius of the Roundhead leader, Cromwell, the King was defeated, tried as a traitor to his country, and condemned to death. You can still see in Whitehall[26] the window through which he walked on to the scaffold to be beheaded.

Charles was a very unvise king, but his execution horrified the nation. Hence, when Cromwell's republican constitution ran into difficulties, and Cromwell himself died, Charles" son, who had escaped death in the Civil War by hiding in an oak tree and fleeing to France, was welcomed back with great rejoicings as Charles II[27], and those responsible for the execution of his father were punished. But never again was the King allowed to go against the interests of Parliament and people.

This lesson was finally brought home in 1688, when the Catholic king James II[28] was forced to flee with his baby son to France, and the throne was offered to his Protestant daughter Mary and her husband William. This was known as the Glorious, or Bloodless, Revolution. For half a century James' descendants lived in hopes of regaining the throne. Most people know the story of their last attempt, when James' young and handsome grandson, Bonnie Prince Charlie, landed secretly in Scotland, and after gathering a few supporters invaded England. In the end he was completely defeated. He wandered for months as a fugitive through the Highlands of Scotland, escaping capture with the help of Scottish friends like the heroic young woman Flora Mac-Donald. But the British as a whole did no want him; they preferred a Protestant king who they knew would respect the Constitution.

The Eighteenth Century

Under Elizabeth, England's great enemy had been Spain. During the whole of the eighteenth century it was France, with which England was continually at war, not only in Europe but also in Canada and India, where they were rival imperialists.[29] The period began and ended with framous victories. The most famous was the Battle of Waterloo, won by the Duke of Wellington over the great Napoleon[30], a victory so important and so complete that today, when we say that a man will "meet his Waterloo", we mean he will encounter final disaster. Equally famous is the great naval victory over Napoleon's fleet won by Lord Nelson—the Battle of Trafalgar[31]. Nelson's Column in Trafalgar Square is one of the best known monuments in modern London.

This supremacy was due not only to military achievements but to certain changes which, in the latter part of the century, were taking place in Britain itself, long before they began to affect any other country. These changes are what we now call the Industrial Revolution, which owed a great deal to the invention of the steam engine. Factories multiplied; so did coal-mines, since steam engines needed coal as a fuel. Big towns were springing up. The nation was able to *produce* more. Some people grew rich. But industrialisation brought its own problems. It created an entirely new social class, the industrial workers, thousands of them, absolutely dependent on a few mine-owners and factory-owners and on the prevailing economic situation. Wages were low, hous were long, working conditions often unhealthy and dangerous, and the big towns ugly and overcrowded.

Even in the military sphere one sad story must be told, for the same century brought the greatest defeat England has ever had—the loss of her American colonies. These were colonies of British settlers, the most famous of whom were the "Pilgrim Fathers", a group of Puritans who had sailed from England in the ship *Mayflower* to escape religious persecution under James I; but many others since then, for various reasons, had left England to settle in various parts of North America's Atlantic coast. Trouble arose when the settlers refused to pay taxes to the British government, arguing that they ought not to have to pay anything to a government in which they were not represented. Eventually, by the Declaration of Independence, the settlers renounced their British citizenship and became Americans, and in the ensuing war the British were defeated. If Britain had won, or if their statesmen had been wiser, the Unites States might perhaps today be a member of the Commonwealth.

The Nineteenth Century

After the Battle of Waterloo and the fall of Napoleon, Britain enjoyed a long period of peace, of which the main historical interest lies in the efforts made: (*a*) to overcome social problems, like those connected with the Industrial Revolution[32] (*b*) to make Parliament more representative of the people, and (*c*) to improve local government and social services. There was, for instance, the anti-slavery movement led by William Wilberforce[33], and the prison reform movement led by Elizabeth Fry[34]. The savage punishments of the eighteenth century, when two hundred separate offences carried the death penalty, were largely abolished, and the modern police force was founded by Sir Robert ("Bobby") Peel: policemen used to be called Peelers, and are still called, rather affectionately, bobbies. Trade unions were allowed to develop, and regulations were made about working conditions in mines and factories, forbidding for example the employment of children; attempts were made to deal with poverty, and to encourage elementary education, though universal and compulsory education was still many years away. A start was made in extending the "franchise", i. e. freedom to vote in general elections. In the eighteenth century Britain was far from being a democracy: it was really an aristocracy, in which only important people were allowed to vote. In the ninteenth century, by a famous Reform Bill, the franchise was extended a little further, and it was to be followed by others. Freely elected town councils, too, were established for the first time.

But the greatest progress of all was made in the field of communications, which are of course the life-blood of a modern state. The steam engine, for the first time, was given wheels and rails to run on, and a railway network quickly developed after the success of George Stephenson's famous locomotive, the "Rocket", gradually replacing the old stage-coach[35], just as the steamship gradually replaced the sailing ship on the sea. Electricity was used to send signals along wires from place to place, and so telegraphy was born, followed later on by the electric telephone, electric lighting, and electric trams. The Penny Post, enabling anyone to send a letter anywhere in the country for only one penny, though not truly an invention, was a revolutionary idea of the greatest importance.

All these tremendous changes will help you to grasp something of the atmosphere of Victorianism, since the monarch of Britain from 1837 to 1901, the longest reign in British history, was the great Queen Victoria[36]. It was an age of national development and national optimism, with only occasional doubts about the future. The working classes, after a great deal of dissatisfaction in the first half of the century, settled down to a period of reasonable stability, despite their slums; and in general the upper and middle classes remained firmly in power, dignified, self-satisfied, kindly disposed towards the rough-mannered workers and simple farm tenants, but very conscious of their own superiority, and, as they supposed, their higher sense of values. True, they were often emparrassed by the pride and ambitions of low-born but successful manufacturers and traders, climbing the social ladder, but embarrassment is not the same as fear[37].

Victorian family life had a similar stability. Each home was like a little kingdom in which the father was king. He expected to be loved, but he also expected to be obeyed. He made all the decisions. His wife was supposed to be his faithful companion, completely submissive, with no interests beyond her husband and children. In novels, the upper-class wife was often depicted as rather frail, subject to fainting and to long days in bed. The highest virtue of the Victorian woman was sexual purity; adultery was the worst of all possible sins. Her dress concealed her whole body except her hands and face, and to show an ankle or a shoulder was considered "improper".

The children were strictly disciplined. Their life consisted of "don'ts"[38]. If they were too noisy or quarrelsome or if they dirtied their clothes or told a lie, they were given a few strokes with a cane, or told to stand in the corner, or given a little sermon by their mother.

The family virtues were a part of religion, for the Victorians were extremely religious. Every family had its Bible and went to church on Sundays. They believed very deeply in God as the Creator of Man and in the life after death. Hence their violent reaction against a book by a certain scientist, one of the most important books ever written, which set out to prove that Man, instead of being a separate creation, had evolved extremely slowly from humbler forms of life according to a simple natural law, and that his nearest relatives were apes! This book was called *The Origin of Species*, *and its author was Charles Darwin*[39]. The average person, not really understanding the issue, remained, like a famous politician. "on the side of the angels"[40], but furious debates were held both in private and in public, and Darwin's theory was destined to outlive Victorianism and to contribute to its decay[41].

It was also, in its later stages, an age of imperialism. Despite her earlier empires in America, India, Australia, and elsewhere, Britain had never been particularly interested in, or even conscious of, the idea of imperial power[42]. Colonies grew up almost by accident, and the British government was very unwilling to take over responsibility for them. When trouble occurred, however, such as the Mutiny in India[43], the British government *had* to take over, and the British began to see themselves as having a sort of mission in the world to spread peace and civilisation through British rule. The difficulties involved were thought of as "the white man's burden", something which it was his destiny to bear. It was at this time that the famous "grab for Africa" occurred, in which almost the whole of Africa was divided into "spheres of influence" among the leading European powers. Britain, of course, had the lion's share[44].

The Twentieth Century

Within a few years of the death of Queen Victoria the Victorian stability had collapsed. The working classes, many of them now well educated, became conscious of their inferior position and eager to claim their rights in full. Why should they be inferior? Given a fair chance, they could be as good as their "bettes". The recently formed Labout Party grew rapidly in strength. The doctrine of socialism became widespread. Serious strikes occurred. The class war was on.

The women woke up too. They, who had been so meek and submissive in Victoria's reign, were now smashing windows, burning houses and whipping members of Parliament in their efforts to gain the right to vote. This was the famous "suffragette" movement[45], not simply a political campaign but a profound revolt against an inferior status.

Meanwhile the trouble in Ireland was going from bad to worse. When Home Rule was again brought up, the Protestant North said it would never consent to be governed by the Catholic South. Civil War there was imminent.

Then in the middle of everything came a catastrophe so great that all else was forgotten: the First World War, 1914 – 1918. The causes of the outbreak were extremely complicated, but it can perhaps be compared to a fight between two people which quickly involves the friends of each, until it becomes far bigger than anyone intended. Britain became involved because she had made friends with her old enemy, France, who was being attacked by Germany; but this was only part of a long story of pride and hatred involving many different European nations. For the British and French it was an almost stationary war fought mainly in trenches, i. e. ditches, dug all the way from Switzerland to the North Sea, with the German grenches running parallel to them a short distance away. If you climbed out of your trench you were liable to sudden death from a rifle bullet or a machine gun, or a bursting shell. Sometimes the shells would be bursting around you for hours at a time, and rain would turn the trench into a gutter of mud. Sometimes you had to go "over the top", i. e. out of the trench and into the thick of the enemy's fire to gain a few hundred yards, where you would dig a new line of trenches and start again.

After three years, neither side had given way. In the fourth year the Germans made a last great effort, which was checked. Then the Americans arrived in strength to help the British and French, and the Germans knew they were beaten. Peace came on November 11th, 1918.

The world seemed very different to the British at the close of the war, which was by far the most terrible war in history. In four years *ten million people* had been killed and many others crippled for life. The British were exhausted, and their joy in victory was surpassed by their deep thankfulness that it was all over. They had two desires: to build a new and better society at home, and to see that war should never break out again. But for very many people, faith in religion had been broken, and the full churches or the Victorian Age became only a memory.

The question of who should have the right to vote was soon settled: the franchise was extended to virtually all adults, including women. Ireland, after a great deal of further trouble, was granted two separate Parliaments, the Southern part of the country becoming completely independent. Althought nobody was completely satisfied with the arrangement, it was accepted by most as the only practicable solution.

But more misery and tragedy lay ahead. The first Labour Government was a failure. Hopes of improving the lot of the workers broke down before economic difficulties. There was a great deal of unemployment, and in 1926 there occurred a General Strike of all industrial workers, which in the coalmining industry lasted for six months. Then, after a brief improvement, the economic situation collapsed completely, not only in Britain, but all over the world. This was the great "slump" of the early 1930's[46], when millions of people in America and Europe were unable to find work, and in other countries food had to be burnt because there was no means of thransporting it where it was wanted. There are many still alive who remember the poverty and the humiliation they suffered in that dreadful period, when they walked from place to place looking for a job and found none.

Meanwhile in international affairs the League of Nations[47], was not truly honoured by the nations which delonged to it, and not really effective in dealing with disputes: pride and hatred remained. As the economic situation slowly improved after the great slump, so the international situation became threatened by fascism. Mussolini in Italy and Hitler in Germany were both fascists. At the time it seemed that Mussolini was the greater nenace, particularly when he invaded Abyssinia. But meanwhile Hitler had already begun his persecution of the Jews, and it was Hitler's constant thirst for power, based on the idea of a German "master-race"[48] that led Europe into the Second World War (1939 – 1945), only twenty years after the end of the first.

Once again the Germans invaded France, and this time within a few weeks France was conquered, and the British army narrowly escaped destruction at Dunkirk. Then Hitler planned to invade Britain. He sent his bombers day after day to bomb airfields and towns in the south, and then night after night, to bomb London. This was the "blitz" of 1940, when sirens wailed every night, and every night hundreds of people lost their lives or their homes. But the British fighter planes fought back heroically: the "Battle of Britain" was won and the planned invasion abandoned.

On the continent of Europe, Hitler was successful everywhere until he made the mistake of attacking a giant: Russia. At last his ambition had gone too far, and shortly afterwards the whole character of the war was altered when Japan treacherously attacked another giant: America. It became a war mainly between Germany and Japan on one side, and Russia and America on the other, with Britain playing a less important part. Eventually, British and American armies sailed from North Africa to invade Italy and from Southern England to invade France, forcing the Germans to fight in the South and West as well as against Russia in the East; and at the beginning of 1945 they were pouring into Germany itself. Germany surrendered in May, and Japan, which was never actually invaded, surrendered in August after being hit by two atomic bombs.

In some ways the Second World War was less terrible than the war of 1914—1918. It was a war of movement: fighting seldom went on long in any one place. But in other ways it was much more terrible. Destruction was more widespread, especially owing to the bombing from the air. And the cruelty of the Germans towards the Jews and other conquered peoples, and that of the Japanese towards their prisoners, filled everyone with horror. It is estimated that by the end of the war about 55 000 000 people had been killed all over the world, many of them innocent men, women and children, deliberately murdered in special camps.

Once again Britain felt there was not only a country, but a whole world to rebuild. The new United Nations Organisation did its best. Europe slowly recovered, and the rest of the world made encouraging progress. India and Pakistan became free, followed later by most of the colonies of the old British Empire. Yet in this century of problems, as soon as one problem was solved another seemed to take its place.

First there was the "Cold War" between Russia and the West, during which everyone feared the outbreak of a nuclear war which would destroy the whole of human civilisation. Then came the horrors of the war in Vietnam, and the dangerous conflict among other countries. And so it goes on.

In the nineteenth century material progress made us eager and optimistic. In the twentieth century it has left us bewildered and a little afraid. New discoveries and new techniques have multiplied. Since the last years of Queen Victoria we have had the motor-car, the wireless, the aeroplane, nuclear power, space rockets, and men on the moon. Entertainment has been made available to everybody by the gramophone, the cinema, radio and television. Social discontent seems to have been abolished by the "Welfare State", whereby, since the Second World War, the state has assumed full financial responsibility for sickness, unemployment and education. The British workman has more money and more leisure today than he has ever had: television sets are in almost every home, and families without cars are becoming fewer and fewer. Yet industrial strikes still occur, crimes with violence are common, politeness seems oldfashioned, religious faith is weak, the new "permissive society" seems ready to tolerate all kinds of sexual immorality and radical behaviour. Many young people, especially in the universities, want a different kind of society altogether, and some are continually taking part in violent demonstrations in an attempt to overthrow the present system. Even the air, the water and the soil around us seem to be threatened by the poisonous products of modern industry, so that fish die in our rivers, and people's health is affected by smoke, chemicals and noise. So behind all the prosperity there is a tendency to wonder whether we are really building a better society and whether it will even survive.

This sort of mood may be incomprehensible to younger nations absorbed in their own progress. Perhaps the future is bright. Britain is a small power now in comparison to America and Russia, but she is still widely respected, and may have an important part to play in organizing a better and a safer world. But for the moment she feels she is living in an age of upheaval and uncertainty.

Words & Expressions

disadvantage/ˌdisədˈvɑːntidʒ/*n.* 不利
enliven/inˈlaivn/*vt.* 使有生气、活跃
Crusade/kruːˈseid/*n.* 十字军东征
infidel/ˈinfidəl/*n.* 异教徒
wield/wiːld/vt. 运用
excommunicate/ˌekskəˈmjuːnikeit/*vt.* （宗教）开除某人的教籍
baron/ˈbærən/*n.* 贵族；男爵
sever/ˈsevə/*vt.* 切断
heir/εə/*n.* 继承人；后嗣
Catholicism/kəˈθɔlisizəm/*n.* 天主教义
embitter/imˈbitə/*vt.* 加剧
heresy/ˈherəsi/*n.* 异教；信奉邪说
devout/diˈvaut/*a.* 虔诚的
Armada/ɑːˈmɑːdə/*n.* （西班牙）无敌舰队
conspiracy/kənsˈpirəsi/*n.* 阴谋
effigy/ˈefidʒi/*n.* 模拟像
divine/diˈvain/*a.* 神的
levy/ˈlevi/*vi.* 征税；征收
condemn/kənˈdem/*vt.* 谴责；判（某人）刑
scaffold/ˈskæfəld/*n.* 断台头
behead/biˈhed/*vt.* 砍头
fugitive/ˈfjuːdʒitiv/*n.* 逃亡者
supremacy/sjuˈpreməsi/*n.* 选举权
franchise/ˈfræntʃaiz/*n.* 选举权
disposed/disˈpəuzd/*a.* 处理，对待
submissive/səbˈmisiv/*a.* 顺从的
stroke/strəuk/*n.* 打
cane/kein/*n.* 棍杖
sermon/ˈsəːmən/*n.* 说教
virtue/ˈvəːtʃə/*n.* 美德
spheres of influence 势力范围
whip/hwip/*vt.* 鞭策
imminent/ˈiminənt/*a.* 迫近的
suffragette/ˌsʌfrəˈdʒet/*n.* 鼓吹妇女参政者
catastrophe/kəˈtæstrəfi/*n.* 大灾难
stationary/ˈsteiʃənəri/*a.* ~war 阵地战
slump/slʌmp/*n.* 暴跌
blitz/blits/*n.* 闪电式袭击
sirens wailed 警报器尖啸
a war of movement 运动战
bewildered/biˈwildəd/*a.* 迷惑不解

Notes

1. enlivened by the author's imagination：作家的想像力使得（历史事件）活生生地再现在读者面前。

2. it has become a sort of joke:1066 年是英国历史的转折点,人们谈到历史,往往从这一年开始,对再往前的历史知之极少,因此 1066 年事件就像(家喻户晓的)笑话那样广为人知了。

3. the Saxon king Harold:哈罗德是英格兰最后一位撒克逊民族的国王,1066 年诺曼底法国人入侵英格兰时,在关键性的 Hastings 战斗中被杀,英格兰从此被征服,诺曼底统治者成了英国国王,即威廉一世。

4. Of the time before that the average person knows little:普通老百姓对 1066 年以前的历史知之甚少。

5. he let the cakes burn ... unrecognized:阿尔弗雷德(849 ~ 899)是英格兰撒克逊民族的一位国王。他成功地阻止了丹麦人的入侵。这里是传说中有关他的一个故事。据说有一次他深入丹麦人占领区时被敌人包围,一位农妇把他掩护起来,让他烤饼。当敌人来搜查时,这位农妇"大骂"这位国王,说把她的饼烧焦了。敌人因此未能认出他来。

6. Arthur ... many legends:亚瑟国王是六世纪时英格兰统治者。有关他的传说很多。这句中提到的就是其中的二则传说。据说亚瑟是不列颠国王和一位叫 Gorlois 妇女的私生子。国王死后,亚瑟由别人秘密抚养,长大成人后,他成功地从石中取出神剑,因此被确认为不列颠国王。亚瑟王和他的骑士们的大圆桌会议是另一则传说。亚瑟的骑士们经常因为开会时的座次问题而争吵不休,因此他命令把他丈人给他的圆桌作为会议桌,这样,骑士们就无法分出高低主次了。

7. the Crusades:在 11 至 14 世纪之间,欧洲基督教徒在罗马教皇鼓动下,进行九次十字军东征,企图把耶稣曾经生活过的圣地巴勒斯坦从穆斯林手中夺回来,真正的动机是欧洲国家企图借此向东扩展,争夺海外领地和财富。

8. the "Infidels" (the Muslims):穆斯林占领巴勒斯坦后,基督教徒受到迫害。欧洲基督教徒们称穆斯林人为"异教徒"。

9. Richard Lion-Heart and Saladin:英王理查一世号称"理查勇士国王"。1190 年他率军进行第三次十字军东征,一直打到耶路撒冷。撒拉丁是埃及君王苏丹。1187 年他带兵占领耶路撒冷,理查一世因该城护卫严密,无法战胜撒拉丁,因此和他签订了三年的停战协定,基督教徒被允许进入耶路撒冷圣地。

10. the Pope in Rome ... eternal damnation:16 世纪新教改革运动以前,罗马天主教会一统欧洲各国,罗马教皇权力极大。根据天主教规,如果一个人被驱逐出教会,他死后就会被打入地狱,永远不得翻身。罗马教皇常常以此胁迫各国君王服从他的意志。

11. the Magna Carta ("Great Charter"):英国《大宪章》。1215 年,英格兰各诸侯在人民的支持下,迫使英王约翰签订大宪章,限制他的权力。《大宪章》一般被认为是英国宪法的基础性文件。

12. a war with France ... for a hundred years:从 15 世纪初英王亨利五世登位开始,英国向法国开战,战争断断续续进行了一百年左右,因此史称"百年战争"。

13. Joan of Arc:圣女贞德(1412 ~ 1431)是英法百年战争期间法国的传奇式的人物。她出身于一个农民家庭,出于爱国心参加抵抗英军对法国的入侵。她多次率兵出击,把英军打得一败涂地。后被英军俘获,被烧死。

14. the Wars of the Roses:1455 至 1485 年,英国又暴发了"玫瑰战争"。内战的双方是

爱德华三世的子孙们。他们为了争夺王位,分为以白玫瑰和红玫瑰为标志的交战两方。这场贵族统治阶级的自戕延续了三十年之久,激起了广大人民的不满。

15. the Middle Ages ... the modern period:欧洲历史上的中世纪一般是指第4、5世纪到15世纪这个时期。17世纪英国资产阶级革命开始后的时期被称为"近代史"。16世纪是个重要的过渡时期。

16. Columbus and vasco da Gama:哥伦布于1492年发现美洲新大陆。1497年瓦·达·伽玛首次经海路从葡萄牙到达印度。1519年麦哲伦开始了环球航行。这些航行把世界五大洲连接了起来。这个时期就称为"地理大发现时期"。

17. Mary:玛丽一世是亨利八世的女儿,但她是天主教徒。她继位后不久,首先宣布与西班牙国王菲力普结婚。和菲力普结婚后,她又与罗马教皇弃嫌修好,任意迫害、烧杀异教徒,所以被称为"血腥的玛丽"。

18. Elizabeth:伊丽莎白一世在玛丽女王死后实行了一系列使英国强盛的政策。她命令心腹船长充当海盗,抢劫西班牙从美洲掠夺回来的船只,用夺得的财富加强海军建设。同时她答应和西班牙国王菲力普结婚,唆使他和法国开战,以获渔翁之利。当她感到英国已经强大到足以抵御西班牙时,又撕毁婚约,菲力普受辱并于1588年对英宣战,却被英国海军击败。这次胜利是英国向外扩张的转折点。从此,英国成了海上霸王,走上了殖民主义的道路。

19. Francis Drake:德雷克是伊丽莎白一世时著名的海军将领,1588年西班牙舰队进攻英国时,他是英国海军副司令。

20. It was a lucky victory in many ways:1588年西班牙无敌舰队向英国进攻,不料遭受暴风,而且处于逆风位置。英国乘势顺风而下,用火船烧得西班牙舰队到处乱窜。最后在英军发明的新战术下,西班牙舰队遭到毁灭性的打击。后来有人说,英国的胜利是风向帮了大忙,因此是侥幸的胜利。

21. one of the most important events in the whole of British history:指英国历史上的资产阶级革命。

22. a "Divine Right" to govern:君权神授论。英国革命时期,詹姆士一世和查理一世极力宣扬这种理论,说他们的统治权是上帝授予的,他们只对上帝负责,不对人民负责,因而人民的反抗是罪恶的。这种理论激起了新兴资产阶级及代表他们利益的议会的反对,因此,议会开始与国王对立,资产阶级革命由此爆发。

23. the "Puritan" elements:英国资产阶级革命又称"清教徒革命",因为革命的领导者大多是清教徒。清教是英国国教内部的一个新教派别。清教教义跟随加尔文主义,认为人人生而有罪,但个人不能拯救自己,也不能通过教会或神父来拯救灵魂,因为人人都是命中注定。也就是说,上帝注定谁是他的选民,谁将进地狱。教会不是上帝的代表,因此不享有至高无上的权力,只有《圣经》才是至高无上的。每个人必须在上帝赐予的神业中工作,而成功与否是一个人是不是上帝选民的重要标志。持这种教义的人要"纯清"英国国教,反对国教中的天主教义,反对国教教会的腐败现象,因而称为"清教徒"。清教派中分两派:一派为分离派,他们决心和英国国教彻底决裂,后来移民到今天美国的新英格兰;另一派则留在英国,参加革命,推翻了斯图亚特王朝。

24. The "Roundheads" and the "Cavaliers":"平头派"支持代表资产阶级利益的议会,

“骑士派”支持国王。

25. the great Civil War broke out:内战于1642年爆发,1649年结束。

26. Whitehall:白厅,英国政府所在地。

27. Charles Ⅱ:查理一世的儿子。1660年英国共和体领导人克伦威尔去世后不久,流亡在外的查理二世乘机回国复辟登位,并大肆镇压资产阶级革命者。

28. the Catholic king James Ⅱ:查理二世死后,由他的弟弟接位,称“詹姆士二世”。他和他的妻子都是天主教徒,遭到议会中资产阶级势力和新教派的强烈反对,因而发生了1688年的“光荣革命”。

29. rival imperialists:(英法)是敌对的帝国主义国家。两国为了争夺海外殖民地曾多次交战,比如“国王威廉之战”(1689~1697)、“女王安妮之战”(1701~1713)以及“七年战争”(1756~1763),还有下文提到的几次战争等。

30. Battle of Waterloo ... Napoleon:1815年,英俄普鲁士和奥地利联军在英国威灵顿公爵领导下,在比利时滑铁卢打败拿破仑的军队,取得了一次决定性的胜利。

31. the Battle of Trafalgar:1805年,英国海军司令纳尔逊在西班牙的特拉法加海角击败法国军队,取得了反对法国海军的一次重大的胜利。他本人在接近胜利时战死。为纪念这位将领,英国在取名为特拉法广场(伦敦)上建立了很高的纳尔逊纪念碑,即Nelson's Column。

32. to overcoma social problems, like those connected with the Industrial Revolution:克服和工业革命有关的一些社会问题,主要是指贫穷和失业问题。

33. William Wilberforce:18世纪末和19世纪初的英国政治家,废奴立法的主要倡议者。

34. Elizabeth Fry:弗赖尔(1780~1845)是英国历史上有名的监狱改革活动家和慈善家。

35. the “Rocket”, gradually replacing the old stage-coach:英国工程师斯蒂文森(1781~1848)于1814年发明机车,1829年他制造的机车“火箭号”,在机车竞赛中名列第一,并使用于铁路,代替了老式交通工具公共马车。

36. Queen Victoria:维多利亚女王(1819~1901),是英国历史上在位时期(1837~1901)最长的君主。

37. but embarassment is not the same as fear:中上阶层,主要是出身于贵族家庭的英国上层统治阶级看不起那些出身低下但在工商业上获得成功而在社会阶梯上向上爬的人,这种人常使他们感到不自在。但这种不自在还没有发展到害怕的程度。

38. Their life consisted of “don'ts”:他们的生活中不许干这干那的规矩很多。

39. Charles Darwin:达尔文(1809~1882),英国博物学家、进化论创立者,他的《物种起源》是其进化论的主要著作。

40. The average person ... “on the side of the angels”:1864年,曾两度任过英国首相的保守政治家迪斯雷利反对进化论思想,在演说中说:“人类是由类人猿进化而来还是上帝创造的天使?……我站在天使一边。”普通英国人不理解问题的实质,因此像这位有名的政治家一样“站在天使一边”,仍相信上帝造人信念。

41. contribute to its decay:(达尔文的理论)促使了维多利亚时代的衰落。作者认为,由于达尔文进化论思想的影响,许多普通人不像维多利亚时代的人们那样相信上帝造人之说了。

42. Britain had never heen ... imperial power:英国对建立一个殖民帝国从来就不特别感兴趣,也没有有意要这么做。作者在这里强调了英国政府,尤其是王室对北美、澳大利亚等殖民地采取不直接参与的方式,这和西班牙殖民方式不同。因此,这些地区的发展和拉美发展有较大的区别。但作者却忽视了很重要的一点,即一切殖民主义者都无一例外地竭力控制殖民地这一重要事实。

43. the Mutiny in India:1857 年,在英军中服役的印度士兵因不满英国的殖民统治,反对英国殖民主义者对印度文化和宗教的破坏而爆发了"印度士兵兵变"。兵变最后被英军残酷镇压,许多人遭屠杀。

44. Britain had the lion's share:英国(在"掠夺非洲"、争夺"势力范围"中)获利最大,取得的殖民地最多,地方最好。

45. the famous "suffragette" movement:1903 年由"妇女社会及政治联盟"发起的旨在争取妇女选举权的"妇女运动"。

46. the great "slump" of the early 1930's:30 年代的大萧条。这个大萧条从 1920 年 10 月 29 日纽约股票市场的暴跌开始,很快波及美国全国、欧洲及世界其他各地;30 年代初是危机最严重的时期。

47. the League of Nations:国际联盟(1920 ~ 1946)是第一次大战后巴黎和约会议的产物。主要鼓吹者是美国总统威尔逊。但美国因与英、法争夺领导权,故参议院否决了参加国际联盟的提议。联盟实为维护侵略政策的工具。1931 年日本侵占中国东北后,联盟没有采取任何行动。所以,所谓联盟旨在维护和平、制止侵略完全是一句空话。

48. the idea of a German "master-race":希特勒法西斯所宣扬的所谓"日尔曼民族优越论",以及所谓日尔曼民族的祖先雅利安人为"世界主子种族"的法西斯种族主义谬论。

Exercises

Ⅰ. Explain the following

1. King Harold
2. Alfred the Great
3. King Arthur
4. the Magna Carta
5. the Wars of the Roses
6. Henry Ⅷ
7. Elizabeth Ⅰ
8. Divine right
9. Charles Darwin
10. Victorianism

Ⅱ. Fill in the blanks

1. ________ were a series of wars in which armies from all over Europe tried to seize Palestine from the Muslims.

2. ________ and ________ were the two famous sailors who started the age of discovery.

3. By the end of ________ England became separated from France and the English language finally took the place of French in all classes in English society.

4. In the English Civil War, the "Roundheads" supported ________ while the "Caveliers" supported ________.

5. The Origin of Species was written by ________.

6. In the early 1930s, ________ brought poverty and humiliation to millions of people in

7. After World War I, an international body called ________ was formed, and after World War Ⅱ, another international organization ________ was founded.

Ⅲ. Choose the correct answer in each of the following

1. One of the following did not take place during the middle ages:

A. The making of the Magna Carta.

B. The defeat of the Spanish Armada by the English navy.

C. The rule of Alfred the Great.

D. The defeat of King Harold by France.

2. In England, the Protestant Reformation began with ________.

A. bloody Mary

B. Queen Elizabeth

C. King Henry Ⅶ

D. King Henry Ⅷ

3. Three of the following were characteristics of the Elizabethan age. Which of the four is the exception?

A. Queen Elizabeth advocated the Divine Right and quarreled with Parliament.

B. Protestantism gradually became the dominant faith.

C. This was the age of literature when Shakespeare lived and when English literature blossomed.

D. This was the age of adventure on the sea.

4. The Industrial Revolution owed a great deal to ________.

A. the invention of printing

B. George Stephenson's famous locomotive, the "Rocket"

C. the invention of the steam engine

D. the springing-up of towns

5. Victorianism was characterized by the following except ________.

A. it was in an age of imperialism

B. it saw the great progress in social sciences with Charles Darwin as a prominent figure

C. it was the age when the great progress was made in the the field of communications

D. it was an age when the Battle of Waterloo was won by the Duke of Wellington

Ⅳ. Answer the following questions briefly

1. What were the main features of the Middle Ages?

2. Why did the Pope in Rome in the Middle Ages have so much power?
3. Why was the sixteenth century so important to English history and European history?
4. What changes took place during the Industrial Revolution? What was the impact of the Industrial Revolution on English society?
5. Explain the atmosphere of Victorianism.

Chapter 3 The English Language

Anyone who has lived a reasonably long time will know that his children and their contemporaries are not using the same words, grammar and pronunciation that he learned as a child, because each generation has a different attitude to its language. In the past, changes in vocabulary, structures and syntax happened so slowly that they were frequently unnoticeable to those speaking the language. But the introduction of widespread education, radio and television, and the greater mobility of the population, have speeded up the process. Young people, especially, use a vast amount of idioms, slang and Americanisms, which are gradually either absorbed into "respectable" English or left behind like any other fashion[1].

Language is a tool which can and must be manipulated to serve the needs of those who use it. In modern times, for example, so many political, social and technological changes have taken place that language too has had to adapt and find new words and expressions. This adaptability has been apparent throughout the long history of the English language whose roots go back to Celtic Britain.

In the time of the Celts, Britain was divided into various tribal kingdoms, each one speaking its own kind of Celtic. But as these ancient people had no written language, they left little that could later be incorporated into English. Relics of Celtic, however, do remain in place names. Some, for instance, derive from the particular tribe that live in the area: Kent from the Cantiaci tribe, Devon from the Dumnonii and Cornwall from the Cornovii. Others are based on Celtic words for specific natural features: several names of rivers, like Avon, Esk, Stour and Usk, come from Celtic words for water; *comb*, Celtic for a deep valley, is found in modern place names like Salcombe, Addiscombe and Wexcombe; and tor, meaning a high rock or peak, persists in Torquay, Torpoint and Torcross. Also some town names, like London, Dover, York, Leeds, Penrith, Carlisle and Catterick, are Celtic in origin. After the Romans invaded Britain in 55 BC, their word for a fortress, *castra* (giving *chester* or *cester*), was added to many existing Celtic place names: modern examples, include Winchester, Manchester, Leicester, Rochester and Gloucester.

Many Celts fled from the Romans and subsequent invaders and settled in the mountains of Wales, the Highlands and islands of Scotland, Ireland, the Isle of Man and Cornwall. Because these areas were so remote, the tribes manage to preserve their languages, which survive today as Welsh, Scottish Gaelic and Irish Gaelic. Manx, another form of Gaelic, was spoken on the Isle of Man until about 1950. The Cornish Celtic language was spoken up to about 200 years ago and a branch of the same language, called Breton, is still used across the Channel in Brittany, a region of north-west France.

As the Romans extended their empire, their language, Latin, became the *lingua franca*[2] of most of western Europe including Britain. Then, from about the third century, the spread of Latin was strengthened by the introduction of Christianity as all prayers and liturgy were in that language. The English alphabet as such, adapted from Roman scripts, appeared sometime between AD 500 and 700.

The history of English really began around AD 450 when the Angles, Saxons and Jutes—tribes from north-west Germany and Denmark—invaded England in succession. The various tribes had their own Germanic dialects but, after they had taken control of the country and settled, four main dialects emerged: Mercian (spoken between the rivers Thames and Humber); Northumbrian (north of the river Humber); Kentish (in the south-eastern corner); and West Saxon (in the south and west). These were the dialects of Old English.

The Evolution of Old English

Old English of Anglo-Saxon, although it is the ancestor of modern English, appears quite different from today's language. Writers of the Old English period—about AD 587-1066—used both Latin and Germanic scripts but always called their language English no matter what their tribe or dialect.

A strong influence entered Old English by way of the Vikings from Scandinavia. During the ninth century they plundered and settled in areas as far apart as Russia, Iceland and the Faroe Islands as well as in the British Isles. As a permanent reminder of the Viking invasion, some 1400 places in England have names of Scandinavian origin. There was a similarity between the Old Norse language[3] of the Scandinavians and the Old English of the Anglo-Saxons and many everyday words were the same. The Scandinavians, however, had developed their own system of writing called the Runic alphabet (other Germanic tribes also used Runic scripts).

The most common words borrowed from Scandinavian are many of those which in modern English have *sk together such as* sky, skin, skill, skull, ski, skip, whish *and* bask. *Old English used the Germanic sh rather than* sk *can be seen in the Old English word* scyrte *becoming* shirt, *whereas the corresponding word in Old Norse*, skyrta, *became* skirt. *Words that retain the hard-sounding* g *and* k *in egg and* kid *are also of Scandinavian origin. Evidence of Scandinavian settlement exists in the many place names (over* 600 *in all) like Derby, Rugby and Grimsby that end in* by *— a Danish word for farm or town. (Two modern everyday words,* by-law *and* by-road, *meaning a local law/road, also derive from the Danish* by).

Old English, by the end of its period, contained a vocabulary of at least 30 000 *words. To compare this with later English: William Shakespeare, in the sixteenth century, used about* 25 000 *words in his plays; John Milton*[4], *in the seventeenth century, used only* 12 000 *for his poetry; and in this century, Sir Winston Churchill*[5] *used a vocabulary of about* 60 000 *words.*

Most of the Old English poetry, prose and records that have survived were composed or written down by scholar-monks; one of the best known was the Venerable Bede (673-735) who lived in a Northumbrian monastery. Around AD 731, *Bede wrote the* Ecclesiastical History of the English People, *which is one of the main sources of information about the history of Anglo-Saxon England.*

The Norman Influence

With the Norman invasion led by William the Conqueror in 1066, Norman French (a dialect of French influenced by popular Latin and old Norse), became the official language of England. After William's victory most important positions, including high offices in the Church, were given to Normans, who organized government and public affairs. As a result, many words connected with administration come from Norman French: words like *realm*, *sovereign*, *tax*, *homage* and *assembly* as well as the names of office holders such as *chancellor*, *chamberlain*, *treasurer*, *marshall*, *governor*, *constable* and *warden*. Many titles of nobility like *baron*, *duke*, *count* and *marquis*, derive from the French of this period; so do the words *court* and *courtier* and titles of respect such as *sir* and *madam*.

Although Norman French became the language of the ruling class, the common people—who far outnumbered the Normans!—continued to speak their own Anglo-Saxon language.

Middle English

The blend of Anglo-Saxon, Latin and French which developed in the three centuries after the Norman conquest is known as Middle English.

In the three centuries following 1066, when the literature of England was trilingual (French, English and Latin), synonymous words took on changes of meaning. For example the Old English words *bull*, *sheep*, *calf*, *swine* and *deer* described the animals themselves; the equivalents from French, *beef*, *mutton*, *veal*, *pork* and *venison* came to mean the meat of these animals used for cooking and eating.

The Kings of England descended from William the Conqueror spoke French, but by 1362, when Parliament was opened in English for the first time, the dominance of French was confined largely to the law and the Court. By the fourteenth century, while French was still to some extent the language of culture and learning, its place had largely been taken by English, which had freely incorporated many French words. This can be seen in the works of the most important Middle English poet, Geoffrey Chaucer[6] (1345 – 1400). He used a vocabulary of more than 8 000 words in his written works, of which just over 4 000 were of Romance (that is, Latin and French) origin. Current English vocabulary is approximately half Germanic (English and Scandinavian) and half Romance. The Middle English dialect used by Chaucer was that of London; it had a strong French accent and intonation.

The difference between Old English and Middle English lies mainly in the abandonment of the system of grammatical inflexions[7]; but the changes from Middle English to Modern English involve mainly pronunciation, vocabulary and spelling.

Pronunciation and vocabulary have been constantly changing. Many present-day pronunciations were not in common use until quite recently. In the eighteenth century *oblige* was pronounced *obleege*; *servant* was *sarvant* (whereas *clerk* is still called *clark*); well into the nineteenth century gold was pronounced gould; and *shown* was *shewn* well into the twentieth. Spelling, too, often gives a clue as to past pronunciation.

At the end of the fifteenth century, with the introduction of the printing press (1476), spellings and written forms began to become standardized. Changes in the spoken language, however, continued to occur.

Modern English

In early modern English, from about AD 1500, the introduction of new words reflected the need for terms to express the advances in learning. The new words were not so much associated with everyday life, but instead were related to subjects like astronomy, philosophy, literature and theology. With the gradual increase in literacy and in the availability of the printed word, the more formal and technical vocabulary of written literature entered common speech.

By the time of William Shakespeare (1564 – 1616), the Renaissance revival of classical learning (ancient Greek and Latin)[8] and a growing interest in literary forms began to influence everyday language. All Shakespeare's works are in Modern English although to today's ears they often need explaining as many of the words he used are now obsolete, or have changed their meaning, or refer to little-known episodes and characters in classical literature.

During the sixteenth and seventeenth centuries scientific investigation brought new words into the language derived from words used in ancient Greece. The vocabulary of modern medicine, astronomy (nearly all stars and planets have names from ancient mythology) and technology, for example, is largely of Greek origin. The suffix *logy*, meaning "the study of", is often joined to parts of Greek words to make scientific and academic words, like *biology*, *physiology* and *psychology*. The prefix *tele*, also Greek, means "from afar" and is used in modern words like *telegram* and, with the Greek root *phone* (meaning voice or sound), *telephone*.

Foreign Elements

After Latin, Scandinavian, French and Greek, the English vocabulary owes most to Italian. Chaucer, who travelled widely in Italy, brought back many words and this borrowing from Italian reached its peak in the sixteenth century. Many current terms relating to architecture (*balcony*, *corridor*), literature (*stanza*, *tanto*), art (*studio*, *profile*, *vista*, *replica*) and especially to music (*opera*, *sonata*, *solo*, *alto*, *piano*) come from Italian.

The development of new sea routes had a lasting effect on the English language. Travellers brought back words like *coffee*, *cotton*, *kiosk* and *turban* from Turkey and Arabia; also *bazaar* and *pyjamas* from Persia.

Likewise, trade with India and the Far East introduced the names of many new commodities such as *tea*, *curry*, *gingham*, *teak*, *bamboo* and *sago*. In the late sixteenth century, Sir Walter Raleigh[9] returned from what is now Virginia in the USA with England's first *potato* and *tobacco*, both names coming from North American Indian words. *Tomato*, *cocoa*, *maize*, *cigar* and *barbecue* came, via sea-going adventurers, from South America. Many of the new commodities arriving in Britain had names related to their places of origin: *port*, wine made in Oporto, Portugal; *madeira*, wine from Madeira island in the Atlantic Ocean; calico, cloth from Calicut in southern India; *muslin*, fine cotton cloth from Mosul, Iraq; *damask*, cloth from

Damascus; *currants*, dried grapes from Corinth, Greece; and *sherry*, fortified wine from Jerez, Spain.

From the Dutch, English acquired words connected with two very different activities: seafaring (*yacht*, *cruiser*, *deck*, *dock*, *skipper*) and painting (*sketch*, *stipple*). From Spanish came *armada*, *guerilla*, *embargo* and *patio*; from Hindi, words like *bungalow*, *yoga*; from Afrikaans (South African Dutch), *tred* and *commando*.

More recently, the enormous increase in travel has brought many foreign foods into British kitchens and restaurants. Foods from France like *gateaux*, *consomme* and *souffle*; from Italy like *spaghetti*, *macaroni*, *lasagne* and *risotto*; *paella*, *gazpacho* and *tortilla* from Spain; *frankfurters* and *hamburgers* from Germany; *chow mein* and *chop suey* from China; *kebabs* from Turkey; *moussaka* and *taramasalata* from Greece; and *curry*, *tandoori* and *poppadoms* from India.

The English language has been borrowing from French ever since 1066 although in modern times the process has, at least, become two-way; the French now use words like *le weekend* and *leparking*. Over the years most French words absorbed into English have become so anglicized that it is easy to forget their origin. Relatively recent adoptions, however, still retain their French pronunciations: examples include *ballet*, *boutique*, *souvenir*, *reservoir*, *gauche*, *rapport*, *repertoire*, *precis*, *avant-garde*, *detente*, *coupd' etat*, *au pair* and *discotheque*.

Standard English and Social Class

When the British Broadcasting Corporation (BBC) was founded in 1927, its motto, *Nation Shall Speak Peace Unto Nation*[10], clearly indicated that the English spoken over the radio should be universally understood. Announcers were chosen whose speech patterns represented the educated southern upper classes. and their particular style of speech came to be recognized as Standard English or Received Pronunciation (RP) English. Although, in recent years, the BBC has been accused of lowering its standards in language, most people still consider that the pronunciation and delivery of BBC announcers is the clearest and most understandable spoken English — and the most appropriate style of speech for a foreigner learning English to copy.

English, perhaps more than any other language, has had a strong association with class and social status. This began as far back as Norman times when the upper classes spoke a completely different language from the common people. All classes at various times used modes of speech, intonation and vowel sounds which were, to any listener, an immediate indication of the speaker's social position.

Since the Second World War, along with a peaceful social revolution, there has been, a considerable change of attitude towards speech snobbery. While successive governments encouraged the idea of a more just and equal society, hallmarks of class distinction such as styles of speech and dress have been gradually discarded, especially by the younger generation. During the "pop" revolution of the 1960s[11] it became fashionable for young people from the upper classes to try to sound and look like members of the ordinary working classes.

As the need has arisen, new words have been invented or found from other languages and incorporated into English. Similarly, old words and expressions have been discarded as their usefulness has diminished or the fashion has passed. This also happens to styles and modes of speech which became fashionable at a particular time and in specific circumstances. Many of the popular, everyday expressions used by the armed forces during the Second World War—now heard only in old war films—sound very silly today, even to the many people who remember using them.

Also during this time, young men and women from relatively humble backgrounds[12] were making an impact on the arts as writers, poets, playwrights and journalists. Young people from the working class were also exerting a great influence on the fashion scene as dress designers and fashion models; many also became successful "pop" musicians and entertainers.

By the second half of the 1960s (the era of swinging London[13], the Beatles and the Permissive Society[14]) it became apparent that it was not necessary to speak Standard English or even correct grammar to become popular, successful and rich. The fashionable speech of the day was no longer the prerogative of a privileged class but rather a defiant expression of classlessness. Most people were quite happy to follow this fashion and retain their own local speech patterns and mannerisms; instead of trying to imitate the speech of the upper classes, as their parents or grandparents might have done, they copied the speech of their cinema, television and pop heroes.

The greatest single influence of the shaping of the English language in modern times is the American accent, idiom and vocabulary exported all over the globe by US films. There can be nowhere in the world today where the expression OK is not used and understood. Over the last 25 years the English used by many people, particularly by those in the media, advertising and show business, has become more and more mid-Atlantic in style, delivery and accent[15].

English Today

In the 1970s, fashion favoured careless enunciation and a language full of jargon, slang and "in" words[16], much of it quite incomprehensible to the outside world. This fashion was encouraged by the popular media and promoted by the many "pop" magazines which appeared at that time. Knowledge and use of a special language, cliches and an "in" vocabulary immediately identified the speaker—perhaps as a politician, a university professor, a psychiatrist, a rock musician... or even a criminal!

Many slang words and expressions have a relatively short life since novelty is part of their appeal. As new expressions appear, old ones are discarded and consequently, their influence on the language is not as drastic as may be thought. On the other hand, by the time today's users of the latest slang expressions reach middle age, some of these expressions will have become absorbed into "respectable" English; furthermore, the same people will probably be complaining about the incomprehensible language spoken by their children. Slang is certainly evidence of a dynamic living language and it brings colour and character to linguistic expression—even if it is not always the best medium for understanding.

All the changes and fashions in style of speech and pronunciation over the centuries are proof of adaptability and versatility. In 1500 years, English has developed from the language of a small, warlike, agrarian people, the Anglo-Saxons, to the language of a highly developed technological civilization and now has one of the richest vocabularies of any language in the world. It has become the most influential and most international language of modern times, spoken by 275 million native speakers, and the language that so many people in the world want to learn. But "which English?" they may well ask. After all, what is considered modern and fashionable in Britain today is often not the kind of English taught in schools and colleges in their own countries. And should it be English or the fast-spreading American English?

The best advice to all those who wish to become proficient in English was given in 1906 by the Fowler brothers in their famous book, *The King's English*. It is just as applicable to today's popular-style English as it was to the "more showy qualities" of Edwardian English. It is still sound advice for any student of English, whether English is his mother tongue or whether it is a foreign language. Their advice is:

"Anyone who wishes to become proficient in English should endeavour, before he allows himself to be tempted by the more showy qualities, to be direct, simple, brief, vigorous and lucid. This general principle may be translated into practical rules in the domain of vocabulary as follows:

Prefer the familiar words to the far-fetched.

Prefer the concrete word to the abstract.

Prefer the single word to the circumlocution.

Prefer the short word to the long.

Prefer the Saxon word to the Romance."

Words & Expressions

syntax/ˈsintæks/*n.* 句法

mobility/məuˈbiliti/*n.* 流动

Americanisms *n.* 美国用词用语

manipulate/məˈnipjuleit/*vt.* 应用

Liturgy/ˈlitə(:)dʒi/*n.* 礼拜仪式

realm/relm/*n.* 王国;领域

sovereign/ˈsɔvrin/*n.* 君主;主权

homage/ˈhɔmidʒ/*n.* 效忠;敬意

assembly/əˈsembli/*n.* 集会;议会

chancellor/ˈtʃɑːnsələ/*n.* 大臣,司法官

chamberlain/ˈtʃeimbəlin/*n.* 国王的内侍

treasurer/ˈtreʒərə/*n.* 司库

marshall/ˈmɑːʃəl/*n.* 元帅

constable/ˈkʌnstəbl/*n.* 警官

warden/ˈwɔːdn/*n.* 总督,大臣

duke/djuːk/*n.* 公爵

count/kaunt/*n.* 伯爵(英国称 earl)

marquis/ˈmɑːkwis/*n.* 侯爵

Romance/rəuˈmæns/*n.* 罗曼语

obsolete/ˈɔbsəliːt/*a.* 过时的

motto/ˈməutəu/*n.* 格言

hallmark/ˈhɔːlˈmɑːk/*n.* 特征

diminish/diˈminiʃ/*vi.* 减小

prerogative/priˈrɔgətiv/*n.* 特征;特权

defiant/difˈaiənt/*a.* 挑战性的

mannerism/ˈmænərizəm/*n.* 言谈举止习惯

enunciation/iˌnʌnsiˈeiʃən/*n.* 发音;发表

jargon/ˈdʒɑːgən/*n.* 专门术语

cliche/ˈkliːʃei/*n.* 陈词滥调

novelty/ˈnɔvəlti/*n.* 新奇

dynamic/daiˈnæmik/*a.* 有活力的

adaptability/əˌdæptəˈbiliti/*n.* 适应性

versatility/ˌvəːsəˈtiliti/*n.* 多面性

lucid/ˈljuːsid/*a.* 清晰易懂的

domain/dəˈmein/*n.* 领域,范围

circumlocution/ˌsəːkəmləˈkiuːʃən/*n.* 累赘;迂回

Notes

1. either absorbed into "respectable" English... fashion:有的成了"高雅"英语的一部分,而另外的则和其他时髦东西一样被淘汰。

2. lingua franca:不同民族之间的通用语。

3. the Old Norse language：指中世纪时期的日尔曼语言。

4. John Milton：弥尔顿(1608～1674)，英国诗人、资产阶级革命家。主要著作有《失乐园》、《复乐园》等。

5. Winston Churchill：邱吉尔(1874～1965)是英国20世纪著名的政治家、作家。第二次世界大战期间及50年代，他曾任英国首相。1953年获诺贝尔文学奖。主要作品有《世界危机》、《第二次世界大战》等。

6. Geoffrey Chaucer：乔叟(约1343～1400)是英国中世纪最著名的诗人。他把属于中古英语的伦敦方言发展成为英国的文学语言。他的著作《坎特伯雷故事集》等作品开创了英国文学的现实主义传统。

7. the system of grammatical inflexions：语法上屈折变化的形式。这个屈折变化主要指数、格、性别和时态的变化。

8. the Renaissance revival of classical learning (ancient Greek and Latin)：13至16世纪，欧洲首先从意大利开始，进行文艺复兴运动，恢复古希腊古罗马时期的古典文化中的人道主义和现实主义，反对封建和教会神权思想，发展资产阶级新兴文化。

9. Walter Raleigh：罗利(约1554～1618)是英国冒险家。他首先把烟草传入今日美国的弗吉尼亚地区，使当地的经济获得新生，以后又是他首先把烟草传入欧洲。

10. Nation Shall Speak Peace Unto Nation：这是英国广播公司成立时的格言，意思是该公司将用大家都能听懂的标准英语向世界各民族传播和平的声音。

11. the "pop" revolution of the 1960s：60年代的"流行音乐"革命起源于英国西北部城市利物浦，下文提到的the Beatles，即由约翰·列农等4人组成的硬壳虫演唱队就是这场革命的先锋。

12. humble backgrounds：贫穷或社会地位低下的家庭。

13. swinging London：(60年代)各种时髦东西(如流行音乐等)在伦敦风靡一时。

14. the Permissive Society：放任社会或译为"无所约束的社会"。这是西方在60年代出现的一种社会思潮。持这种思想的人主张性自由，对一切传统的清规戒律、社会习俗等进行坦率自由的讨论。

15. mid-Atlantic in style, delivery and accent：在风格、说话腔调以及发音上美国化。

16. "in" words：时髦用语。

Exercises

Ⅰ. Explain each of the following

1. Old English
2. Middle English
3. Geoffrey Chaucer
4. Nation Shall Speak Peace Unto Nation
5. Modern English
6. Standard English

Ⅱ. Fill in the blanks

1. The Old English period lasted from ________ to ________.
2. Old English used both ________ and ________ scripts.
3. The official language of England after 1056 was ________.
4. The combination of the three languages, ________, ________ and ________, is known as Middle English.
5. Geoffrey Chaucer used ________ English while William Shakespeare used ________ English.
6. Modern English started from about ________.
7. Standard English is based on the speech patterns of ________.

Ⅲ. Choose the correct answer in each of the following

1. Which of the following is not true?
   1066 was important in English history because ________.
   A. England was conquered in the Norman invasion
   B. the Norman French became the official language of England
   C. this was the beginning of Middle English
   D. Anglo Saxon language was beginning to die
2. The 1960s was characterized by three of the following except ________.
   A. the fashion of speaking Americanisms
   B. the Permissive Society
   C. the Beatles
   D. swinging London
3. The greatest single influence of the shaping of the English language in modern times is ________.
   A. the "pop" revolution in the 1960s
   B. the enormous increase in travel
   C. American English
   D. the French language
4. In what period of English did John Milton write?
   A. Old English. B. Middle English.
   C. Modern English. D. BBC English.

Ⅳ. Answer the following questions briefly

1. Why has the English language changed so fast in this century?
2. Why did Anglo-Saxon become a language of low social status after 1066?
3. What are the basic differences between Old English and Middle English. and between Middle English and Modern English?
4. Why has the English language had a very strong association with class and social status? What difference have modern ideas of social equality made to language in Britain?

Chapter 4 British Political System

Britain is arguably the oldest representative democracy in the world, with roots that can be traced over a thousand years[1]. Other countries also have long political histories but these histories are marked by periods of sudden, and often violent, change. Although Britain too has had its periods of political instability, in contrast to say, France, the United States, or China, the process of statc-building has been one of evolution rather than revolution[2]. This long, unbroken history is still apparent in Britain's current political institutions and in its political culture[3].

The Monarchy

The oldest institution of government is the Monarchy . This dates back to the Saxons who ruled from the fifth century AD until the Norman Conquest in 1066. The present Queen, Elizabeth II, is directly descended from King Egbert[4], who united England under his rule in 829.

The power of the monarchy was largely derived from the ancient doctrine of the "divine right of kings"[5]. It was held that the sovereign derived his authority from God, not from his subjects. Because of this divine right, although there were sometimes battles between different families who insisted they were the legitimate heirs to the throne, the actual existence of the monarchy has seldom been questioned. For a thousand years Britain has had a hereditary king or queen as the head of state, although there was one brief exception. In the 17th century there was a civil war in England between republican "roundheads"[6] (so-called because the men defied popular fashion and wore their hair cut very short) led by Oliver Cromwell, who wanted to abolish the monarchy, and royalists who wanted it to continue. The Roundheads succeeded in ousting the monarch, Charles I[7], in 1642 and ruled for just eighteen years before the monarchy was restored.

While the King in theory had God on his side, in practice even in medieval times it was thought that he should not exercise absolute power[8]. Instead, the sovereign should be willing to receive advice from prominent men. The monarch's willingness to do this led to many battles between the king and other powerful groups like the Church and powerful, land-owning feudal barons.

It was a gang of feudal barons and the Church which opposed some of King

John's (1199—1216) policies. This opposition was so powerful that the king finally granted them a charter of liberty and political rights, still known by its medieval Latin name of Magna Carta[9]. Magna Carta placed some limits on the king's ability to abuse his royal power. This is still regarded as Britain's key expression of the rights of citizens against the Crown.

The Parliament

The word "parliament" comes from the verb "to parley", that is, to discuss or talk. The term was first used officially in 1236 to describe the gathering of feudal barons and representatives from counties and towns which the king occasionally summoned if he wanted to raise money. Traditionally, medieval kings were supposed to meet their own royal expenses out of their own wealth. If extra resources were needed—for example, if a king wanted to wage a war, which he frequently did—he would try to persuade the Great Council[10], a gathering of leading, wealthy barons which met several times a year, to give him some extra money. By the 13th century, kings found they could not make ends meet by asking for money from this quite small group, and so they widened the Great Council to include representatives of counties, cities and towns, to get them to contribute to his projects. It was in this way that the Great Council came to include both those who were summoned "by name"[11] (the House of Lords) and representatives of communities (the House of Commons). These two houses exist today and collectively we call them the Parliament. The Commons quickly gained in political strength. They were willing to help the King by raising taxes and passing laws, but in return they wanted an increasing say in what the king was doing. In recognition of this, Henry IV decreed in 1407 that all money grants should be considered and approved by the Commons before being considered by the Lords, a formula which is almost the same today. The Commons also acquired law-making powers by the 15th century, a prerogative which had once belonged only to the King and his Councillors.

The civil war which brought the roundheads to power in the 17th century was rooted in a dispute over the power of the king vis-a-vis Parliament. James I[12] and his successor Charles I both insisted on their divine right as kings. They felt Parliament, representing the community, had no real political right to exist, but only existed because the king allowed it to do so. It was the effort to reassert the rights of Parliament that led to the Civil War[13]. The royalist armies were defeated and King Charles I was executed in 1649. But by 1660, Charles I's son was restored to the throne as Charles II[14].

The next King, James II[15], having apparently learned little from the experience of the previous decades, also tried to govern without the consent of Parliament. Leading politicians and church authorities asked James' son-in-law, William of Orange[16], to replace him. In return, William promised these representatives that he would declare governing without parliamentary consent to be illegal. This might have led to another civil war, but James ran away and William took over. In 1689 Parliament passed the Bill of Rights[17] which ensured that the King would never be able to ignore Parliament.

The Prime Minister and Cabinet

To ensure good relations between Crown and Parliament, the king or queen met regularly with a group of important Parliamentarians, a group which became known as the Cabinet[18]. While Cabinet ministers were appointed by the sovereign, they had to have enough support in the House of Commons to enable them to persuade Parliament to pass laws and vote for taxes.

In 1714, the ruling Queen died without producing an heir to the throne and so Britain had to "import" a member of the royal family from Germany to rule Britain. The new King George I[19] spoke English very badly and was not very interested in politics anyway, so he left the job of chairing cabinet meetings to one of his miniters. In time he came to be called the Prime Minister.

While a king or queen who was interested in politics remained very influential, the Parliament was slowly becoming more powerful, especially as it became more organizd. In 1832, when a system for choosing the House of Commons by popular election replaced the monarch's job of appointing representatives, the modern political system was born. Members of Parliament (MPs) assembled themselves into groups which eventually would become political parties, organized groups which presented their policies and ideas to the electorate for approval[20]. The party with the most supporters in the Commons forms the government, and by tradition, the leader of that party becomes Prime Minister.

The British Government Today

From this brief history we can see that British government today is deeply influenced by its long past. Britain is both a parliamentary democracy and a constitutional monarchy[21]. While the official head of state is the Queen, her powers are largely traditional and symbolic. The government at national and local levels is elected by the people and governs according to British constitutional principles.

Because of Britain's imperial past, when many other corners of the globe were ruled from London, we find similar systems of government in many former colonies[22]. Other countries which are governed according to the principles of British parliamentary democracy are Australia, Canada, New Zealand and India. All but India recognise the Queen as their head of state, and a representative of the Crown, called the Governor-General, is present in such constitutional monarchies in order to fulfil the role of the monarch.

The Constitution

British governance today is based upon the terms and conditions of the constitution. Israel and Britain are the only two countries without written constitutions of the sort which most countries have. Instead of having one particular document which lists out the basic principles of how a country should be governed, the foundations of the British state are laid out in statute law[23], that is, laws passed by Parliament; the common laws[24], which are laws which have been established through common practice in the courts, not because Parliament has written them; and conventions[25], which are rules and practices which do not exist legally, but are nevertheless regarded as vital to the workings of government.

Parliament

Parliament has a number of different functions. First and foremost, it passes laws. Another important function is that it provides the means of carrying on the work of government by voting for taxation[26]. Its other roles are to scrutinize government policy, adminitration and expenditure and to debate the major issues of the day.

Parliament is supreme in the British state because it alone has the power to change the terms of the Constitution[27]. For example, the decision for Britain to join the European Union (EU) required a constitutional change because it meant recognizing that EU law would in particular cases be more important than British law.

There are no legal restraints upon Parliament. It can make or change laws, change or overturn established conventions or even prolong its own life without consulting the electorate[28]. However, it does not assert its supremacy, but bears the common law in mind and acts according to precedent.

Strictly speaking, the Parliament today consists of the Queen, the House of

Lords and the House of Commons. These three institutions must all agree to pass any given legislation.

However, most everyday references to Parliament refer to the workings of the Lords and/or the Commons, with the Monarchy regarded as a separate institution. This is because even though the Queen must consent to pass a law, this consent is given as a matter of course[29]. The last royal refusal was in 1707.

The Monarchy

The role of the monarch today is primarily to symbolise the tradition and unity of the British state. Obviously the prime minister and governing party at any given time will only represent the part of the population that voted in their favour[30]. The Queen, however, because she is non-political, belongs to everybody. Under the terms of the constitution her other roles are as follows: she is legally head of the executive, an integral part of the legislature, head of the judiciary, commander in chief of the armed forces and "supreme governor" of the Church of England[31].

In a 1988 poll, most Britons felt the Queen's most important job was to represent Britain at home and abroad; her second most important job was to set standards of good citizenship and family life. While the Queen has indeed led an exemplary life, her children have been criticized for their poor behaviour. Her successor and son, Prince Charles, divorced his wife, Princess Diana. Stories came out in the press alleging that they had both been having extramarital affairs. Her middle son, Andrew, also divorced his wife, Sarah Ferguson (popularly known as Fergie). Andrew and Fergie in particular were both criticized for their jet-setting lifestyles and the way they squandered money.

While the Queen is independently wealthy, much of the financial support for the Royal Family comes from the taxpayer, supposedly in recognizance of the fact that the royal family fulfils its role on behalf of the British people[32]. This had led to great controversy in recent years. In 1992, after Andrew and Fergie had separated, newspapers published a picture of a topless Fergie and her "financial advisor", a wealthy Texan, lounging around a swimming pool. People were outraged because their tax money was used to support such decadence. Shortly afterwards, Charles and Diana also announced they were separating and allegations about their extramarital affairs began to appear in the press.

Criticism of the Queen's children led to a more general criticism about the monarchy and the debate came to a head in November 1992 when a fire did a great deal of damage to Windsor Castle[33]. The government immediately offered 50 million pounds' worth of taxpayers' money to pay for repairs. The electorate was very angry: Britain was in a recession and basic things like hospitals and schools had been forced to cut their services because public money was so scarce. They thought it was very unfair that the Queen, who is incredibly wealthy and does not have to pay taxes herself, should not have to pay for at least part of the repairs. The taxpayer was already paying for the running costs of Buckingham Palace, Windsor Castle, three other palaces, a royal yacht, a royal train and a royal plane. As a result of the controversy, the Queen offered to start paying taxes and to accept less public money to support her family. She also began to open Buckingham Palace to tourists in the summer months in order to raise money to pay for repairs. Her willingness to give in to popular demands once again endeared her to her subjects[34], although her children still remain quite unpopular.

A less well known role of the queen, which is nevertheless very important to British politics, is that of a confidante to the Prime Minister. Every Tuesday the Prime Minister attends the queen privately at Buckingham Palace. In her 40 years on the throne, the Queen has had weekly chats with 9 different Prime Ministers and they have said that her long experience and her political neutrality make her a good source of informed observation on the day to day problems of governance[35].

Interestingly, it is said that the Queen gets on much better with Labour Prime Ministers than with Conservative Prime Ministers.

The House of Lords and the House of Commons

Below the Queen is the House of Lords. It consists of the Lords Spiritual, who are the Archbishops and most prominent bishops of the Church of England; and the Lords Temporal, which refers to everyone else[36]. Lords, usually called peers, are not elected and are not considered to represent anyone besides themselves. They sit in the Lords either because they have inherited the seat from their forefathers (peerages can only be passed through the male line) or because they have been appointed by the sovereign, at the suggestion of the Prime Minister (a practice created in 1948). These latter are called life peers[37].

Because peers are appointed or given the right by their birth into a particular family, in Parliament they speak and vote as individuals, not as representatives of the greater interests of the country—although of course civic-minded peers do try to serve their country rather than their own interests. Unlike those who serve in the

House of Commons, they do not receive salaries and many do not attend Parliament at all. In 1993 there were 1213 Lords: 776 were hereditary peers, 391 were life peers, 20 were Law Lords (a special group chosen to assist the House in its judicial duties) and the remainder were Lords Spiritual. Only 375 on average regularly attended the sittings.

Nowadays the composition of the House of Lords is seen as being both sexist and elitist because of the way the majority of peerages are passed down through aristocratic patrilineal lines[38]. It is very likely that efforts will be made to reform the House of Lords to make it a more effective and modern institution in the next decade.

Finally, there is the House of Commons which currently consists of about 650 Members of Parliament (MPs) elected by the people to represent them. MPs represent voters in a particular area, known as a constituency or seat. The number of seats varies a little bit because of changes in the population. MPs are only allowed to sit for the lifetime of the parliament, that is, the length of time between General Elections when a new set of MPs is elected. However, MPs can be reelected a limitless number of times and so popular MPs have veritable careers as parliamentarians. Unlike the Lords, MPs receive a salary of about £ 31 000 a year. This is about the same pay as an average middle class professional such as a doctor or an accountant would earn and it is thought that MPs will thus be able to identify with the "typical" voter they represent. They also receive allowances for secretaries and researchers, travel and so on.

Most MPs belong to political parties—Labour, the Conservatives and the Liberal Democrats are the major ones. The Prime Minister is of course the leader of the political party which wins the most seats in a general election. His or her Cabinet nowadays consists of usually around 20 MPs in the governing party who are chosen by the Prime Minister to become government ministers in the Cabinet. The Cabinet carries out the functions of policy-making, the coordination of government departments and the supreme control of government[39]. The House of Commons is the real centre of British political life—it is the place where elected representatives make and debate policy—and so its role is discussed in greater detail in the chapter on British Politics.

Words & Expressions

arguably/ˈɑːgjuəbli/*ad.* 可论证地;可能,大概

instability/ˌinstəˈbiləti/*n.* 不稳定性,不稳固

state-building/steitˈbilidiŋ/*n.* 创立国家,建

国
monarchy/ˈmɔnəki/n. 君主政体,君主制
sovereign/ˈsɔvrin/n. 君主,最高统治者
legitimate/liˈdʒitimət/a. 合法的,法律认可的
throne/θrəun/n. 宝座;王位,帝位
hereditary/hiˈreditəri/a. 承袭的,世袭的
defy/diˈfai/v. (公然)违抗;藐视
oust/aust/v. 驱逐,罢黜
medieval/ˌmediˈiːvəl/a. 中世纪的,中古(时代)的
prominent/ˈprɔminənt/a. 重要的,著名的
baron/ˈbærən/n. (由国王直接敕封领地的)贵族
charter/ˈtʃɑːtə/n. 宪章,共同纲领
parley/ˈpɑːli/v. 会谈,谈判
wage/weidʒ/v. 进行,开始
contribute/kənˈtribjuːt/v. 捐(款等),捐助
community/kəˈmjuːnəti/n. 社区;团体
say/sei/n. 发言机会,发言权
decree/diˈkriː/v. 命令,颁布
grant/grɑːnt/n. 授予物(如补助金等)
formula/ˈfɔːmjulə/n. 惯例,常规
prerogative/priˈrɔgətiv/n. 特权,独有的权利
councillor/ˈkausələ/n. 顾问;(市、镇等的)政务会委员
vis-a-vis/ˌviːzɑːˈviː/prep. 同…相对,同…相比
reassert/ˌriːəˈsəːt/v. 再断言,重申
execute/ˈeksikjuːt/v. 将…处死
consent/kənˈsent/n. 同意,准许
parliamentarian/ˌpɑːləmenˈtɛəriən/n. 国会议员
cabinet/ˈkæbinit/n. 内阁
chair/tʃɛə/v. 担任(会议等的)主席
assemble/əˈsembl/v. 召集,聚集
electorate/iˈlektərit/n. (总称)选举人,选民
governor-general/ˈgʌvənəˈdʒenərəl/n. (英国殖民地或英联邦国家的)总督
governance/ˈgʌvənəns/n. 统治方法,管理方法
statute/ˈstætjuːt/n. 成文法,法令,法规
working/ˈwəːkiŋ/n. (常用复数)运转,运行,活动
scrutinise/ˈskruːtinaiz/v. 详细检查,仔细观察
expenditure/ikˈspenditʃə/n. (时间、金钱等的)花费,支出
restraint/riˈstreint/n. 限制,约束
overturn/ˌənvəˈtəːn/v. 推翻,废除,使无效
supremacy/sjuˈpreməsi/n. 至高无上,最高地位
precedent/priˈsiːdənt/n. 先例,前例
executive/igˈzekjutiv/n. (政府的)行政部门,行政当局
integral/ˈintigrəl/a. 基本的,不可缺少的
legislature/ˈledʒisleitʃə/n. 立法机关,议会
judiciary/dʒuːˈdiʃiəri/n. 司法部,司法系统
successor/səkˈsesə/n. 继承人,继任者
allege/əˈledʒ/v. 声称,断言
extramarital/ˌekstrəˈmæritəl/a. 婚外的
jet-setting/ˈdʒetsetiŋ/a. 乘坐喷气机飞来飞去的阔佬的
squander/ˈskwɔndə/v. 浪费,挥霍
recognisance/riˈkɔgnisəns/n. 承认,确认
controversy/ˈkɔntrəvəːsi/n. 争议,争论
Texan/ˈteksən/n. (美国)得克萨斯(州)人
lounge/laundʒ/v. 闲逛,闲荡
outrage/ˈautreidʒ/v. 激怒,激起…义愤
decadence/ˈdekədəns/n. 堕落,颓废
allegation/ˌæliˈgeiʃən/n. 指控,宣称
come to a head (事情)达到决定性阶段;达到顶点
recession/riˈseʃən/n. (经济的)衰退,衰退期
endear/inˈdiə/v. 使受喜爱,使受钟爱
confidante/ˌkɔnfiˈdænt/n. 知己的女友
neutrality/njuːˈtræləti/n. 中立,中立地位

Lord Spiritual 上议院的神职议员（指主教或大主教）

archbishop/ˌɑːtʃˈbiʃɔp/n. 大主教，主教长

Lord Temporal 上议院的世俗议员（指非主教或大主教的贵族议员）

civic-minded/ˈsivikˈmaindid/a. 关心公益的，热心公民事务的

Law Lord 上议院执掌最高司法职务的议员，上议院法官

sitting/ˈsitiŋ/n. （议会的）开会

elitist/eiˈliːtist/a. 杰出人物统治（论）的

patrilineal/ˌpætriˈliniəl/a. 父系的，父子相传的

veritable/ˈveritəbl/a. 名副其实的，十足的

allowances/əˈlauəns/n. 津贴，补贴，零用钱

coordination/kəuˌɔːdiˈneiʃən/n. 协调，协同

Notes

1. Britain is arguably the oldest representative democracy ... a thousand years：英国可以说是世界上最古老的代议民主制国家，其代议民主制度起源于1000多年以前。

2. Although Britain too has ... one of evolution rather than revolution：尽管英国历史上也曾有过政治不稳定时期，但相对法国、美国或中国而言，英国的建国历程是一个逐渐演变而不是革命性剧变的过程。法国历史上曾有法国大革命以及拿破仑一世发动的雾月政变；美国历史上有1775～1783年的独立战争。其实，英国也有过革命性的剧变，如17世纪的英国革命。

3. This long, unbroken history ... in its political culture：这样长久持续的历史在英国现今的政治体系和政治文化中仍然有所体现。政治文化是指一个国家有关政权、政府制度及政策制定的理论和价值观等。

4. King Egbert：埃格伯特国王，西撒克逊国王（802～839）。即位后为巩固其独立统治，使韦塞克斯脱离麦西亚联盟，825年大败麦西亚国王，使韦塞克斯成为英格兰最强大的王国。

5. The power of the monarchy ... the "divine right of kings"：君主政体的权力主要是依古老的"君权神授"理论而来。"君权神授论"认为国王的统治权是上帝赋予的，所以人民对其统治的怀疑和反抗是罪恶的。这种理论引起了英国新兴资产阶级及代表其利益的议会的强烈反对。

6. roundheads：以奥立佛·克伦威尔为首的圆颅党人，1642～1652年英国内战期间的议会派成员，因剪短发而得名。支持国王的一派称为"骑士派"（the "Cavaliers"）。

7. Charles I：查理一世，英国斯图亚特王朝国王（1625～1649），因对抗国会，压迫清教徒而引起内战，被以克伦威尔为首的圆颅党人打败，被国会处以死刑。克伦威尔领导的共和体持续了18年，1660年克伦威尔去世后不久，流亡在法国的查理一世之子回国重新登位，又恢复了君主制。

8. While the King in theory ... should not exercise absolute power：尽管在理论上国王有上帝站在他一边，但早在中世纪时，人们就已认为国王不能无限行使权力。

9. Magna Carta：（the Great Charter）英国大宪章。1215年，英国大封建领言和教会反对英王约翰的一些政策，迫使他签署了保障部分公民权和政治权利的文件，限制国王的权力。

《大宪章》被认为是维护公民权不受王权侵犯的重要文件。

10. the Great Council:大议会。中世纪时,国王们需用钱时,常召集一些上层富裕的大封建领主筹钱,这些人组成了大议会。后来发现这些人人数太少,无法要到更多的钱,13 世纪前后,国王们开始把各县、市、镇的代表纳入大议会。

11. those who were summoned "by name":这里是指那些享有世袭贵族头衔的家族,大封建领主。

12. James I:詹姆斯一世。英国斯图亚特王朝第一代国王(1603~1625),他和他的儿子查理一世都极力宣扬"君权神授"理论,招致新兴资产阶级的反对,从而引发了资产阶级革命。

13. the civil war:内战。为了保障议会的权力,1642~1646 年和 1648~1652 年,议会派圆颅党人在克伦威尔的领导下,与支持查理一世的保皇党人之间爆发了内战,议会派获胜,查理一世于 1649 年被处死。

14. Charles II:查理二世。英国斯图亚特王朝国王(1660~1685),查理一世之子,1660 年王政复辟,回国继承王位,恢复了君主制。

15. James II:詹姆斯二世。英国国王(1685~1688),查理二世的弟弟,继位后置议会的权利不顾,被 1688 年的"光荣革命"推翻。

16. William of Orange:即威廉三世。原为尼德兰联省共和国执政,后应英国资产阶级和新教派的邀请,在 1688 年的"光荣革命"后,与其妻玛丽(詹姆斯二世之女)共同执政,接受国会通过的《权利法案》,确立了英国君主立宪制度。

17. the Bill of Rights:《权利法案》。1689 年,英国议会通过的限制国王权力,确立英国君主立宪制的宪法性文件。

18. To ensure good relations between Crown and Parliament ... as the Cabinet:为使王室和议会保持良好关系,国王或女王常定期与议会一些主要议员碰面,这些人后来逐渐被称为"内阁"。

19. George I:乔治一世。英国汉诺威王朝第一代国王(1714~1727)。即位后组成以辉格党占统治地位的内阁,沃波尔(Walpole)成为英国第一任首相。

20. Members of Parliament ... to electorate for approval:议员们组成各种团体,向选民宣扬他们的政策和观点以取得支持,这些团体最终逐渐演变成政党。

21. Britain is both a parliamentary democracy and a constitutional monarchy:英国既是一个代议民主制国家,又是一个君主立宪制国家。

22. Because of Britain's imperial past ... in many former colonies:由于过去大英帝国的历史,世界上其他许多国家曾被英国统治过,人们发现在许多前殖民地国家存在着类似的政体。

23. statute law:成文法。指由议会通过的一些法案,如 1679 年通过的《人身保护法》(Habeas Corpus Act)等。

24. the common laws:普通法,判例法。指英国法庭历来通过的判决而形成的法令,而非议会通过的法案。

25. conventions:习惯法。指法律上没有明文规定,但对政体的运行非常重要的一些传统的规则和习惯。

26. Another important function is that ... by voting for taxation:另一个重要作用是通过投

票决定税收制度,为政府工作的开展提供资金。

27. Parliament is supreme ... to change the terms of the Constitution:由于议会能独立修改宪法的条款,因此在英国政体中具有最高地位。

28. It can make or change laws, ... without consulting the electorate:议会可以制定或修改法律,修改或推翻已成定规的习惯法,甚至可以不用征得选民同意而推迟选举日期。

29. This is because even though ... as a matter of course:这是因为尽管必须经女王同意方能通过一项法律,但是女王总是理所当然同意的。

30. Obviously the prime minister and governing party ... voted in their favour:显然,首相及执政党任何时候都只会代表投票选举他们的那部分人。

31. Under the terms of the constitution ... the Church of England:按宪法规定,女王的其他职责是:她是法律意义上的行政首脑,立法机构的不可缺少的一部分,司法机构首脑,军队最高统帅,以及英国国教的"最高领袖"。

32. While the Queen is independently wealthy ... the British people:尽管女王本人很富有,但王室的许多资金开支来源于纳税人,大概是对王室代表英国人民利益尽责的一种承认。

33. Criticism of the Queen's children ... to Windsor Castle:对女王子女行为的指责引起人们对君主制的广泛批评,1992 年 11 月温莎堡遭火灾破坏,更使这场争论达到了高潮。Windsor Castle:温莎堡,英国王室住所,在离伦敦不远的温莎城。

34. Her willingness to give in to ... endeared her to her subjects:她乐意接受大众要求的行为再次使她得到了人民的爱戴。

35. In her 40 years on the throne ... on the day to day problems of governance:40 年在位期间,女王曾先后与 9 位首相坚持每周交谈。这些首相声称,女王长期积累的经验和她政治上的中立态度,使她能为日常国家管理事务提出有价值的意见。

36. It consists of the Lords Spiritual ... which refers to everyone else:上议院由神职议员和世俗议员组成,前者是指英国国教的大主教和知名主教,后者是指其他非主教或大主教的贵族议员。

37. life peers:终身贵族。1958 年英国议会通过了《终身贵族爵位法》,对那些为英国社会做出杰出贡献的人,由首相提名,王室授封他们为终身贵族,但其爵位不能传给后代。

38. Nowadays the composition of ... through aristocratic patrilineal lines:现在,人们认为上议院的组成成分既表现出性别歧视,又体现出高人一等的优越感,因为大多数贵族爵位是父子相传的。

39. The Cabinet carries out the functions ... the supreme control of government:内阁履行制定政策、协调政府各部位工作,以及对政府全面管理等职责。

Exercises

Ⅰ. Explain the following

1. the divine right of kings
2. the "roundheads"

3. the Great Council
4. the Constitution
5. the House of Lords
6. the House of Commons

Ⅱ. Fill in the blanks

1. ________, the ancestor of the present Queen, Elizabeth II, united England under his rule in 829.
2. The doctrine of the "divine right of kings" held that ________, ________.
3. During the civil war in the 17th century, those who represented the interests of Parliament are called ________, and those who supported the King were called ________.
4. In 1215, some feudal barons and the Church forced King ________ to sign the ________ to place some limits on the King's power.
5. In medieval times, kings would summon a group of wealthy barons and representatives of counties, towns and cities—called ________ to raise money.
6. In 1689, Parliament passed ________ to ensure that the King would never be able to ignore Parliament.
7. In the 18th century, King George I left the job of chairing cabinet meetings to one of his ministers who later came to be called ________.
8. In Britain, the official head of state is ________ while the real centre of political life is in ________.
9. The British Constitution consists of ________, ________ and ________.
10. The most important function of the Parliament is to ________.
11. Strictly speaking, the Parliament today consists of ________, ________ and ________.
12. The fund the Queen received to repair the fire damage to ________ caused a lot criticism from the public about the monarchy, and the queen later decided to open ________ to summer tourists to raise money.
13. Life peers should be nominated by ________, and appointed by ________.
14. According to tradition, most peerages can only be passed through the ________ lines.

Ⅲ. Choose the correct answer in each of the following

1. Which of the following is NOT characteristic of British government?
   A. It offers the Queen high political status and supreme power.
   B. It is both a parliamentary democracy and a constitutional monarchy.
   C. It is the oldest representative democracy in the world.
   D. It has no written form of Constitution.
2. Which of the following king was executed in the civil war?
   A. James I
   B. James II
   C. Charles I
   D. Charles II

3. What happened in 1215?

A. It was the year of Norman Conquest in British history.

B. Forced by barons, King John signed the Magna Carta.

C. Henry IV granted the Commons the power to review money grants.

D. King Egbert united England under his rule.

4. Which of the following is NOT true about the Great Council?

A. They included barons and representatives from counties and towns.

B. They were sometimes summoned by the kings to contribute money.

C. They late developed into what we now know as the Cabinet.

D. They represented the aristocrats as well as the communities.

5. Under whose reign was the Bill of Rights passed?

A. James II.

B. William of Orange.

C. Oliver Cromwell.

D. George I.

6. Which of the following is NOT true about the Constitution?

A. It is a document which lists out the basic principles for government.

B. It is the foundation of British governance today.

C. Conventions and Laws passed by Parliament are part of the Constitution.

D. The common laws are part of the Constitution.

7. Which of the following about the Parliament is NOT true?

A. There are no legal restraints upon Parliament.

B. Strictly speaking, the queen is part of the Parliament.

C. Parliament has the supreme power of passing laws.

D. Parliament has no power to change the terms of the Constitution.

8. Which of the following about the Queen is NOT true?

A. The Queen selects the Prime Minister and the Cabinet.

B. The Queen symbolizes the tradition and unity of the British state.

C. The Queen acts as a confidante to the Prime Minister.

D. The Queen is the temporal head of the Church of England.

9. Which of the following about the House of Lords is NOT true?

A. Lords do not receive salaries and many do not attend Parliament sittings.

B. It consists of the Lords Spiritual and the Lords Temporal.

C. The lords are expected to represent the interests of the public.

D. Most of the lords in the House of Lords are males.

10. Which of the following about the House of Commons is NOT true?

A. Members of Parliament elect the Prime Minister and the Cabinet.

B. MPs receive salaries and some other allowances.

C. MPs are elected to represent the interests of the public.

D. Most MPs belong to the major political parties.

Ⅳ. Answer the following questions briefly

1. What are some of the characteristics of the British constitutional monarchy?
2. How did the doctrine of the "divine right of kings" lead to the English Civil War?
3. What role did the parliament play in the Civil War?
4. What role does the Queen (King) and the Prime Minister play in British government?

Chapter 5 Industry, Agriculture and Business

Absolute Decline and Relative Decline[1]

By the 1880s the British economy was dominant in the world, producing one third of the world's manufactured goods, half its coal and iron, half its cotton. The amount of British shipping was greater than that in the rest of the world put together. But even by 1900 this was no longer the case, the UK having been overtaken by both the United States and Germany; and certainly from 1945 until the present, the story of the UK economy is usually thought of as one of decline. This is understandable but rather misleading, as it has in fact been a period of steady economic growth and rapidly increasing living standards. Britain remains one of the Group of Seven large industrial economies[2]. But there are reasons for describing this period as one of decline. Britain entered the post-war world as one of the successful allies of the Second World War, with some of its chief competitor nations such as Germany and Japan, economically destroyed. Also Britain was the centre of a still vast empire. According to the figures, the UK was second only to the United States in the international economy. Thus Britain was then in an apparently strong economic position, a position it clearly no longer occupies, which indicates some sort of decline.

But the basic positive-seeming facts describing the size of the economy, the high proportion of world trade that was British, and so on, in 1945, did not reveal important negative facts about the UK's position even then[3]. Firstly the country had gone heavily into debt in order to finance the war, selling many of its accumulated overseas assets[4], and borrowing large amounts from the United States and Canada. These debts meant that the UK entered the post-war era with a major economic problem.

Secondly, the era of empire was over. India, popularly known as "The Jewel in the Crown" of the British Empire, gained its independence in 1947, only 2 years after the end of the war. This was the largest element in the empire, providing raw materials and a big market for British goods. This relationship with India was no longer available, and the rest of the empire quickly followed India to independence[5], leaving Britain as just a medium-size European country, with a population only one fifth the size of the U. S.

Thirdly, despite the relatively rapid and trouble-free process of decolonization, Britain was still forced to maintain a substantial and expensive military presence in many overseas locations until the process was completed (mostly) by the end of the 1960s[6]. Also its position as one of the shapers of the post-war world required substantial military contributions—both as one of NATO[7]'s major partners, and as a member of the UN Security Council. All this had the result that Britain spent a higher proportion of its national wealth (and especially of its research and development budget) on the military than most of its competitors. Military expenditure tends not to generate an economic return in quite the same way as other industrial investment[8].

Fourthly, although Britain was quite badly damaged by German bombing during the war, its industry survived comparatively unaffected. This contrasted greatly with some of its competitors—especially the main losers in the conflict, Germany and Japan, who almost had to start again from nothing. This apparent disadvantage for them may have worked in their favour in that as they had to invest, they could invest in the most modern equipment and new products[9]. British industry however could continue with its older factories and pre-war products, and given its other economic problems, did so—a problem in the long-term[10]. It also meant that output was initially very low in these two potentially large economies: so while Britain looked securely wealthier than them in 1945, a catching-up with the UK was inevitable as they recovered.

This failure to invest sufficiently in industry also reflects a longstanding and continuing problem in the UK economy. Even without the particular circumstances of the post-war world, relatively low rates of investment (the amount of money businesses put aside from profits to reinvest in the business in new products and production methods) were characteristic of the British economy in relation to other developed economies[11]. Economists have pointed to the lack of a close relationship between industry and banks in the UK—again a contrast, particularly with the two most successful post-war economies, Japan and Germany, where banks and industrial firms have very close links. Economic historians have suggested that this may be due to the fact that the UK was the first economy to industrialise, and industrial firms, without foreign competition, grew used to financing their own development, without need to borrow from banks. Banks therefore, not able to find good investment opportunities in the UK, looked overseas for investment opportunities. A low rate of domestic industrial investment coupled with a very high rate of overseas investment is still a characteristic of the UK economy. So, amongst European nations, Britain is the largest investor in China, but sells fewer of its own manufactured goods here than Germany or France do.

The point to note is that the comparatively strong economic position Britain found itself in 1945 was in many ways deceptive. So the decline from Britain's apparently good fortunes at that point until now is thus not as extraordinary as it might seem, being the result of already existing basic problems[12]. And it should also be remembered that this was not an absolute decline: Britain is not poorer, or producing less than it was in 1945, in fact (like most countries) it is a lot wealthier and more productive than it was then. The problem is that though it has improved, other countries have improved more rapidly, hence the slide from being the 2nd largest economy (after the United States) to being the sixth, as it is at present. And even many smaller economies have overtaken the UK in terms of output per head of population[13]. So the UK has experienced economic decline, but this decline is relative to some other economies rather than absolute. Nevertheless, this relative failure is a serious cause of concern to the UK governments.

Recent History

The British economy went through a particularly bad period in the 1970s. The oil price rises at that time led to very high rates of inflation (up to 25%). This caused many workers to strike for more pay. The fall in the value of the UK currency (The Pound) even forced the Labour (socialist) government to borrow from the International Monetary Fund[14]. British industry, notably the car industry, appeared to be doing badly, with increasing imports relative to exports. All these negative economic facts led to a change of government at the next general election, in 1979, when the British people voted in the Conservative party under Margaret Thatcher[15], with the promise of a radical programme of reform. Bureaucracy was reduced (foreign exchange controls were lifted, rules governing banks loosened, for example). And throughout the 1980s an extensive programme of privatization was carried out, with many state-owned businesses (such as steel, telecom, gas, aerospace) joining the private sector. It seemed in some ways to be successful in that inflation came under control, and businesses, especially the newly privatized businesses, made profits. The negative aspect was a rapid increase in unemployment, rising to almost 12% at its worst. So while companies were more efficient, producing the same amount with less workers, and therefore being able to pay higher wages and make higher profits, the cost was paid by the unemployed who had to live on low incomes from state support. The national economy as a whole continued to grow at lower rates than its competitors. In the recession 1990 – 1992, the economy even shrunk by 2.3%.

Since then, however, the picture has been brighter, with four years of steady growth, at rate's higher than that in the rest of the European Union. Unemployment has now fallen to 7.7%, which is among the lowest in the European Union. Inflation has remained under control at very low levels. Investment has increased, encouraged by low interest rates. Britain's membership of the EU has also made it an attractive location for inward investment by companies from outside the EU (especially the U.S. and Japan), of which it has received a larger share than any other EU countries. Overall it is second only to the U. S. as a destination for international direct investment[16]. It is also itself a major source of international investment—in fact it is the second biggest international investor in the world (1995).

The Current UK Economy

National economies can be broken down into three main areas: "primary" industries, such as agriculture, fishing, and mining; "secondary" industries, which manufacture complex goods from those primary products; and tertiary industries[17], often described as services, such as banking, insurance, tourism, and the selling of good.

Britain's agricultural sector is small (producing 1.4% of the national wealth) but efficient, producing 58% of the UK's food needs with only 2% of its workforce. Three quarters of Britain's land is used for agriculture, with about a quarter of that under crops—wheat and barley are the two commonest. The rest is grazing for animals, including cattle (both dairy and beef), though sheep are the most numerous livestock. The beef industry has been hit badly by BSE disease[18] in cattle leading to a 1996 ban on beef exports. The best agricultural land is in the southeast of England.

The fishing industry provides 55% of the UK demand for fish. Scottish ports land the majority of the fish caught.

Energy production is an important part of the UK economy, accounting for 5% of the national wealth. Since the 1970s, when oil and gas were discovered under the North Sea, Britain has become a major oil and gas producer, in addition to its older coal mining industry, which now only accounts for about 1/4 of energy supplies, the rest being divided between oil, gas, and nuclear energy. This abundance of energy resources means that the UK has become an overall exporter of energy. The technology required to extract oil from the difficult offshore conditions has given UK companies a strong position in the offshore oil industry around the world. Three of the biggest ten companies in Britain are to be found in the energy sector: Shell (half Dutch), British Petroleum (BP), and British Gas[19]. The world's largest mining company, RTZ, is a UK company which operates mines all over the world.

In the secondary sector of the economy, manufacturing industry remains important, producing 22% of national wealth. British companies are active in all major fields of manufacturing industry, but are particularly strong in pharmaceuticals (the British company Glaxo-Welcome is the biggest drug company in the world), chemicals (ICI[20] is the second largest paint manufacturer in the world), aerospace (overall the UK industry is third in size in the world) and food and drink (Scotch whisky being a major export). Britain has a big electronics industry (the fourth largest in the world) but like the car industry (which includes Ford, GM, Peugeot, Nissan, Toyota[21]) this is in many cases foreign-owned. Britain's last major independent car company, Rover, was recently bought by the German company BMW[22]. A high-technology engineering industry has developed around the motor-racing business, with many of the world's racing cars, both for Formula One, and the American Indycar series[23], being designed and built in Britain. McClaren and Williams are two of the most successful of these companies. The recently privatised British Steel is the world's fourth largest steel company.

Like most developed economies Britain has seen a relative shrinking of the importance of secondary industry and a spectacular growth in tertiary or service industries, which now produce 65% of national wealth. A lot of this is domestic activity such as retailing, tourism and so on, but Britain is also a major international provider of services, accounting for about 10% of the world's exports of such services. 70% of the UK's workforce are employed in the service sector. The financial sector is an important part of this service industry, as London is one of the top three financial centres in the world. It has the greatest concentration of foreign banks in the world, accounts for 20% of all international bankloans, and is the world's largest foreign exchange market. As well as banking, dealings in commodities and insurance are important processes in "The City"[24]—the name given to the historic area at the centre of London where all this business is concentrated, at the heart of which is the London Stock Exchange[25], one of the busiest share-dealing centres in the world. Advertising is another major business service in which UK companies are highly successful.

The Aerospace Industry: the Highlight of British Economy

After those of the U. S. and Russia, the UK's aerospace industry is the next largest, capable of producing the full range of aerospace products from civil and military aircraft (including helicopters) to missiles, satellites, and jet engines. It produces 2% of UK national output, accounting for 8% of manufactured export goods.

The first powered flight in the world was made by the Wright Brothers[26] in the U. S. in 1903. It was in 1908 when the first such flight was made in the UK. But only a few years later came the First World War which forced the rapid development of the aviation industry, and by 1918 the British industry was the biggest and most sophisticated in the world, producing 1250 aircraft each month.

After the war the new aircraft types provided the base for the development of the civil aviation industry. A converted First World War bomber crossed the Atlantic Ocean in 1919[27], and a civil airline, Imperial Airways, was started in 1924. International air races provided an incentive for technological development, and a British plane, the Supermarine S6B, powered by a Rolls Royce engine, broke many speed records[28]. Rolls Royce became the most successful aero-engine manufacturer at this time. The aircraft-building industry was reduced to a few major companies by a series of mergers.

One of the most significant developments of the inter-war period was the development of radar by the UK's Marconi company in 1922. And when Englishman Frank Whittle[29] developed the world's first practical jet engine in 1937, the foundations had been laid for the three major branches of the aviation industry: aircraft, engines and aviation electronics, with British companies prominent in each field.

Sadly, in 1939 war came again to provide another spurt of technological change, with many successful British aircraft designs in action, such as the Spitfire fighter and Lancaster bomber, and culminating in the jet-powered Meteor. The Rolls Royce Merlin engine became the best-selling aero-engine of all time with 166 000 produced. The wartime government, seeing the importance that the aircraft industry had gained (in employed 1. 8 million workers by the end of the war), planned a range of civil aviation types to take over from wartime production. These included the world's first jet-powered civil airliner: The Comet.

However, the years following the Second World War were problematic for the UK industry. It continued to produce the full-range of products, even selling some of its aircraft to the United States. But in most markets British companies were in head on competition with American companies such as Boeing and McDonnel-Douglas, which were larger, having the advantage of being preferential customers for the enormous U. S. market, both civil and military[30]. The British industry merged into two main aircraft groups: the British Aircraft Corporation, and Hawker-Siddeley Aviation, with Rolls-Royce as the main engine builder, and Westland in helicopters. Nevertheless British civil airliners of the 1960s such as the Trident and the VC10 sold much less well than their American equivalents. Nor did British military aircraft sell very well overseas, with the exception of the unique Vertical Take-off and Landing Harrier, bought by the U. S. Marines amongst others.

The answer to the problem lay in collaborative projects with other European aircraft manufacturers which faced the same problems. The first of these was between Britain and France to produce the world's first supersonic civil airliner, Concords[31]. The aircraft was a technical success but a commercial failure, only 16 being built for British Airways and Air France. However the successful collaboration led to more such programmes between Britain and France, including the Jaguar combat aircraft, and three types of helicopter, including the Lynx, which holds the world speed record for helicopters.

Many other collaborative programmes between Britain and other European countries developed, including the Tornado combat aircraft—a project between Britain, Germany, and Italy. The current European Fighter Aircraft is another such venture. Westland has developed their latest helicopter in association with an Italian company.

But the most successful programme has been in civil airliners where the Airbus series of aircraft has effectively competed with American companies. This is an ongoing programme between France, Germany, Britain and Spain. British companies build the wings. British Aerospace build their own range of regional jets, including the successful 146 (popular with Chinese airlines) famous for being the quietest jet airliner. It is likely that these smaller aircraft will go into a European joint-venture too.

The industry has been through some major changes of ownership in the last twenty-five years. Rolls-Royce, in attempting to build a revolutionary new engine for the American company, Lockheed, went bankrupt, and had to be rescued by the government in 1971. BAC and Hawker Siddeley were also nationalised—as one company, British Aerospace, in 1977 by the Labour government. But both Rolls-Royce and British Aerospace were privatized in the 1980s by the Conservatives and have since been very successful both in individual projects and in international joint-ventures. The third main arm of the current industry is GEC Avionics, producing a wide range of electronic systems including the technologically advanced cockpit of the latest Boeing 777 airliner[32]. Smaller companies produce a wide range of equipment from ejection seats to landing gears.

The Aerospace industry is now profitable, with over 300 companies employing 170 000 people. Its overseas sales account for around 12% of total world aerospace exports. It has been through difficult times, particularly in the 1970s, moving in and out of public ownership. But it has found success in links with Europe—a pattern it shares with the rest of the UK economy.

Words & Expressions

ally/ˈælai/*n.* 同盟国,同盟者

accumulate/əˈkjuːmjuleit/*v.* 积累,积攒,累积

asset/ˈæset/*n.* (常用复数)资产

decolonization/diːˌkɔlənaiˈzeiʃən/*n.* 非殖民(地)化

substantial/səbˈstænʃəl/*a.* 大量的,可观的,相当数目的

budget/ˈbʌdʒit/*n.* 预算,预算拨款

expenditure/ikˈspenditʃə/*n.* 经费,费用,支出额

catching-up *n.* 竞争;(尤指工业生产方面的)定额

sufficiently/səˈfiʃəntli/*ad.* 充足的,足够的

long-standing *a.* (已持续)长时间的,为时甚久的

in relation to 与…相比

deceptive/diˈseptiv/*a.* 骗人的,造成假象的

slide/slaid/*n.* 滑落,下落

per head 每人,按人

inflation/inˈfleiʃən/*n.* 通货膨胀,物价飞涨

general election 大选,普选

bureaucracy/bjuˈrɔkrəsi/*n.* (行政部门的)权力集中;政府机构

foreign exchange 外汇;国际汇兑

lift/lift/*v.* 撤销,解除,停止

privatization/ˌpraivətaiˈzeiʃən/*n.* 私有化,私人化

telecom/ˈtelikɔm/*n.* telecommunication 电信

aerospace/ˈɛərəuspeis/*n.* 航空航天工业(或技术)

recession/riˈseʃən/*n.* (经济的)衰退,衰退期

interest rates 利率

tertiary/ˈtəːʃəri/*a.* 第三的,第三产业的

dairy (beef) cattle 乳(菜)牛

offshore/ˈɔfʃɔː/*a.* 近海的,近岸的

pharmaceutical/ˌfɑːməˈsjuːtikəl/*n.* 药品,药物

retail/ˈriːteil/*n.* 零售,零卖

share-dealing 股票交易

jet engine 喷气发动机

convert/kən'vəːt/v. 改建,改装

incentive/in'sentiv/n. 刺激,鼓励

merger/'məːdʒə/n. (公司,企业等的)兼并

spurt/spəːt/n. (活动等的)突发性开展;急剧上升

culminate/'kʌlmineit/v. 达到顶点,到达高潮

preferential/ˌprefə'renʃəl/a. 优先的,优待的

collaborative/kə'læbəreitiv/a. 合作的,协力完成的

supersonic/ˌsjuːpə'sɔnik/a. 超音速的,超声速的

cockpit/'kɔkpit/n. (飞行员)座舱

ejection seat (飞机的)弹射座椅

landing gear (飞机)起落架

Notes

1. absolute decline and relative decline:绝对衰退和相对衰退。作者认为,英国经济一直在不断发展中,但因其他国家发展速度较之英国更快,所以英国的世界经济地位才相对衰退。

2. Britain remains one of the Group of Seven large industrial economies:英国仍为世界七大工业国之一。西方七国集团指美国、英国、德国、法国、日本、意大利和加拿大。

3. But the basic positive-seeming facts ... the UK's position even then:但是显示 1945 年英国的经济规模,以及它在当时世界贸易中所占的高比例等等的那些看似乐观的数据,掩盖了当时英国已处于极为不利地位的重要事实。

4. accumulated overseas assets:长期积累的海外资产。英国在历史上有很多海外殖民地,故有此说。

5. ... and the rest of the empire quickly followed India to independence:继 1947 年印度独立以后,其他原英属殖民地相继独立。

6. Thirdly ... was completed (mostly by the end of the 1960s):第三,尽管非殖民化的过程相对迅速,相对平静,英国还是被迫在此过程结束之前(大多是到了 60 年代末)在许多海外殖民地区驻扎大量军队,军费开支巨大。

7. NATO:其全称是"North Atlantic Treaty Organization",北大西洋公约组织(简称"北约组织"),建立于 1949 年,英国是其成员国;the UN Security Council:联合国安理会。

8. Military expenditure ... other industrial investment:军费开支往往不会像其他工业投资那样产生经济收益。

9. This apparent disadvantage ... the most modern equipment and new products:这看似不利的条件却可能反而对他们有利:正因为他们不得投资,所以他们可以投资于最现代化的设备和新产品。

10. British industry however ... a problem in the long-term:而英国工业能够靠旧工厂和战前的产品生存下去,再加上其他经济问题,也确实这样做了,所以就造成了一个长期的问题。did so 即等于 did continue with its older factories and pre-war products。

11. Even without the particular circumstances of the post-war world ... other developed economies:即使不是在战后这种特殊情况下,英国经济与其他发达国家相比,投资额还是相对较低。括号中的话是用来解释 rate of investment 的,意思是:企业从利润中抽取的用于再

投资于新产品和新生产方式的那部分钱。

12. So the decline from Britain's apparently good fortunes ... basic problems:所以,英国从当时的表面繁荣到现在的衰退,就显得比较正常了,因为这是那些早已存在的主要原因造成的。

13. And even many smaller economies ... output per head of population:甚至许多小国经济在人均产量上也超过了英国。per head of population:per capita

14. The fall in the value of the UK currency ... the International Monetary Fund:英国流通货币(英镑)的贬值甚至迫使工党政府向国际货币基金组织借款。the International Monetary Fund(联合国)国际货币基金组织。1945 年成立,是联合国管理和协调国际金融业务的专门机构,总部设在华盛顿。

15. Margaret Thatcher:玛格丽特·撒切尔,英国历史上第一任女首相(1979~1990),保守党领袖(1975~1990)。任首相期间推行自由放任的经济政策(laissez faire),促进国有企业的私有化,使经济有所回升,但失业率迅速上升。

16. Overall it is ... international direct investment:总体而言,英国是国际直接投资的第二大目标,仅次于美国。

17. tertiary industries:第三产业,也称"服务性行业"。

18. BSE disease:俗称"疯牛病",始发于牛的一种传染性大脑疾病。

19. Shell (half Dutch), British Petroleum (BP), and British Gas:壳牌公司(英国和荷兰合资)、英国石油公司(原属国有,1987 年私有化)、英国煤气天然气公司(1986 年私有化)是英国三大能源公司。

20. ICI: Imperial Chemical Industries 帝国化学工业公司,又称"卜内门化学工业公司"。英国最大的化学公司,创建于 1926 年,主要经营药品、油漆、塑料和石油化工产品。

21. Ford, GM, Peugeot, Nissan, Toyota:福特(美国)、通用(General Motors,美国)、标致(法国)、尼桑(日本)、丰田(日本),这些都是世界有名的汽车公司。

22. Britain's last major independent car company ... the German company BMW:英国最后一家独立的(指英国独资的)大汽车公司 Rover(罗孚)公司,最近被德国的 BMW(宝马)公司买下了。

23. Formula One, the American Indycar series:前者是一级方程式赛车世界锦标赛,1950 年设立,属职业性比赛。后者全称是 Indianapolis 500,印第安纳波利斯 500 英里汽车大赛,1911 年设立,每年一届,是美国举办的重要国际汽车赛。

24. "The City":"伦敦城"。英国首都伦敦的市中心区的一部分,是全国金融业和工商业中心,在一平方英里的地区集中了许多家大银行和金融公司。

25. the London Stock Exchange:伦敦证券交易所,1802 年开业,是世界著名的证券交易所之一。

26. the Wright Brothers:赖特兄弟(Orville and Wilbur),美国飞机发明家、航空先驱者,于 1903 年成功地试飞了第一架可操纵的动力飞机,开辟了飞行器重于空气的飞机时代。

27. A converted First World War bomber crossed the Atlantic Ocean in 1919:一架改装过的第一次世界大战时的轰炸机于 1919 年飞越了大西洋。英国战后利用军用飞机的优势发展民用航空工业。

28. International air races ... broke many speed records:国际航空竞赛刺激了技术的发展,一架装备有罗尔斯-罗伊斯发动机的英国飞机 Supermarine S6B 打破了许多飞行速度的记录。Rolls Royce:著名的汽车和发动机公司,生产的该品牌小轿车属高档昂贵车,其发动机为世界航空工业界广泛采用。

29. Frank Whittle:弗兰克·惠特尔,英国飞行员、工程师、发明家,1941 年发明飞机喷气发动机。

30. But in most markets ... both civil and military. 但在多数市场,英国公司遭到了来自美国波音、麦道(这两家公司已于 1996 年合并)等公司的激烈竞争,这些公司规模更大,在巨大的美国民用和军用市场占有特惠客户的优势。

31. The first of these ... first supersonic civil airliner, Concorde:第一个此类合作项目是英法合作生产的世界第一架超音速客机:协和式飞机。

32. the technologically advanced cockpit of the latest Boeing 777 airliner:最新波音 777 大型客机的技术先进的座舱。

Exercises

Ⅰ. Explain the following

1. privatization in the 1980s
2. Margaret Thatcher
3. "The City"
4. Concorde

Ⅱ. Fill in the blanks

1. "The Jewel in the Crown" of the British Empire—________, which provided ________ and a big market for British goods, gained independence in 1947.
2. A low rate of ________ coupled with a very high rate of ________ is a characteristic of the UK economy.
3. Since 1945, the UK economy has experienced ________ decline rather than ________ decline.
4. In the 1970s, the devaluation of the UK currency forced the Labour government to borrow money from ________.
5. In 1979, the Conservative party under ________ came into power and carried out a programme of ________.
6. In recent years, Britain is second only to the U. S. as a destination for ________
7. The UK economy can be divided into three main sectors: ________ industries, secondary industries and ________ industries.
8. The beef industry was hit badly by ________ which caused a ban on beef exports in 1996.
9. Since the discovery of oil and gas under the ________, Britain has gained a strong position in the offshore oil industry.

10. Glaxo-Welcome is the biggest ________ company in the world while ________ is the second largest paint manufacturer in the world.

11. ________ is one of the busiest share-dealing centres in the world.

12. Englishman Frank Whittle developed the world's first practical ________ in 1937.

Ⅲ. Choose the correct answer in each of the following

1. Which of the following statements about the UK economy is NOT true?
   A. Britain remains one of the Group of Seven large industrial economies.
   B. Britain has experienced a relative economic decline since 1945.
   C. There has been a period of steady decreasing of living standards.
   D. Some smaller economies have overtaken the UK in terms of output per capita.

2. Which of the following was NOT the reason for the relative economic decline since 1945?
   A. Britain did not invest in modern equipment and new products.
   B. Britain spent a high proportion of its national wealth on the military.
   C. Britain had been heavily in debt to finance the war.
   D. Britain had carried out the nationalisation of the businesses.

3. Which of the following livestock has the biggest number in the UK?
   A. Beef battle.
   B. Dairy cattle.
   C. Chicken.
   D. Sheep.

4. Where is the best agricultural land in Britain?
   A. In the southeast of England.
   B. In the northeast of England.
   C. In the southeast of Scotland.
   D. In the northeast of Scotland.

5. Which of the following is NOT a company in the energy sector?
   A. Shell.
   B. ICI.
   C. RTZ.
   D. British Gas.

6. Which of the following used to be the last independent car company in the UK?
   A. Ford.
   B. Peugeot.
   C. Rover.
   D. BMW.

7. In aerospace industry, which two countries are ahead of Britain?
   A. The U. S. and Germany.
   B. The U. S. and Russia.
   C. Germany and Russia.

D. France and Russia.

8. which civil airline was started in 1924 after the First World War?

A. Imperial Airways.

B. British Airways.

C. Hawker-Siddeley Aviation.

D. The British Aircraft Corporation

9. What did Frank Whittle do in 1937?

A. He invented the first jet plane.

B. He developed the first jet engine.

C. He made the first powered flight.

D. He made the trans-Atlantic flight.

10. Which company became an important aero-engine manufacturer after WWI?

A. Boeing.

B. Rolls Royce.

C. McDonnel-Douglas.

D. Hawker-Siddeley Aviation.

11. British Aerospace was the merger of which two companies?

A. The British Aircraft Corporation and Hawker-Siddeley Aviation

B. The British Aircraft Corporation and Rolls Royce

C. Hawker-Siddeley Aviation and GEC Avionics

D. Hawker-Siddeley Aviation and Rolls Royce

Ⅳ. Answer the following questions briefly

1. How does the author explain the reasons for the absolute decline and relative decline?

2. What did the Conservative Party under Mrs. Margaret Thatcher promise to do to the UK national economy in 1979?

3. What are the three main areas in national economy?

Chapter 6 British Literature

Early Writing

Much early British writing was concerned with Christianity: Anglo-Saxons produced beautifully illustrated (or "illuminated") versions of the Bible: the most famous of these is the Book of Kells, partly written on the Scottish island of Iona[1]. Today it is kept in the library of Trinity College in Dublin, the capital of Ireland. Outside of the church, few people in this period were literate. Even today early British literature (that dating from before the sixteenth century), is little read outside of university literature departments, because the English language then was rather different—closer to its German roots[2]—making it quite difficult even for native English speakers to read today. But there are a few well-known literary works from those times. One of the oldest of these early "Old English" literary works[3] is a long poem from Anglo-Saxon times called *Beowulf*[4]. The earliest copy dates from 1000 AD, but there are pieces of the 8th century texts in existence. It tells the story of the 6th century Swedish warrior Beowulf and his conflict with a family of dragons.

With the Norman conquest in 1066 Britain entered the Middle Ages (1066 – 1485), and the language of the royal court became French. So literature of that period was written in French or Latin. But one work from these times often studied today by middle school students is *The Canterbury Tales* by Geoffrey Chaucer[5] (1340 – 1400). He was the first court poet to write in English. Written in a more recognizable version of English (known as "Middle English"[6]) than "Beowulf", it is made up of a series of stories told by pilgrims to entertain each other on their way to the important Christian Church at Canterbury in southeast England. It is notable for its diversity, both in the range of social types amongst the 31 pilgrims[7], and the range in style of the stories they tell. The tale of *The Wife of Bath*[8], for example, is a romance concerning King Arthur's times.

The legend of King Arthur became established in literary form with the publication in 1138 of Geoffrey of Monmouth's *History of the Kings of Britain*, a Latin work which, though calling itself a work of history, invented material to fill the broad gaps in the historical records[9]. The stories of King Arthur's court, his knights and their famous round table, and the quest for the Holy Grail in the 5th century[10], are mostly invention around a very few vague "facts". The best-known version of this story comes from around 1470 when Thomas Malory[11] completed his *Morte D'Arthur* (*Death of Arthur*), making the story of Arthur's Queen Guinevere, and her love affair with his best friend and greatest knight Sir Lancelot, the stuff of the British imagination for centuries to come[12]. Locations mentioned in the legends such as the ruined castle at Tintagel in Cornwall are popular tourist destinations.

King Arthur also features in the most famous of early Welsh literary works: a series of folk-tales known as *The Mabinogion*[13], (a "Mabinog" was a poet's apprentice in Welsh culture). Although these tales draw on earlier Celtic myths, they are first known in written form in the 14th century.

Irish literature in Gaelic has its own early heroic literature: *The Ulster Cycle*[14], recorded from the 9th to 13th centuries (but probably pre-5th century in origin), features the legendary, unbeatable warrior, Cuchulain[15], and his efforts to defend the northern Irish kingdom of Ulster from the King and Queen of Connaught.

Elizabethan Drama

There was a general flowering of cultural and intellectual life in Europe during the 15th and 16th centuries which is known as "The Renaissance[16]" ("rebirth"). In British culture one of the most successful and long-lasting expressions of this development lay in drama. The first professional theatre opened in London in 1576, and others followed, producing the work of many notable playwrights, including Christopher Marlowe[17], Ben Jonson[18], and, of course, William Shakespeare.

Marlowe (1564 – 1593) was the earliest of this great trio, and his style is thought to have been a great influence on Shakespeare. His most famous play is *Dr Faustus*[19], the story of a man who sold his soul to the devil in return for power. It is thought that Marlowe had another career as a government agent, and that his death by murder in a Deptford (part of London) pub may have had something to do with that political activity.

William Shakespeare[20] (1564 – 1616) is probably the best-known literary figure in the world, but little is known of his life. He came from a middle-class family in Stratford, but somehow he became a successful playwright and director of a theatre company in London. Records show him as a shareholder in the famous Globe Theatre (which has recently been faithfully reconstructed and puts on Shakespearean plays in the style which Shakespeare knew) and wealthy enough to buy his father the largest house in Stratford. His many plays include tragedies, comedies and history plays[21].

Among the best-known are *Hamlet*[22], the most performed play in the world: the story of a Danish prince seeking revenge upon his uncle for the murder of his father; and *Romeo and Juliet*[23], the story of two young lovers from feuding families which ends in a tragic double suicide.

Elizabethan drama, and Shakespeare in particular, is considered to be among the earliest work to display a "modern" perception of the world: full of moral doubts and political insecurities, where the right of those who wield power to do so is put in question.

The Nineteenth Century Novel

The nineteenth century was a very rich literary period. The early decades saw the great poets of the Romantic movement[24], such as Keats[25], Shelley[26], and Wordsworth[27]. The Romantics saw themselves as free spirits, emphasizing nature, originality, the emotional and personal, rather than the "rational"[28], in their work. This was a change from the emphasis on imitating classical (meaning Ancient Greek and Roman) conventions and forms that had been typical of the 18th century[29].

This spirit of Romanticism also occurred in the novel, notably in Mary Shelley's (the poet's wife) *Frankenstein*[30] (1817), the story of science gone wrong through the disastrous consequences of an arrogant scientist's (Dr Frankenstein) attempts to create life. In the process he only creates a monster. But the novel's sympathies are with the monster's struggle to make sense of his existence in a world that rejects him.

Jane Austen[31] wrote six novels published between 1811 and 1818.

These stories (often set in the pretty south-west town of Bath) of middle-class women in search of husbands are known for their fine writing and subtle characterisation. In the spirit of the 18th century, rationality is praised, but in the contemporary spirit of Romanticism, this is balanced with imaginative and the personal. This balance is seen in the title of one of the best-known of her novels: *Sense and sensibility* which was recently made into a highly successful film by a Taiwan director, Ang Lee[32].

Perhaps the most famous literary family in British history are the Bronte sisters, and they too were influenced by the Romantic movement. They were three daughters (Charlotte, Emily and Ann[33]) of the vicar of a village church in Haworth in Yorkshire, and as such, poor, but educated and respectable. They had a brother who was a failed painter and alcoholic, and two other sisters who died in childhood.

All were tragically to die before their father. Given their short lives they did not produce much, but among their works are some of the best-loved novels in English: Charlotte Bronte's *Jane Eyre* and Emily's *Wuthering Heights* (both 1847) being the most successful. Both have been filmed several times. Their novels reflect both their local geography: the wild high moors of the Yorkshire hills, which their home backed onto, and their uncertain economic position, because of which they could not hope for a respectable marriage of equals, being too poor. Thus *Jane Eyre* tells the story of an orphan, who has a loveless childhood at a terrible boarding school, and who goes to work for a rich man as a governess to his child. He becomes attracted to her because of her independence and free spirit. However, he has a secret in his past: a mad former wife locked up in the attic of his house. The secret discovered, Jane runs away. Later she becomes the object of a vicar's attention, who wishes to marry her as he feels she will make a suitable wife for a missionary. But in true Romantic fashion, this worthy but passionless lover is rejected, and Jane returns to the darker, but passionately romantic, figure of her previous employer, Mr Rochester.

The Brontes had trouble getting published, and in fact had to use male pseudonyms in order to gain acceptance. But one of Charlotte's friends was another female novelist, Elizabeth Gaskell[34]. She represents a more realistic aspect of the 19th century novel, concerned with social comment, not just personal freedom. A vicar's daughter from Manchester, she was concerned with the situation of the workers in the new industrial cities. Her novel *North and South* describes the division that this economic change was emphasizing in British society at that time, both in terms of class, and geography—the north was the industrial part of England, and those in the south, where power laid, remained ignorant of it. She was supported in her work by the greatest British storyteller of the 19th century, Charles Dickens[35]. He too was concerned with the state of the nation, and having suffered as a child worker himself when his father was imprisoned for debt, he had personal reasons for bringing the suffering of the poor to light. He wrote many well-known novels, including *Oliver Twist*, the story of an orphan child drawn into crime in the London underworld, and *Bleak House*, which describes the tragic unfolding of an endless lawsuit concerning an inheritance. The novel is a powerful criticism of the legal system at that time. These writers could be thought of as novelists first and social critics second. But there is one nineteenth century novelist who can be thought of as a social critic first, who used his novels to demonstrate his political ideas. His name was Benjamin Dirraeli[36], and his best known novel is perhaps *Sybil* (1845). Of

Jewish descent he became leader of the Tory party, and was a successful Prime Minister for two periods in the 1860s and 1870s. Like Gaskell he saw Britain as a society divided between the rich and poor, and used the term "Two Nations" to describe this situation. There are still Tory (Conservative) politicians today who call themselves "One Nation" Tories, meaning that their aim is to heal that rift.

The most famous Scottish novelist, Sir Walter Scott[37] (1771 - 1832), wrote many novels in the early decades of the nineteenth century. The first were romances concerned with Scottish history, such as *Rob Roy*[38] and have been very influential as being among the first novels which set about realistically recreating whole historical societies. Later, to pay off huge debts he had incurred through a business failure, he turned to more commercial English medieval topics, such as *Ivanhoe*[39], a story of conflict between Saxon and Norman. The novels remain popular today, and several have been the subject of Hollywood films. There is a monument to him in a prominent position in Edinburgh.

Later in the nineteenth century Robert Louis Stevenson[40] also wrote Scottish historical romances, but his most famous work was *Doctor Jekyll and Mr. Hyde*[41], a novel again concerned with the conflict between the rational and the emotional, sensual side of man's nature, represented in the single person of the scientist Dr Jekyll, who transforms himself into the wild Mr Hyde.

Twentieth Century Literature

Twentieth century literature can be broadly divided into two stylistic periods: Modernism[42], and Postmodernism[43]. These periods roughly correspond to literature written before the Second World War (1939 - 1945) and literature written after it. Both are characterized by a high degree of experimentation[44].

Modernism in literature can be seen as a reaction against the nineteenth century forms discussed above, which can be thought of as assuming understanding between writer and reader, resulting in the simple communication of an agreed version of the "world"[45]. This approach to writing is known as "Realism"[46]. Instead, Modernist writers express the difficulty they see in understanding and communicating how the world works. Often, therefore, Modernist writing seems disorganized, hard to understand. It often portrays the action from viewpoint of a single confused individual, rather than from the viewpoint of an all-knowing impersonal narrator outside the action[47],

One of the most famous of English Modernist writers is Joseph Conrad[48]. He was raised in Poland, but became a sailor, and ended up as the Captain of a British ship. He got British citizenship and settled in England, where he wrote his books in English. They are Modernist in their concerns with moral uncertainty: what is right? And in their concerns with factual uncertainty: what is true?

Conrad's most famous novel is *The Heart of Darkness*[49] (1902), a story of a riverboat journey in central Africa to investigate an exploitative European ivory trader called Mr. Kurts. The journey is a symbolic one representing the darkness at the heart of man. Mr Kurtz's last words, "The horror! The horror!" are among the best known in English literature. A film based on the novel has been made by the American director, Francis Ford Coppola, but set in Vietnam in the 1960s, and called *Apocalypse Now*.

Virginia Woolf[50] is another writer associated with Modernism, and one of the most famous writers of the century. She was part of the intellectual "Bloomsbury group" named after the fashionable area of London in which they lived, which included other writers, philosophers, painters, and the economist, J. M. Keynes[51]. Her work was concerned with the individual consciousness, especially the female consciousness. Her novels have become important to feminists for the way they show women's personalities to be limited by society. *Mrs. Dolloway*[52] (1925) is one of her best-known works. She sometimes used what has been called the "stream of consciousness[53]" technique: the apparently unorganised flow of thought onto page.

Less experimental, D. H. Lawrence[54], and E. M. Forster[55] both wrote novels in this period which are critical of the modern world. In Forster's *Howard's End*[56] (1910 - recently made into a very successful film) he contrasts the artistic, romantic Schlegel sisters with the forceful, unethical business-people, the Wilcoxes. But in what we might see as a typical move for a British writer, the two families are brought together to create a new "hybrid".

Moving into the post-war period, one of the most famous novels in English appears: George Orwell's *1984*[57] (1949) is a powerful satire on the totalitarian tendency in modern states. It is set in an extremely unpleasant England ruled absolutely by "Big Brother". This depressing story is characteristic of the post-war years, and begins "Postmodernism". The horrors of the Second World War undermined ideas of human progress, and of meaning in life, however well hidden. So while Modernists were scientists of human existence, looking for buried meaning below confusing surfaces, Postmodernists can be thought of as abandoning that search[58]. Meaning does not exist outside of the human head, likewise it does not exist inside a book, waiting to be discovered, instead it is made in the process of reading a book, or of making sense of the world[59].

So writers like John Fowles[60] play a game with the reader, constantly demonstrating the fictionality of their writing, and inviting the reader to put together different pieces freely. Fowles' most successful novel, *The French Lieutenant's Woman*[61] (1968), set in the small holiday resort of Lyme Regis, describes a Victorian gentleman's education into his own freedom by the mysterious girl, Sarah. It was also made into a well-known film. The story's main postmodern "trick" is that the reader is offered a choice of endings.

Not all writers can be squeezed into the definitions Modern or Postmodern. Many post-war writers continue traditional themes: Graham Greene[62] (1904 – 1991) wrote novels of morally and religiously troubled expatriates, sometimes concerned with spies. Spy fiction in general is one of the strong points of contemporary British fiction: the best known is John Le Carre[63]. His novels (such as *Smiley's People*[64] — 1980) have been made into internationally distributed TV serials. In popular fiction, Ian Fleming's fantastic *James Bond*[65] stories are even better known, especially for their numerous film versions.

The best-known Welsh writer is the poet Dylan Thomas[66] (1914 – 1953), whose compelling rhythms and rich natural imagery make his poetry very accessible and popular. Scotland too has produced many writers of note in recent times. Irvine Welsh's 1993 novel, *Trainspotting*, tells a shocking and powerful story of drug abuse, crime and unemployment amongst young people in Edinburgh. Written in the local dialect, it was made into a controversial (and popular!) film in 1996. The Northern Irish playwright, Brian Friel[67], has had recent international success with his investigations of Irish history and Irishness such as *Dancing at Lughnasa*.

To look at a list of the most respected contemporary British writers is to be struck by the variety of many of their origins: Salman Rushdie (India), Grace Nichols (Guyana), Kazio Ishiguro (Japan), V. S. Naipaul (Trinidad) amongst many others. This too is an aspect of the postmodern world: a mixing of cultures on a grand scale. But this mixture, this "hybridity" as I have called it, has always been a part of British writing, with its multinational and class-divided internal status, its imperial past, and its current highly international economy. British literature continues to reflect that complexity.

Words & Expressions

annual/ˈænjuəl/*a*.　每年的
Christianity/ˌkristiˈæniti/*n*.　基督教
pilgrim/ˈpilgrim/*n*.　朝圣者
destination/ˌdestiˈneiʃən/*n*.　目的地
apprentice/əˈprentis/*n*.　初学者
myth/miθ/*n*.　神话
the Renaissance　文艺复兴
playwright/ˈpleirait/*n*.　剧作家
trio/ˈtriːəu/*n*.　三人(一组)
perception/pəˈsepʃən/*n*.　观念;感觉
wield/wiːld/*vt*.　使用
subtle/ˈsʌtl/*a*.　微妙的
characterisation/ˌkæriktəraiˈzeiʃən/*n*.　性格描写
contemporary/kənˈtempərəri/*a*.　当代的
vicar/ˈvikə/*n*.　教区牧师
alcoholic/ˌælkəˈhɔlik/*n*.　酒鬼
missionary/ˈmiʃənəri/*n*.　传教士
pseudonym/ˈpsjuːdənim/*n*.　假名;笔名
unfolding/ʌnˈfəuldiŋ/*a*.　展开的
lawsuit/ˈlɔːsjuːt/*n*.　诉讼
descent/diˈsent/*n*.　后裔
prominent/ˈprɔminənt/*a*.　突出的
sensual/ˈsensjuəl/*a*.　好色的
transform/trænsˈfɔːm/*v*.　改变
feminist/ˈfeminist/*n*.　女权主义者
unethical/ˌʌnˈeθikəl/*a*.　不道德的
hybrid/ˈhaibrid/*n*.　不同文化的混合
satire/ˈsætaiə/*n*.　讽刺
totalitarian/ˌtəutæliˈtɛəriən/*a*.　极权主义的
expatriates/eksˈpætriəts/*n*.　被流放者;侨民
compelling/kəmˈpeliŋ/*a*.　有强烈吸引力的
accessible/əkˈsesəbl/*a*.　可以理解的;易懂的

Notes

1. the Scottish Island of Iona:苏格兰爱奥那岛。

2. closer to its German roots:更接近德文的词源。盎格鲁·撒克逊祖先居住在德国北部一带,他们讲类似德语的方言。因此,移居英国后,他们的语言深受德语的影响。

3. old English literary works:古英语文学作品。古英语是指公元6世纪至11世纪盎格鲁·撒克逊的英语。古英语文学作品主要是指8世纪至11世纪的文学作品。作品的素材来源于丹麦和其他北欧国家。主要作品有《贝奥武甫》和《盎格鲁·撒克逊年鉴》。

4. *Beowulf*:《贝奥武甫》是盎格鲁·撒克逊时期的一首英雄史诗,古英语文学的最高成就,同时标志着英国文学的开始。史诗分两部分:第一部分讲述瑞典青年王子贝奥武甫来到丹麦,帮助丹麦国王赫罗斯加杀死了12年来常来进行夜袭的巨妖格伦德尔及他的母亲;第二部分简述了贝奥武甫继承王位,平安统治50年。后来,他的国土被一条喷火巨龙蹂躏,老当益壮的贝奥武甫与火龙交战,杀死火龙,自己也受了致命伤。

5. Geoffrey Chaucer:杰弗里·乔叟(1340 ~ 1400)是英国莎士比亚时代以前最杰出的作家和最伟大的诗人之一。主要作品有《坎特伯雷故事集》等。他的作品突出主题、题材、风格、笔调的多样性及描写人对生活的追求的复杂性,内含幽默感,同时对重要的哲学问题进行了严肃而宽容的讨论。乔叟的诗在当时普遍受到推崇,特别是《坎特伯雷故事集》,对后世影响很大。

6. Middle English:中古英语,产生于11世纪至15世纪,是英国文学的真正开始。

7. It is notable ... 31 pilgrims:《坎特伯雷故事集》以其丰富多彩的故事而出名,不仅体现了31位朝圣者的各种社会阶层,而且也反映出他们叙述故事的不同风格。

8. *The Wife of Bath*:《巴斯夫人的故事》。传说很久以前,亚瑟王的一名骑士因犯强奸罪而被判死刑,但王后提出,只要他在一年内找出"女人最想要什么"这一答案,即可豁免。经过努力,骑士终于从女巫口中获得答案。但女巫要求嫁给骑士,骑士因女巫丑陋而不从,但因有约在先,只好接纳。女巫教育了骑士在择偶上的道理,骑士欣然接受。女巫即变成了美丽的姑娘。这是《坎特伯雷故事集》中的故事之一。

9. a Latin work which ... in the historical records:这部用拉丁文写成的著作,尽管称之为一部史书,但实际上这些素材都是编造的,用以填补历史的空白。

10. the Holy Grail:圣杯,传说是耶稣在最后晚餐时用过的。

11. Thomas Malory:托马斯·马洛礼,以《亚瑟王之死》一书而闻名。此书叙述亚瑟王成败兴衰及其圆桌骑士们的伙伴关系,是此类著作的第一部英国散文作品。

12. the stuff of the British imagination for centuries to come:这些英国人想像出来的故事流传了几个世纪。

13. The Mabinogion:《马比诺吉昂》是11个中世纪威尔士故事的总称,以神话、民间传说的英雄传奇为基础,记录12世纪下半叶到13世纪末的流传故事。这些故事提供有关凯尔特人(Celtic)、诺曼人和法国人的早期相互交流的趣事。其中重要的故事有13世纪的本地亚瑟王传奇《罗纳布威之梦》。凯尔特人是西欧及北欧的古老部族居民。

14. *the Ulster Cycle*:《厄尔斯特故事集》,古爱尔兰文学,用Gaelic语(盖尔人语言)写成。盖尔人是西欧及北欧的古老部族人。本书叙述一组爱尔兰北部尤莱德族时代的传说和故事。

15. Cuchulain:库丘林是传奇故事康纳尔王骑士中的主要英雄。在康诺特,有一个由利艾尔国王和梅得布王后统治的朝廷,与康纳尔王统治的厄尔其特人对立并发生冲突。库丘林为了保卫厄尔期特及厄尔斯特人的利益,英勇作战。

16. The Renaissance:文艺复兴。发端于14至15世纪的意大利。城市的新兴资产阶级为维护和发展其政治、经济利益,要求在意识形态领域里开展反对教会精神统治即封建文化的斗争,以新的世界观推翻神学、经院哲学以及僧侣主义的世界观。这种新的世界观推动文学、艺术及科学技术的发展,形成文艺复兴运动。它对欧美乃至世界现代文明的发展有着不可磨灭的影响。

17. Christopher Marlowe:克里斯托弗·马洛(1564~1593),英国重要诗人和戏剧家,他推动了伊丽莎白时代英国戏剧的迅速发展。在他之前,英国戏剧中的无韵诗体还很呆板,是他使之具有高度的灵活性。他才华横溢,性格狂暴,生活放荡,持无神论观点。他的主要作品有《帖木儿》、《浮士德博士》、《爱德华二世》、《巴黎大屠杀》等。

18. Ben Jonson:(1572~1637)本·琼森,英国剧作家,诗人、评论家。他被公认为伊丽莎白一世时期和詹姆斯一世时期仅次于莎士比亚的剧作家,是驾驭戏剧情节、运用语言和刻画人物性格大师。他的主要作品有《人人高兴》、《人人扫兴》、《黑假面剧》、《炼金术士》和《卡塔林的阴谋》等。

19. *Dr. Faustus*:《浮士德博士》是马洛最受人重视的一部作品。浮士德确有其人,生活在1488年~1541年间的德国，据传是个魔术师或巫师，慢慢地成了一位半神话式的人物。剧的大意是浮士德对中世纪经院所传授的知识感到不满，向往“魔术”，同魔鬼歃血为约：为了获得知识，他可以驱使魔鬼24年，到期魔鬼就把他的灵魂劫往地狱。

20. William Shakespeare：威廉·莎士比亚(1564~1616)是文艺复兴时期英国著名的剧作家和诗人。他创作了大量的作品，其中包括喜剧、悲剧和历史剧。他的剧本至今仍在许多国家上演，并为人们所普遍阅读。莎士比亚的作品文才横溢，创造的喜、怒、哀、乐场面使人印象深刻，历久难忘。

21. His many plays include tragedies, comedies and history plays：莎士比亚创作的主要悲剧有《奥赛罗》、《哈姆雷特》、《麦克白》和《罗密欧与朱丽叶》等；创作的喜剧有《仲夏夜之梦》、《威尼斯商人》、《无事生非》和《皆大欢喜》等；历史剧包括《亨利六世》三部曲、《理查二世》、《理查三世》和《亨利四世》等。

22. *Hamlet*：悲剧《哈姆雷特》的故事是根据13世纪初丹麦历史学家 Saxo Grammaticus 的记载，叙述了丹麦王子哈姆雷特替父报仇，杀死篡夺王位的叔父的故事。莎士比亚改造了丹麦的历史故事，创造了哈姆雷特这个复杂深刻的人物。通过这个人物和他周围环境之间的冲突，反映了文艺复兴时期人文主义思想家的理想和资本主义原始积累时期社会现实中的无法调和的矛盾。

23. *Romeo and Juliet*：《罗密欧与朱丽叶》。莎士比亚的这一悲剧描写了一对青年男女因家族间的世仇而不能联姻，结果自杀的故事。揭露了封建制度的残酷无情，同时，歌颂了青年男女纯洁坚贞的爱情，表达了作者早期的人文主义思想。

24. the Romantic movement：浪漫主义作为一种文艺思潮，产生于18世纪末19世纪初的欧洲资产阶级革命时代，是文学艺术的基本创作方法之一。在文学艺术史上，浪漫主义与现实主义是两大主要思潮。浪漫主义在反映现实上，善于抒发对理想世界的热烈追求，常用热情奔放的语言、瑰丽的想象、夸张的手法来塑造形象。

25. Keats：济慈(1795~1821)是英国浪漫主义诗人。他出身贫苦，做过医生的学徒，后来才以写诗为业。他对当时英国社会的现实不满，希望在一个“永恒的美的世界”中寻找安身立命之处。但他对人生态度是严肃的，不是像有些人认为的唯美主义者。他的诗特别以文辞声调之美著称，在艺术上对后代的英国诗人影响很大。主要作品有《伊沙贝拉》、《夜莺颂》、《心灵》、《梦》和《秋颂》等。

26. Shelley：雪莱(1792~1822)是英国浪漫主义诗人。他生于贵族家庭，早年深受卢梭、潘恩和葛德文等人的思想影响，诗才横溢。他既有富于政治思想性的诗，也有优美的抒情诗，特别是爱情诗，显示了不羁的想象，瑰丽的色彩和动人的音韵，使他成为英国文学史上最有才华的抒情诗人之一。他的主要作品有《麦布女王》、《伊斯兰的叛变》、《解放了的普罗米修斯》和《西风颂》等。

27. Wordsworth：华兹华斯(1770~1850)，18~19世纪之交英国浪漫主义运动最伟大和最有影响的诗人，其作品的主题是人与大自然的关系。1796年~1806年是华兹华斯诗歌创作的全盛时期，其所有最优秀的作品几乎都是在这一期间完成的。1813年他接受政府长期津贴，1843年又被封为桂冠诗人。他的主要作品有《抒情歌谣集》、《我们七个》、《彩虹》、《水仙》和《序曲》等。

28. The Romantics saw ... rather than the “rational”：浪漫主义作家把他们自己当做自

由人,强调真实和独创性,强调情感和个性,而不强调理性。

29. This was a change . . . 18th century:对于18世纪流行的强调遵循典型传统与模式的写作方法来说,这种浪漫主义的写作方法是一种变化。

30. *Frankenstein*:《弗兰肯斯坦》是M. W. 雪莱运用了哥特式浪漫故事和科学幻想小说相结合的手法写成的一本恐怖小说。在书中,弗兰肯斯坦是一个专攻秘术的瑞士学者,他人工制造了一个由各部分肢体组成的怪物,而最终却被他所造的怪物杀死。后来弗兰肯斯坦却成了这个怪物的名字,以后又成了著名电影的怪物角色。

31. Jane Austen:珍妮·奥斯丁(1775~1817),英国现实主义小说家。她是乡村牧师的女儿,一生住在乡间,对乡村绅士地主的生活了解很深,平生写过六部小说,多以此为背景,而更以婚姻问题为中心题材。她的作品情节结构情密紧凑,人物描写深刻生动,戏剧场面精彩,对话巧妙。主要作品有《理智和情感》、《傲慢与偏见》、《曼斯菲尔德花园》、《爱玛》、《诺桑觉寺》和《劝导》。

32. Ang Lee:李安,1954年生于台湾,1978年移民美国,获伊利诺斯州立大学戏剧系学士学位,后又获纽约大学电影制作硕士学位。1985年他所导演的《分界线》获得纽约大学毕业影展最佳导演及最佳影片双项奖。1994年他编导的《喜宴》获美国影片协会提名的奥斯卡最佳外语片。1995年,他导演的外语影片《理智与情感》获当年美国奥斯卡最佳剧本改编及最佳女演员奖。

33. Charlotte, Emily and Anne:夏洛蒂、爱米丽和安妮姐妹三人出身贫寒,幼年丧母,不得不在慈善学校度过童年。姐妹三人先后当过收入微薄的教师和家庭教师。夏洛蒂38岁才结婚,次年去世。两个妹妹终生未嫁。夏洛蒂的代表作《简爱》是她的自传体小说,小说问世后立即产生了巨大影响。小说坦率而热情地塑造了同自己的人生欲望和社会地位发生冲突的妇女形象。爱米丽的《呼啸的山庄》被誉为第一部社会革命小说。小妹安妮的小说具有平静的力量和现实性,也得到了一些评论者的称赞。

34. Elizabeth Gaskell:伊丽莎白·盖斯凯尔(1810~1865)是英国小说家,出生牧师家庭,母亲死后由姨妈抚养成人。1832年同W·盖斯凯尔结婚,定居曼彻斯特。她的主要作品有《玛丽·巴顿》、《克兰弗德》、《露丝》和《妻子与女儿》等。

35. Charles Dickens:查理·狄更斯(1812~1870),19世纪英国伟大的小说家。幼年家贫,曾作徒工,成名后仍接近贫苦人民。一生创作辛勤,留下了20多部小说,包括《匹克威克外传》、《奥立弗·特维斯特》、《双城记》、《艰难时世》和《大卫·科波菲尔》等。狄更斯的小说情节曲折动人,人物形象鲜明生动,写景叙事真切而又富想象,既有尖刻的讽刺,又有幽默的夸张。

36. Benjamin Disraeli:本杰明·迪斯累里(1804~1881),英国政治家和小说家,生于伦敦,双亲为意大利籍犹太人。他曾两度任首相。他写过许多部小说,其中包括《威尼斯》和《罕丽达神殿》。1875年获贵族爵位,1878年获嘉德骑士勋章。

37. Sir Walter Scott:瓦尔特·司各特(1771~1832)是英国19世纪初浪漫主义时期的著名诗人、小说家和戏剧家。他从小就喜爱诗歌,从1796年起,陆续发表了他所翻译的外国诗和搜集到的苏格兰民歌。接着出版了他自己创作的诗,享有盛名。他的主要成就是历史小说。《艾凡赫》是他的代表作,主要作品还包括《威佛利》、《盖伊·曼纳林》、《苏格兰边区歌谣集》和《米德洛西恩的监狱》等。

38. *Rob Roy*:《罗布·罗伊》,描写1715年詹姆斯党人第一次起义前夕苏格兰山地人民反抗英国政权的斗争。罗布·罗伊是"苏格兰的罗宾汉",本是山地氏族领袖,在封建压迫下成了反抗统治阶级、杀富济贫的绿林好汉。

39. *Ivanhoe*:《艾凡赫》出版于1819年,被认为是司各特的最有代表性的一部历史小说。它以12世纪的英国为背景,描写当时的盎格鲁·撒克逊人和在上一世纪征服了英国的诺曼人之间的民族矛盾,以及统治阶级和穷苦农民之间的阶级矛盾。它通过各式各样的人物和错综复杂的情节,描绘了一幅中世纪社会生活的广阔画面。

40. Robert Louis Stevenson:罗伯特·路易斯·斯蒂文森(1850.11.13～1894.12.3)。英国著名的冒险故事和散文作家。作的作品种类繁多,构思精巧,其成熟小说富有独创性和感染力。他对苏格兰的风土人情感情浓厚,曾深入研究18世纪苏格兰历史,写了一系列以苏格兰为背景的小说,如《黑箭》、《绑架》、《巴伦特雷少爷》和《卡特林娜》等。他的成名作《金银岛》更是男孩们爱不释手的好书。

41. *Doctor Jekyll and Mr. Hyde*:《吉基尔医生与海德先生》是一部反映人性复杂特征的心理浪漫小说。吉基尔本是一位人品出众、心地善良的医生。正是这种品质使他内心深处的丑恶面得到抑制。然而在后来的药物试验中,由于他吃了一种可以使人性变恶乃至杀人的药,结果他变成了杀人犯——海德先生。当他意识到这种试验一发不可收拾时,在极度矛盾之下,只好自杀,了结一切。

42. Modernism:现代派是本世纪初以来陆续出现的各种文学流派的总称。它包括象征主义、未来主义、超现实主义、意识流小说、存在主义文学、黑色幽默等流派。现代主义的大多数作品情节若有若无,人物形象扑朔迷离,思想含义晦涩难明。

43. Postmodernism:后现代主义派是二战以后,60年代至70年代期间出现的一种文学流派,其特点是试图摆脱传统保守模式的束缚,否定权威,否定中心,提倡多元化。代表人物有英国的格雷厄姆·格林、多丽斯·莱辛和玛格丽特·德拉布尔。

44. Both are characterized by a high degree of experimentation:现代派和后现代派在很大程度上具有试验性特点。

45. Modernism in literature ... an agreed version of the "world":文学上的现代主义可以被看做对上面讨论过的19世纪写作方式的一种反叛。这可以被认为是在作者与读者之间存在一种理解,从而达到对世界一致看法进行简单的交流。

46. Known as "Realism":现实主义是文艺的基本创作方法之一,侧重如实地反映现实生活,客观性较强。它提倡客观地、冷静地观察生活,按照生活的本来样式精确细腻地加以描写,力求真实地再现典型环境中的典型人物。

47. It often portrays ... outside the action:现实主义的写作方法往往从个人自身矛盾观点来描写行为,而不是从一个了解内情,但又是局外人的角度来描写行为。

48. Joseph Conrad:约瑟夫·康拉德(1857～1924),英国航海家和小说家。他出生在俄国的波兰人家庭,姓克尔泽尼奥夫斯基,康拉德是他的笔名。他自幼向往海上生活,先后在不同的商船上工作,担任过水手、大副和船长等职务。他在海上传奇式的经历给他的写作提供了丰富的素材。他的作品有《黑暗的中心》、《群岛上的被遗弃者》、《机会》和《胜利》等。

49. *The Heart of Darkness*:《黑暗的中心》写船长马洛指挥一艘汽船沿刚果河深入非洲。

一路上不断听说非洲腹地有一个名叫库尔兹的白人脱离了“文明世界”，被土著奉若神明，尊为领袖。马洛历经艰险终于见到了他，原来他早已堕落。这部书表现了文明与原始的对立，在许多地方对殖民主义表示不满。

50. Virginia Woolf：维吉尼亚·沃尔夫（1882～1941），英国女作家。她对小说的写作形式曾做出独特贡献，也是当时最优秀的评论家之一。她在伦敦的住地布鲁姆斯伯里成为文学中心，座上客都是当时著名作家和文人。1912 年与列诺德·沃尔夫结婚，1917 年夫妻成立了著名的“何加斯”出版社。维吉尼亚于 1941 年 3 月投河自杀。她的小说着重写人物的内心世界，常用“意识流”手法。主要作品有《远航》、《夜与日》、《奥兰多》、《幕与幕之间》和《黛洛维夫人》等。

51. J. M. Keynes：凯恩斯（1883.6.5～1946.4.21），英国著名经济学家、经济政策的制定者和评论家、有成就的金融家。1902 年入剑桥大学，先学习数学，转而对政治学和经济学感兴趣。1915 年以前一直教经济学，成绩卓著。第一次世界大战期间，在英国财政部任职。他发表的《凡尔赛和约的经济后果》和《就业、利息和货币通论》著作使他获得了不朽的声誉。

52. *Mrs. Dolloway*：《黛洛维夫人》是维吉尼亚·沃尔夫早期的佳作，写黛洛维夫人一天 24 小时之内的生活。情节简单，风格特点是抒情、深邃、细致的，对人物的描写带有讽刺。小说有主要人物和次要人物，但很难说有什么正面人物。她感兴趣的是人物的内心深处的活动，用“意识流”这一创作方法深刻、细腻地描绘了人物的思想感情、个性及弱点。

53. the stream of consciousness：意识流，20 世纪心理小说的一种叙事技巧。以意识流作结构，有意忽略故事情节的连贯和完整，让人物在主观的时空框子里活动，采用内心独白、自由联想、象征暗示、时序颠倒以及现实与回忆、事实与虚幻互相穿插等手法来展现人物的意识流动轨迹。意识流小说的著名代表作家有：爱尔兰的乔伊斯、英国的沃尔夫、美国的福克纳等。

54. D. H. Lawrence：D. H. 劳伦斯（1889～1930）是当代英国文学的一位大师，著名的现代派作家代表之一。他在创作上摒弃了英国传统的艺术表现形式，语言质朴、句子结构简单，大量使用淳朴的生活语言。他在作品中揭示了人性中的本能力量，并辛辣地批评了现代工业社会。他一生写了 10 部长篇小说，其中最伟大和最有代表性的是《虹》和《恋爱中的女人》。

55. E. M. Forster：福斯特（1879.1.1～1970.6.7），英国小说家、散文家。生于伦敦，毕业于剑桥大学。初期小说反映了英国文学摆脱维多利亚时代影响的特点。他摒弃了 19 世纪人们喜爱的繁缛辞藻和复杂的细节描写，采取更为流畅自如、更加口语化的写作风格。主要作品有《霍华德庄园》、《印度之行》、《天使不敢涉足的地方》、《最长的旅行》、《一间可以看到风景的房间》和《莫里斯》等。

56. *Howard's End*：《霍华德庄园》是 E. M. 福斯特的成名小说，现在已拍成电影，搬上银幕。故事讲述了富有浪漫主义色彩和自由想像力的玛格丽特和追求商业利益而濒于精神崩溃的亨利结婚，玛格丽特把亨利带回到以前的旧居，希望重建想像力与土地的联系。

57. George Orwell's *1984*：乔治·奥威尔（1903～1950），英国讽刺小说家、新闻记者、自传作者。他的主要讽刺作品有《兽园》和《一九八四》。《一九八四》发表于 1949 年，该书描写了一个过分集权的社会如何歪曲真相和不断地否定历史。

58. So while Modernists were . . . as abandoning that search:因此现代派是人类生存的科学家,探求在混乱的表面现象下的生活意义,而后现代派则可以被认为要放弃这种追求。

59. Meaning does not exist outside of . . . or of making sense of the world.:生活的意义并不存在于人们的大脑之外,同样也不存在于书本之中等待人们去发现,而是在阅读一本书的过程中获得,或者是在了解世界的过程中获得。

60. John Fowles:约翰·福尔斯(1926.3~),英国小说家。1950年毕业于牛津大学,曾在希腊、法国和英国教学。他的作品把心理描写和社会生活巧妙地结合起来。他的第一部小说《收藏家》出版后,立即受到读者欢迎。除此之外,他还写了《占星家》、《法国中尉的女人》和《丹尼尔·马丁》。

61. *The French Lieutenant's Woman*:《法国中尉的女人》,描写19世纪中叶的一个富有传奇色彩的三角恋爱故事。故事叙述对古生物学和地质学颇感兴趣的查尔斯与被人们称之为"法国中尉的情妇"萨拉邂逅相遇,为了追求萨拉,他毅然同富有的商人之女蒂娜决裂,撕毁婚约,抛弃垂手可得的荣华富贵。但是当他与萨拉情意绵绵时,萨拉却悄然离他而去。经过一番周折,查尔斯找到萨拉并向她求婚,却遭到萨拉婉拒。

62. Graham Greene:格林(1904~1991),英国小说家,毕业于牛津大学,1929年开始专门从事写作。惊险小说《斯坦布尔列车》出版后,崭露头角。此后他又出版了《一支出卖的枪》、《秘史》。电影剧本《第三个人》是第二次世界大战后著名的间谍影片。《布赖顿硬糖》和《权力和荣耀》都以天主教为主题。《病毒发尽的病例》是他后期小说中最重要的作品。

63. John Le Carre:约翰·勒卡雷(1931~)。真名为大卫·康威尔,约翰·勒卡雷是他的笔名。他毕业于牛津大学。曾一度执教于伊顿公立学校,后从事外交工作。他的作品有《德国小镇》、《叛徒》、《士兵》和《间谍》等。

64. *Smiley's People*:《史秘雷的同僚》主要描写功勋卓著的英国反间谍能手乔治·史秘雷在退休之后倚仗其大量的间谍情报和同僚的协助,成功地将前苏联头号间谍卡拉策反到西方国家的故事。该书歌颂了史秘雷等英国特工人员的忠诚和高超的反间谍技术。

65. James Bond:詹姆斯·邦德,英国侦探系列小说的主人翁。邦德是英国情报机构的侦探,代号007。他常常受命执行十分艰巨而危险的任务。每次执行任务中,他都能历经艰险,出生入死,克服重重困难而化险为夷。这部侦探系列小说已被搬上银幕,深受观众喜爱。

66. Dylan Thomas:迪伦·托马斯(1914~1953),英国诗人。他生于英国威尔士一个中产阶级的家庭,早年谙熟英国诗歌,显露出文学天才。他憎恶富豪,同情穷人,自称是和平主义者。托马斯是英国最后一位浪漫派抒情诗人。早年在威尔士的生活对托马斯有极大的影响,使他的主要作品独树一帜,不同于一般的英国文学的风格与情趣。他的主要作品有《诗十八首》和《诗集》等。

67. Brian Friel:布赖恩·弗里尔,爱尔兰当代著名剧作家和小说家,大学毕业后就开始创作生涯。他的作品多以泰隆县和多尼尔县为背景,内容融合现实与想象,人物多为农民和穷苦民众,他所使用的幽默和讽刺更使作品增加了浓厚的爱尔兰色彩。他的小说与剧本在一定程度上反映了爱尔兰这个古老民族在本民族文化失落、宗教民族矛盾冲突不得解决时的心态。

Exercises

Ⅰ. Explain the following

1. Elizabethan drama
2. The Canterbury Tales
3. the Romantic Movement
4. Modernism
5. Postmodernism

Ⅱ. Fill in the blanks

1. One of the oldest of the early "old English" literary works is called ________.
2. ________ is generally regarded as Geoffrey Chaucer's masterpiece.
3. Shakespeare's plays fall into three categories. They are ________, ________ and ________.
4. Name two of the tragedies written by Shakespeare: ________ and ________.
5. Charlotte Bronte and Emily Bronte are noted for their novels ________ and ________ which are largely the love stories of a woman for a man.
6. Charles Dickens and Elizabeth Gaskell are regarded not only as ________ but also as social ________ in the 19th century.
7. The author of *Ivanhoe* was ________; *Doctor Jekyll and Mr. Hyde* was done by ________; Charles Dickens wrote ________ and among many other works.
8. Twentieth-century literature can be broadly divided into two stylistic periods: ________ and ________.
9. Virginia Woolf was one of the most famous writers of the ________ century. Her work was concerned with the individual consciousness, especially the ________ consciousness. She sometimes used the technique called ________ in her writing.
10. *The Heart of Darkness* was written by ________; *the French Lieutenant's Woman* was done by ________ and the author of 1984 was ________.
11. The most famous novel by John Fowles was called ________.
12. *Smiley's People* was written by ________.

Ⅲ. Choose the correct answer in each of the following

1. Which of the following books is written by Geoffrey Chaucer?
   A. *The Canterbury Tales.*　　B. *Beowulf.*
   C. *The Ulster Cycle.*　　D. *Morte D'Arthur.*
2. What flourished in Elizabethan age more than any other form of literature?
   A. Novel.　　B. Essay.
   C. Drama.　　D. Poetry.
3. Among the following writers, who was NOT one of the great trio?
   A. Ben Johnson.　　B. William Shakespeare.

C. Geoffrey Chaucer. D. Christopher Marlowe.

4. Which of the following did NOT belong to Romanticism?

A. Keats. B. Shelley.

C. Wordsworth. D. E. M. Foster.

5. Which of the following is a tragedy written by Shakespeare?

A. *Dr. Faustus.* B. *Hamlet.*

C. *Frankenstein.* D. *Sense and Sensibility.*

6. Which of the following was the most famous Scottish novelist?

A. D. H. Lawrence. B. Charles Dickens.

C. Robert L. Stevenson. D. Walter Scott.

7. Several gifter women played a part in 19th-century literature. Which of the following is an exception?

A. Virginia Woolf. B. Emily Bronte.

C. Jane Austen. D. Charlotte Bronte.

8. Which of the following writers was NOT associated with Modernism?

A. D. H. Lawrence. B. E. M. Forster.

C. Charles Dickens. D. Virginia Woolf.

9. Which of the following is generally considered to be the masterpiece by Joseph Conrad?

A. *Sybil.* B. *The Heart of Darkness.*

C. *Bleak House.* D. *Wuthering Heights.*

10. Which of the following was a Postmodernist writer?

A. George Orwell. B. Robert L. Stevenson.

C. Jane Austen. D. Virginia Woolf.

Ⅳ. Answer the following questions briefly

1. What are some of the characteristics of the early writing in English Literature?
2. Why was Geoffrey Chaucer so significant in English Literature?
3. Why do you think that the legend of King Arthur was so popular in the early writing of English Literature?
4. What are some main features of Elizabethan Drama? Who was the best known figure in Elizabethan Drama?

Chapter 7 Religion and Beliefs

Christianity

The British are of course Christians—in name at least—and the following very brief summary of Christianity is given for the benefit of non-Christian readers[1].

Jesus Christ was a Jew who lived in Palestine 2,000 years ago and is accepted by Christians as the son of God. He was miraculously conceived by a virgin named Mary[2], became a carpenter by trade, and then started preaching and performing miracles[3]. The things he taught conflicted with orthodox Jewish laws and doctrines, and at the age of about thirty-three he was executed by crucifixion[4]. It is believed that he rose from the dead, ascended into Heaven, and sent his spirit into the hearts of his twelve apostles[5] to inspire them to spread his teaching.

Christ's teaching was based on love: love of God, and love of our neighbour, i. e. of all our fellow-men regardless of race. Love, humility, repentance and prayer lead to everlasting happiness in Heaven.

The Bible, which is the holy book of Christianity, consists of two "testaments"[6]. The Old Testament contains the Jewish writings before the coming of Christ. The much shorter New Testament contains four accounts ("gospels") of the life of Christ, followed by the writings of the early Christians, of whom St Paul[7] was the greatest. Christian doctrine as developed by St Paul and the early Church states that Jesus Christ was in fact God in the form of a man, and that God, Jesus and the Holy Spirit are three aspects of the same one God (the Trinity). In dying, Jesus took upon himself the punishment of the sins of men. Thus, his death saves us from sin, and proves that God loves us. Moreover, the coming of his spirit enables God to be revealed to anyone who believes in him.

The Christian Church in Britain

The Church of England, or *Anglican* Church, is one of the many "Protestant" sects which broke away from the more ancient and more orthodox Roman Catholic Church several centuries ago, during the great religious upheaval called the Reformation. It is an "established" Church[8], which means that it represents the official state religion, having certain duties towards the state, and receiving certain privileges from it, though no financial support. Its temporal (i. e. non-priestly) head is the Queen[9], and twenty six of its highest priests sit in the House of Lords[10].

But the Church of England is not as strong as might at first appear. For one thing, it is "established' only in England, not in Scotland, Ireland or Wales. Scotland has its own established Church, the Church of Scotland, which in organisation is Presbyterian[11]. Then too, in spiritual matters the Church of England has no strong central authority. Roman Catholics throughout the world recognise the supreme holy authority of the Pope in Rome and of the Church or priesthood in general (e. g. in personal confession of sins), but the Anglican Church relies more on the Bible, which is not always easy to interpret, and leaves many questions to individual consciences[12]. Certain Roman doctrines have of course been generally rejected by Anglicans. The central one concerns the celebration of Holy Communion[13], in which there is a symbolic eating of bread and drinking of wine. Roman Catholics believe that the bread and wine actually become the body and blood of Christ, whereas most Anglicans think they are simply representations. But there may be wide differences of opinion within the Anglican Church on such matters as the Virgin Birth, the Miracles, the Resurrection and the Ascension; and some even more difficult questions like everlasting torment in Hell as the punishment of sin, and the imminent coming down to earth of the Kingdom of Heaven, tend to be avoided altogether.

Moreover, even in England, the Church of England is only a minority. There are several million Roman Catholics in Britain, and even more members of one or other of the "free" or "nonconformist" Churches. These include the many independent Presbyterian organizations, the Methodist Church[14], the Congregational[15] and Baptist Churches[16], and many others. All these sects agree on the essentials of Christianity as described earlier, but have different methods of organization or forms of service of points of interpretation and emphasis.

One characteristic of many non conformist Churches, like the Methodist, the Presbyterian, and especially the "Quakers"[17], is best described by the old-fashioned word "puritanism[18]". The Puritans were originally an extreme Protestant sect, determined to "purify" the English Church of all the corruption and ceremonial pomp of the Roman Church of that time. As an attitude of mind, Puritanism indicates stern simplicity and strict morality. Puritanical people are for instance very keen to protect the Sabbath, or the Lord's Day (Sunday)[19] against sacrilege like work, commerce, games and entertainment. They form "temperance societies' to combat the evils of strong drink, for they are strict teetotallers, and some even disapprove of smoking and dancing. All forms of gambling are forbidden, including football pools and national lotteries. They believe in plain food and plain clothing: women should not wear high-heeled shoes, or too much make-up, or clothes which expose their bodies. Puritans have a reputation for absolute honesty, but they are often lacking in humour and warmth of heart, and are often condemned as "kill-joys". Puritanism today is not a sect. It is just, as we said, a characteristic which you may notice in some people.

Some of the smaller sects in Britain have beliefs which most people find rather odd. There are for instance the Christian Scientists[20]. They believe in faith-healing, i. e. healing the sick by faith through prayer. There are the Seventh-Day Adventists and the Jehovah's Witnesses[21], who both believe in an imminent "second coming" of Christ to earth, when the forces of evil will be finally defeated. There are the Latter-Day Saints (or Mormons)[22], with their own religious system and even scriptures of their own. Remarkably enough, all the sects just mentioned originated in nineteenth-century America. Their representatives may quite commonly be seen in Britain walking the streets and knocking on people's doors with pamphlets or warning notices about repentance and judgment. On the edge of Christianity are the spiritualists, who claim to be able to summon the spirits of the dead to advise and comfort the sad and the bereaved[23].

Attempts to unite the larger Christian denominations have been partly successful, but the Roman Catholic Church does not admit the validity of other churches at all. Thus, Christianity in Britain has many voices. Everybody is of course completely free to worship as he pleases, and the different sects certainly suit different kinds of people. It might be said that they lead by different paths to the same goal.

The Decline of Religion

But the most striking thing about religion in Britain today is that a large proportion of people are not really interested in it a all. This situation is comparatively new. During the last century religion was very popular; during the present century it has seriously declined, and today only a minority go to any kind of church regularly. The successes of modern science are partly responsible for this, the prime example being the development of Darwin's famous theory of evolution, which shows to the satisfaction of most thinking people (including Church leaders) that man, far from being separately created by God as a unique being, has evolved extremely slowly from humbler forms of life. Science seems to be taking the mystery, and therefore the holiness, out of the universe[24]. Then, too, the general improvement in social conditions and the variety of modern entertainment have made religion appear rather irrelevant.

Most of the large majority who do not go to church still believe in God and Heaven in a confused sort of way. They like to get married in church and perhaps have their children christened in church, and they would certainly like to have a Christian funeral when they die. But they never go to church otherwise, and they may never even pray. Some will tell you frankly that they do not believe in the miraculous element of religion, such as the fact that Jesus rose from the dead, and they cannot see that religion has any use. Others, perhaps most, never really think about it: they have certain vague beliefs, but they cannot really justify themselves—and the same thing might be said of some church-goers[25]. None of these people are of course necessarily immoral in any way. Among intellectuals, at one end of the scale there are some who manage to reconcile reason with religion[26] and these include the greatest leaders of the modern Church. At the other end of the scale there are many who are convinced atheists or agnostics, and some of these believe that the world would actually be a better place if Christianity and other religions died out altogether.

This does not of course deny the sincerity and devotion of those quite ordinary Christians of all denominations, both priests and laymen, who for instance, spend their whole lives in unpleasant districts at home, or in remote places abroad, sometimes in difficult conditions and on very low salaries, simply to help others. Even here, however, one finds that the purely *social* work like peacemaking, education, the fight against crime and disease, the protection of children and animals, and so on, is taken over more and more by the state, and by voluntary organizations like the Red Cross which may have no religious connections at all.

As for non-Christian religions, the only one which is widespread in Britain is that of the Jews, for whom religion is largely a matter of race. But even the Jews have sects, and are finding that not all their people remain faithful to their ancient beliefs. There are also in Britain a few Muslims and Buddhists, but it is most uncommon for a Briton to be converted to any of these faiths.

Superstition

Superstition is a difficult question. We cannot quite say that superstition in

Britain is dead. Its history is too long and too recent for that, and indeed you will find many relics of it in modern Britain. But they are connected chiefly with vague notions of good luck and bad luck. It is unlucky, for instance, to walk under a ladder, or to spill salt, or break a mirror, or to have anything to do with number 13; whereas a horseshoe brings good luck, and people jokingly "touch wood" to prevent the return of a past misfortune. There are still many strange country remedies against sickness which are obviously superstitious. Most striking of all, there is still a surprising amount of interest in fortune-telling, e. g. in the form of "horoscopes" in newspapers and women's magazines—though for most people this is nothing more than an amusement, which they may well be slightly ashamed of.

But the real measure of superstition is fear. In this sense there is no superstition in Britain. British people as a whole do not believe in evil influences or evil spirits. Sickness and misfortune are not the result of witchcraft, but of dirt or chance of foolishness or inefficiency. Witches belong only to history books. Ghosts exist only in the mind—usually the minds of others. Magic is simply a sensational word for conjuring tricks. Fairies are pretty little winged creatures in "fairy stories" for children, and any adult who believe in fairies or magic or witches would be considered slightly mad. Thus, modern Britain has largely emerged from superstition, and the future seems to consist not of ghosts, but of matter and machines[27].

Words & Expressions

Christianity/ˌkristiˈæniti/*n.* 基督教
Jesus Christ/ˈdʒiːzəs kraist/ 耶稣基督
Jew/dʒuː/*n.* 犹太人
Palestine/ˈpælistain/*n.* 巴勒斯坦
virgin/ˈvəːdʒin/*n.* 处女
preach/priːtʃ/vt/*vi.* 布道
orthodox/ˈɔθədɔks/*a.* 正统的
crucifixion/ˌkruːsiˈfikʃən/*n.* 在十字架上钉死
ascend/əˈsend/*vi.* 上升,升天
apostle/əˈpɔsl/*n.* 使徒
humanity/kju(ː)ˈmæniti/*n.* 人的美德;人性
repentance/riˈpentəns/*n.* 忏悔
prayer/ˈpreiə/*n.* 祈祷
testament/ˈtestəməmt/*n.* 圣约书
gospel/ˈgɔspəl/*n.* 福音
trinity/ˈtriniti/*n.* (圣父、圣子、圣灵)三位一体
reveal/riˈviːl/*vt.* 启示
upheaval/ʌpˈhiːvəl/*n.* 动荡
Anglican/ˈæŋglikən/*a.* 英国国教的,英国圣公会的
presbyterian/ˌprezbiˈtiəriən/*a.* 长老制的
the Pope 教皇
conscience/ˈkɔnʃəns/*n.* 良心
communion/kəˈmjuːnjən/*n.* 圣餐
Resurrection/ˌrezəˈrekʃən/*n.* 耶稣复活
Ascension/əˈsenʃən/*n.* 耶稣升天

torment/ˈtɔːmənt/n. 折磨
Hell/hel/n. 地狱
imminent/ˈiminənt/a. 即将来临的
non-Conformis/nʌn kənˈfɔːmist/a. 非国教的
Methodist/ˈmeθədist/a. 卫理公会的
Congregational/ˌkɔŋgriˈgeiʃənl/a. 公理会教派的
Baptist/ˈbæptist/a. 浸礼会的
sect/sekt/n. 派别
Quaker/ˈkweikə/n. 贵格会教徒,教友会教徒
puritanism/ˈpjuəritənizm/n. 清教主义
sacrilege/ˈsækrilidʒ/n. 渎圣行为
Sabbath/ˈsæbəθ/n. 安息日
temperance/ˈtempərəns/n. 戒酒,节制
teetotaller/tiːˈtəutlə/n. 绝对戒酒主义者
pool/puːl/n. 赌注
lottery/ˈlɔtəri/n. 彩票
Adventist/ˌædˈventist/n. 相信基督再度降临教徒
Jehovah/dʒiˈhəuvə/n. 《圣经》中的耶和华,即上帝
scripture/ˈskriptʃə/n. 经文
summon/ˈsʌmən/vt. 传唤
bereaved/biˈriːvd/a. 丧失亲人的
denomination/diˌnɔmiˈneiʃən/n. 派别
validity/vəˈliditi/n. 合法性
worship/ˈwəːʃip/vt. 信仰,崇拜
christen/ˈkrisn/vt. 为…施洗礼
atheist/ˈeiθiist/n. 无神论者
agnostic/ægːnɔstik/n. 不可知论者
layman/ˈleimən/n. 俗人
Muslim/ˈmʌzlim/n. 穆斯林教徒
Buddhist/ˈbudist/n. 佛教徒
superstition/ˌsjuːpəˈstiʃən/n. 迷信
touch wood 用手碰碰木头以免遭坏运气
remedy/ˈremidi/n. 治疗方法
fortune-telling 算命
horoscope/ˈhɔrəskəup/n. 占星术
witchcraft/ˈwitʃkrɑːft/n. 巫术
ghost/gəust/n. 鬼魂
sensational/senˈseiʃənl/a. 耸人听闻的
conjure/ˈkʌndʒə/vt. 变换戏法

Notes

1. the following ... non-Christian readers:下面关于基督教的简单概述是为非基督教读者而写的。

2. He was ... Mary:一名叫玛丽亚的未婚处女奇迹般地怀了孕,生下了耶稣。这是《圣经》里的有关耶稣出生的传说。基督教徒称耶稣的母亲为“圣母玛丽亚”。

3. Started preaching and performing miracles:(耶稣)开始布道,同时表现了创造奇迹的本领,如能使盲人立刻见到光明等。

4. The things ... crucifixion:他布讲的东西和正统的犹太法律和信念发生矛盾,因此他在33岁时被当局在十字架上钉死。耶稣在布道时,攻击犹太统治者,同情穷人,赶走在寺院的钱币兑换商。因此,统治者收买了他的第13个信徒犹大。耶稣被他出卖而被捕,并以亵渎罪判处死刑。

5. twelve apostles:耶稣有12个使徒,为他传播福音。这12个使徒有圣彼得、圣安德烈等,包括犹大。因为犹大出卖了耶稣而死,他的缺位被选出的马提亚(Matthias)充任。

6. two “testaments”:《圣经》包括《旧约》和《新约》两部分。《旧约》有39卷,原是犹太教的圣经,内容有《摩西五经》即《创世纪》等5卷,其次是历史,如《士师记》等10卷,再次是

先知书,如《小赛亚书》等15卷,还包括诗文集。《新约》共27卷,内容包括《马太福音》、《马可福音》、《路加福音》和《约翰福音》,《新约》还包括《信徒行传》、《启示录》等。

7. St. Paul:圣保罗是耶稣12个使徒以外的另一名信徒,他受耶稣启示而积极传播基督教义,传播圣父(上帝)、圣子(耶稣)及圣灵三位一体的思想。

8. It is an "established" Church:英国国教是依法确立下来的宗教。1534年,英国议会通过"最高权威法案",正式确认英王享利八世切断英国教会与罗马教皇的一切关系的要求,宣布英国君主为新确立的英国国教的首脑。

9. Its temporal head is the Queen:英国国教的世俗领袖是君王,现在是女王伊丽莎白二世。而它的宗教领袖是英国大主教(the Primate of All England of the Archbishop of Canterbury)。所有主教必须忠于君主,而不是像宗教改革运动以前那样忠于罗马教皇。

10. twenty-six of its highest priests sit in the House of Lords:在上议院有26个主教议员,但他们不代表任何党派,也很少参加会议。

11. Scotland has ... presbyterian:苏格兰有其自己依法确立的宗教,苏格兰教会的组织称为"长老会"。教会不设主教,而是由长老负责。长老有教士长者,负责传教、教育及教会管理,还有教会成员选举产生的非教士管理长者,协助教士长者管理教会。

12. leaves many questions to individual consciences:英国国教教义认为《圣经》包含了拯救灵魂的一切,信徒主要应依据《圣经》行事。但到底怎样解释《圣经》,各人理解不一。因此在许多情况下,信徒根据各人的心灵、各自的认识解释《圣经》。

13. Holy Communion:圣餐仪式。天主教与新教的圣餐仪式很不相同。前者认为,面包与酒就是耶稣的血肉,而后者认为这只是象征的表示,是仪式。在新教各派里,对圣餐看法也很不一致,如教友会就拒绝一切有关教堂的仪式,甚至认为教堂都是多余的。

14. the Methodist Church:卫理公会是新教中的一个教派。这个教派起源于18世纪初的英国,其创始人主张教徒的生活和宗教教育都要遵循一定的"方式方法",牧师可在任何地方传教,非本派教徒可以经过上课训练成为卫理公会派。

15. Congregation Church:公理会是新教的另一教派。它起源于16世纪末、17世纪初的英国,旨在反对国家控制的国教组织形式。它不设主教,也没有长老。各地方教会独立处理教务,各教会只不过是以上帝为首的大家庭中的平等成员。

16. the Baptist Church:新教的又一教派"浸礼会",因为"圣水洗礼"仪式而得名。浸礼会要求其会员接受洗礼,使其获得新生,赦免罪恶,成为该会正式成员。

17. the Quakers:贵格会又称"教友会教徒"。新教中的一派,起源于17世纪中期的英国。这一教派认为,上帝与个人心灵之间不应有任何教会或牧师作桥梁。圣灵可以进入每个人的内心,因此他们拒绝任何教会的权威。教友会不设教堂,不设牧师,只有教徒的"聚会所",这个聚会所可设立在任何地方。他们相信人人生来平等的思想等。

18. Puritanism:清教主义是英国国教中的一个新教派教义。它起源于16世纪中期的英国。他们以加尔文学派为基础,要求"纯洁"英国国教中的天主教教规和礼仪。他们强调人人"生前命中注定论"思想。宣称一部分人命中注定是"上帝的选民",另外的人命中注定进地狱。他们认为《圣经》是信仰的惟一依据,个人在神授的职业中的成功是上帝选民的标志。清教主义对英美两国的政治、经济和文化起过极其深刻的影响。

19. the Sabbath, or the Lord's Day:基督教的安息日(星期日)。根据《圣经》传说,上帝

从星期一到星期六创造了世界，星期日休息。

20. the Christian Scientists：基督教科学派，创建于19世纪末期美国。他们认为，疾病和罪恶可以用信仰来得到治疗和克服。他们生病时拒绝去医院看病。

21. the Ceventh-Day Adventists and the Jehovah's Witnesses：前者是“耶稣第二次降临派”中主张星期六为安息日的一派，创建于19世纪中期。这个新教派的主要教义是耶稣即将再次降临，以拯救人类，《圣经》是教徒信仰和活动的惟一依据。后者称为“耶和华作证派”，建于19世纪末期的美国。教派成员都称自己是先和派牧师，相信“耶稣第二次降临”已经开始，人类罪人只要忏悔，太平盛世就会到来。

22. the Latter-Day Saints (or Mormons)：“现代圣人派”（或称“摩门教派”）创立于1830年美国的一个教派。今日摩门教的中心在美国犹他州的盐湖城。教徒严格按照自己的《摩门圣经书》行事，有严格的教规和教堂组织，在早期还实行一夫多妻制。

23. On the edge of Christianity ... the bereaved：接近于基督教的还有招魂灵派。他们声称能招来死者的灵魂以安慰死者亲人，传达死者意图。现代招魂灵派创立于19世纪中期的美国。这一派认为人死后人魂继续存在，它可以通过一种渠道或灵媒和活人取得联系。

24. Science seems ... out of the universe：看来科学正在揭去宇宙的神秘面纱，它那由宗教赋予的圣神性也因而消失。

25. the same thing might be said of some church-goers：一些常去教堂做礼拜的信徒也有类似的情况，即上文所说的信念很模糊的那些人。

26. Among intellectuals, ... with religion：在知识分子中，一部分人力图把理性与宗教统一起来。在这里，理性是指不信那些宗教上的神秘因素，比如耶稣死后升天等说法。

27. the future seems ... machines：未来似乎不会包括那些鬼神，而是物质、是机器。

Exercises

Ⅰ. Explain the following

1. Christianity
2. Jesus Christ
3. the Bible
4. The Church of England
5. Roman Catholic Church
6. Protestant Reformation

Ⅱ. Fill in the blanks

1. In Europe, Christianity is divided into two major groups, ________ and ________.
2. The Bible consists of two parts, ________ and ________.
3. ________ is the non-priestly head of the Church of England and ________ is the spiritual leader of the Church of England.
4. The Trinity, according to the Christian doctrine as developed by St Paul and the early Church, refers to the three aspects of the same one God, ________, ________ and ________.

5. The Church of Scotland in organization is ________.

6. ________ is the supreme holy authority of the Roman Catholic.

7. Point out five major Protestant sects that are mentioned in the text: ________, ________, ________, ________ and ________.

8. According to Darwin's theory of evolution, man has evolved extremely slowly from ________.

Ⅲ. Answer the following questions briefly

1. What are some of the differences between the Catholic Church and the Church of England?

2. What are some of the characteristics of the Protestant sects?

3. Why has religion declined in Britain during the present century?

4. Cite a few examples from the text to show that there are many relics of superstition on modern Britain.

Chapter 8 Character and Manners

English Characteristics

To other Europeans, the best known quality of the British, and in particular of the English, is "reserve". A reserved person is one who does not talk very much to strangers, does not show much emotion, and seldom gets excited. It is difficult to get to know a reserved person: he never tells you anything about himself, and you may work with him for years without ever knowing where he lives, how many children he has, and what his interests are. English people tend to be like that. If they are making a journey by bus, they will do their best to find an empty seat; if by train, an empty compartment, If they have to share the compartment with a stranger, they may travel many miles without starting a conversation. If a conversation does start, personal questions like "How old are you?" or even "What is your name?" are not easily asked, and it is quite possible for two people to know each other casually for years without ever knowing each other's name. Questions like "Where did you buy your watch?" or "What is your salary?" are almost impossible. Similarly, conversation in Britain is in general much more quiet and restrained than, say, in Africa, and loud speech is considered ill-bred.

This reluctance to communicate with others is an unfortunate quality in some ways, since it tends to give the impression of coldness, and it is true that the English (except perhaps in the North) are not noted for their generosity and hospitality. On the other hand. they are perfectly human behind their barrier of reserve, and may be quite pleased when a friendly stranger or foreigner succeeds for a time in breaking the barrier down. We may also mention at this point that the people of the North and West, especially the Welsh, are much less reserved than those of the South and East.

Closely related to English reserve is English modesty. Within their berates. the English are perhaps less conceited than anybody else, but in their relations with others they value at least a show of modesty[2]. Self praise is felt to be ill-bred. If a person is , let us say, very good at tennis, and someone asks him if be is a good player, he will seldom reply "Yes", because people will think him conceited. He will probably give an answer like, "I'm not bad", or "I think I'm quite good", or "well, I managed to reach the finals in last year's local championship." Even a definite achievement like the last-mentioned will often be stated in such a manner as to suggest that it was only due to an incomprehensible piece of good luck[3]. This self-deprecation is typically English, and, mixed with their reserve, it often produces a sort of general air of indifference which appears to foreigners as a pose[4], difficult to understand and even irritating.

The famous English sense of humour is similar. Its starting point is self-deprecation, and its great enemy is conceit. Its ideal is the ability to laugh at oneself-at one's own faults, one's own failures and embarrassments, even at one's own ideals. Here perhaps we are departing somewhat from the world of everyday people and straying into realms of literature and philosophy[5], but the quality is observable in individuals, and the criticism. "He has no sense of humour" is very commonly heard in Britain, where humour is so highly prized. Prince Philip[6] during a visit to Ghana in 1959, both praised it and illustrated it when he talked of "God" s greatest gift to mankind-a sense of humour'. It is an attitude to life rather than the mere ability to laugh at jokes. This attitude is never cruel or disrespectful or malicious. The English do not laugh at a cripple or a madman, a tragedy or an honourable failure. Sympathy or admiration for artis' tic skill are felt to be stronger than laughter.

Sinse reserve, a show of modesty, and a sense of humour are part of his own nature, the typical Englishman tends to expect them in others. He secretly looks down on more excitable nations, and likes to think of himself as more reliable than them. He distrusts exaggerated promises and shows of affection, especially if they may write to him. To those who are fond of these kinds of exaggeration, therefore, the English-man may appear disconcertingly cold and skeptical, and they may be bewildered when his sense of humour is arouzed by airs of dignity and importance.

Finally, sportsmanship. Like a sense of humour, this is an English ideal which not all Englishmen live up to[7]. It must be realised that sport in its modern form is almost entirely a British invention. Boxing, rugby, association football, hockey, tennis and cricket were all first organized and given rules in Britain. Rules are the essence of sport, and sportsmanship is the ability to practise a sport in obedience to its rules, while also showing generosity to one's opponent and good temper in defeat, the high pressure of modern international sport makes these ideals difficult to maintain, but they are at least highly valued in Britain and are certainly achieved there more commonly than among more hot-blooded races. Moreover. sportsmanship as an ideal is applied to life in general. This is proved by the number of sporting terms used in ordinary speech. To take boxing alone: a well-aimed and vigorous criticism is said to be "straight from the shoulder"[8], while an unfair one is "below the belt[9]. One of the most elementary rules of life is "never hit a man when he"s down"-in other words, never take advantage of another ' s misfortune. English school-boys often show this sense of sportsmanship to a surprisingly high degree in their relations with each other. And or course everybody talks of "fair play" and "playing the game"[10], or "playing fair".

The English Class System

As regards social conventions, we must say a word about the well-known English class system. This is an embarrassing subject for English people, and one they tend to be ashamed of, though during the present century class-consciousness has grown less and less. and the class system less rigid. But it still exists below the surface. Broadly speaking, it means there are two classes, the "middle class" and the "working class". (We shall ignore for a moment the old "upper class", including the hereditary aristocracy, since it is extremely small in numbers: but some of its members have the right to sit in the House of Lords, and some newspapers take a surprising interest in their private life.) The middle class consists chiefly of well-to-do business men and professional people of all kinds. The working class consists chiefly of manual and unskilled workers.

The most obvious difference between them is in their accent. Middle-class people use slightly varying kinds of "received pronunciation" which is the kind of English spoken by B. B. C. announcers and taught to overseas pupils. Typical working-class people speak in many different local accents which are generally felt to be rather ugly and uneducated. One of the biggest barriers of social equality in England is the two-class education system, which is treated in another chapter. To have been to a so-called "public school" immediately marks you out as one of the middle class. The middle classes tend to live a more formal life than working-class people , and are usually more cultured. Their midday meal is "lunch" and they have a rather formal evening meal called "dinner", whereas the working man ' s dinner, if his working hours permit, is at midday, and his smaller, late-evening meal is called supper.

As we have said, however, the class system is much less rigid than it was, and for a long time it has been government policy to reduce class distinctions. Working-class students very commonly receive a university education and enter the professions, and working-class incomes have grown so much recently that the distinctions between the two classes are becoming less and less clear. However, regardless of one's social status, certain standards of politeness are expected of everybody, and a well-bred person is polite to everyone he meets, and treats a labourer with the same respect he gives an important businessman. Servility inspires both embarrassment and dislike. Even the word "sir", except in school and in certain occupations (e. g. commerce, the army, etc.) sounds too servile to be commonly used.

Politeness in Britain

British habits of politeness are on the whole very informal There are no complicated greetings. For instance: a simple "good morning" or a cheery wave of the hand across the street is quite satisfactory. Handshakes are only exchanged on a first introduction, or on special occasions, or as a token of agreement or congratulation. All politeness is based on the elementary rule of showing consideration for others, and fitly acknowledging the consideration they show to you. "Excuse me" is used as an advance apology for troubling somebody, as when passing in front of him or interrupting his conversation, or when putting a question to a stranger. "Sorry" expresses regret for an accidental disturbance or breach of manners. It also takes the place of "no" when you cannot accede to a request or an implied request like "May I borrow your pen?" or "Do you know the time?" or "Have you any size seven shoes?" "Pardon?" is the polite way of asking somebody to repeat what he has said. In Britain, except at school, "please" is on longer used in asking permission to speak, and the phrase "No, please", so common abroad, would sound most unusual in Britain itself. "Yes, please" is the commonest use of the word, and is the opposite of "No, thank you" when replying to an offer. A bare "Yes" or "No" sounds very rude in this case, Similarly, a polite request does not begin with "I want" or "I think", but with a phrase like "Will (or would, can, could) you please..." or "Would you mind..." When the request is granted, and at any time when you are receiving something, however obviously you are entitled to it, you are always expected to say "Thank you".

British people do not readily ask each other to do anything which would involve real inconvenience: they prefer to wait for such service to be offered, rather than ask for if. If they do ask, then the request is accompanied by an implied apology like,

"I don't really like asking you, but..." or, "I know the trouble I'm causing you, but would you mind?" and so on. Similarly it is often polite to refuse an offer of service by means of such a reply as, "Oh! please don't bother", followed by an explanation of why you can do without it. In fact, without being conscious of it, British people sometimes make offers purely out of politeness, not really expecting them to be accepted, and offers of this kind are automatically refused with corresponding politeness.

If you are invited into a person's home, there are other questions to consider. For instance, what time should you arrive? If it is a social occasion, not a business one, it is not polite to arrive early. Your hostess will be preparing for you, and will be most embarrassed if you arrive before she is quite ready. Ten minutes late is excellent. Half an hour late is excessive, and requires apologies. Then too, the British are rather particular about table manners. The main thing is to sit up straight, copy everyone else, gaily asking what to do if you are not sure, and keep the conversation going. What time should you leave? There are no rules, but it is most impolite to stay too late, as it implies a lack of consideration for your hosts. If it is simply an invitation to an evening meal and conversation, you will probably take your leave between ten and eleven o'clock. If you have been asked to stay for several days, you will conform as far as possible to the routine of the house, and your hostess will be very pleased if you give her a bunch of flowers, specially purchased, before you leave. If the invitation has been made purely to give you pleasure, a gift of money would be refused with some embarrassment.

Gifts are not the same as "tips". The tipping system is an evil in most European countries, and consists of a small extra payment made to certain employees. In Britain it is confined chiefly to waiters and taxi-drivers, to whom you give an extra tenth or eighth of the price of the meal or fare. Hotel servants and railway porters, too. expect a small tip if they are of service to you. Apart form these special cases, gifts of money are given only cautiously. This is because the offer of money makes an act of kindness seem like a mean desire for gain. If a kindly act has actually involved expense, it is only right to offer reimbursement[11], but most British people feel that kindness itself can only be repaid with gratitude, not with money. Thus, you do not offer money to a driver who gives you a lift, or to someone who stops to help you to mend a puncture or to give you first aid, though if you feel sufficiently grateful you might buy the person some cigarettes or a drink or some other small gifts. As for a more important act like finding somebody a job or saving him from drowning—to expect money for doing something like that is almost unthinkable.

Politeness towards women is less observed today than it used to be. It is still considered polite to give up one's seat to a woman who is standing, to open doors for her, help her alight from the bus, carry things for her, to protect her from the traffic, and so on , and the maxim "Ladies first" is well known; but now that women are the equals of men in having the vote, taking paid employment and receiving higher education, they receive much less consideration than formerly. for the whole basis of politeness towards woman is the feeling that they need protection.

The same principle applies to old people. If they are respected in Britain. it is because they are felt to be in need of protection and support . Old age and seniority alone do not command authority[12] among the British: in fact modern life has been developing so fast that old people often appear tiresome and out of date. Thus, "We need some young blood" is often heard in organizations where the energy and modern methods of younger men are felt to be more likely to succeed than the long but partly irrelevant experience of older ones. The wisest of the older generation realize this. They either make an effort to remain young in heart and keep pace with the times, or else they let younger men take their place.

It follows that mature Europeans have no desire to grow old or to look older than they are. Women especially, for reasons of sexual attraction, long to "stay young", and there is no greater compliment to a mature woman than to be told "How young you look!"[13] On the other hand, if a woman's hairstyle, make-up and clothes reveal an obvious effort to look artificially young, she is said to "look common", and is regarded with disapproval.

We have said enough already to show that the British are very different in some ways from people of other continents. This is partly because they are Europeans: all Europeans have certain things in common.

Words & Expressions

reserved 沉默寡言的

compartment /kəm'pa:tmənt/n. 火车车厢

restrained/ris'treind/a. 拘谨的

ill-bred/'il-'bred/a. 没有教养的

generosity/ˌdʒenə'rɔsiti/n. 慷慨大方

hospitality /'hɔspi'tæliti/n. 好客

incomprehensible /inˌkɔmpri'hensibl/a. 不可理解的

deprecation /ˌdeˌpri'keiʃən/n. 贬低,否定

pose /pəuz/n. 做作,装腔作势

irritating/'iriteitiŋ/a. 令人不愉快的

disrespectful/ˌdisris'pektful/a. 不尊重

malicious/mə'liʃəs/a. 恶意的

cripple/'kripl/n. 残废人

disconcertingly/ˌdiskənˈsəːtiŋli/*adv.* 令人为难

sceptical /ˈskeptikəl/*a.* 怀疑的

sportsmanship/ˈspɔːtsmənʃip/*n.* 运动员的诚实公正的品质

association football 英式足球,即现今世界各国的足球运动

hockey/ˈhɔki/*n.* 曲棍球

cricket/ˈkrikit/*n.* 板球

hot-blooded 容易激动的

convention/kənˈvenʃən/*n.* 习俗

class consciousness 阶级意识

hereditary/hiˈreditəri/*a.* 世袭的

cultured /ˈkʌltʃəd/*a.* 有文化有教养的

servility/səːˈviliti/*n.* 卑从

cheery/ˈtʃiən/*n.* 愉快的

token/ˈtəukən/*n.* 象征

breach/briːtʃ/*n.* 违反

a mean desire 卑劣的要求

reimbursement/ˌriːimˈbəːsmənt/*n.* 偿还,报销

Notes

1. they are perfectly human behind their barrier of reserve：他们表面上有一道沉默寡言的屏障,但透过屏障,他们完全和普通人一样。

2. in their relations with others they value at least a show of modesty：在和别人的关系上,他们至少重视外表的上谦虚。

3. Even a definite achievement... good luck：即使取得了上面提到的那样明显的成绩,人们也可能把它归结为不可捉摸的好运道所起的作用。

4. it often produces... as a pose：(这种自我贬低的态度)常常使人产生一种漠不关心的神态,在外国人看来,是一种装腔作势的姿态。

5. we are departing... philosophy：我们正远离普通人的世界,进入文学和哲学的领域。意思说,幽默感不是现实生活,而是带有文学和哲理色彩的东西。

6. Prince Philip：菲力普亲王是英国女王伊丽莎白二世的丈夫。

7. which not all English men live up to：(和幽默感一样,)在现实生活中不是每个英国人都具备诚实公正的品德的。

8. to be "straight from the shoulder"：在拳击运动中,运动员必须准确地狠狠地出拳打击对方,所以准确无误的直截了当的批评也可用此成语。

9. below the belt：在拳击运动中,打击对方的下身是犯规行为。因此,它常用来形容采用不正当手段对待别人,或暗箭伤人。

10. playing the game：原指运动中每人都要遵守比赛规则,现在也指要光明正大。

11. If a kindly act... reimbursement：如果别人友好的举动使人家破费太多,你自然应该提出你愿意给予补偿。

12. old age and seniority alone do not command authority：单靠年高资深不会获得权威。

13. there is no greater compliment..."How young you look!"：就一位中年妇女来说,对她讲一句"你长得真年轻!"就是最好的赞美了。

Exercises

Ⅰ. Explain the following

1. English modesty
2. Sportsmanship as an English ideal
3. The English class system
4. The English sense of humour

Ⅱ. Fill in the blanks

1. Loud speech in Britain is considered ______________________.
2. In their relations with others, Englishmen value at least a show of ______________________, whose enemy is ______________________.
3. Prince Philip once said that ______________________ is "God's greatest gift to mankind."
4. The terms such as "never hit a man when he's down" and "playing the game", or "playing fair" reflect sense of ______________________.

Ⅲ. Answer the following questions briefly

1. What are some of the characteristics of a reserved English man?
2. What are some of the differences between the middle class and the working class?
3. What are the major characteristics of the Englishman?
4. Why does the Englishman value a sense of humour?

Chapter 9 British Education

Introduction

Many people think school is just about teaching children what are often called "the three R's"—"reading, 'riting and 'rithmetic" (reading, writing and arithmetic). In other words, the purpose of school is to provide children with literacy and the other basic skills they will need to become active members of society. But the purpose of the British education system is also to socialise children. Children are taught practical skills; but in school they also learn the rules and values they need to become good citizens, to participate in the community, and to contribute to the economic prosperity of an advanced industrial economy.

It is no surprise, then, that the state is heavily involved in deciding when, where, how and what children are taught. It is also, be no surprise that these decisions are often very controversial. Should naughty pupils be punished physically? Corporal punishment is currently banned in the UK, but some people—including the government minister responsible for education—would like to see the return of the cane.[1] What sort of English should children learn to speak? Should children be forced to speak in a standardized way rather than with regional accents and idioms? Or do local variations in the way people talk contribute to the richness of British culture?

Such controversies are not just about education. They reflect the deeper divisions in British society as a whole. Britain is a society in which social class is still very important: class inequality can be erased or continued according to educational policy[2]. If you understand the importance of the relationship between education and social class, you can understand a great deal about British culture and society.

The enduring feature of British education is the continuing debate over how "equal" educational opportunity should be. Sociologists have found that 51 per cent of British people are working class and 49 per cent are middle class. While the split is about half and half, the opportunities for working class and middle class people can be very different. In Britain, the accent you speak with, the clothes you wear, and the schools you attend are all markers that identify your social class.[3]

The school(or college)the is a clear marker of social class. Even on informal occasions you will sometimes see men wearing their attendance at a certain school. To have attended the "right" schools—particularly the famous boys' public schools like Eton and Winchester—and the "right" universities—Oxford and Cambridge[5] (these two rival universities have been nicknamed "Oxbridge")—is still the single best way to guarantee a successful career. In 1994, 46% of Conservative Party Members of Parliament were graduates of Oxbridge, as were three-quarters of the Government executive. Most senior civil servants are also Oxbridge graduates. When people in Britain talk about "the old boys network"[6], they mean this elite group of men who went to school and university together. Not only do they dominate government, but they are also very influential in banking, the media, the arts and education. In Britain, where you are educated is still very important to your future.

History

Fans of great British novels will already know something about how education in Britain used to be in the past, and how even then class differences could be seen in the way people were schooled. Jane Austen's *Emma*[7] is about the relationship between a rich young woman who has been taught the womanly subjects of the time—reading poetry, playing the piano, sketching, and speaking a little bit of French—and a lower class woman she befriends and decides to "educate" in order to make her more marriageable. Charlotte and Anne Bronte's novels frequently have governesses as their heroines, while Thomas Hardy's *Jude the Obscure*[8] is about a poor man who dreams of attending Oxford University (called Christminster in the novel).

Nowadays, the British education system is run by the state, which provides funding, oversees standards, and tries to make sure that all British children receive a quality education. One of the largest, most important government departments is the Ministry of Education.

In 1989 – 1990 state expenditure on education was 24 billion pounds, or about 4.6% of the UK's Gross Domestic Product.[9]

But the state was not always involved in educating British children. Historically, education was voluntary and many of the schools that existed were set up by churches. The influence of the Church on schooling is still strong: until very recently, religious education was the only subject which the state insisted all schools teach their pupils (other subjects were left up to schools to decide upon). Daily prayers and singing hymns is still a regular part of school life, In keeping with changes to British society, however, Christianity is no longer the only religion officially recognised. In some cities, the state funds schools which have the Islamic religion rather than the Christian religion as their creed.

Before 1870, only 40 per cent of children under 10 went to school regularly. The main receivers of a more advanced education were the sons of the wealthy. One of the changes to British society brought by the Industrial Revolution was the government's decision to become increasingly involved in taking responsibility for the education of children. In 1870 the government passed a law which called for government funded education. By 1880, attendance at school for children between 5 and 10 was compulsory rather than voluntary; and by the end of the First World War, the school leaving age was raised to 14 in order to dissuade children from leaving school in order to work to support their families.

Other major changes to the British education system were caused by World War Ⅱ。When the Germans began dropping bombs on British cities, 750 000 school children were "evacuated" to live in the countryside where it was hoped they would be safer. Schools were closed or used for war purposes and education continued in the countryside on an ad hoc basis. As a result of this disruption of the old system, the government, with the assistance of the Church (a conservative force) and newly powerful trade unions (a more socialist influence) began planning to reconstruct the education system. This time, the new system would emphasize equality.

The result was the 1994 Education Act which made entry to secondary (middle) schools and universities "meritocratic"[10]. Children would be admitted to schoolsnot because they were of a certain social class or because their parents possessed a certain amount of money, but because of the abilities they displayed. All children were given the right to a free secondary education and the main concern was to make sure more children had access to good education.

This first attempt to try to create a less elitist school system failed. In spite of the government's high hopes, working class children still left school at a younger age and with fewer qualifications than middle class children. Because entrance to schools was based upon exam performance, the children of the middle classes performed better. They had more free time, more access to help if they were having trouble (their parents could hire tutors, for example) and valued education more than their working class peers who were often under pressure to quit school and find jobs in order to help their families.

Central governments, working with teachers and local government officials continued to experiment with policies to try to raise the quality of education of all pupils, not just the middle classes, In the 1960s, comprehensive schools[11] were introduced all over the country, which ended the division between grammar schools[12]—where the most academically capable pupils were sent to be prepared for university—and vocational schools[13] where less successful pupils were sent to learn trades. Entrance exams were abolished and schools were no longer allowed to let children "compete" for places.

In 1976 British education was the focus of a new controversy when the Labour Party started "the Great Education Debate" about national standards and styles of teaching. The Labour Government was concerned about the inadequate skill level of the labour force and a new initiative to prepare children for employment was launched. Just three years later, with the victory to the Conservative government of Margaret Thatcher, education again became a big political issue. While the new government thought that job training was very important, it felt schools were not paying enough attention in teaching pupils the traditional "three Rs." Therefore, in 1989 the government introduced a National Curriculum. Now all children throughout the country must study the following subjects: English, mathematics, science, religious education, history, geography, technology, music, art, physical education, and a modern foreign language. They must also pass national tests and schools are ranked according to the success of their pupils in reaching national targets.

This is a very big change: previously, the central government only set broad education policy guidelines and provided funds. Practical decision-making was carried out by Local Education Authorities (LEAs), located at regional or city levels, which based their policies on local conditions. Teachers also had a lot of individual power to decide on what to do in the classroom. Now all teachers are told what to teach and their schools are now ranked according to how well they perform this task. Thus the National Curriculum has reintroduced competition between schools. Good schools attract good pupils and therefore attract more funding. More funding means they can hire better teachers, buy more books and equipment and therefore produce even better pupils.

The Present Education System

Education in the UK is compulsory. Children are legally obliged to attend school form the ages of 5(4 in Northern Ireland) to 16. In 1992 there were 9. 5 million full-time school/college students.

Parents can choose between sending their children to state schools or to private schools. State schools ate funded by local and central government. About 93% of pupils receive free education form the public sector. The government also sometimes assists schools established by religious groups.

Since 1993, parents have the right to express a preference for a particular state school for their children[14]. A system of "league tables"[15]—comparative tables which rank schools according to public examination results, truancy rates, destinations of school leavers, and so on—are published in order to help parents make choices. While children usually attend the school they live closest to , now ambitious parents sometimes move to a different neighbourhood in order to be close to a well performing school. Needless to say, good schools tend to be in middle class neighbourhoods and it is the wealthier middle classes who can most easily afford to move if they think it is necessary.

In the private sector there are independent schools which are commonly, but confusingly, called public schools. [16](They are called public schools because they were originally seen as "public" alternatives to having private tutors in aristocratic households.) Independent schools receive their funding through the private sector and through tuition rates, with some government assistance, Independent schools are not part of the national education system, but the quality of instruction and standards are maintained through visits from Her Majesty's Inspectors of Schools. [17]Parents choose to pay fees in order to send their children to these schools because the quality of education is such that their children have a better chance of getting into good universities and/or getting better jobs when they lave school.

Up to age 5, children may have some pre-primary schooling in nursery schools, daycare, or play groups. The government has no obligation to provide such facilities and so many are private enterprise arrangements. However, the state realises such provision is important, especially now that many mothers work, and so they provide some financial support.

Between the ages of 5 to 11, pupils mainly attend state sector primary schools. These schools are called co-educational or mixed schools because they admit both boys and girls.

Form the age of 11 up to around the age of 19, students attend secondary schools. More than 80% of pupils in secondary schools in England and Wales attend mixed schools;60% in Northern Ireland;Scotland, nearly all.

About 90% of secondary schools are comprehensive schools which admit children without reference to their academic abilities. Such schools provide a general education. Pupils can study everything from academic subjects like literature and sciences, to more practical subjects like cooking and carpentry.

Foreign languages are taught as an integral part of the National Curriculum, reflecting the importance of Britain's relationship with Europe.[18]

Those children who do not attend comprehensive schools attend grammar schools instead. Grammar schools select children, usually at the age of 11, through an examination called"the 11 puls". Those who show academic potential are admitted to the grammar schools where the emphasis is on advanced academic work rather than the more general curriculum of the comprehensive schools. In Northern Ireland the grammar school/non-grammar school division is still common, but throughout the rest of Great Britain grammar schools are becoming increasingly rare.

After 5 years of secondary education, (at about age 16) English, Northern Irish and Welsh students sit their GCSE exams (General Certificate of Secondary Education[19]). GCSEs are the main means of assessing pupils' progress in their final 2 year of compulsory education. Based on these results, pupils then decide what avenue of education they would like to follow[20]. They have a number of choices. At the age of 16, they can decide to quit school and find a job; or they can prepare to sit exams for university entrance; or they can concentrate on vocational training. Every 16 & 17 year old is guaranteed a place in full-time education or training.

Pupils who hope to attend university carry on their academic study in the sixth form for a further two years and then sit A-levels exams (General Certificate of Education-Advanced[21]). Most pupils try to achieve 3 or 4 A-levels in the subjects they are most proficient at.[22] Since admittance to universities depends largely on A-level results, the two years spent in the Sixth Form are very important and often very stressful for British pupils. Among first year university getting to know each other, the most common question after"What's your name?" and"Where are you from?" is "What A-levels did you take."

Other pupils who decide not to go to university may choose to take vocational training. The vocational equivalent of A-levels are GNVQs (General National Vocational Qualifications[23]), which provide a broadly based preparation for work or for taking further vocational training.

Higher Education

British universities are public bodies which receive funds from central government. This differs from the United States which, in addition to public universities, also has privately funded universities which are often very wealthy. In the UK, the amount of funding each university receives is based on its size, the number of stuedents it teaches, and the research it conducts, So far, the UK has only one privately funded university, the University of Buckingham.

Higher education has a long history in the UK. Oxford and Cambridge date from the 12th and 13th centuries, while the Scottish universities of St Andrews, Glasgow, Edinburgh and Aberdeen from the 14th and 15th centuries. The rest were founded in the 19th and 20th centuries. In the 1960s there was a large expansion in the numbers of universities and many new universities were built. In 1992 the number grew again when polytechnics[24] and other higher education establishments were given the right to become universities. By 1994, Britain had 83 universities.

University campuses are full of people of different ages and nationalities studying many different things. In 1990/1 there were 353 000 full-time students, 87 000who came from overseas. While most of the students are studying for their first degrees,[25] about 64 000 were working on postgraduate qualifications. There are about 30 000 full time university teachers paid wholly from university funds. The government tries to encourage the best overseas students to study in Britain by offering scholarships. In 1991, nearly 25 000 overseas students received some kind of help.

Universities, reflecting the trend throughout the education system, have traditionally been rather elitist. Most students were from the middle classes, attended good schools, performed well in their A-levels and received a fully-funded place in a university. In recent years, great efforts have been made to increase the numbers of and kinds of people that pursue higher education. For example, whereas in 1980, 1 in 8 pupils went on to university, by 1990 it was 1 in 5, and by 2000 will be 1 in 3. Access for mature students and students without traditional A-level qualifications is widening.[26]

The Open University[27] offers a non-traditional route for people to take university level courses and receive a university degree. People can register without having any formal educational qualifications. They follow university courses through textbooks, TV and radio broadcasts, correspondence, videos, residential schools and a network of study centres, Tens of thousands of Britons, from housewives to coal miners, form teachers to ballet dancers "attend" the Open University each year. It was the Open University which provided the inspiration for the founding of China's TV and Radio University. First degree courses are mainly full time and last three years, except in Scotland where they take four years. Degree titles vary, but usually one receives a Bachelor of Arts (BA) or a Bachelor of Science (BSc), for a second degree Master of Arts (MA) or Science (MSc) and Doctor of Philosophy (PhD). In the older Scottish universities, Master is used for a first degree in Arts subjects, and in Oxford and Cambridge the BA converts to an MA several years later, upon payment of a fee.[28]

Words & Expressions

literacy/ˈlytərəsi/*n.* 识字;有学问
participate /pɑːˈtisipeit/*vi.* 参加;参与
controversial/ˌkɔntrəˈvəːʃəl/*a.* 有争议的
corporal/ˈkɔːpərəl/*a.* 肉体的
corporal punishment 体罚
came/kein/*n.* 手杖;笞杖
erase /iˈreiz/*vt.* 消除
sociologist/səusiˈɔləŋist/*n.* 社会学家
guarantee /ˌgærənˈti/*vt.* 保证;担保
executive/igˈzekjutiv/*n.* 行政人员
elite/eiˈliːf/*n.* 社会精英
expenditure /iksˈpenditʃə/*n.* 经费;开销
prayer /ˈpreiə/*n.* 祷告者;恳求者
hymn/him/*n.* 圣歌;赞歌
Islamic/izˈlæmik/*a.* 伊斯兰教的
compulsory/kəmˈpʌlsəri/*a.* 义务的;必修的
dissuade/diˈsweid/*vt.* 功阻;劝止
evacuate/iˈvækjueit/*vt.* 搬空;腾出
ad hoc/ædˈhɔk/*a.* 特别的;专门的
access /ˈækses/*n.* 途径
peers/piəz/*n.* 同事;伙伴
abolish/əˈbɔliʃ/*vt.* 取消;废除
initiative/iˈniʃətiv/*n.* 第一步;着手
launch/lɔːntʃ/*vi.* 开始
curriculum/kəˈrikjuləm/*n.* 课程
truancy/ˈtruːənsi/*n.* 逃学;旷课
aristocratic/ˌəristəˈkrætik/*a.* 贵族的
facilities/fəˈsilitiz/*n.* 设备;设施
integral/ˈintigrəl/*a.* 完全的;缺一不可的
proficient/prəˈfiʃənt/*a.* 熟练的;精通的
polytechnics/ˌpɔliˈtekniks/*n.* 工艺学校
register/ˈredʒistə/*vt.* 登记

Notes

1. but some people... to see the return of the cane: 有些人,包括教育部长,仍然希望学校能够重新使用体罚。the return of the cane 意为 the use of corporal punishment.

2. class inequality can be erased of continued according to educational policy: 教育政策可以铲除地位的不平等,也可以使这种不平等继续存在。这说明在英国,是否受到良好教育直接影响到你的社会地位。

3. In Britain, the accent you speak with... identity your social class：在英国，你说话的口音、你穿的衣服、你所上的学校都标志着你的社会地位。

4. Eton and Winchester：伊顿公学位于伦敦以西；温切斯特公学位于英格兰南部。这些公学都是英国培养贵族的私立学校。

5. Oxford and Cambridge：牛津和剑桥大学是英国最老的两所大学，分别建立于12世纪和13世纪。这两所大学有着悠久的历史，在世界上都享有盛誉。英国大部分的政治家和政府官员都毕业于这两所大学。

7. *Emma*：《埃玛》，讲述了一个受过良好教育的有钱人家的小姐交了一位来自下层社会的女朋友，她没有文化知识。为了让她找到一户好人家，埃玛开始对她传授知识。

8. *Jude the Obscure*：《微贱的裘德》，描写了一位立志攻读牛津大学的年轻人，由于环境及家庭的影响，他希望入高等学府之梦终未实现。这一故事说明了牛津、剑桥等这样的高等学府只是面向中产阶级以上家庭的子弟的，与工人阶级家庭的子弟无缘。

9. the UK's Gross Domestic Product：英国的国内生产总值。

10. The result... "meritocratic"：1944年教育法的颁布使中学和大学都录取出类拔萃的学生。二次世界大战期间，英国进行了教育改革，1944年颁布了教育法。新的教育法强调平等就学的机会，无论家庭出身如何、父母财富多少，只要有真才实学就可以上中学和大学。

11. comprehensive schools：综合学校，本世纪60年代在英国广泛推行。此类学校不论学生能力如何均可入学，学生可以学习多种科目。二至三年之后，可以选学自己最喜欢的专业。目前这些学校在英国中学中占90%，并正在推行新的教学方法。

12. grammar schools：文法学校，一种采取旧的优选制的中学。儿童在11岁时就参加升入中等学校的考试，成绩最好者可进入文法学校。这些学校主要教授专业课程，使学生能够通过考试进入高等学校。其余学生进入职业技术学校，毕业后不允许进入高校学习。这种考试制度现已改变。

13. vocational schools：职业学校。英国政府十分重视职业技术教育，为提高职业技术教育的地位，在体制上不断进行了改革。一方面把职业技术教育渗透在整个教育体系，使每个学校都注意职业技术教育。义务教育阶段（16岁前），技术课是学生的必修课程。另一方面不断完善职业考核制度，制订了五级国家专业资格证书标准。

14. parents have the right... school for their children：家长有权替他们的孩子选择某一个国立学校。

15. public schools：公学，也叫"私立学校"。学费很贵，一般有钱人家的子女才上得起这样的学校。英国有名的公学有伊顿、哈罗和拉格贝。

17. Inspectors of Schools：学校检查员。英国政府的教育科学部的主要职责是确定各类学校必须达到的标准，定时派检查员到各学校检查视察，并负责向教育科学部报告视察结果。

18. Foreign languages... with Europe：外语教学是全国教学大纲不可缺少的组成部分，反映了英国与欧洲国家之间关系的重要性。

20. pupils then decide what avenue of education they would like to follow：学生可以对自己愿意接受的教育途径做出选择。avenue of education：教育途径

21. General Certificate of Education-Advanced：高级水平测试结业证书。16岁的学生通过中学毕业考试后，想继续深造进高等学府，必须通过高级水平测试。从16岁到18岁的两年时间里，学生根据自己想读的大学专业选定数门有关课程学习，一般选3门。通过A级水平考试合格者都可入大学深造。

22. Most pupils... most proficient at：大部分学生试图在自己学得最好的课程中有三至四门的课程取得A级水平。A-level：advanced level；即高级水平。

23. General National Vocational Qualifications：国家专业资格证书。这一证书是专为职业技术学校毕业的学生设置的，共分5个级别，这就便于人们按阶梯逐级攀登，根据自己条件通过实际工作和专业培训，由低级向高级发展。获四级国家专业资格证书相当于学士学位；获五级国家专业资格证书相当于研究生水平。

24. polytechnics：多科性技术学院。

25. most of the students are studying for their first degrees：大部分的学生只是为了拿到学士学位。first degree：初级学位。即学士学位。second degree：硕士学位或博士学位。

26. Access for mature students... is widening：对于成人以及没有通过传统的A级测试的学生，进入高等学校的渠道正在拓宽。

27. the Open University：开放大学。对任何人都开放，无需正式学历。完成大学的必修课程后均可拿到大学文凭。开放大学的特点就在于通过电视、广播、录像、函授等方式为学生提供就地学习的条件。开放大学不限年龄，最小的不到20岁，最大的90岁有余，大多在20岁至40多岁之间。

28. in Oxford and Cambridge the BA... upon payment of a fee：牛津和剑桥大学的硕士学位制有其特殊之处，在这两所大学获得学士学位的毕业生，四年后，只要申请并交纳一定费用，就可以获得硕士学位，不需在校学习。

Exercises

Ⅰ. Explain the following

1. comprehensive schools
2. grammar schools
3. independent schools
4. Open University

Ⅱ. Fill in the blanks

1. The two oldest universities in Britain are ________ and ________.
2. Two famous public schools in England are ________ and ________.
3. Children in Britain must receive a full-time education legally from the age of ________ to ________.
4. Pupils from the age of ________ to ________ mainly attend state-run ________ schools.
5. Students attend ________ schools from the age of 11 up to around the age of ________.

6. Parents can choose between sending their children to __________ schools or __________ schools.

7. Parents from the wealthier middle class prefer to send their children to __________ schools so as to have better __________.

8. Comprehensive schools provide a __________ education, teaching students everything from __________ subjects like literature and science to more __________ subjects like cooking and carpentry.

9. Name two of the four Scottish Universities dating from the 14th and 15th centruies: __________ and __________.

10. In Britain, people can go to the __________ without having any formal educational qualifications.

11. GCSE stands for __________.

12. GCEA stands for __________.

13. GNVQs stands for __________.

Ⅲ. Choose the correct answer in each of the following

1. In Britain, the great majority of parents send their children to ________.
   A. private schools C. state schools
   B. independent schools D. public schools

2. In Britain, children from the age of 5 to 16 ________.
   A. can legally receive partly free education
   B. can legally receive completely free education
   C. can not receive free education at all
   D. can not receive free education if their parents are rich

3. If a student wants to go to university in Britain, he will take the examination called ________.
   A. General Certificate of Education-Advanced
   B. General Certificate of Secondary Education
   C. the common entrance examination
   D. General National Vocational Qualifications

4. Which of the following is a privately funded university in Britain?
   A. The University of Cambridge.
   B. The University of Oxford.
   C. The University of Edinburgh.
   D. The University of Buckingham.

5. Which of the following is NOT true?
   A. Parents send their children to public schools because they are rich.
   B. Parents send their children to public schools because their children can get better jobs when they leave school.
   C. Parents send their children to public schools because their children can have a better

chance of getting into a good university

D. Parents send their children to public schools because their children prefer to go to public schools.

6. Which of the following is NOT a characteristic of the Open University?

A. It's open to everybody.

B. It requires no formal educational qualifications.

C. No university degree is awarded.

D. University courses are followed through TV, radio, correspondence, etc.

7. In the examination called "the 11 plus", students with academic potential go to ________.

A. grammar schools

B. comprehensive schools

C. public schools

D. technical schools

8. Which of the following is NOT included in the National Curriculum?

A. Children must study the subjects like English, mathematics, science and so on.

B. Children must sit in A-level exams.

C. Children must pass national tests.

D. Teachers must teach what they are told.

9. Which of the following is NOT true about the British education system?

A. It's run by the state.

B. It's funded by the state.

C. It's supervised by the state.

D. It's dominated by the state.

10. Which of the following schools would admit children without reference to their academic abilities?

A. Comprehensive schools.

B. Secondary schools.

C. Independent schools.

D. Grammar schools.

Ⅳ. Answer the following questions briefly

1. What are the purposes of the British education system?
2. How does the British education system reflect social class?
3. What are the major changes that have taken place since World War Ⅱ?
4. Why does the author say that universities in Britain have been rather elitist?

Chapter 10 The Commonwealth

The Commonwealth of Nations contains three groups of territories as follows:

(*a*) "White" territories, whose inhabitants are mainly of British descent, and who speak English as their mother tongue, viz. Canada (with Newfoundland[2]), Australia and New Zealand.

(*b*) "Non-white" territories, where the British have never settled, except temporarily as traders and administrators, e. g. India, Pakistan, Sri Lanka, West African countries and Malaya.

(*c*) Mixed territories, whose inhabitants are partly British and partly non-British, e. g. the Central African East African countries.

All three groups have either achieved independence or are moving towards it. For group(*a*) it has been a very gradual and a remarkably peaceful development. For group(*b*) it has not always been peaceful and the final steps have been taken rather hurriedly. Group(*c*) has provided the greatest problems of all problems which have yet to be solved. Until they are solved, the transition from Empire to Commonwealth, i. e. from imperialism to freedom, cannot be regarded as complete.

Let us look a little more closely at each of our three groups. The "white" territories are of course not completely white. Each country had and still has its more purely native peoples. Canada has its "Indians" and Eskimos, Australia its "Aborigines" and New Zealand its Maoris. But their numbers have always been small. When the British first arrived, many generations ago, they found a pleasant climate, not unlike home, with huge tracts of productive but largely untouched land, thinly populated, where they were able to thrive, multiply and expand in comparative peace, joined from time to time by fresh immigrants from the mother country(i. e. Britain herself).

At first, these colonies depended entirely on Britain for their survival. Gradually, however, they grew more self-sufficient, and developed interests of their own. Britain's failure to recognize this in the eighteenth century resulted in her losing the most valuable territory she had—the territory which is now the United States of America. But Canada, Australia and New Zealand have never broken away because Britain has respected their interests; and today they are sovereign states within the Commonwealth. Their attitude to Britain is illustrated by the fact that they all freely entered the Second World War in Britain' s support, and they would probably do the same again if necessary. Moreover, they are still quite eager to attract British immigrants. If you go to Britain today you will often see advertisements like "Come to Canada!" (or to Australia or New Zealand), addressed mainly to specialists and skilled workmen of one kind or another, and thousands of British families do emigrate to these places every year.

What about the non-white territories? Why have the British not settled there permanently as they have elsewhere? Chiefly, of course, because of climate. Canada, Australia and New Zealand are mainly temperate like Britain itself; India, Africa and Malaya are mainly tropical and sub-tropical. Why did the British go there in the first place? Chiefly, of course, to trade and to establish plantations. Why did they not develop democratic government there from the first, as they did for example in Canada? Obviously, because foreign, but only with making bargains. They became involved only gradually in the general administration of native people. In Ghana, for instance, the British government did not finally take over from the traders until 1844[3], and in India not until 1858[4]. And it was only with the spread of education and the growth of a national consciousness that democracy and independence could develop, for these are not like coins which can be given by one person to another: they are part of a nation' s character-they must grow.

The final steps to independence in almost all of these countries have now been taken. Did the British have to be persuaded to agree? Of course they did. On the one side were the young leaders of newly developing nations, eager and optimistic, inspired by the progress already made; on the other were representatives of a nation whose own development had been extremely slow, and who were naturally cautious, preoccupied with progress still to be achieved[5]. Some persuasion was inevitable. But the final steps have been taken, and more than that, taken systematically and cordially; and the average Briton is content, and even rather proud of it.

There are some. of course, who lament the "loss of the Empire". But the British as a whole feel that the Commonwealth is something better, because it is based on freedom. They are ashamed of some of the past effects of colonialism, the greed, the big-power rivalries, the sense of superiority, the bloodshed, the slave trade. They are embarrassed at the short period during the late nineteenth and early twentieth centuries when they tended to glorify their own imperialism, the flag waving period of "empire builders" like Cecil Rhodes[6] and writers like Rudyard Kipling[7]. But at the same time they feel that their colonial record was by no means wholly bad.

For they believe they also brought with them pacification, law, education and material progress, and that the best of their administrators showed great integrity and a deep respect for the people under their control. Hence their embarrassed sense of injustice when they hear "colonialism" and "imperialism" used as political catchwords standing only for aggression, oppression, exploitation and inhumanity; and hence their hurt feelings when people whom they respect fail to regard them in any other way than as "wicked imperialists"[8].

Mixed Territories: the Present Situation

There remains, however, our third group of territories, those whose inhabitants are partly white and partly non-white. It is here that colonialism has created the greatest difficulties. The basic problem here is not self-government. It is democracy. Countries like Rhodesia[9] are not democratic, because government lies in the hands of a white minority. Those who say, "Send the white men home" have completely failed to understand the situation. Rhodesia is their home. Britain is no more home to them than it is to a Canadian, or a New Zealander. Most of them have never seen Britain. Rhodesia is their home not only because they were born and bred there, but also because they have built it with their own efforts into something approaching a modern industrial state. But since they are heavily outnumbered by the non-whites they are convinced that if they accept democracy in the sense of "one man one vote" they will lose control of their own achievements and of their whole way of life, and will be left with no home at all.

Britain herself is in a difficult position. Whatever she does or advises with regard to these mixed Commonwealth territories, she is almost bound to be attacked by the whites for going too far, and by the non-whites for not going far enough[10]. In any case, nobody in Britain professes to know the ideal solution to the problem, and even if they did they would have neither the power nor the right to force anyone to accept it. But one thing the British are sure of: they hate any doctrine of racial superiority, and any system in which one man has less opportunity than another. It was these opinions which caused the Republic of South Africa to withdraw from the Commonwealth in 1961, and Rhodesia to declare its independence illegally in 1965[11]. Eventually some kind of solution based on racial equality *must* be found.

The Commonwealth as a whole, therefore, is an astonishing mixture. It is already completely different from the old Empire, and now that nearly all its members are independent is will certainly change even further. It contains a wide variety of governments, races, colours, languages, opinions and levels of development, Even the Queen is no longer the central figure that she once was, since republics like India and Ghana, while still recognising her as head of the Commonwealth, no longer recognise her as head of their own separate nation. In any case, as the Commonwealth is composed of fully self-governing states, there is no central political leadership of any kind.

What, therefore, is the Commonwealth? What binds it together? It has often been said that the Commonwealth is a sort of club, and this is probably the best way of looking at it. You are not forced to become or to remain the member of a club. You belong to it because you like the other members and because you somehow find membership useful to you. It is the same with the Commonwealth. If you are a member of the Commonwealth, you have, for example, powerful friends to help you in time of trouble, all speaking English as *lingua franca*: you can use established trade channels; you can draw freely on the experience of others in developing, for example. universities and public services like broadcasting and the police; you can command a certain respect in the world at large through belonging to an established organization instead of being isolated[12], you can exchange your ideas with others, thereby both extending your influence and gaining a more objective view of yourself and a clearer idea of where you are heading. The departure of South Africa shows that the Commonwealth has certain ideals, and an organization with ideals is bound to be of some value. Hence the significance of the Conference of Commonwealth Heads of States, which meets about once a year, where nobody forces anybody to do anything, but where useful ideas do "get across" from one nation to another.

As we have said, the character of the Commonwealth is bound to change. Perhaps, some more of its members will grow away from it and leave it. Perhaps wider international associations will supersede it. But whatever happens, the Commonwealth, beginning in imperialism and ending in freedom and equality, will be regarded as a symbol of progress in the history of the world.

Colour Problems in Britain

The existence of the Commonwealth means, of course, that large numbers of overseas students and officials come to Britain to train, take part in conferences, and so on, and in recent years (starting in the 1950's particularly) their numbers have been greatly increased by a steady influx of West Indians, mostly Jamaicans[13], coming to Britain to find work and to settle down more or less permanently. Indeed, more people from the Commonwealth want to come to live in Britain than there are jobs and houses available. so for the past few years immigration has been limited to the close relatives of people already living in Britain. Traditionally, there has been no discrimination of any kind in Britain against such people, whatever their race or colour. The British like to feel that an African or an Indian, for example, can do exactly the same things in Britain as they do themselves, and any kind of colour bar evokes loud public protests[14].

And yet misunderstandings do sometimes occur. Why? First, because the British area reserved race. They do not mix easily even with each other, especially if they feel that the other person is different from them in speech or manner. They talk with each other in a perfectly friendly way when necessary, but there is always a sort of barrier between them until they become properly acquainted. Now a foreigner is always felt to be different from them, and a coloured foreigner is obviously so by his appearance. So the barrier is bound to exist, and is easily mistaken for pride or active unfriendliness.

At closer quarters, further misunderstanding is often caused because the foreigner does not conform to conventional British ideas of politeness. This has nothing to do with character—it is simply a question of social habit. Thus, for example, if someone fails to say "Excuse me" or "Thank you" at the right times. he creates an unnecessarily bad impression; and if he calls on people uninvited at awkward times, or always seems to be praising himself in conversation, will certainly be disliked, even though in another country the same behaviour might be considered perfectly normal.

But the real test of good relations occurs where the foreigner actually makes his home, especially with his landlady. The landlady-lodger relationship is a precarious one even when the two people concerned are of the same race and perhaps even same family, so when the tenant is foreign it is even more precarious. Here is one small example. A West African is used to bathing every day. In his country people sweat in the heat, and the sweat not only makes them fell dirty, but it makes dust stick to their body, which in its light clothing is not well protected. But in Britain people do not sweat so freely, and in any case their bodies are shielded from dirt by beaver clothing. Moreover bath water has to be heated: this costs money in fuel and may be troublesome. So most working-class people have a complete bath only once a week. Now the West African tenant may ask his landlady to heat a bath for him every day, and the landlady may refuse. She thinks he is unreasonable. He thinks she is mean and dirty. Neither is right and neither is wrong—it is just a misunderstanding. And there are many others. Hence the trouble that some foreigners have in finding lodgings, and as always the coloured foreigners tends to have the greatest trouble because he is so *obviously* foreign. Indeed, some landladies are actually afraid of him, just as some African villagers are afraid of the colour of a white man.

Finally there are the difficulties which occur when a whole family of foreign people settles in a particular house, or when many families settle in whole district. It often happens that these people were formerly used to a certain way of life which is completely different from that of the people now around them, this comes out in various ways[15], and one of the commonest is what the British call overcrowding. Overcrowding tends to cause noise, lack of privacy, and an appearance of poverty which perhaps does not really exist. So the neighbours complain. They say their district is losing its respectability, and so on.

The government is very concerned that no one living in Britain should be unfairly treated, and has made all discrimination illegal. The Race Relations Board was set up to enforce this law: and if anyone feels he has been made the victim of any kind of prejudice, he can complain to the Board, who will investigate, and may bring court proceedings against the offender.

These, in brief, are the main colour problems in Britain. It is important to realise that *foreignness* is the fundamental difficulty. Colour simply aggravates it. It is also important to remember that if you are a coloured visitor to Britain, your experience that if *you* are a coloured visitor to Britain, you experience will depend on : (*a*) the particular people you happen to meet—there are good and bad in every community; (*b*) luck; (*c*) your own tact and understanding of British ways. On three things will depend whether you return to your own country saying, "I hate those British—they are proud, and they despised me for my colour"; or saying, "The British have some funny ways until you get to know them, but they are really very kind, and I made lots of friends."

Words & Expressions

The Commonwealth of Nations　英联邦

desent/di'sent/*n*.　血统

transition/træ'siʒən/*n*.　过渡

Eskimo /'eskiməu/*n*.　爱斯基摩人

Aborigines /ˌæbə'ridʒiniːz/*n*.　土著居民

Maori /'mauri/*n*.　新西兰土著居民毛利人

self sufficient /self sə'fiʃənt/*a*.　自给自足的

temperate /'tempərit/*a*.　气候温和的

tropical/'trɔpikəl/*a*.　热带气候的

sub tropical *a*.　亚热带的

plantation /plæn'teiʃən/*n*.　种植园

permanent/'pəːmənənt/*a*.　永久性的

bargain/ˈbaːgin/n 成交贸易

cordially/ˈkɔːdjəli/adv. 真诚地,友好地

lament/ləˈment/vi. vt. 痛惜

glorify/ˈglɔːrifai/vt. 荣耀

pacification /ˌpæsifˈkeiʃən/n. 安定

integrity /inˈtegriti/n. 正直

catchword/ˈkætʃwɔːd/n. 时髦话

wicked/ˈwikid/. a 凶恶的

outnumber/autˈnʌmbə/vt. 在数量上超过

profess /prəˈfes/vt. 声称,表示

influx/ˈinflʌks/n. 涌进

bar/baː/n. (色)带

evoke/iˈvəuk/vt. 隔阂

precarious/priˈkɛəriəs/a. 不稳定的,困难的

lodger/ˈlɔdʒə/n. 房客

enforce/inˈfɔːs/vt. 实行

proceedings/prəˈsiːdiʤz/n. (复)诉讼

aggravate /ˈægrəveit/vt. 加剧

Notes

1. The Commonwealth of Nations：英联邦是1931年成立的。第一次世界大战后,英国殖民体系土崩瓦解。为了维持其既得利益,英国政府把那些新近独立的或正在独立的英属殖民地拉在一起,成立英联邦,企图通过政治经济和外交上的所谓协商和合作达到控制的目的。女王名义上仍是不少成员国的元首,但各国都保持内政外的主权。本文作者和不少英国人一样,在谈到英国过去的对外帝国主义性质的扩张、侵略,对殖民地所进行的残酷掠夺时总是遮遮掩掩,时时加一些粉饰之词,这也反映了大英帝国没落腐朽的情绪。

2. with Newfoundland：1931年,英联邦成立时,纽芬兰仍是英属自治领,1949年成为加拿大第十个行政区。

3. Ghana. . . 1844：加纳原属英国,是西非的一个殖民地。1844年以前,英国、葡萄牙等国在加纳进行残忍的奴役和掠夺黄金的贸易。1844年后,英国政府开始进行殖民地的政治活动。

4. India. . . 1858：1813年英国成立对印度贸易垄断性公司"东印度公司"。1857年镇压了印度士兵起义后,英国加紧了对印度的政治统治。事实上,大英帝国在印度的殖民主义活动早在1757年就已开始。

5. On the one side. . . to be achieved：一方面,新兴发展中国家的年轻领导人由于受到已经取得成绩的鼓舞而要求迫切,并且充满信心;另一方面,一个国家的代表看到本国发展一直非常缓慢,他们主要考虑今后如何发展,因此,这些代表当然很谨慎小心。意思是说,英国政府出于无奈而不得不承认各殖民地的独立。

6. Cecil Rhodes：罗兹(1853 ~ 1902)是赤裸裸的英国帝国主义者。南非金刚石公司以及其他英国在南部非洲矿业的老板。曾任英国首相,梦想建立从好望角到埃及的英国殖民地。罗德西亚(非洲人称为"津巴布韦")就是以他的名字命名的英国殖民地。所以作者说他这类人就是高举帝国大旗,到处扩展殖民地的"帝国建造者"。

7. Rudyard Kipling：吉卜林(1865 ~ 1936)出生于印度的英国作家。1907年获诺贝尔文学奖,是英国第一个获此奖的作家。在他的作品中,帝国主义分子被描写为勇敢的、有良心的、能自力更生的、真正的英国人。

8. Hence their embarrassed sense. . . "wicked imperialists"：当他们听到别人说到"殖民主义"和"帝国主义",并把这两个词仅仅当成代表侵略、压迫、剥削和非人性般的残忍的政

治时髦话时,就感到有一种很难说出口的受到不公正对待的感觉。当他们所尊敬的人(意为殖民地人民)把他们当成“邪恶的帝国主义分子”而不是从别的角度看待他们时,就大伤感情。这是今天那些留恋大英帝国,希望原殖民地人民感谢英国帝国主义者、殖民主义者,感谢为他们带来所谓好处的英国人。

9. Rhodesia:非洲人称之为“津巴布韦”,现已获得独立。

10. she is almost bound... far enough:她总是受到两面夹击,白人(居住在殖民地的白人)批评英国走得太远,而非白人却又说做得不够。

11. It was... in 1965:正是英国人的这些思想(痛恨种族优越论、要求人人机会均等)促使南非于 1961 年退出英联邦,罗得西亚于 1965 年宣布非法独立。但事实上,南非退出英联邦主要是因为成员国强烈反对南非的种族隔离政策。1965 年,白人统治的罗得西亚宣布独立,英国拒绝了这种非法独立。

12. you can command... isolated:由于属于一个大家确认的组织,而不是处于孤立状态,成员国可以在世界范围内获得大家的某种尊敬。

13. a steady influx of West Indians, mostly Jamaicans:西印度群岛位于北美与南美之间,这里不少岛屿原属英国殖民地,如牙买加。1962 年,牙买加正式成为独立的英联邦成员国。这些原英属殖民地的不少人从 50 年代起涌入英国,寻找工作或定居下来。这些有色人员大批涌入,种族矛盾开始尖锐起来。

14. any kind of colour bar evokes loud public protests:任何对有色人种的歧视都会引起大家的激烈的反对。colour bar 原指有色带,这里指对有色人种的区分,歧视。

15. This comes out in various ways:这种情况反映在各个方面。

Exercises

Ⅰ. Explain the following

1. the Commonwealth of Nations
2. the Race Relations Board

Ⅱ. Fill in the blanks

1. The Commonwealth of Nations contains groups of territories as follows: ______________, ______________ and ______________.
2. In Canada the true native peoples are called ________ and ________, in Australia the true native people are ________, and in New Zealand they are called ________.
3. In the "white" territories of the Commonwealth of Nations, there are three major countries, ____________, ____________ and ____________. In these countries, ____________ is their mother tongue.
4. In Asia, ____________, ____________, ____________ and ________________ are members of the Commonwealth of Nations.
5. The author believes that the fundamental difficulty in the racia, relations is ________________. ________________ simply worsens the situation.
6. The head of the Commonwealth is ______________________.

Ⅲ. Answer the following questions briefly

1. Why did the British go to Africa and India? Why have the British not settled permanently in the non-white territories of the Commonwealth?
2. What is the attitude of the British towards independence in the former colonics of the British Empire?
3. What, according to the author, binds the Commonwealth together? What is the character of the Commonwealth?
4. What is the major difference between "non-white" territories and mixed territories in the Commonwealth?
5. How did colour problems come into being?

Part Ⅱ

The United States of America

Chapter 11 The Land of the U. S. A.

In its vast area the United States comprehends most of the physical conditions known to men; heat and cold, forest and desert, tropical swamp and Arctic waste, mountains and endless plains, empty spaces and megalopolis, and the world's largest river system. Yet the most remarkable contrast of all is the contrast between the variety inevitable in so great an area and the similarity of the people and of the things that they have made in all these diverse parts.

the United States in bigger in area than the whole of Europe, and includes a spread as from Paris to Karachi in Pakistan. Evidently life in the hot southern sub-tropical forests is very different from life in the north, where the winters are colder than anywhere in western Europe.

It would not be easy to talk in general terms about western Europe as a unit, with its differences of climate and culture, its mountains, plains and coasts. One would have to describe the various parts one by one, and it would take a long time to do so. In the far bigger area of the United States, with far greater diversity of climate there are also contrasts: there are too many characteristics to be described in a single generalization. And the diversity of the people themselves is immense. It is not only that some came originally from Britain, others from Italy, Germany, Ireland or

Poland; first generation immigrants are still close to their diverse origins, while most long established Americans are wholly assimilated; first-generation Italians differ not only from long-established Dutch, but from fourth-generation Italians—and even they differ according to the degree of intermarriage. Yet there is at the same time a lack of cultural difference among the regions, because all these varied people are scattered everywhere, with only minor local ethnic concentrations.

The great Republic of the United States is not the same country even in area, as it was at the time of its foundation in the 1780s[1]. The original Union consisted of thirteen states along the eastern seaboard. *The thirty-five continental states*[2] *which* have been added since independence occupy an area eight times as great as the original thirteen, and more than two-thirds of all Americans now live in these thirty-five states, in an area which 180 years ago was mainly unexplored, except for some Spanish and French coastal settlements here and there. But the founders of the Constitution foresaw that, as settlement spread westwards and new areas were developed by stable populations capable of self-government, so new states would be allowed to join the Union. The process began almost at once. Kentucky and Tennessee, southwards and across the mountains from Virginia, were added in 1792 and 1796, and further north the admission of states west of Pennsylvania began with Ohio in 1803.

The story of the addition of new states in the nineteenth century is also the story of the conquest of the west, with the wagons and then the railroads, the cowboys and the sheriffs and that piece of human experience which the Western movie constantly revives[3]. The last block of north-western states was not incorporated until after 1890. With Arizona in 1912 the list of forty-eight continental states was at last complete, and recently, in 1959, the first separate territories were granted statehood-Hawaii in the Pacific Ocean and the great northern pioneers' land of Alaska, bigger than France, Germany, Italy and Austria together—and still with only a quarter of a million people.

Our study of the growth of the Union reminds us that within the United States there is a difference between old and new. To Europeans America may look a new country, but it is not all new in the same way. Even in Europe, apart from churches and castles, there is not so very much left from more than 200 years ago. Houses, shops, factories, stores, means of transport—almost all the buildings and the things people use are less old than the United States. From four million at the time of independence the population there has grown to 215 million, but this does not mean that all parts have grown at the same rate. The State of Virginia now has six times as many people as in 1787, but modern England has five times as many as it had then. If we exclude the part of Virginia which consists of suburbs of Washington, we find a rate of increase about the same as in England itself over this period. In most aspects of everyday life, Virginia is not really newer than the mother country[4]. But with the western states things are quite different. There, hardly anything man-made goes back 100 years, and few adult inhabitants have roots going back more than one generation. So there is a contrast within the United States between old and new, less obvious than many other contrasts but significant and interesting all the same.

Although the country is so big and its people have so many different ethnic backgrounds, it is in some ways less varied than Europe. The national origins of the people are by now fairly well mixed all over the country, though there are exceptions on small and large scales. The English language is virtually universal in its American form. The American way or speaking has developed independently of England and is on the whole closer to what can be heard in Ireland than to the speech of any other part of the British Isles. Regional variations of accent are slight, and to a German or an Italian the difference between the accent of the deep south and that of the "Yankee" is less evident than the difference between two Englishmen from places two hours' journey apart[5]. Some Americans speak rather indistinctly, not pronouncing consonants properly, others show by their speech that English is not their mother tongue, and Irish or Negro accents can often be recognised; but the lack of real regional or class variety in speech or usage is one of the characteristics that tend to make the whole country very obviously one.

Another instance of uniformity is in habits and ways of living. From Boston to Los Angeles is as far as from France to Central Asia. and from east to west there are four time zones[6], but everywhere people get up and go to bed at about the same time, eat the same kind of food, bought in the same kind of shops, work and rest at the same times of the day and have the same pattern of holidays, In general they share the same ideas, ideals and objectives, In most of the things that matter there is less difference between rich people and ordinary people, or between town and country, than in any single European nation. It is fairly easy to imagine a typical American; most individuals deviate from this "type" in some ways, but are fairly near to it in others. It is not that this personal uniformity is boring. It is after all superimposed on original diversity, and where single pattern involves much friendly informality in personal relations there is little cause to feel oppressed.[7]

Althouth the United States covers so much land and the land produces far more food than the present population needs, its people are by now almost entirely an urban society. Less than a tenth of the people are engaged in agriculture and forestry, and most of the rest live in or around towns, small town may still be very like other small towns, and the typical small town may embody a widely accepted view of the country, but most Americans do not live in small towns any more. Half the population now live in some thirty metropolitan areas (large cities with their suburbs) of more than a million people each—a larger proportion than in Germany or England, let alone France—and if we add another 200 or so quite large towns with their suburbs we see that the small town has been superseded by the large town as the typical environment—or, to be more exact, by the suburban section of a large town. The statistics of urban and rural population should be treated with caution, because so many people who live in areas classified as rural travel by car to work in a nearby town each day[8]. As the rush to live out of town continues rural areas within reach of towns are gradually filled with houses[9], so that it is hard to say at what moment a piece of country becomes a suburb. But more and more the typical American lives in a metropolitan rather than a small town environment—with no single metropolis to Moscow or Tokyo; every great city shares in a single metropolitan quality[10].

The fact that the United States has always been a single economic unit, with no tariffs to restrict trade, has contributed to uniformity. Modern industry favours large organizations. and it is no accident that the world' s biggest commercial firms are American. Massmarkets are efficient; the constituent pieces are interchangeable[11], The people are interchangeable too. They can choose between the products of competing manufacturers, but the products are all much alike. The smooth-running automatic comfortable car, the one—stored house in its pleasant piece of land, with its plate-glass windows and its swimming pool—all these things are good, but each has many others like it, just as there are too many car-parks and garages and signs about things for sale. The different parts and communities of the United states are like one another in the same way as big airports all over the world are like one another—and after all mass air travel developed in America before it did anywhere else. Except, up to a point, in the south, there is not much really distinctive regional architecture or cookery, music or literature, This is why Americans are so impressed by a Mediterranean fishing port or hilltop town. North America belongs to people who came there across the Atlantic, most from Europe, some as slaves from Africa. So when we look at this vast country there is good reason for beginning with the east coast, where the first and later immigrants landed. Beginning with the north we have first the area known as New England, which runs from the Canadian shore to New York, with a coastline 800 kilometers long (in direct line) and stretching inland for 300 kilometers at its widest point. This area is about the same size as England and Wales, and resembles old England in many ways. Some of the earliest settlement was here, and urban. In character we can divide New England roughly into two parts. The southern section. consisting of the states of Connecticut, Massachusetts and Rhode Island, is the most "English". The ten million people of these states are as crowded as the English, and most live in towns—a quarter of them in and round Boston and another fifth (or nearly so) in the outer parts of the great sprawl that runs up the coast from New York City. Boston already had a quarter of a million people 100 years ago, and in its central part many streets are well over 100 years old. In this old-established part the scenery is rather English, with flat country near the coast and hills up to 1 000 metres inland.

Northern New England is rather different, emptier, wilder, more picturesque. The states of Maine, New Hampshire and Vermont together have only two million people in an area as big as England. The southern parts of New Hampshire and Maine are suburan, but everywhere else, with lakes and hills up to 1 300 meters in Vermont, spectacular rocky coasts in Maine, this is more than anything an attractive holiday country for the town-dwellers further south: country for enjoyments like yachting, swimming, fishing, skiing and enjoying rural peace—particularly in the "fall" (autumn), when the colours are glorious.

The southern end of New England merges into the suburbs of New York City, and to the west the great state that takes its name from the city at its southernmost tip[12]. Some say that New York is the world's biggest "town", but it is rather pointless to argue whether or not it is bigger than Tokyo. It all depends how many areas which are more or less attached are included. Manhattan Island[13] includes everything that most people think of when they say "New York": Wall Street[14] and the office skyscrapers clustered around it, Fifth Avenue running up the centre of the island, with Broadway slanting from it, the Empire State Building, [15]Rockefeller Centre[16], the United Nations Building, the museums and central shops, Central Park (where at times it is dangerous to walk alone), the Negro quarter of Harlem, the docks and the slums behind them: but Manhattan has only around two million residents. New York City is composed of five boroughs: Manhattan, Brooklyn (on the south of Long Island), the Bronx, Richmond and Queen's. Immense bridges join the boroughs with each other and with the suburbs in New Jerscy across the Hudson. The city population of nearly eight million has not changed much for a long time, but the area of continuous has not changed much for a long time, but the area of continuous town can be taken to include in addition about seven million people in New York State, New Jersey and southern Connecticut. In the mid-1970s the population fell rapidly.

Eastern New York State is really the same thing as the valley of the Hudson River, but the State extends 500 kilometers to the west to Lakes Ontario and Erie andCanada, and finally Niagara Falls. The state is as big as England. Half of its eighteen million people live in or near New York City, while the rest are mainly concentrated in the line of Hudson valley towns and near the Great Lakes, leaving much of the hill and lake country empty. If has sometimes been argued that New York City might as well be a state on its own. To the south of the state is Pennsylvania, which also spreads out to the borders of the middle west, with well-separated areas of coal mining and heavy industry among its hills. Philadelphia, well up the Delaware River, is the metropolis of Pennsylvania, with five million people in its metropolitan area, or city plus suburbs. In the western part of the state the steel area around Pittsburgh is already across the mountains and on the Ohio River; wate flows south to the Gulf of Mexico. Pennsylvania is the main part of the mid-Atlantic area, which includes New Jersey and Maryland, bounded at the south by the Potomac River. This is the clearest dividing-line in the United States, because across the river is the south.

It was on this border that the founding fathers chose the site for the national capital city of Washington. They set apart for it a square territory which they called the District of Columbia[17] taken out of the states of Maryland and Virginia to from the national capital territory, outside the jurisdiction of any state and subject only to the control of the Federal Congress.

The whole of New England and the mid-Atlantic states together can conveniently be regarded as a single section of the United States, comprising eleven states together with the District of Columbia. This is the base from which America was built and it still has more than a quarter of the whole population, in one-fifteenth of the land area.

The north-east as a whole is slightly smaller than France in area but larger in population. More than half of its fifty-five million people are concentrated in the coastal area of early settlement. The train from Boston through Providence, New

York, Philadelphia and Baltimore to Washington travels between buildings for most of the way, and the part from Philadelphia to New York, Philadelphia and Baltimore to Washington travels between buildings for most of the way, and the part from Philadelphia to New York, and a good way beyond in each direction, is almost solidly built up[18]. Whit good roads and universal car ownership each of the big cities in this string spreads out its suburbs towards its neighbour, and people talk of this as megalopolis

It hardly seems sensible to talk of Boston and Washington as parts of a single urban complex, when they are 600 kilometers apart, but this area contains the political capital of the United States as well as the commercial capital and most of the established centres of culture[19].

On southwards down the Atlantic coast are the tobacco and cotton states, with Washington on the border between south and north. This was slave-owning country before the civil war, and has not prospered much since then. Economically these south-eastern states are notoriously backward, with much rural poverty surviving among whites as well as Negroes; more recently they have attracted a great new wave of industrial development, helped by federal plans and hydro-electric power.

Rather different from the rest of the south is its most extreme part. the state of Florida, with its swamps and pine forests, its orange plantations, its beaches, inland springs and waterways in a Caribbean climate. Thousands of retired northerners live in Southern Florida, enjoying the warm winter climate and hoping not to see their homes destroyed in a hurricane some autumn[20]. Miami, with its long row of huge holiday hotels, is now not only a holiday resort but also a great centre of prosperous new industries, as well as being the home of 400 000 refugees from Castro's Cuba.

Behind and through the eastern states runs the range of the Appalachian mountains, beginning far south in Georgia and continuing, with slight interruptions, northwards to Vermont and Canada. Sections of the range have different names, but the different parts have much in common. Rounded hills and forests are the main feature. The highest point is only 2 000 metres above the sea.

The mountains were a barrier to early movement westwards for the early generations, but beyond the mountains the vast central plain stretches all the way to the Rocky Mountains, with the water from the Ohio and Missouri Rivers joining the Mississippi to flow down to New Orleans and the Gulf of Mexico. Half the area of the United States lies in this vast basin bounded by the Appalachians on the east and the Rocky Mountains to the west, with, to the north, the scarcely perceptible watershed which divides the Mississippi waters from those that flow north into the Great Lakes and St Lawrence.

The north-eastern part of this great basin is known as the Middle West. The term is confusing because in fact it describes the north-eastern quarter of the United States except for the states close to the Atlantic. But in 1776 all this area was still west of the fully-settled territory of the original states. The great "mid-western" plain was first developed for farming, and Chicago, with its navigable water route east across the Great Lakes to the St Lawrence River, and its central position, soon became its chief town. Now Chicago is an industrial and commercial city comparable with Paris or London, dominating the five industrial mid-western states east of the Mississippi. Each of these five states, Illinois, Michigan, Indiana, Wisconsin and Ohio, includes huge, sparsely-populated open spaces. Together they have a total area slightly greater than France, but more than half of their forty million people live in a dozen industrial cities with their suburbs. The biggest of these (next to Chicago) is Detroit, Michigan, home of the great American gods, Ford, General Motors and Chrysler[21]. More than two million people produce more murders each year than the whole of Britain or West Germany. By the standards even of the Atlantic states these great Western inner cities may be new, but parts of their central areas already suffer from decay.

Further west still the great plain which occupies the middle of the United States from Canada down to Texas is empty, featureless country, where one can drive for hours with little change of scene, and where the vastness of America is palpable. The plains run from the Gulf of Mexico in the south up to the Canadian border and beyond—an endless open space comparable with Siberia. Few places in the world can compare with these great plains for uniformity and monotony, and they are onlypart of a continuous system which goes northwards to the barren lands of the Arctic. The eastern part has a moderate rainfall, but in general the rainfall declines towards the mountain barrier of the Rockies in the west. Although there are great extremes of cold in winter and of heat in summer the plains are more favourably placed than those of Siberia. Running from thirty to forty-nine degrees north they can produce wheat in large quantities, and the endless space is good for the use of mechanisation on a huge scale. One can well imagine the sense of isolation of the early settlers in this region, but the new developments of isolation of the early settlers in this region, but the new developments of road transport have changed all this for the modern farmer. The four states forming the heart of the plains, North and South

Dakota, Nebraska and Kansas, have a combined area nearly as great as France and Italy together, and only five million inhabitants including those who live in and around the two big cities on the Missouri river, which joins the Mississippi from the west at St Louis.

At the southern end of the plains is the huge state of Texas, largest in the Union until surpassed in size by the addition of sub-arctic and arctic Alaska. Texas is relatively arid, and has always had a distinctive quality, first with is cowboys and cattle, then with the rapid development of oil and industry. The population is growing fast and has now surpassed that of Pennsylvania. making Texas the third most populous state in the Union, but most of the state is still empty, with the people concentrated in a few big cities, famous for their millionaires, their brashness and their violence.

To the west the plains merge into rising land, the cattle country of the old wild west, the Rocky Mountains and the great deserts, much emptier yet than the plains, An area as big as Europe has fewer people than the Netherlands. Yet in some of these deserted areas, such as the states of Arizona, New Mexico and Nevada, we can now see new jobs multiplying and new inhabitants pouring in. Some of these areas have had ups and downs in the past, mostly because of some spectacular gold rush which produced a sudden boom town, now deserted. Nevada had nearly as many people in 1880 as in 1920, after some fluctuations, but the population has quintupled in the last thirty years.

The desert states have boom towns again, and the boom is not based only on unrestricted gambling or easy divorce laws[22]. Being easily accessible to California is an advantage, and with their remarkable scenery they have obvious attractions for holidaymakers. They can still identify themselves with the old wild west, at the same time as they give conducted tours of canyons and breath-taking shapes of mountain and rock under ever-blue skies. For all their newness these areas represent a little of the American's image of his country. Here the frontier seems real, and in a sense it is, though now mixed with air-conditioning.

But for the fullest, most significant representation of the modern American image we must go to the Pacific coast and to the southern part of it in particular. Steinbeck's Okies in The Grapes of Wrath[23], driven out of the dust-bowl land of Oklahoma, saw this as the promised land because of the hope of some work picking fruit. But now it is not just oranges that bring people west, nor just Hollywood. Roaring, fast-growing America has its centrepiece here[24], and each year until 1970 half a million people joined the search for the Californian dream. Glorious mountains, sea with majestic cliffs as well as inviting expanses of sand, scenery which leaves the east coast and the mid-west looking very dull by comparison, warm winters, sunshine, the world's biggest trees (Redwoods)—these are only part of the story. The oranges and grapes and fertile land are still important, but the electronics industry, aeroplane factories, defence plants of many kinds, and a whole new industrial complex are more important still. The trouble is that southern California is being ruined by its own success. In what was once the best area of all, around Los Angeles, there will soon be ten million people in one continuous ruban development 100 kilometres across; and there are more motor-cars than in the whole of Asia and the Soviet Union. Northern California, with San Francisco as its centre, is less brash, more sensitive, its people less prone to follow political or religious extremists or cranks. California's population, now the biggest in the Union, passed 20 million in 1970, but then immigration slowed down.

Surprisingly, the northern Pacific states of Washington and Oregon, which only became states in 1889, have not progressed as rapidly as California, although they too, like British Columbia[25], have everything in their favour. They do not want to grow too fast. They are just above the average for the whole country in wealth and population-growth. Boeing's factories at Seattle suffered from the decline in the growth of air travel in the mid-1970s, but these northwestern states, along with Wyoming and Idaho, work to preserve their natural advantages.

In all this western part[26], although fruit-growing was the first activity and is still immensely flourishing, life is mainly urban, based on specialised industries flourishing, life is mainly urban, based on specialised industries demanding high-level skill and training. In the far west everything man-made is new, and although, as everywhere else, city streets and suburban houses look much the same as in all the rest of the United States, the newness belongs unquestionably here. This is a land made by modern man for his enjoyment, although the process brings unpleasant features with it, such as a crime rate double the national average, But without the west modern America would not be complete; both geographically and sentimentally there is a sense in which it all leads out to California.

California has one place whose fame goes back to the early days of the great rush to prosperity and growth: Hollywood. No institution has ever before been such an instrument for conveying images and myths about any one country to every corner of the world. There must be few people anywhere who have not seen America's past and present represented in films and television serials. The picture may be partly false or misleading, with too much emphasis on crime and violence: but however much one may criticise the mass media of entertainment, it is appropriate that they started in California and have grown up with it. Hollywood has a good claim to interpret America to the world, because it is in the place where all American civilisation is distilled into an image of its own destiny[27].

Words & Expressions

comprehend/ˌkɔmpriˈhend/*vt.* 包括
physical conditions 自然条件
swamp/swɔmp/*n.* 沼泽
megalopolis/ˌmegəˈlɔpəlis/*v.* 特大都市
assimilate/əˈsimileit/*vt.* 同化
ethnic/ˈeθnik/*a.* 少数民族的
the Union/ˈjuːnjən/*n.* 美利坚合众国,美国联邦
seaboard/ˈsiːbɔːd/*n.* 沿海
sheriff/ˈʃerif/*n.* 地方(县)行政司法长官
statehood/ˈsteithud/*n.* 州地位
superimpose/ˈsjuːpərimˈpəuz/*vt.* 添加
embody/imˈbɔdi/*vt.* 包含
metropolis/miˈtrɔpəlis/*n.* 大城市
magnet/ˈmægnit/*n.* 吸引力
town-dweller/taunˈdwelə/*n.* 城里人
Broadway/ˈbrɔːdwei/*n.* 百老汇街
borough/ˈbarə/*n.* 行政区
Ontario/ɔˈɛəriəu/*n.* 安大略湖
Erie/ˈiəri/*n.* 伊利湖
Niagara Falls/naiˈægərə/*n.* 尼亚加拉大瀑布
jurisdiction/ˌdʒuərisˈdikʃən/*n.* 管辖范围
hydro-electric/ˈhaidrəu-iˈlektrik/*a.* 水力发电的
Caribbean/ˌkæriˈbi(ː)ən/*a.* 加勒比海的
palpable/ˈpælpəbl/*a.* 容易觉察出来的
Siberia/saiˈbiəriə/*n.* 西伯利亚
barren/ˈbærən/*a.* 荒芜的
arid/ærid/*a.* 干旱的
quintuple/ˈkwintjy(ː)pl/*vt.* 增加五倍
canyon/ˈkænjən/*n.* 峡谷

Notes

1. The great Republic... in the 1780s: 美利坚共和国和 18 世纪 80 年代建国时相比已发生了很大的变化,就是在地域上也大不相同了。

2. the thirty-five continental states: 美国大陆上的 35 个州,不包括阿拉斯加州和夏威夷。阿拉斯加州位于北美北端,它与美国大陆中间隔着加拿大。夏威夷州位于太平洋北部洋面。

3. that piece... revives: 西部影片经常描写的美国人征服西部过程中的故事。

4. the mother country: 英国被称为英属北美十三个州的母国。

5. Regional variations... apart: 美国英语中各地口音差别不大。最南部的美国人的口音与"北方佬"的口音之间的差别,在德国人或意大利人看来,还不如居住在两小时路程以外的两个英国人的口音明显。the deep south 指美国最南部地区,如佐治亚、密西西比等州。

the Yankee 原来泛指新英格兰人，南北战争以后，南方人贬称北方人为“北方佬”，第一次世界大战时，英国人称美国人为“美国佬”，现在，世界不少地区的人，尤其是和美国关系紧张地区的人贬称美国人为“美国佬”。

6. four time zones：美国大陆本土划分为四个时区，即东部标准时间，中部标准时间，山区标准时间和太平洋沿岸标准时间，从东到西，每个时区相差一小时。

7. It is not that... feel oppressed：这并不是说个人的生活习惯的一致性令人厌烦。这种一致性是建立在原先的多样性之上的。单一的方式使人与人之间的关系变得很友好随和，不会使人感到压抑。

8. The statistics... each day：对于城乡人口的统计数字要作仔细的分析，因为许多人住在农村，但每天驱车到城里上班。

9. As the rush... with houses：因为大批人搬出城市，涌向农村，而且这种趋势还在继续，因此，在接近城镇的那些农村地区，出现了越来越多的房屋。

10. every great city... quality：而每一个大城市都是一个单一的都市。

11. the constituent pieces are interchangeable：（超级市场上的）各种货物都很相同，可以互相替代。constituent pieces 原指组成整体的各个部件。

12. the great state that takes its name from the city at its southernmost tip：纽约市位于以该市命名的巨大的纽约州的最南端。

13. Manhattan Island：曼哈顿位于纽约市内的东南部，哈得逊河与东河之间的岩岛，是纽约的市中心。

14. Wall Street：纽约市华尔街位于曼哈顿地区，是美国的主要金融中心。

15. the Empire State Building：帝国大厦是位于纽约市曼哈顿中部的一座办公大楼，建于 1930 ~ 1931 年，高 102 层(381 米，不包括 1951 年在楼顶上修建的高 68 米的电视塔)。

16. Rockefeller Centre：洛克菲勒中心大楼群，其中 14 幢包括 70 层高的美国广播公司大厦建于 1931 ~ 1939 年。这些大楼里有办公室、商店、饭店、展览厅、广播室、电影院等。

17. District of Columbia：哥伦比亚特区为纪念哥伦布而命名。美国首都所在的行政区域。

18. The train from Boston... built up：火车从波士顿出发，穿过普罗维登斯市，到纽约，再到费城和巴尔的摩，最后到首府华盛顿。中间经过的大部分地区都是人口集中，建筑林立。从费城到纽约之间以及这两个城市周边的一大片几乎全是密集的建筑。

19. the commercial capital and most the established centres of culture：商业之都是指纽约市，传统的文化中心在这里指波士顿地区、纽约地区以及费城等。

20. hoping not to see their homes .. autumn：（这些退休的北方人）不想呆在北方，不想在秋天看到他们的家被飓风所毁(北方秋天常有飓风发生)。

21. home of the great American gods... Chrysler：底特律是大家所崇拜的三大汽车公司的所在地，这就是福特汽车公司、通用汽车公司和克莱斯勒汽车公司。

22. Unrestricted gambling and easy divorce laws：在美国的某些地区如内华达州，赌博是合法的，政府对赌博没有任何限制。另外，有些州根据本州法律，离婚比别的州容易得多，如内华达州的赌城雷诺(Reno)。该城被称为“世界离婚之都”。

23. Steinbeck's Okies in The Grapes of Wrath：Okies，流动的季节性农工，尤指 30 年代

由于干旱从俄克拉何马及大平原的其他地区迁往西部的流动农工。

24. Roaring, fast-growing America has its centrepiece here：生气勃勃、飞跃发展的美国在这里有最吸引的人地方。centrepiece 意为引人注目之物。

25. British Columbia：加拿大西部的一个省，和美国西北部的华盛顿等州相邻，森林，矿产等资源极其丰富。

26. western part：美国西部地区（the west）由 11 个州组成，即 Montana, Wyoming, Colorado, New Mexico, Idaho, Utah, Nevada, Arizona 8 个州加上太平洋东岸的 3 个州：Washington, Oregon, and California。

27. Hollywood... its own destiny：好莱坞可以宣称它最有资格向全世界介绍美国，因为在这里，美国文化的每一方面都以它自身的特点被提炼成形象的东西向世界推出。

Exercises

Ⅰ. Explain the following

1. New England
2. the Mid-Atlantic area
3. Washington, D. C.
4. the Great Plain states

Ⅱ. Fill in the blanks

1. The Republic of the United States consists of __________ states with __________ states at the time of independence, __________ continental states which have been added since independence, __________ and __________ which were granted statehood in 1959.
2. The largest state in terms of area is __________ and the largest state in terms of population is __________.
3. In the United States, there are four time zones from east to west: 1 __________, 2 __________, 3 __________, 4 __________.
4. New England consists of these six states: __________, __________, __________, __________, __________ and __________.
5. The mid-Atlantic states refer to these five states: __________, __________, __________, __________ and __________.
6. The dividing line between the north and the south is __________ River, with the city __________ on the border between the two parts.
7. __________ mountains run from far south in Georgia northwards to __________ and __________.
8. __________ The __________ mountains are situated in the east and the __________ mountains are in the west.
9. The Pacific coast these three states, __________, __________, and __________.
10. The United States continent is divided into the following major parts: __________, __________, __________, __________, __________ and __________.

Ⅲ. Choose the correct answer in each of the following

1. How many of the states in the Republic of the Untied States are on the continent of North America?

   A. 50.

   B. 49.

   C. 48.

   D. 35.

2. Which of the following is not true about the characteristics of New England?

   A. Economically backward.

   B. Long established.

   C. Small-scale.

   D. Urban.

3. Which of the following is the most "English"?

   A. The east coast of the U. S. .

   B. The mid-Atlantic states.

   C. Northern New England.

   D. Southern New England.

4. Which of the following is not in New York City?

   A. Wall Street.

   B. The Empire State Building.

   C. The Black quarter of Harlem.

   D. Niagara Falls.

5. Washington. D. C. is named ______

   A. after the U. S. President George Washington

   B. after Christopher Columbus

   C. after both George Washington and Christopher Columbus

   D. after none of them

6. Texas is famous for three of the following except ______.

   A. unrestricted gambling and easy divorce laws

   B. cowboy tradition

   C. many millionaires

   D. oil industry

Ⅳ. Answer the following questions briefly

1. How has the Republic of the United States grown in terms of area since the time of its foundation in the 1780s?

2. What are some of the characteristics of the uniformity in American culture?

3. What are some of the characteristics of the Great Plain states?

4. Why have so many people joined the search for the California dream?

Chapter 12 American History

What is an American? This has become a classic question asked not only by foreigners visiting the united States, but more often by Americans themselves. When Americans feel confused or when they are in a crisis, they ask who they are and try to find out what being an American means. In fact, this famous question was first asked by a Frenchman called J. Hector St. John de Crevecoeur[1] who settled in Pennsylvania in the 18th century. In 1782, this French farmer published a book in London entitled Letters from an American Farmer in which he posed the question and answered it himself: "What then is the American, this new man? He is either a European, or the descendant of a European, hence that strange mixture of blood, which you will find in no other country. I could point out to you a family whose grandfather was an Englishman, whose wife was Dutch, whose son married a French woman, and whose present four sons have now four wives of different nations. He is an American, who leaving behind him all his ancient prejudices and manners, receives new ones from the new mode of life he has embraced, the new government he obeys, and the new rank he holds[2]... Here individuals of all nations are melted into a new race of men, whose labors and posterity will one day cause great changes in the world[3]... The American is a new man, who acts upon new principles; he must therefore entertain new ideas, and form new opinions[4]... This is an American." According to Crevecoeur, the American in those days had the mixed blood of Europeans or their descendants without taking into consideration other nationalities such as American Indians and blacks. Today, the picture of an American is more complex. In American families, there may be sons-in-law or daughters-in-law with European descendants or Afro-Americans[5] or Asian immigrants although these mixed blood families of whites with other blacks or Asians are in the minority. To understand this American, let us go back to American past.

A New Land

The American continents were peopled as a result of two long-continuing immigration movements, the first from Asia, and the second from Europe and Africa. This first movement began probably 25 000 years ago when Siberian tribes, in search of new hunting grounds or of refuge from pursuing enemies, crossed over the Bering

Strait to Alaska[6]. By 1492, over 10 to 20 million people, mistakenly called Indians by Christopher Columbus, inhabited the Americas[7]. They developed their own aboriginal cultures, which ranged from the simple to the complex, from those of the primitive tribes to the brilliant civilizations of the Aztecs, the Incas and the Mayas[8]. But their technological development had lagged behind that of Europe and Asia.

The second migration to the Americas began with the expansion of Europe at the start of the modern period from the 16th century. In 1492, Columbus persuaded the king and queen of Spain to finance his voyage. he believed that by sailing west from Europe, he could reach the Far East. he never succeeded, but instead he landed on one of the Bahama Islands in the Caribbean Sea and "discovered" the new World. Based on Columbus' discovery, the Spanish king could claim the territory in the Americas and later Spain conquered the new land and established a huge empire and grabbed enormous wealth from the Indians. In 1497, another Italian sailor, John Cabot[9] who was in the service of the English king, arrived in today's Canada and the English king claimed that the whole of the territory of North America belonged to England. Enforcing this claim, the Englishmen began to establish permanent settlements in North America by the beginning of the 17th century.

Europe in the 16th and 17th Centuries

The English permanent settlements in North America began in the 17th century when Western Europe was undergoing great changes. During the Middle Ages (between A. D. 500 and A. D. 1500), Europe was under the single spiritual authority of the Roman Catholic Church[10]. The feudal system of serfdom prevailed. The peasants, or the serfs, were tied to the soil and worked in the fields for their lords. Merchants and craftsmen were handicapped by the social disorders. Art and learning were controlled by the Church. By the 16th century, some new and powerful social forces began to emerge which led to the awakening of Europe and the discovery of America. The first new force was the development of capitalism. The growth of capitalism produced two new classes — the bourgeois class and the working class. With the fast development of commerce and trade, the bourgeoisie became increasingly powerful in politics as well as in economy. They wanted to share power with feudal lords and in some countries such as England they wanted to have more power from the king so that they could have free development. The English Revolution was the result of this growth of capitalism.

The second major force that brought about the modern development of Europe was the Renaissance, which was marked by a changing outlook on life[11]. The God-centered world was challenged by the great progress in natural and social science. People began to be more confident in themselves and show more interest in the world about them. Many challenged the authority of the Bible[12] and were willing to observe, experiment and test truths for themselves. This attitude pushed the development of technology.

The third influential force was the Religious Reformation, a religious reform movement that started from Germany. In 1517, Martin Luther[13], a German professor of theology, put up "95 Theses" on the church door in protest against abuses and corruption in the church. He argued that the Pope had no right to sell "indulgences" for the remission of sins[14]. He believed that sinful men could win salvation neither by good works nor through the church or the Pope, but only by faith in Jesus Christ and through a direct relationship to God[15]. And the only true guide to the will of God was the Bible. Because Martin Luther protested against the Catholic Church, the Reformation came to be called the Protestant Reformation. Soon after Martin Luther began his revolt, John Calvin[16], a Frenchman, who had fled to Switzerland, started his reform movement. Calvinism which had many followers in England will be dealt with later. In England, King Henry VIII, because of the political disputes with the Roman Catholic Church and because of his personal marital problems, broke away from the Roman Catholic Church and set up the Church of England[17], and he became the head of the Church of England himself. These religious reforms had much in common. They all challenged the authority of the Pope and the Catholic Church which controlled people's religious beliefs and interfered in political affairs of the nation states. The individual Christian believers who supported the Reformation believed that human beings could be saved only by faith, by establishing a direct contact with God, not through the church or its priests. These reforms reflected the rise of nationalism in Europe, represented the demand of the bourgeois class for free development and expressed the desire of ordinary working people, especially the serfs, for the liberation from the feudal control[18]. Therefore, the Protestant Reformation was welcomed by leaders, middle class and working people in Europe, especially in Western European countries. As a result, the Protestants and their denominations spread far and wide.

Against the background of those emerging new forces, the 13 English colonies that would become the United States of America were planted in North America.

The Settlement in Virginia

The first English permanent settlement was founded in 1607 in Virginia. This was organized by the London Company[19] with a charter from the English king James I. The company sent three small ships with 144 English men to Virginia. During the long voyage across the Atlantic Ocean, 44 people died and 100 survivors landed by the side of a river, the James River, which they named after their king and began to build a town called Jamestown. Most of the 100 colonists were adventurous English gentlemen including some business people who refused to do any manual labour, and very few of them were willing laborers. Yet the London Company had wished to have a quick return for its investment and had instructed them to hunt for gold and other wealth as soon as they landed in Virginia. When the colonists settled down, they did not grow food. Instead, a few laborers among them started to dig for gold and look for other riches while those English gentlemen were idle, doing nothing. Unfortunately, nothing was found. Soon they ran into the shortage of food. When the second group of men were sent by the London Company with supplies, all but 38 of the first arrivals were dead. Jamestown was in a great crisis. Then Captain John Smith took the leadership. He imposed discipline by making everyone work. A few years later, another colonist, John Rolfe began to experiment with the West Indian Tobacco and this plant grew well in Virginia soil. Tobacco cultivation quickly spread up and down the settlement and yielded profits by selling tobacco to Europe. Meanwhile, John Rolfe married the princess of an Indian tribe chief [20]. This marriage led to the ending of hostility between the white people and Indians for some time[21]. The plantation of tobacco saved the settlers and the marriage gave time to the colonists for development.

In 1619, two events took place in Virginia, which would influence the shaping of American culture a great deal. On July 30, 1619, in the Jamestown church, the delegates elected from various communities in Virginia met as the House of Burgesses to discuss, along with the governor and his council members[22] who were appointed, the enactment of laws for the colony. This was the first example for the future United. States, the first meeting of an elected legislature, a representative assembly, in North America. It was thought to be the brilliant example of self-government of Americans although white servants did not have their representatives. A month later there occurred in Virginia another event. A Dutch ship brought in over 20 Negroes, who were bought to be held as servants for a term of years. Thus a start had been made toward the enslavement of Africans within what was to be the American republic. The two events combined constituted a unique American phenomenon[23]. On the one hand, the English and other Europeans went to North America for seeking freedom. But on the other hand, these very white people who were seeking and fighting for their own freedom deprived black Africans of their freedom. George Washington[24] was a great fighter for American freedom, and Thomas Jefferson[25] was a chief author of the Declaration of Independence, and yet both of them were slave owners, each with over 200 black slaves.

Puritan New England

New England today includes Massachusetts, Connecticut, new Hampshire, Vermont, Maine and Rhode Island in the Northeast of the United States. The second enduring English settlement was established in Massachusetts Bay in 1620. It was founded by English puritans who separated themselves from the Church of England. As mentioned above, King Henry VIII cut off the political relationship with the Pope in Rome and set up the Church of England, but there was no reform in religious beliefs and practices. A group of people thought that the Church of England was too catholic and wanted to "purify" the church, hence the name "puritans"[26]. These puritans were Protestants who followed the doctrine preached by John Calvin. They had some different religious beliefs from the Catholic Church. They believed that God was incomprehensible to man, and the power of God was all-knowing, yet hidden and unknown to man, while Catholics believed that God could be reached through his representative on the earth — the Pope[27]. Puritan salvation was different from that of Catholics. Puritans were convinced that human beings were predestined by God before they were born[28]. Some were God's chosen people while others were predestined to be damned to hell. Therefore no good works could save anyone, and nobody knew if he or she was God's elect[29]. But Catholics argued that a person could confess his or her sin, do good works and give money to the church and buy back his or her soul. Was there any evidence for Puritans to show that some people were God's chosen people? Puritans believed that everyone had a calling, which was given by God. The success of one's work or the prosperity in his calling was the sign of being God' select[30]. Therefore, everyone must work hard, spend little and invest for more business. Working hard and living a moral life were their ethics[31]. How could Puritans find God's will and establish a direct contact with God? They concluded that the Bible was the authority of their doctrine. So every Puritan must read the Bible in order to find God's will and search for one's individual contact with God[32]. To be able to read the Bible and understand God's will, education was essential for Puritans.

Such Puritan beliefs were heretical to the Church of England, so they were cruelly persecuted. Some of them were thrown into prison and even executed for their religious beliefs. Some of them fought back and started the English Revolution. Oliver Cromwell, one of the Puritans, became the revolutionary leader, overthrew the monarchy, had King Charles I beheaded and founded a republic. Some other Puritans thought that England was too corrupted and hopeless and decided to separate themselves from England. They fled to Holland where there was religious freedom[33]. There they were allowed to meet and hold their services without interference. But as foreigners, they were not allowed to join the Dutch guilds of craftsmen[34], and so they had to work long and hard at unskilled and poorly paid jobs. They were further troubled as their children began to speak Dutch, marry into Dutch families, and lose their Englishness[35]. Some of the Puritans decided to move again, this time across the Atlantic, where they might find an opportunity for a happier living and also worship as they pleased. The leaders of this group of Puritans found the necessary funds for the voyage from some merchants in London. In 1620, 35 Puritans and 67 non-Puritans took the ship Mayflower and left Holland for north America. Before they reached their destination, one of the Pilgrim Fathers[36] drew up an agreement which was called the Mayflower Compact[37] and was signed by 41 of the passengers. They formed their own religious community and set up a civil government for the general good of the colony they were going to found in the new land[38]. They settled at Plymouth, Massachusetts. A much larger Puritan colony was established in the Boston area in 1630 and by 1635 more Puritan settlers were migrating to nearby Connecticut.

Puritanism in New England changed gradually due to the frontier environment and the mobility of the population[39]. As time went on, many of the new generations no longer adhered to the orthodox Puritanism. Many moved to the West and other parts of the United States. Today, Puritans are no longer in existence. But their legacies are still felt in American society and culture. For example, the Puritans hoped to build "a city upon hill" — an ideal community[40]. Since that time, Americans have viewed their country as a great experiment, a worthy model for other nations. This sense of mission has been very strong in the minds of many Americans[41]. New England also established another American tradition — a strain of often intolerant moralism. The Puritans believed that governments should enforce God's morality. They strictly punished drunks, adulterers, violators of the Sabbath and other religious believers different from themselves[42]. Roger Williams[43], one of the Puritans who protested that the state should not interfere with religion, was driven out of Massachusetts. In 1635, he set up Rhode Island colony, which guaranteed religious freedom and the separation of church and state. The American values such as individualism, hard work, respect of education owe very much to the Puritan beliefs[44].

Catholic Maryland

Following the two patterns of early American culture in Virginia and New England was the pattern in the colony of Maryland founded by the Catholics. The founder was the second Lord Baltimore, his father, George Calvert, was born into an ordinary English family, not from the nobility nor from a Catholic background[45]. While at oxford, he came to know some influential people, and upon his graduation, he became the secretary of state in the king's Privy Council[46]. During his service to the throne, the was converted to Roman Catholicism. This conversion created some problems for his service to the English king. In England, the king was both the head of state and the head of the Church of England. Anyone who served the king must take the oath of supremacy recognizing the monarch as the supreme head of state and church[47]. As a Catholic, Calvert could not take the oath because his religious supreme head was the Pope in Rome. So he was driven out of the court. But the English king Charles I personally excused him and made him a noble with the title of Baron Baltimore[48]. As he had the experience of being suppressed for his Catholic beliefs and witnessed the persecution of his fellow Catholics, he decided to find a haven in North America for his persecuted fellow religious believers. He went to his old friend King Charles I and asked for his help. In 1623, he was granted a charter from the king and was allowed to set up a colony in today's Maryland. But before he could do so, he died. his son, the second Lord Baltimore, carried out his father's will in 1632. he became the owner of the colony, captain-general of the armed forces, head of the church and disposer of all offices and the governor. In fact, he had the power comparable to that of the king in England. All the had to do was the promise of one-fifth of all the gold and silver discovered in Maryland and two Indian arrowheads a year to the king[49].

Lord Baltimore wished to introduce a feudal system similar to the manor system in Europe to his colony. His plan was that each gentleman who brought 5 servants with him settled in his land was allowed to establish a manor of 2 000 acres. This gentleman had the privileges received in England, the privileges such as wearing distinctive medals to set the manor lord apart from the common herd[50]. Lord Baltimore also declared that each freeholder was given 100 acres of land plus another 100 acres for his wife, 100 acres for a servant, and 50 acres for each of his children. But the freeholders could not enjoy the rights and privileges as the gentlemen, Both lords and freeholders must pay some rent to Lord Baltimore. Gentlemen's lands were to be tilled by indentured servants[51].

this feudal plan was bound to be doomed as were other feudal plans experimented with in North America due to various factors in the new World. In order to develop his colony, Baltimore had to attract as many settlers as possible to his land. So he encouraged the immigration of Protestants as well as Roman Catholics. Since relatively few of the Catholics were inclined to leave England, the Protestant settlers soon far outnumbered the Catholics. In 1648, Lord Baltimore appointed a Protestant governor, and the next year, the Maryland Toleration Act, which assured freedom of worship to all who believed in Jesus Christ, was passed[52]. Because the Protestant majority were capitalistic-minded people and refused to carry out the feudal plan[53], and because the wilderness of North America provided plenty of land while labor was scarce, it was impossible for Lord Baltimore to have his feudal plan executed. Not long after the founding of his colony, the feudal experimental plan was dropped, and the colony, like other colonies in North America, followed a capitalist development road.

Quaker Pennsylvania

The fourth colonial pattern in North America was set by William Penn, an English Quaker who had been looking for a place for his fellow believers to live according to their religious faith. The term "Quakers" was coined by their enemies because the Quakers were so faithful to God that when they spoke of God, they trembled. These Quakers, though they were Protestants, had very different religious beliefs not only from the Catholics, but also from Puritans and other Protestant sects. They denied both the church and the Bible as the highest authority. They believed that people could communicate directly with God because everyone had an inner light and God was in everyone's soul and in man's heart[54]. They believed in God through their faith without the help of church and priests. They did not build and church and did not train any priest. Their religious place of worship was called a meeting place, which could be anywhere[55]. Since everyone had a divine light in his heart, all were born equal, and all were brothers and sisters[56]. People were not born sinful. Quakers had their own way of life too. They lived a simple life, with thrifty and self-denial. They believed that God required everyone to work hard and have a productive life. Even in jail, they busily set about working at crafts[57]. They refused all forms of war and followed a passive resistance. Their religious beliefs taught them that everyone was equal, so they refused to take off their caps to nobles when they met them and even refused to bow to the king[58]. They wore plain clothes and used plain language. They rejected all the polite forms which were used in high society. As they rejected the authority of church, they refused to pay taxes for the support of the church. As a result, they were persecuted, and many of them were put into prison. William Penn, the founded of Pennsylvania, was such a Quaker.

William Penn's father was the admiral of England and a member of the Church of England. When a soot Penn was at Oxford, he was converted and became a confirmed Quaker. For this, he was thrown into jail, and his father threatened to cut him off financially. All this could not prevent him from his religious determination. In 1681, after his father's death, he used the debt of 16 000 pounds King Charles II owed to his father as an excuse and asked the king to grant him a right to plant a colony in North America[59]. He received the grant from the king and decided to found a colony for his persecuted fellow Quakers in today's Pennsylvania, a name after his father. Before he went to Pennsylvania, he wrote a pamphlet called "Some Account of the Province of Pennsylvania", which was translated into several European languages and circulated far and wide. In the pamphlet, he explained his plan. All those who settled in his land would enjoy religious freedom. This was a great attraction to thousands of people with different religious backgrounds who were being persecuted for their religion in Europe. Another great appeal to Europeans, especially to those peasants hungry for land, was that he offered very easy terms for land. Anyone who would settle in his colony could get some land almost for nothing. many Europeans were attracted to go to live in Pennsylvania, Germans, French people, Irish people, Northern Europeans as well as the English. When Penn arrived in his colony, he started to carry out what the called "the Holy Experiment". From his religious belief that man was not born sinful and everyone was born equal, he encouraged the spirit of liberty and equality. he set no restrictions on immigration, and naturalization was made easier for non-English people. So many American historians believe that the idea of the melting-pot was first practiced here[60]. William Penn also established a liberal self-government. In his colony, there was a representative assembly elected by the landowners, and death penalty was imposed only for the two crimes of treason and murder, as compared with about 200 crimes leading to capital punishment in England at the time. The Quakers argued that religion was a person's private business with God, therefore no government should interfere in his or her religious beliefs. In accordance with Quakerism, William Penn carried out the policy of separation of state and church in his colony. Penn's holy experiment had great impact on American culture. Voltaire[61] always held this colony up as proof that man could lead a good life without absolute monarch, feudalism or religious and racial uniformity. Some American founding fathers such as Thomas Jefferson and Benjamin Franklin[62] were inspired by Penn's experiment.

The American Revolution

Those four patterns set by the early colonial leaders were filled with meanings for the future development of the United States. By the early 1760s, the 13 English colonies in North America had developed a similar American pattern in politics, economy and cultural life and enjoyed the same frontier environment. The English people and Europeans had become Americans and the were ready to separate themselves from the Old World. The American Revolution officially proclaimed the birth of a new nation of Americans.

On the eve of the American Revolution, while the 13 English colonies occupied the Atlantic coast, from New Hampshire in the north to Georgia in the south, the French controlled Canada and Louisiana[63]. Between 1689 and 1815, France and Britain fought several wars, and North America was drawn into every one of them. In 1756, England and France began to fight the Seven years' War, known in America as the French and Indian War. The English government invested soldiers and money in North America and won a great empire. The British forces captured several Canadian strong points such as Quebec and Montreal. The Peace of Paris, signed in 1763 between Britain and France, gave Britain title to Canada and all of North America east of the Mississippi River.

Britain's victory led directly to a conflict with its American colonies. The British government argued that Britain had spent large sums of money to defend their American colonies in those wars, and that the colonists therefore should pay a part of those expenses. As a result, the British government began to charge new taxes on sugar, coffee, textiles and other imported goods. For instance, with the passage of the Stamps Act, special tax stamps had to be attached to all newspapers, pamphlets, legal documents and licenses[64]. The Quartering Act passed by British Parliament forced the colonies to house and feed British soldiers[65]. But the Americans feared that new taxes would make trading difficult, and that British troops stationed in the colonies might be used to crush the civil liberties which the colonists had heretofore enjoyed[66]. The colonial Americans insisted that they could be taxed only by their own colonial assemblies. "No taxation without representation" was their rallying cry[67]. The colonists refused to obey the British laws, so British soldiers were sent to Boston.

In 1773, a group of patriots responded to the tea tax by staging the "Boston tea Party"[68]. Disguised as Indians, they boarded British merchant ships and tossed 342 crates of tea into Boston harbor. British Parliament then passed the Intolerable Acts: The independence of the Massachusetts colonial government was sharply curtailed[69], and more British soldiers were sent to the port of Boston, which was now closed to shipping. In September 1774, the First Continental Congress, a meeting of colonial leaders who opposed British oppression in the colonies, met in Philadelphia. These leaders urged Americans to disobey the Intolerable Acts and to boycott British trade. At the same time, the colonists began to organize militias and collect and store weapons and ammunition in order to defend themselves. On April 19, 1775, the first shot was fired when 700 British soldiers went to capture a colonial arms depot in a small town of Concord near Boston. Thus the American War of Independence began.

In May 1775, a second Continental Congress met in Philadelphia and began to assume the functions of a national government[70]. It founded a Continental Army and Navy under the command of George Washington. On July 2, 1776, the Congress finally resolved that "these United Colonies are, and of right ought to be free and independent states"[71]. Thomas Jefferson of Virginia, assisted by John Adams[72] and Benjamin Franklin, drafted *Declaration of Independence*, which the Congress adopted on July 4, 1776. The Declaration officially proclaimed the independence of 13 North American colonies. it solemnly declared that "We hold these truths to be self-evident, that all men are created equal; that they were endowed by their Creator with certain unalienable rights; that among these, are life, liberty and the pursuit of happiness"[73]. Most importantly, it explained the philosophy of governments: "to secure these rights, governments are instituted among men, deriving their just powers from the consent of the governed;"[74] "whenever any form of government becomes destructive of these ends, it is the right of the people to alter or to abolish it, and to institute a new government, laying its foundation on such principles, and organizing its powers in such form, as to them shall seem most likely to effect their safety and happiness."[75] This theory of politics and a guiding principle of the American Revolution came from John Locke[76], an English political philosopher in the 17 th century.

The War of Independence came to end in 1781 with the victory of North Americans. The Treaty of Paris was signed in 1783 and Britain had to recognize the independence of the United States. A new American nation was thus born.

Words & Expressions

Dutch /dʌtʃ/ *adj.* 荷兰
posterity /pɔs'teriti/ *n.* 后代
Bering Strait 白令海峡
Alaska /ə'læskə/ *n.* 阿拉斯加
migration /mai'greiʃən/ *n.* 迁移
Bahama Islands 巴哈马群岛
Caribbean Sea 加勒比海
serfdom /'səːfdəm/ *n.* 农奴制
bourgeoisie /ˌbuəʒwaː'zi/ *n.* 资产阶级
Calvinism /'kælvinizəm/ *n.* 加尔文义
burgess /'bəːdʒis/ *n.* 议员(美史)
enactment /'inæktmənt/ *n.* 立法
enslavement /in'sleivmənt/ *n.* 奴役
elect /i'lekt/ *n.* 上帝的选民
nobility /nəu'biliti/ *n.* 贵族
privy /'privi/ *n.* 顾问,王室
supremacy /sju(ː)'preməsi/ *n.* 最高地位
indentured /in'dentʃəd/ *adj.* 定有契约的
naturalization /ˌnætʃərəlai'zeiʃən/ *n.* 入国籍
Old World 旧世界(欧洲)
Quebec /kwi'bek/ *n.* 魁北克(加拿大一省)
Montreal /ˌmʌntriː'ɔːl/ *n.* 蒙特利尔(加拿大一城)
boycott /'bɔikət/ *v.* 抵制

Notes

1. J. Hector St. John de Crevecoeur:赫克托・圣约翰・德克雷夫科尔是美国革命时期移居宾夕法尼亚地区的一位法国农人。他根据自己的生活经历,于1782年写了《美国农人书简》一书,提出了有关美国民族特性的这样一个经典性问题。

2. he is and American ... the new rank he holds:美国人是这样的人:他把所有过去的偏见和习俗抛在脑后,而从他所热爱的新的生活方式、他所依附的新政府、他享有的新地位中接受新的一套。leave behind:遗忘,抛在脑后

3. Here individuals of all nations ... great changes in the world:来自各个种族的人,在此熔化为一个新的民族,他们的劳动及他们的后代必将给世界带来巨大变化。不少历史学家认为,美国是大熔炉的思想源于此话。当然,德克雷夫科尔的所谓民族大熔炉的思想史包括欧洲白人,他把印第安人和黑人安全排除在外。

4. The American is a new man ... form new opinions:美国人是一种新型的人,他按新的

原则办事，他因此必须吸取新的思想，形成新的见解。这里讲的新思想、新见解实际上就是《独立宣言》中阐述的思想原则。

5. Afro-Americans：非洲裔美国人。这是美国黑人通过长期斗争使自己的社会地位有所改善之后，当今美国社会和官方对黑人的不带种族主义色彩的一种称谓。

6. The first movement began ... the Bering Strait：向美洲的第一次人口迁移运动开始在大约25 000年以前，当时在西伯利亚的部族为了寻找新的猎场或逃避追赶的敌人，越过白令海峡，到达阿拉斯加。当时的白令海峡是一片陆地，后来被海水淹没。

7. over 10-20 million people ... inhabited the Americas：大约1 000 ~ 2 000万土生土长的美洲人生活在美洲，他们被哥伦布错认为印度人。哥伦布相信地球是圆的，从大西洋向西航行就可以到达东方，到达印度。到达美洲后，他见美洲土著人像印度人，因此把他们错认为东方的印度人。中文译为“印第安人”。这些印第安人后被欧洲殖民主义者征服，在他们的灭绝性屠杀及残酷奴役掠夺下，又经不起欧洲人带来的疾病的袭击，印第安人人口急剧下降。

8. the brilliant civilizations of the Aztecs, the Incas and the Mayas：印第安人创造的辉煌的阿兹台克文化（墨西哥地区）、印加文化（秘鲁地区）及玛雅文化（中美洲）。这些文化当时在许多方面比欧洲还先进，但后来被欧洲殖民主义者摧毁。

9. John Cabot：约翰·卡伯特。意大利航海家，1497年他为英王亨利七世航行到达今天的加拿大，他却以为到了亚洲的东海岸。第二年他到达今天的美国东海岸。他向英王报告发现了新的领土。英王根据他的报告宣称北美大陆属英国所有，为以后英国的殖民主义活动打下了所谓“合法”的基础。

10. Europe was under the single spiritual authority of the Roman Catholic Church：欧洲当时处于罗马天言教的单一精神权威统治之下。16世纪的宗教改革运动打破了这种局面。

11. which was marked by a changing outlook on life：文艺复兴的显著特点是人们的人生观的变化。人们开始注意个人在世的生活，而不像以前只注意死后是否进天堂的问题。

12. many challenged the authority of the Bible：许多人向《圣经》的权威性发起了挑战。不少科学家对“上帝创世说”开始怀疑，他们注意科学实验，在天文、物理等领域取得了许多重大发现。

13. martin Luther：马丁·路德。16世纪宗教改革运动的发起者，德国神学院教授。他发起的宗教改革运动对欧美资本主义及其文化的发展起了极其重要的作用。

14. sell “indulgences” for the remission of sins：出售“赎罪券”以减免罪孽。中世纪天主教教廷向教徒出售“赎罪券”，说教徒因此可以免罪或减少在地狱中的痛苦。他们以此办法弥补财政亏空，遭到路德等宗教改革派的强烈批判。

15. through a direct relationship to God：通过个人与上帝的直接联系获得拯救。路德认为，所谓“积德”只会产生出售“赎罪券”的腐败行为，教会或教皇也不是上帝在人间的代表，因此不可能代表教徒与上帝取得联系。

16. John Calvin：约翰·加尔文。法国神学家，后移居瑞士。他是16世纪宗教改革运动中最重要的人物之一，对美国影响极大的清教主义来源于他的学说。

17. In England, King Henry VIII ... the Church of England：在英国，国王亨利八世因与罗马教皇的政治争论和自己的婚姻问题同罗马教廷决裂，成立英国国教。亨利八世认为，教皇不应干涉英国内政,他自己要离婚或结婚不得由教皇决定,所以宣布在政治上脱离与教皇的关系,但在教义及宗教仪式上没有作任何变动。

18. These reforms ... for the liberation from the feudal control:这些改革反映了欧洲高涨的民族主义情绪,代表了资产阶级要求自由发展的呼声,表达了普通劳动者、特别是农奴们要求从封建统治中获得解放的愿望。所以,宗教改革运动得到了中下阶层的欢迎。

19. the London Company:伦敦贸易公司。英国是最早成立合股贸易公司进行资本主义经营的欧洲国家之一。

20. John Rolfe married the princess of an Indian tribe chief:约翰·罗尔夫与印第安人一部族首领的公主 Pocahontas 结为伉俪。

21. This marriage ... for some time:这桩婚事暂时结束了白人与印第安人之间的敌对活动。不久,这两个民族之间的战事又起,其根本的原因是英国殖民主义者企图征服、消灭印第安人。

22. met as the House of Burgesses ... his council members:弗吉尼亚民选代表聚会组成议会,同总督及他任命的议事们一起治理这块殖民地。这是北美议会民主制的畸形。

23. The two events combined constituted a unique American phenomenon:这两个事件构成了独特的美国现象。白人移民一方面为自己的自由平等而努力奋斗,另一方面却又剥夺黑人及印第安人的自由和平等,奴役他们。

24. George Washington:乔治·华盛顿。弗吉尼亚人,美国的开国元勋,独立战争时期的大陆军总司令,美国制宪会议的主席,美利坚合众国首任总统(1789~1798)。任职8年后决定不再竞选,回乡务农,管理他自己的种植园。

25. Thomas Jefferson:托马斯·杰斐逊。弗吉尼亚人,美国的开国元勋之一,《独立宣言》的主要作者。美国第三任总统(1801~1809),他被认为是美国民主的创始者。他在起草《独立宣言》时曾把反对奴隶制这一点写进文件,终因南方奴隶主的反对而未能如愿。

26. to "purify" the church, hence the name "puritans":要求"纯洁"教会,因此才有"清教徒"之名。清教徒不仅要求英国国教在政治上割断和罗马教皇的联系,而且在教义和仪式上进行改革。

27. They believed that God was incomprehensible to man ... the Pope:清教徒相信上帝对人类来说是不可知的,上帝的力量无所不能,为人所不知。而天主教却认为人可以通过上帝在人间的代表教皇同上帝取得联系。

28. Puritans were convinced ... before they were born:清教徒深信人的命运是生前就由上帝注定的。这是清教主义的命运天定说。

29. Some were God's chosen people ... if he or she was God's elect:一些人是上帝的选民,而另一些人则注定进地狱。所以,任何公德不可能拯救人,也没有人知道谁是上帝的选民。

30. The success of one's work ... the sign of being God's elect:一个人工作上的成功或事业上的兴旺是上帝选民的标志。所以清教徒必须努力工作,千方百计地挣钱,多积累。

31. Working hard and living a moral life were their ethics:清教徒的道德原则就是勤奋工作,品行端正。因为这也是上帝选民的标志之一。

32. So every Puritan ... for one's individual contact with God:清教徒必须人人读《圣

经》,从中探索上帝的意志,建立自己与上帝的联系。这是清教徒个人与上帝直接联系的方法,他们不通过教会或教士。他们强调个人,因此,美国的个人主义在很大程度上是从清教主义而来。

33. They fled to Holland where there was religious freedom:他们逃到享有宗教自由的荷兰。

34. join the Dutch guilds of craftsmen:参加荷兰手工艺人的行会。行会是封建社会的一种经济组织,目的是保护本行业和行业成员的利益。在荷兰,外国人不能参加行会,因此无法找到技术性强、报酬高的工作。

35. lose their Englishness:丢了英国的特性。在荷兰的英国人的下一代开始不讲英语,举止行为也变得荷兰化了。

36. the Pilgrim Fathers:清教移民先驱。Pilgrim 原意是朝圣者,现意新来的移民。

37. the Mayflower Compact:"五月花公约"。这是有关北美移民团体的第一个自治性公约,也是有关北美移民的最早的历史文献。这些移民先驱们起草了生死与共的公约,民主选举了总监,为尔后成立自治政府打下了基础。

38. set up a civil government ... found in the new land:为了大众的利益建立即将在新大陆诞生的殖民地的民事政府。根据"五月花公约"建立的自治政府和宗教有紧密的关系。

39. Puritanism in New England ... the mobility of the population:由于边疆的荒野环境及人口的流动,新英格兰清教主义逐渐发生变化。在人烟稀少、人口不断变化的荒野环境中,宗教观念越来越淡薄,清教主义对年轻人及后代的吸引力也越来越小。

40. build "a city upon hill" — an ideal community:清教徒希望把他们的殖民地建成一座"山巅之城",成为一个理想的社会。这种传统对后来的美国人产生很大的影响。至今,美国仍有一些人总把自己的政治制度说成是世界上最好的,并企图强加于人。

41. This sense of mission ... in the minds of many Americans:许多美国人的这种使命感很强。

42. They strictly punished ... different from themselves:他们严厉惩罚醉汉、通奸者、违反安息日规定者及宗教信仰不同于他们的人。这是清教徒在道德上的不容忍主义的表现。the Sabbath 是安息日,基督教定为星期日。他们相信,星期日应是教徒上教堂,向上帝祈祷的一天,不应进行任何商业或娱乐活动。犹太教的安息日是星期六。

43. Roger Williams:罗杰·威廉斯原是马萨诸塞地区的清教徒,但他主张宗教自由和政教分离,因而被正统清教教会驱逐出境。他随后到今天的罗得岛州,建立了北美宗教和政治上最自由的一个殖民地。

44. The American values ... owe very much to the Puritan beliefs:美国的价值观,如个人主义、勤奋工作、尊重教育等,在很大程度上源于清教主义。个人主义来源于清教的个人与上帝直接联系的教义;勤奋工作观来自清教的富裕和成功是上帝选民的象征的信念;尊重教育源于阅读《圣经》以求理解上帝旨意的清教思想。

45. not from the nobility nor from a Catholic background:既不是出身于贵族家庭,也不是出身于天主教家庭。

46. the king's Privy Council:英国国王的枢密院。这是英王的顾问委员会。

47. Anyone who served the king ... as supreme head of state and church:王室官员必须宣

誓承认国王是国家及教会的最高权威。但作为天主教徒的卡尔弗特只承认罗马教皇的最高权威而不能宣誓,因此他被驱逐出朝廷。

48. the title of Baron Baltimore:巴尔的摩男爵。英国贵族分公、侯、伯、子、男等爵位。

49. two Indian arrowheads a year to the king:每年向国王进贡两支印第安人箭头。英国国王爱好打猎,而印第安人的箭头是世界上最好的,因此国王才有此要求。

50. This gentleman ... from the common herd:绅士享有英国所有的特权,如佩带各种显耀的贵族勋章,以此把庄园主与普通老百姓区分开。the herd 是对普通百姓的蔑称。

51. indentured servants:白人契约奴。北美殖民地初期,一些英国穷人家境贫困而无力移居北美,北美的有钱人家为他们支付路费,这些人卖身为契约奴。根据契约,他们必须为有钱人家无偿劳动 5 ~7 年,在这期间他们没有自由。不久,白人契约奴被黑奴代替。

52. the Maryland Toleration Act .. was passed:马里兰宗教容忍法被通过。该法规定,凡是信仰耶稣基督的人都可以享有信仰自由。也就是说,基督教徒以外的人没有宗教自由。但和欧洲相比,这仍不失为一个进步。

53. Because the Protestant majority ... to carry out the feudal plan :因为马里兰的多数居民是新教徒,他们都是有资本主义思想的人,拒绝执行这一封建性计划;还因为北美荒野的大陆有大量土地,加上劳动力缺乏,因此,巴尔的摩勋爵无法实施他的封建制规划。

54. everyone had an inner light ... in man's heart:每个人都有灵光,上帝就在每个人的灵魂里,在每个人的心中。因此,贵格派认为他们不需要教会或教士,也不认为《圣经》是权威,他们只靠自己对上帝的信念。

55. which could be anywhere:贵格派的宗教聚会所可以设在任何地方。他们不需建设任何教堂。

56. Since everyone had a divine light ... all were brothers and sisters:既然每个人的心里都有上帝的神光,因此人人生来平等,人人都是兄弟姐妹。

57. Even in jail, they busily set about working at crafts:即使在监狱里,他们仍然忙碌着干一些手工活。他们相信,一天不干活就是对上帝缺乏虔诚。

58. refused to bow to the king:拒绝向国王鞠躬行礼。按照贵格派的教义,人人都是平等的,国王也不例外。因此,人们不必向国王脱帽行礼。

59. he used the debt of 16 000 pounds ... to plant a colony in North America:他(威廉·潘恩)以英王查理二世欠他父亲 16 000 英镑为由,要求国王在北美大陆赐给他一片土地,抵消这笔债务,他可以建立一个殖民地。国王因受议会限制不能控制国家财政收入,所以他常常向富人借钱。

60. So many historians ... first practiced here:所以许多历史学家认为,民族大熔炉的思想是首先从这里实施的。"大熔炉"一词来自剧作家以色列·赞格威尔写的同名话剧。这部描写美国民族大熔炉的话剧 1908 年在纽约上演时很叫座,如黑人、印第安人、亚裔人等。许多学者认为美国民族应是"色拉缸"。最近,多元文化论兴起,学者们认为应把多元化文化主义作为美国民族的特征。

61. Voltaire:伏尔泰。法国 18 世纪最伟大的作家和政论家,他宣传宗教和政治自由,强烈反对暴虐。

62. Benjamin Franklin:本杰明·富兰克林。美国开国元勋之一,参与起草《独立宣言》,

是制宪会议的重要成员。他出身贫穷，后在印刷业上获得成功，并在政治、科学及哲学等领域里有卓越建树，因此，他被奉为“美国梦”成功的代表。

63. Louisiana：路易斯安那地区。杰弗逊任美国总统时（1803 年）用 1 600 万美元从法国拿破仑手中购买而来的密西西比河以西的大片土地，它南起今天的路易斯安那州，北到加拿大边境，是当时美国领土的一倍。

64. with the passage of the Stamp Act ... and licenses：印花税通过以后，北美殖民者必须向英国交纳报刊、传单、法律文件及各种执照税。

65. the Quartering Act ... feed British soldiers：英国议会通过的驻军食宿法强迫殖民地老百姓为英军士兵提供食宿。

66. to crush the civil liberties which the colonists had heretofore enjoyed：剥夺殖民者（北美居民）一向享有的公民自由。英国殖民方式与西班牙不同。英国王室不直接控制北美殖民地，也不派军队。因此，殖民地白人相对比较自由。现在英国派驻军队显然是对殖民地人民自由的巨大威胁。

67. “No taxation without representation” was their rallying cry：“没有代表权就不纳税”是号召北美人民团结起来一致抗英的口号。英国一方面要殖民地人民纳税，另一方面又剥夺他们选派代表进入英国议会的权利。因此，纳税与不纳税成了殖民地人民与英国政府之间的政治斗争。

68. the “Boston Tea Party”：“波士顿茶党”。“茶党斗争”：北美殖民地人民在波士顿把英国商人的茶叶倾入大海的斗争。

69. The independence ... was sharply curtailed：马萨诸塞政府的独立受到严重限制。英国议会通过的一条法令宣布，马萨诸塞议会等官员由代表英国王室的总督任命，剥夺了人民选举自己代表的权利。

70. to assume the function of a national government：担当全国政府的功能。当时的 13 个州没有统一的领导机构，因此，大陆会议承担了这个机构的职能，领导美国革命的斗争。

71. On July 2, 1776 ... and independent states：1776 年 7 月 2 日，大陆会议做出决定：“这些联合一致的殖民地从此是自由和独立的国家。”

72. John Adams：约翰 · 亚当斯。美国的开国元勋之一，第二任美国总统（1797 ~ 1801）。

73. We hold these truths ... the pursuit of happiness：我们认为以下这些真理是不言而喻的：人人生命平等，造物者赋予他们若干不可剥夺的权利，其中包括生命权、自由权和追求幸福的权利。

74. to secure these rights ... from the consent of the governed：为了保障这些权利，人类才在他们之间建立政府，而政府之正当权力是经被统治者的同意而产生的。

75. Whenever and form of government ... to effect their safety and happiness：当任何形式的政府对这些目标具有破坏作用时，人民便有权利改变或废除它，以建立一个新的政府，其赖以奠基的原则、其组织权力的方式，务使人民认为唯有这样才最可能获得他们的安全和幸福。

76. John Locke：约翰 · 洛克（1632 ~ 1704）。英国哲学家、政论家，著有《论宽容的信札》、《政府论文》及《人类理智论》等。上述《独立宣言》中的基本原则主要来自洛克的社会契约论及他的其他思想。

Exercises

Ⅰ. Explain the following

1. Columbus' "discovery" of America
2. the Religious Reformation
3. Puritanism
4. the Pilgrim Fathers
5. Quakerism
6. the Declaration of Independence

Ⅱ. Fill in the blanks

1. In 1782, the Frenchman who settled in Pennsylvania first asked the question "what is an American" in his book ______.
2. The New World of America was peopled as a result of two long-continuing immigration movements, the first one from ______ and the second from ______ and ______.
3. American Indians had developed three brilliant civilizations before the Europeans arrived. These three civilizations were ______, ______ and ______.
4. Columbus discovered the new World in the year of ______.
5. The English king claimed the territory of North America based on the voyage of ______.
6. ______ was the first to start the Religious Reformation and the next important leader of the Reformation was ______.
7. The first permanent settlement in North America was established in today's ______ in the year of ______.
8. The crop ______ that was transplanted from the West Indian saved Virginia.
9. Lord Baltimore who set up the colony of ______ was ______ in religion.
10. New England was founded by a group of religious believers called ______ while Pennsylvania was planted by ______ who was a ______ in religion.
11. Two most important principles of the Holy Experiment were ______ and ______.
12. ______ officially proclaimed the birth of a new American nation.
13. Name two of the taxes imposed on North American colonies by the British Parliament on the eve of the American Revolution: ______ and ______.
14. The institution that began to assume the function of a national government during the American Revolution was ______.

Ⅲ. Choose the correct answer in each of the following

1. Which of the following statements was correct around the time of the American Revolution?

A. The American had the mixed blood of Europeans or their descendants.

B. The American had the mixed blood of Europeans with American Indians.

C. The American had the mixed blood of Europeans with blacks.

D. The American had the blood of English and their descendants only.

2. Which of the following was NOT one of the three forces that led to the modern development of Europe?

A. The growth of capitalism.

B. The Renaissance.

C. The Religious Reformation.

D. The spiritual leadership of the Roman Catholic Church.

3. The following were the main Reformation leaders except ________.

A. Martin Luther

B. Martin Luther King

C. John Calvin

D. The English King Henry VIII

4. The following were some of the characteristics of Protestantism except ________.

A. challenging the authority of the Pope

B. salvation through faith

C. salvation through the church

D. establishing a direct contact with God

5. Which of the following American values did NOT come from Puritanism?

A. Separation of state and church.

B. Respect of education.

C. Intolerant moralism.

D. A sense of mission.

6. Lord Baltimore's feudal plan failed because ________.

A. there were more Protestant than Catholics in Maryland

B. the wilderness of the continent made the plan impossible

C. there was plenty of land while labor was scarce

D. the English king did not like the plan

7. The following were the founding fathers of the American Republic except ________.

A. George Washington

B. Thomas Jefferson

C. William Penn

D. Benjamin Franklin

8. The theory of American politics and the American Revolution originated mainly from ________.

A. George Washington

B. Thomas Jefferson

C. John Adams

D. John Locke

9. Which of the following was NOT a denomination of Protestantism?

A. Catholics.

B. Puritans.

C. Quakers.

D. Church of England.

10. "No taxation without representation" was the rallying cry of ________.

A. the settlers of Virginia

B. the people of Pennsylvania

C. the colonists in New England

D. the people of the 13 colonies on the eve of the American Revolution

Ⅳ. Answer the following questions briefly

1. What is an American? Comment on the answer to the question by Crevecoeur.
2. How did modern development in Europe influence the settlement of North American colonies?
3. What was the unique American phenomenon?
4. In what way did Puritanism influence American culture?
5. How is it that American development was characterized with capitalism from the very beginning?
6. Comment on the Holy Experiment by William Penn.
7. What were some of the causes of the American Revolution?

Chapter 13 American Political System

The peace treaty of 1783 recognized the independence of the United States and the former 13 British colonies along the east coast of the Atlantic became 13 states of the new nation. These 13 states were: Massachusetts, Connecticut, Rhode Island and New Hampshire in New England in the Northeast; Maryland, Pennsylvania, Delaware, new York, and New Jersey in the Mid-Atlantic, and Virginia, north Carolina, South Carolina and Georgia in the South. Although the Declaration of Independence proclaimed that 13 united colonies "are, and of right ought to be, free and independent states", they were not very clear about the future political system of the United States and about the relationships between the states and the government of the new nation. A constitution was badly needed.

Articles of Confederation

When the war of Independence was over, the United States was not one unified nation as it is today. Each new state had its own government and was organized very much like an independent nation. Each made its own laws and handled all of its internal affairs. During the war, the states had agreed to work together by sending representatives to a national congress patterned after the "Congress of Delegates" that conducted the was with England. After the war was won, the Congress[1] would handle only problems and needs that the individual states could not handle alone. It would raise money to pay off debts of the war, establish a money system and deal with foreign nations in making treaties. The agreement that set this plan of cooperation was called the Articles of Confederation[2].

The Articles of Confederation failed because the states did not cooperate with the Congress or with each other. When the Congress needed money to pay the national army or to pay debts owed to France and other nations, some states refused to contribute. The Congress had been given no authority to force any state to do anything. It could not tax any citizen. Only the state in which a citizen lived could do that.

Many Americans worried about the future. How could they win the respect of other nations if the states did not pay their debts? How could they improve the country by building roads or canals if the states would not work together? They believed that the Congress needed more power.

The Congress asked each state to send delegates to a convention in Philadelphia, the city where the Declaration of Independence had been signed, to discuss the changes which would be necessary to strengthen the Articles of Confederation.

The smallest state, Rhode Island, refused, but delegates from the other 12 states participated. The meeting, later known as the Constitutional Convention, began in may of 1787. George Washington, the military hero of the War of Independence, was the Presiding officer. 54 other men were present. Some wanted a strong, new government. Some did not.

Constitution

In the course of the Convention, the delegates designed a new form of government for the United States. The plan for the government was written in very simple language in a document called the Constitution of the United States. The Constitution set up a federal system with a strong central government. A federal system in one in which power is shared between a central authority and its constituent parts, with some rights reserved to each. The Constitution also called for the election of a national leader, or president. It provided that federal laws would be made only by a Congress made up of representatives elected by the people. It also provided for a national court system headed by a Supreme Court.

In writing the Constitution, the delegates had to deal with two main fears shared by most Americans.

One fear was that one person or group, including the majority, might become too powerful or be able to seize control of the country and create a tyranny. To guard against this possibility, the delegates set up a government consisting of three parts, or branches, the executive, the legislative and the judicial. Each branch has powers that the others do not have and each branch has a way of counteracting and limiting any wrongful action by another branch.

Another fear was that the new central government might weaken or take away the power of the state governments to run their own affairs. To deal with this the Constitution specified exactly what power the central government had and which power was reserved for the states[3]. The states were allowed to run their own governments as they wished, provided that their governments were republican.

The Constitution opens with a statement, called a Preamble, which makes it clear that the government is set up by "We, the People" and its purpose is to "promote the general welfare and secure the blessing of liberty to ourselves and our posterity."

Before the new government could become a reality, a majority of the citizens in 9 of the 13 states would have to approve it. Those in favor of the adoption of the Constitution argues long and hard in speeches and writing[4]. They finally prevailed, but the states made it clear that one more change would have to be made as soon as the new government was established.

Representatives of various states noted that the Constitution did not have any words guaranteeing the freedoms or the basic rights and privileges of citizens. Though the Convention delegates did not think it necessary to include such explicit guarantees, many people felt that they needed further written protection against tyranny. So, a "Bill of Rights" was added to the Constitution in 1791.

Legislative Branch

The legislative branch is made up of elected representatives from all of the states and is the only branch that can make federal laws, levy federal taxes, declare war or put foreign treaties into effect. It consists of a Congress that is divided into two houses:

The House of Representatives comprises lawmakers who serve two-year terms[5]. Each House member represents a district in his or her home state. The number of districts in a state is determined by a count of the population taken every 10 years[6]. The most heavily populated states have more districts and, therefore, more representatives than the smaller states, some of which have only one. In the 1980s, there were 435 representatives in the House of Representatives.

The Senate comprises lawmakers who serve six-year terms. Each state, regardless of population, has two senators. That assures that the small states have an equal voice in one of the houses of Congress. The terms of the senators are staggered[7]. so that only on-third of the Senate is elected every two years. That assures that there are some experienced senators in Congress after each election.

The main duty of the Congress is to make laws, including those which levy taxes that pay for the work of the federal government. A law begins as a proposal called a "bill". It is read, studied in committees, commented on and amended in the Senate or House chamber in which it was introduced. It is then voted upon. If it passes, it is sent to the other house where a similar procedure occurs. Members of both houses work together in "conference committees" if the chambers have passed different versions of the same bill. Groups who try to persuade congressmen to vote for or against a bill are known as "lobbies". When both houses of Congress pass a bill on which they agree, it is sent to the president for his signature. Only after it is signed does the bill become a law.

Executive Branch

The chief executive of the United States is the president, who, together with the vice president, is elected to a four-year term. Under a Constitutional Amendment passed in 1951, a president can be elected to only two terms[8]. Except for the right of succession to the presidency, the vice president's only constitutional duties are to serve as the presiding officer of the Senate; the vice president may vote in the Senate only in the event of a tie.

The powers of the presidency are formidable, but not without limitations. The president, as the chief formulator of public policy, often proposes legislation to Congress. The president can also veto any bill passed by Congress. The veto can be overridden by a two-thirds vote in both the Senate and House of Representatives. As head of his political party, with ready access to the news media, the president can easily influence public opinion regarding issues and legislation that he deems vital.

The president has the authority to appoint federal judges as vacancies occur[9], including members of the Supreme Court. All such court appointments are subject to confirmation by the Senate.

Within the executive branch, the president has broad powers to issue regulations and directives regarding the work of the federal government's many departments and agencies. He also is commander in chief of the armed forces.

The president appoints the heads and senior officials of the executive branch agencies; the large majority of federal workers, however, are selected through a nonpolitical civil service system[10]. The major departments of the government are headed by appointed secretaries who collectively make up the president's cabinet. Each appointment must be confirmed by a vote of the Senate. Today these 13 departments are: State, Treasury, Defense, Justice, Interior, Agriculture, Commerce, Labor, Health and Human Services, Housing and Urban Development, Transportation, Energy and Education[11].

Under the Constitution, the president is primarily responsible for foreign relations with other nations. The president appoints ambassadors and other officials, subject to Senate approval, and with the secretary of state, formulates and manages the nation's foreign policy. The president often represents the United States abroad in consultations with other heads of state, and, through his officials, he negotiates treaties with other countries. Such treaties must be approved by a two-thirds vote of the Senate. The president also negotiates with other nations less formal "executive agreements" that are not subject to Senate approval.

Judicial Branch

The judicial branch is headed by the Supreme Court, which is the only court specifically created by the Constitution. In addition, the Congress has established 11 federal courts of appeal and, below them, 91 federal district courts. Federal judges are appointed for life or voluntary retirement, and can only be removed from office through the process of impeachment and trial in the Congress[12].

Federal courts have jurisdiction over cases arising out of the Constitution[13]; laws and treaties of the United States; maritime cases; issues involving foreign citizens or governments; and cases in which the federal government itself is a party. Ordinarily, federal courts do not hear cases arising out of the laws of individual states.

The Supreme Court today consists of a chief justice and eight associate justices. With minor exceptions, all its cases reach the Court on appeal from lower federal or state courts. Most of these cases involved disputes over the interpretation of laws and legislation. In this capacity, the Court's most important function consists of determining whether congressional legislation or executive action violates the Constitution[14]. This power of judicial review is not specifically provided for by the Constitution, it is the Court's interpretation of its Constitutional Role as established in the landmark Marbury v. Madison case of 1803[15].

Checks and Balances

When Americans talk about their three-part national government, they often refer to what they call its system of "checks and balances"[16]. This system works in many ways to keep serious mistakes from being made by one branch or another. But sometimes they do not work the way as they are supposed to work. Here are a few examples of checks and balances.

If Congress proposes a law that the president thinks is unwise, the president can veto it. That means the proposal does not become law. Congress can enact the law despite the president's views only if two-thirds of the members of both houses vote in favor of it.

If Congress passes a law which is then challenged in the courts as unconstitutional, the Supreme Court has the power to declare the law unconstitutional and therefore no longer in effect.

The president has the power to make treaties with other nations and to make all appointments to federal positions, including the position of Supreme Court justice. The Senate, however, must approve all treaties and confirm all appointments before they become official. In this way the Congress can prevent the president from making unwise appointments.

Bill of Rights

To all American, another basic foundation in their constitution is the Bill of Rights, adopted in 1791. This consists of 10 very short paragraphs which guarantee freedom and individual rights and forbid interference with lives of individuals by the government. Each paragraph is an Amendment to the original Constitution.

In the Bill of Rights, Americans are guaranteed freedom of religion, of speech and of the press. They have the right to assemble in public places, to protest government actions and to demand change. They have the right to own weapons if they wish. Because of the Bill of Rights, neither police nor soldiers can stop and search a person without good reason. They also cannot search a person's home without legal permission from a court.

The Bill of Rights guarantees Americans the right to speedy trial if accused of a crime. The trial must be by a jury and the accused person must be allowed representation by a lawyer and must be able to call in witnesses to speak for him or her. Cruel and unusual punishment is forbidden.

There are 16 other amendments to the Constitution as of 1991[17]. The changes are not many considering that the Constitution was written in 1787. Only a few need to be mentioned here. One forbids slavery and three others guarantee citizenship and full rights of citizenship of all people regardless of race. Another gives women the right to vote and another lowered the national voting age to 18.

Political Parties

There is one more very important part of the American political scene which is not part of any formal written document: the political party system.

Political parties are organized groups of people who share a set of ideas about how the United States should be governed and who work together to have members of their group elected in order to influence the governing of the country. When members of a political party form a majority in Congress, they have great powers to decide what kinds of laws will be passed. With exceptions, presidents tend to appoint members of their party or supporters of the views of their party to executive branch positions, including those of secretaries (heads of federal executive agencies) within the presidential cabinet.

The writers of the Constitution feared that parties representing narrow interests rather than the general interest of all the people could take over the government[18]. They hoped the government would be run by qualified people who did not have a second loyalty — a loyalty to a party. They believed their government would work well without parties. Despite this, parties began to form shortly after the Constitution went into effect.

Today, the United States has two major political parties. One is the Democratic Party, which evolved out of Thomas Jefferson's party, formed before 1800[19]. The symbol of the party is the donkey. The other is the Republican Party, which was formed in the 1850s, by people in the states of the North and West, such as Abraham Lincoln, who wanted the government to prevent the expansion of slavery into new states then being admitted to the union[20]. The symbol of the Republican Party is the elephant.

Most Americans today consider the Democratic party the more liberal party. By that they mean that Democrats believe the federal government and the state governments should be active in providing social and economic programs for those who need them, such as the poor, the unemployed or students who need money to go to college. The Democrats earned that reputation in the 1930s when there was a worldwide economic depression[21]. Under President Franklin Roosevelt's "New Deal" plan, Democrats set up government programs that provided paid employment for people building dams and roads and public buildings[22]. The government under the Democratic Party established many other programs, including Social Security[23], which ensures that those who are retired or disabled receive monthly payments from the government.

Republicans are not necessarily opposed to such programs. They believe, however, that many social programs are too costly to the taxpayers and that when taxes are raised to pay for programs, everyone in hurt. They place more emphasis on private enterprise and often accuse the Democrats of making the government too expensive and of creating too many laws that harm individual initiative[24]. For that reason, Americans tend to think of the Republican Party as more conservative.

Americans do not have to join a political party in order to vote or to be a candidate for public office. However, running for office without the money and campaign workers a party can provide is difficult. Many voters become members of a party because they feel strongly about the party goals or want a voice in selecting its candidates. Whether or not they belong to a party, voters may cast ballots for any candidate they wish. Everyone votes in secret, and no one can know how another votes or force another person to vote for any particular program or candidate[25].

One concern many Americans have about their political system is the high cost of campaigning for public office. These costs have risen sharply in recent years, in part because most candidates, in order to reach a large number of voters, buy advertising time on television. In 1990, the average winning candidate for election to the House of Representatives spent \$406 000 — more than four times the average spent in 1976. People worry that the high cost of getting elected may force candidates to spend more time raising money that dealing with important issues and may discourage many qualified people from running for public office. They are also concerned because much of the money to fund political campaigns comes from organized interest groups rather than individuals. Many Americans question whether, after election, these officials will feel more beholden to the groups which gave them money than to the people they represent[26].

The concerns of the public and of elected office-holders themselves have started a movement to change the financing of elections. Some people advocate voluntary spending limits. Others want the government to set limits. It is uncertain exactly what changes will be made, but public concern is so great that reforms in political campaign spending are bound to come soon.

Words & Expressions

confederation /kənˌfedəˈreiʃən /n. 邦联

article /ˈaːtikl /n. 条款

federal system 联邦制

tyranny /ˈtirəni /n. 专制，暴政

executive /igˈzekjutiv /n. ; adj. 行政

legislative /ˈledʒisˌleitiv /adj. 立法

judicial /dʒuːˈdiʃəl /adj. 司法

levy /ˈlevi /v. 征收

putinto effect 生效

lawmaker 立法者

amend /əˈmend /v. 修正

chamber /ˈtʃeimbə /n. 议院

procedure /prəˈsiːdʒə /n. 程序

version /ˈvəːʃən /n. 文本

lobby /'lɔbj /n. 院外游说集团
signature /'sijnitʃə /n. 签字
succession /sək'seʃən /n. 继任
tie /tai /n. 双方票数相等,平局
treasury /'treʒəri /n. 财政部
interior /in'tiəriə /n. 内政部
ambassador /æm'bæsədə /n. 大使
consultation /ˌkənsəl'teiʃən /n. 协商
negotiate /ni'gəuʃieit /v. 谈判
appeal /ə'piːl /n. 上诉
remove /ri'muːv /v. 免职
impeachment /im'piːtʃmənt /n. 弹劾
jurisdiction /ˌdʒuəris'dikʃən /n. 审判权
maritime /'mːeritaim /adj. 海事的
chief justice 首席大法官(最高法院)
associate justice 大法官(最高法院)
jury /'dʒuəri /n. 陪审团
cast /kaːst /v. 投(票)
ballot /'bælət /n. 选票
interest group 利益集团

Notes

1. the Congress:国会。这里指美国独立战争结束后由第二届大陆会议转变而来的美国全国领导机构。它由各州代表组成,没有行政和司法机构,权力很小。

2. the Articles of Confederation:邦联条款。这是1777年11月国会通过的美国第一部宪法性文件,规定联合新独立的13个州的松散的邦联政府的职能。1787年美国制订联邦宪法,邦制随之终止。

3. To deal with this ... for the states:为了消除这种害怕心理,宪法明文规定哪些权力属于中央联邦政府,哪些权力保留给各州政府。各州仍然保持各自的州宪法,实施自己州的权力。后来,"权利法案"又对州权作了规定。

4. Those in favor ... in speeches and writing:赞同批准宪法的人通过演讲和撰写文章进行了长期艰苦的努力。他们写文章说服公众支持宪法,争取得到13个州中至少9个州的批准。

5. The House of Representatives ... two-year terms:众议院由任期两年的立法者组成。

6. The number of districts ... taken every 10 years:每个州选区的多少由每隔10年一次的人口普查而决定。

7. The Terms of the senators are staggered:参议员的任期是交错的。每隔两年改选三分之一。

8. Under a Constitutional Amendment ... only two terms:根据1951年通过的第22条宪法修正案,总统连任不得超过两任。美国历史上只有富兰克林·罗斯福因第二次世界大战而连任三次。

9. The president has the authority to appoint federal judges as vacancies occur:联邦法官席位出现空缺时,总统有权任命新的法官。联邦法官是终身制。当联邦法官死亡或自愿退休时,或当他们经过合法程序被弹劾免职时,总统有权任命新的联邦法官。

10. the large majority ... civil service system:联邦政府大部分工作人员通过非政治性的公务员制(文官制度)挑选的。"非政治性"是指不受政党或大选的影响,不管谁当选总统,他们的工作不变。

11. Today these 13 departments ... Energy and Education:现在美国联邦政府的13个部

分别为:国务院、财政部、国防部、司法部、内政部、农业部、商业部、劳工部、卫生与公共服务事业部、住房与城市发展部、交通部、能源部及教育部。

12. the process of impeachment and trial in the Congress:国会弹劾及审判程序。当联邦法官犯有重大罪行时,他们可以被弹劾免职。其程序是由众议院提出起诉,参议院进行审判。

13. Federal courts have jurisdiction over cases arising out of the Constitution:联邦法院对涉及联邦宪法的案件有审判权。

14. In this capacity ... violates the Constitution:最高法院在这方面的最重要的职能包括决定国会法案或行政法令是否违宪。这种职能被称为"司法复审权"。从本世纪30年代以来,美国最高法院已多次宣布国会通过的法案违宪。

15. Marbury v. Madison case of 1803:1803年马伯里对麦迪逊案。美国第二任总统约翰·亚当斯任命马伯里为首都哥伦比亚特区法官。任命书在总统离任前两天签署生效。但下届总统杰斐逊命令当时的国务卿麦迪逊扣发任命书。马伯里因此向最高法院提出起诉,要求麦迪逊立即下发任命书。最高法院裁决马伯里败诉。此案例确立了最高法院解释宪法及裁决被通过的法案法令是否违宪的司法复审权力,确立了行政、立法与司法各部门间的均势。

16. "checks and balances":"制约与平衡"的原则。这个原则的确立是为了防止专制。但在实施过程中出现不少问题,比如联邦调查局及中央情报局侵犯人权的事常有发生,也没有得到制约。

17. There were 16 other amendments to the Constitution as of 1991: 到1991年为止还有另外16条宪法修正案,截至今日,美国宪法仍然只有26条修正案。

18. The writers of the Constitution ... take over the government:制宪者们担心,代表狭隘利益而不是代表人民整体利益的党派会控制政府。所以他们反对成立党派。

19. which evolved out of Thomas Jefferson's party, formed before 1800:民主党是从杰斐逊在1800年前成立的党逐步演变而来的。杰斐逊成立的党的名称是民主共和党。19世纪20年代末,后任美国总统的安德鲁·杰克逊在此基础上成立了民主党。他们以驴作为党的象征。

20. who wanted ... to the union:新成立的共和党人要求政府制止南方奴隶制向正在加入联邦的新州扩张。当时新加入联邦的州有加利福尼亚州等。

21. a worldwide economic depression:世界性的经济萧条。这是资本主义世界最严重的一次经济危机。美国的经济大萧条从1929年底纽约的股票暴跌开始,一直延续到30年代初。罗斯福总统为摆脱这次经济危机,挽救资本主义,在他就任总统后开始实施"新政"计划。

22. Under President Franklin Roosevelt's "New Deal" plan ... public buildings:按照富兰克林·罗斯福总统的"新政"计划,民主党人确定了各种政府规划,为人们提供获得收入的就业机会,如建设大坝、道路及公共设施等。罗斯福总统来自民主党,他主张以工代赈,而不是单纯地发放救济金。

23. Social Security:社会安全保障。这是罗斯福总统"新政"中的一部分。根据这个计划,政府从职工的工资中扣除一部分,并根据雇主向雇员发放的工资的总额向雇主征税,把这两项收入作为退休后的老年人的退休金。享受退休金的老人死后,其配偶可享受一定比例的养老金。

24. They place more emphasis ... individual initiative：共和党人更注重个人的首创精神,常常指责民主党人耗费巨资把政府搞得过于庞大,指责他们制定了许多伤害个人积极性的法律。美国的两大政党在本质上没有什么区别,他们只是不同的资产阶级利益集团的代表,在具体政策上有时强调的侧面不一样。

25. to vote for any particular program or candidate：投票支持某项计划或某个候选人。美国人投票选举美国总统或国会议员时,偶尔还要在同一张选票上表明是否支持当地推出的某项计划,如教育计划、基本建设计划等。

26. Many Americans question ... to the people they represent：许多美国人怀疑,选举结束后那些当选的官员可能只代表赞助他们的利益集团,而不是为他们所代表的人民谋利益。

Exercises

Ⅰ. Explain the following

1. the Articles of Confederation
2. the U. S. Constitution
3. the legislative branch
4. the executive
5. the judicial branch
6. the Bill of Rights

Ⅱ. Fill in the blanks

1. After the War of Independence was won, the national government was called ____________, and the agreement that guided the government was ____________.
2. The city where the Declaration of Independence was signed and where the U. S. Constitution was made is ____________.
3. The Constitutional Convention was held in the year of ____________ and the president of the Convention was ____________.
4. The Constitution set up a federal system with ____________.
5. A federal system is one in which ____________ is shared between ____________ and ____________ with some rights reserved to each.
6. The U. S. federal government consists of the following three branches: ____________, ____________ and ____________.
7. The Congress is divided into ____________ with ____________ members who serve two-year terms, and ____________ with ____________ lawmakers who serve six-year terms.
8. Groups who try to persuade Congressmen to vote for or against a bill are known as ____________.

9. The Supreme Court is composed of ____________ chief justice and ____________ associate justices.

10. The Supreme Court has the function of determining whether Congressional legislative or executive action violates the Constitution. This power is called ________________.

11. There are ________ amendments to the U. S. Constitution.

12. Two major political parties are ____________, which is thought to be more liberal, and ____________, which is believed to be more ____________.

Ⅲ. Choose the correct answer in each of the following

1. Which of the following statements was NOT correct when the War of Independence was over?

   A. Each new state had its own government.

   B. Each new state made its own laws and handled all of its internal affairs.

   C. The national government was called the Congress with little power.

   D. The relationships between the states and the national government were clearly defined.

2. According to the author, the Articles of Confederation failed because of the following reasons. Which is not true?

   A. The new states did not cooperate with the Congress or with each other.

   B. Some new states wanted to be free from the Union.

   C. The Congress could not raise money to pay the national army and to pay debts owed to France and other nations.

   D. The Congress had no power to tax any citizen.

3. Which of the following states refused to participate in the Constitutional Convention?

   A. Virginia. B. Rhode Island.

   C. New York. D. Maryland.

4. Which of the following statements was NOT correct. when the Constitution was written.

   A. There was a Bill of Rights in the Constitution.

   B. There was no Bill of Rights.

   C. The Constitution did not have any words guaranteeing the freedoms or the basic rights and privileges of citizens.

   D. A "Bill of Rights" was added to the Constitution 4 years after the Constitution was made.

5. Which of the following is the only branch that can make federal laws, and levy federal taxes?

   A. The executive. B. The legislative.

   C. The Judicial. D. The president.

6. Which of the following is NOT a power of the president?

   A. The president can veto any bill passed by Congress.

   B. The president has the authority to appoint federal judges when vacancies occur.

C. The president can make laws.

D. The president has broad powers, with the executive branch, to issue regulations and directives regarding the work of the federal departments.

7. The Bill of Rights consists of ________.

A. 10 very short paragraphs in an amendment

B. 10 amendments adopted in 1787

C. 10 amendments added to the Constitution in 1791

D. the amendments concerning the freedom of speech, the freedom of the press and the freedom of religion

8. Which of the following is NOT guaranteed in the Bill of Rights?

A. The freedom of religion.

B. The freedom of searching a person's home by police.

C. The freedom of speech and of the press.

D. The right to own weapons if one wishes.

9. The following were NOT written into the Constitution in 1787 except ________.

A. The Bill of Rights

B. The judicial review

C. The political party system

D. The powers of the president

10. The New Deal was started by ________.

A. Franklin Roosevelt

B. J. F. Kennedy

C. George Washington

D. Thomas Jefferson

Ⅳ. Answer the following questions briefly

1. Why did the Articles of Confederation fail?
2. What are some of the major differences between a federal system and a confederation?
3. What are some of the major powers of each of the three branches of the U. S. government?
4. What are the two political parties in the United States?

Chapter 14 American Literature

From the beginning of American history to the present day, American literature has recorded the story of a quest. At different times the quest has taken different forms. In the 16th century Europeans came to the New World in search of the lost continent of Atlantis. [1] They came looking for the golden " cities of Cibola " that haunted Coronado ' s imagination[2]. They searched for the fabled Northwest Passage to the Orient[3].

These fantastic dreams changed in time to more down-to-earth dreams of success. These dreams brought millions of young men and women from farms and small to cities in the hope of winning fame and fortune. At times the quest was a religious pilgrimage. For example, the Puritans hoped the New World would become a New Canaan[4], where a chosen people might at last build a society of which god would approve. The Mormons who trekked across the plains to Utah were inspired by a similar vision[5]. Other pioneers (and many later Americans as well) were pulled westward neither by financial nor by religious ambitions. They were simply restless. Whether they traveled by covered wagon or by automobile trailer, they believed that being on the road was better than staying put. The questing of the American people has indeed been a drama of many parts. In one way or another, however, it has always been a " pursuit of happiness ". American literature is the continuous narrative of that pursuit.

Early Fiction

Writers of the post-Revolutionary period had been embarrassed that America did not have much of a history. Washington Irving[6] solved this problem by inventing a history. His History *of New York* (1809) is supposedly an account of the Dutch settlement of Manhattan Island. With this work Irving furnished America with its first myth-hero, Father Knickerbockers. In *Rip Van Wrinkle and The legend of Sleepy Hollow*, Irving contributed even more memorable characters to his legendary recreation of the American past: Rip Van Winkle, Brom Bones, and Ichabod Crane. In his accounts of his history of The Alhambra (1832), the fabulous palace of the Moors in Granada, Spain[7], Irving also demonstrated that an American writer need not write only America in order to remain a patriot.

His *Tour on Prairies*(1835) showed Irving's interest in the literary possibilities of the West. Here, however, he was poaching on the literary territory of fellow New Yorker James Fenimore Cooper. [8] Cooper's novel *The Spy*(1821) was an exciting story of espionage in New York during the Revolution, but he did not really hit his stride as an author until he turned to The Pioneers(1823). This was the first of the five great romances known as *the Leatherstocking Tales.* Surpassing Irving as a mythmaker, Cooper introduced in *The Pioneers* the fabulous woodsman, Natty Bumppo. He was the forerunner of all heroic forest scouts, bear hunters, and cowboys of later forerunner of all heroic forest scouts, bear hunters, and cowboys of later American novels and films. *The Last of the Mohicans* (1826), *The Prairie* (1827), *The pathfinder*(1840), *and The Deerslayer*(1841) pursued Natty's career both forward and backward in time, from the first flush of manhood to his death as an old man on the western plains.

Transcendentalists

The country was expanding westward, but in the older cities of the northeastern states—still referred to as "New England"—the in influence of early Puritan teachings remained strong. However, such authoritarian religious organizations inevitably produce dissenters. In 1836, an ex-minister named Ralph Waldo Emerson[9](1803 – 1882)) published a startling book called *Nature.* In this volume, Emerson claimed that by studying and responding to nature individuals could reach a higher spiritual state without formal religion[10]. For the next several years, Emerson's essays made him extremely influential, not only upon other thinkers and writers, but upon the general population as well, thanks to growing popular lecture circuit that brought controversial speakers to small towns across the country[11]. In his poetry, Emerson developed a freeform, natural style, using symbols and imagery drawn from nature. His work had an immense impact on other poets of the time.

A circle of intellectuals who were discontented with the New England establishment soon gathered around Emerson. They were known as "the Transcendentalists," based on their acceptance of Emerson's theories about spiritual transcendence. One of Emerson's most gifted fellow-thinkers was Henry David Thoreau[12](1817 – 1862).

Thoreau was passionate about individuals' learning to think for themselves and being independent, both traditional American values, He carried out this ideal by going to live by himself for two years in a simple cabin beside a wooded pond, where he survived essentially by his own labor and meditated in solitude. The book he wrote about this experience, *Walden*, was published in 1854, but many of its statements about the individual's role in society —simply put, that the dictates of an individual's conscience should take precedence over the demands, even the laws, of society[13]—sound radical even today.

Power of Imagination

White these new England intellectuals presented perspectives of literature and life, other writers were concentrating upon human imagination and emotion rather than the intellect. A young Virginian, Edgar Allan Poe[14] (1809 – 1849), was publishing poems of musical language and extravagant imagery, which made him a worthy rival of the European Romantic poets. Brilliant but unstable, Poe earned his living as a journalist, often writing devastating reviews of other writers' works. In 1835, he also began writing bold, original short stories, such as *The Musque of Red Death and the Fall of the House of Usher*. These suspenseful, sometimes terrifying tales plunged deep into human psychology, and explored the realms of science fiction and the mystery story long before such genres were recognized.[15]

Meanwhile, in 1837, a young writer in new England named Nathaniel Hawthorne[16] (1804 – 1864) published a volume called *Twice-Told Tales*, stories rich in symbolism and peculiar incidents. Although he knew the Transcendentalists, Hawthorne did not share their beliefs. His way of rebelling against the traditional new England outlook on life was to write imaginative "romances," stories and novels which were not necessarily realistic but which were designed to explore certain moral themes such as guilt, pride and emotional repression. His masterpiece was *The Scarlet Letter*, a novel published in 1850. Set in the Puritan past, it is the stark drama of a woman harshly cast out from her community for committing the sin of adultery.

Hawthorne's writing had a profound impact upon another writer, originally from New York, who was living at the in New England. Herman Melville[17] (1819 – 1891), whose wealthy father had gone bankrupt, had worked at many jobs before signing on in 1839 for the first of several sea voyages.[18] Seven years later, he began writing accounts of his adventures on the open seas and in exotic ports, which won him instant success. Yet Melville longed to write something more serious. Inspired by Hawthorne's example, he began writing novels which were fundamentally allegories on politics and religion. The public rejected them, however, and, discouraged, Melville published little except poetry for the rest of his life. Ironically, the very books that proved unacceptable during his lifetime are the ones most admired today.[19] *Moby Dick*, published in 1851, uses a story of a whaling voyage to explore profound themes such as fate, the nature of evil, and the individual's struggle against the universe. It is considered an American masterpiece.

New Visions of America

Poe, Hawthorne and Melville all struggled to find their individual voices, and through them American literature began to acquire its own personality. One more figure emerged in the 1850s to assert a truly American voice, one that celebrated the American landscape, the American people, their speech and democratic form of government. His name was Walt Whitman[20] (1818 – 1892), and like so many other of these writers, he had had to work hard for a living as a school teacher, printer and journalist. In 1848, he took a trip to the southern city of New Orleans, at the mouth of the Mississippi River, that great waterway flowing through the heart of the country. There Whitman gained a new vision of America and began writing poetry that would embody his vision. In 1855, he published a ground-breaking book called *Leaves of Grass*. Readers were amazed by the free-flowing structure of this poetry, with its long irregular lines. Like Melville in *Moby Dick*, Whitman ventured beyond traditional forms to meet his need for more space to express the American spirit.[21] Some readers were disturbed by Whitman's egotism (one main poem in *Leaves of Grass* is called "Song of Myself"), but Whitman dwelt on himself simply because he saw himself as a prototype of "The American." Startling as this poetry was, it won Whitman admirers across America and in Europe. Through out the rest of his life, he kept rewriting and republishing editions of Leaves of Grass. He celebrated a sweeping panorama of the American landscape and sang almost mystically of the rhythms of life uniting all citizens of the democracy.[22]

Reform and Liberation

New England intellectuals had, in fact, a tradition of involvement in liberal reform, In the 1850s, this took the form of a movement to end the institution of slavery, which by that time was practiced chiefly in the southern states. In 1852, a New England woman named Harriet Beecher Stowe[23] (1811 – 1896) wrote *Uncle Tom's Cabin*, an antislavery novel that galvanized political opinion across the nation. Sentimetal and melodramatic as it was, Uncle Tom's Cabin portrayed black slaves as sympathetic, suffering figures, and created an image of the cruel slaveowner in the character of Simon Leree[24]. Largely as a result of this bestselling novel, the slavery question became a passionately debated political issue. Eventually the Southern states determined to secede from the Union and to establish themselves as an independent country in order to preserve their way of life, which included an agrarian economy based in great part on slave labor. The result of Northern reaction to this secession was the Civil War (1861 – 1865), fought to preserve the Union. One consequence of the South's defeat in that war was the abolition of slavery in the United States.

Regionalism

In many ways, this bloody divisive war dimmed American optimism, and for a time writers retreated from national themes, the country had been growing: as pioneers settled in new territories in the West, writers now focused on the differences between the various regions of the United States rather than on a single vision of the expanding country. One of the most important leaders of this "regionalism" movement was William Dean Howells[25] (1837 – 1920), who in 1866 became editor of the influential Atlantic magazine. Howells published stories from all over the United States, and in his literary reviews he praised writers who described local life realistically. The raw mining camps and settlements of the far West were brought to life by storytellers such as Bret Harte, in *The Luck of Roaring Camp*, and a newspaper correspondent named Samuel Clemens (1835 – 1910), who wrote under the pen name of Mark Twain.[26]

Mark Twain was the first major American writer to be born away from the East Coast. He grew up in small town on the banks of the Mississippi Rive and received only a basic public school education. He began working in a printer's shop when he was still a boy, and this experience led to a series of newspaper jobs in the Midwest and the West. Twain was a new voice, an original genius, a man of the people, and he quickly won readers. He captured a peculiarly American sense of humor, telling outrageous jokes and tall tales in a calm, innocent, matter-of-fact manner. He sometimes used local dialect for comic effect, but even his normal prose style sounded distinctively American—rich in metaphor, newly invented words and drawling rhythms.

Twain had a cynical streak that matched the country's skeptical post-Civil War mood. He soon developed beyond merely "regional" stories and turned to comic novels. His shrewd social satire was most apparent in books such as A *Connecticut Yankee in King Arthur's Court*, but perhaps his greatest book is *The Adventures of Huckleberry Finn* (1884). This is the story of a boy running away from home and steering a raft down the Mississippi River, but it is more than that. The people the boy meets cover the entire spectrum of humanity[27], and his voyage down the river becomes a metaphor for a journey through life. Funny, powerful, humane and laced with social commentary and criticism, Huckleberry Finn has been called the greatest novel in American literature.

While prose fiction in the United States was developing in vital imaginative ways. poetry seemed to recede as an art form. The poetic giant Whitman died in the 1880s, as did a poet who has been admired by later generations, but who was barely known while she lived. This unrecognized poet was Emily Dickinson[28] (1830 - 1886). Her poetry mixed gaiety and gloom. During the last 25 years of her life, she rarely left the grounds of the Dickinson household in Amherst, Massachusetts. But her imagination took her on long flights of fancy. Her verses are filled with the names of faraway, exotic places that she visited only in imagination. On the other hand, she could make poetic drama out of things close at hand—a cracked plate on a shelf in the dining room of the sound of a honeybee in the garden. She was fascinated by life. She was also more than a little in love with death[29]. Of the 1 500 poems she composed, more than 600 have to do with dying. Almost all of poems are brief, rarely more than 12 or 15 lines long. But in small spaces she packed an emotional charge of surprising force.

A New Ware

As the wounds of the Civil War slowly healed, many Americans became discontented with the growing materialism of society in the United States. Henry James[30] (1843 - 1916), an American who lived in Europe, examined American society by observing the divergence between American and European culture in novels like *The American and Portrait of a Lady*.

"Regional" writers began to drop their narrow provincial focus, while still using realistic descriptions of everyday life, As they concentrated increasingly upon the grimmer aspects of reality and a deterministic view of life, they were called "naturalists," linking them to European naturalists such as French novelist Emile Zola[31]. Again, William Dean Howells led the American realistic movement, both with his magazine criticism and with his own novels, such as The Rise of Silas

Lapham(1885), a probing but sympathetic portrait of an American businessman. Stephen Crane's[32] (1871 – 1900) *Maggie*, *A Girl of the Streets*, in 1893, and Theodore Dreiser's[33] (1871 – 1945) *Sister Carrie*, in 1900, were considered shocking because they described young urban women who fell into sexual sin. Crane's next novel, *The Red Badge of Courage*(1895) was set during the Civil War. By limiting itself to a young soldier's confused impressions of battle, it became the first impressionistic novel in America. Upton Sinclair's[34] *The Jungle*(1906) exposed the horrible lives of meat-packing factory workers. Jack London's [35] *Call of the Wild* (1903), the tale of a sled god, was set in the snowy wilderness of the Northwest, where the discovery of gold had caused a rush of greedy prospectors. In this novel and other celebrated tales set in Alaska and in the South Pacific, London expressed his sense that primitive urges underlie all of life, reducing even humans to the level of animals. [36]

While these controversial books disturbed the reading public, other writers were quietly exploring the fate of the individual. After the turn of the century, Henry James, still living in Europe, wrote three brilliant novels, *The Wings of the Dove*, *The Ambassadors and The Golden Bowl*, in which he plunged deep into the characters of the naturalists' novels, James' people were trapped in their environment, struggling to find happiness, James' interest was psychological rather than social, however. Recording characters' mental and emotional processes. His writing style became increasingly complex, but this focused attention away from action and setting and onto what the characters were feeling. [37]

Edith Wharton[38] (1862 – 1937) was one of Jame's close friends and literary followers. She came from a socially prominent New York family and had married into an equally important Boston family. This-high-toned social circle disapproved of her writing, but eventually she defied her peers and produced insightful novels and stories. One of her finest books, *The House of mirth*(1905), tells the tragic story of a fading beauty hunting desperately for a rich husband and falling victim to the hypocritical high society of New York. *The Age of Innocence* (1920) is another successful novel written by Wharton, who exposed her upper-class world as only an insider could.

Sympathetic Views

Three other women, in different parts of the country, were also writing sympathetic psychological studies. Though influenced by regionalism. they didn't emphasize setting so much as they did their characters, individuals who often felt out of place in their environments. Kate Chopin's[39] *The Awakening* (1899) is set set in the heart of the South, in New Orleans; Willa Cather's[40] *O Pioneers!* (1913) depicts life on the sweeping plains of Midwestern Nebraska. Cather went on to write several novels and establish herself as a major American writer, but Chopin stopped writing after her book was condemned by literary critics.

American literature entered the 20th century not as optimistic or patriotic as it had been a century earlier, yet full of democratic spirit, There were some voices still to be heard, however. Black Americans were just beginning to make in literature in the wake of the Civil War's having freed them slavery. In 1903, W. E. B. Dubois[41] (1869—1963) published *Souls of Black Folk*, a series of sketches of the common lives of his people which was the first glimpse many white Americans had had of the social condition of blacks since slavery.

Rebellious Spirit

In the first decades of the 20th century the United States became increasingly urban. Two major works of literature expressed this new attitude of rebellion against the limited life of the typical small American town. In 1919, a writer named Sherwood Anderson[42] published a book of short stories called *Winesburg, Ohio*. This was a series of portraits of different personalities in one midwestern town, creating an overall impression of narrow-minded ignorance and frustrated dreams. The second "revolt from the village" work was a novel called *Main Stre*et, by Sinclair Lewis,[43] published in 1920. Again, the setting was a small midwestern town, this one called *Gopher Prairie*,[44] a name that suggested crudeness and lack of culture. In this book, and in others such as *Babbitt and Arrowsmith*, Lewis drew vivid caricatures and satirized the traditional "American dream" of success. To urban Americans and Europeans both, Lewis seemed to sum up what small-town America was all about. He was awarded the Nobel Prize for Literature in 1930, the first American to be so honored.

The Modernists

One important literary movement of the time was "Imagism," whose poets focused on strong, concrete images. Ezra Pound[45] began as an Imagist but soon went beyond, into complex, sometimes obscure poetry, full of references to other art forms and to vast range of literature. Living in Europe, Pound influenced many other poets, especially T. S. Eliot. [46]

Eliot was born in St. Louis but settled in England. He wrote spare, intellectual poetry, carried by a dense structure of symbols. His 1922 poem, *The Waste Land* spun out, in fragmented, haunting images, a pessimistic vision of post-World War I society. From then on, Eliot dominated the so-called "Modern" movement in poetry[47]. Another Modernist, E. E. Cumming, [48] called attention to his poetry by throwing away rules of punctuation, spelling, and even the way words were placed on the page. His pocms were songlike but satiric, humorous and anarchistic. Wallace Stevens, in contrast, wrote thoughtful speculations on how man can know reality. Stevens's verse was disciplined, with understated rhythms, precisely chosen words and a cluster of central images. The poetry of William Carlos Williams, with its light, supple rhythms, was rooted in Imagism, but Williams, a New Jersey physician, used detailed impressions of everyday American life.

Lost Generation

In the aftermath of World War I many novelists produced a literature of disillusionment. Some lived abroad and were know as "the Lost Generation." [49] F. Scott Fitzgerald's[50] novels captured the restless, pleasure-hungry, defiant mood of the 1920s. Fitzgerald's great theme, expressed poignantly in *The Great Gatsby*, was of youth's golden dreams turning to disappointment. His prose was exquisite, yet his vision was essentially melancholy and nostalgic. John Dos Passon came home from the war to write long novels that attempted to portray all of American society, usually with a critical eye. In three novels combined under the title *U. S. A*, he interwove many plots, characters and settings, fictional and nonfictional, cutting back and forth between them in style much like the new popular art-form, motion pictures. [51]

War had also affected Ernest Hemingway[52]. Having seen violence and death colse at hand, Hemingway adopted a moral code exalting simple survival and the basic values of strength, courage and honesty. In his own writing, he cut out all unnecessary words and complex sentence structure, concentrating on concrete objects and actions, His main characters were usually tough, silent men, good at sports or war but awkward in their dealings with women. Among his best books were *The Sun Also Rises*(1926), *A Farewell to Arms* (1929) *and For Whom the Bell Tolls*(1940). He eventually won the Nobel Prize and is considered one of the greatest American writers.

A Southerner, William Faulkner[53], found in one small imaginary corner of the state of Mississippi, deep in the heart of the South, enough material for a life time of writing. His social portraits were realistic, yet his prose style was experimental. To show the relationship of the past and the present, he sometimes jumbled the time sequence of his plots; to reveal a character ' s primitive impulses and social prejudices, he recorded and edited the rambling of his or her consciousness. [54] Some of his best novels are the *The Sound and the Fury* (1929) and Light in August (1932). Faulkner, too, won a Nobel Prize.

Harlem Renaissance

The 1920s also saw the rise of an artistic black community centered in New York City in Harlem, a fashionable black neighborhood. African-Americans had brought a lively. Powerful music called jazz with them as they moved to northern cities; the jazz clubs of Harlem became chic night spots in the 1920s. The nation suddenly discovered " the new Negro, " an articulate urban black, conscious of his or her racial identity. Magazines and newspapers dedicated to black writing sprang up. New poets such as Langston Hughes and Countee Cullen wrote about what it meant to be black. They used exotic images drawn from their African and slavery pasts. And incorporated the rhythms of black music such as jazz, blues and the folk hymns called " spirituals ". The Harlem Renaissance gave African-American culture prominence and an impetus to grow.

New Drama

There was another burst of intense literary activity in the 920s in drama. Although the premiere theater town was the large eastern city of new York, most cities had their own theaters. Professional actors toured the United States, performing British classics, musical entertainments or second-rate melodramas. But there had not yet been an important American dramatist. Then , in 1916, a company called the Provincetown Players began to produce the works of Eugene O ' Neill[56]-plays that were more than just entertainment.

O ' Neill borrowed ideas from European playwrights. Like the Modernists, he used symbolism, adapted stories from classical mythology and the Bible, and drew upon the new science of psychology to explore his characters ' inner lives. What made O ' Neill unique was his incorporation of all these elements into a new American voice and dramatic style. His characters spoke heightened language—not realistic, yet not flowery. To express psychological undercurrents, he had characters speak their thoughts aloud or wear masks, to represent the difference between public self and private self. He wrote frankly about sex and family relations, but his greatest theme was the individual's search for identity. Among his major plays were *Desire Under the Elms* (1924), *Mourning Becomes Electra* (1931), *The lceman Cometh* (1946) *and Long Day's Journey into Night* (1956). O'Neill won a Nobel Prize in 1936 for literature.

Depression Realism and Escapism

The Depression caused novelists to focus on social forces. In the West, john Steinbeck[57] told sympathetic stories about drifting farm laborers and factory workers. His 1939 masterpiece, *The Grapes of Wrath*, depicted an impoverished midwestern family joining a stream of poor farm laborers heading west to the "land of opportunity," the state of California. By interweaving chapters of social commentary with his story, Steinbeck made this portrait of the Joad family into a major statement about the Depression.

Historical fiction became increasingly popular in the Depression for it allowed readers to retreat to the past. The most successful of these books was *Gone with the Wind*, a 1936 best-seller about the Civil War by a southern woman, Margaret Mitchell.

In 1939, war broke out in Europe, and eventually the entire world wad embroiled in conflict again. The United States joined the war in December 1941, fighting both in Europe and in the Pacific. Right after the war, a series of young writers wrote intelligent novels showing how the pressures of war highlight men's characters. These included Norman Mailer's *The Naked* and *the Dead* and Herman Wouk's *Caine Mutiny*. By 1961, Joseph Heller[58] published his satiric war novel Catch-22, in which war is portrayed as an absurd exercise for madmen.

Postwar Voices and the "Beat Generation"

The new receptivity of American society to a diversity of voices incorporated black writers and black protest into the mainstream of American literature. Richard Wright's[59] disturbing novel Native Son, published in 1940, revealed a new black hero, whose character had been warped by this violent and cruel society. The hero of Ralph Ellison's[60] *Invisible Man* (1952), is also driven underground by the values of white society. James Baldwin's[61] characteristic themes, hatred of racism and celebration of sexuality, were expressed in novels like *Go Tell It on the Mountain*

(1953) *and in essays like The Fire Next Time*(1963).

American Jews also began to raise their literary voices at this time. Writers such as Saul Bellow[62] (*The Adventures of Augie March*, 1953), Bernard Malamud (*The Assistant.* 1957), and Philip Roth (*Good-bye*, *Columbus*, 1959) not only focused upon Jewish characters and social questions, but brought a distinctively Jewish sense of humor to their novels, Their prose often carried echoes of Yiddish, the language used by European Jews which had helped preserve Jewish culture, isolated but intact, until the early 20th century. Another Jewish writer, Isaac Bashevis Singer,[63] who was born in Poland but had emigrated to the United States in 1935, continued to write in Yiddish, though his stories were quickly translated into English and became part of the national literature. Both Singer and Bellow won the Nobel Prize for Literature.

In the theater, Tennessee Williams,[64] beginning with *The Glass Menagerie* (1945), expressed his southern heritage in poetic yet sensational plays, usually about a sensitive woman trapped in an insensitive environment. Arthur Miller portrayed the common man pressured by society; his greatest play, *Death of a Salesman*(1947), turned a second-rate traveling salesman, Willy Loman, into a quasi-tragic hero.

The San Francisco writers were part of a large group called the "Beat Generation,"65a name that referred simultaneously to the rhythm of jazz music, to their sense that society was worn out, and to their interest in new forms of experience, through drugs, alcohol or Eastern mysticism. Poet Alan Ginsberg's *Howl*(1956) set for them a tone of social protest and visionary ecstasy, in elaborate language reminiscent of Whitman.

While other writers did not espouse the life style of the Beats, they also viewed the world on a comic, absurd light, In J. D. Salinger's *The Catcher in the Rye* (1951), a sardonic teenage boy resists the hypocrisies of adult society. Funny as the novel is, there is something tragic in the boy's hopelessness about his world.

New American Voices

The feminist movement of the 1960s and 1970s fueled creative energies for many women writers. Some poets, with their personal poetry, revealed the pain and joy of being a woman, As the women's movement gained more acceptance, however, women wrote less in protest and more in affirmation—particularly black women writers, such as Toni Morrison(*Beloved*, 1987) and Alice *Walker*(*The Color Purple*,

1982), who portrayed strong black women as the source of continuity, the preservers of values, in black cultured. Only in the 1970s did other ethnic groups begin to find their literary voice. Magazines and anthologies were dedicated to the works of American Hispanics, who had come largely from Mexico and the Caribbean. Chinese-American Maxine Hong Kingston wrote about her ancestors in the books *The Woman Warrior and China Men.* And writers from foreign ethnic backgrounds did not occupy the fringe of American literature—they were very much in the mainstream. Amy Tan, a Chinese-American writer, told of her parents' early struggles in China and in the United States in The Joy Luck Club(1989), which quickly climbed to the top of the best-selling book list.

Toni Morrison(1931 –), a professor at Princeton University, has published six novels up to now, of which *Song of Soloman*(1977) and *Beloved* are considered her best works. Although they are descriptions of African-American experience, her novels are widely read all over the world by people of all colors, ages and creeds, She won the Nobel Prize for Literature in 1993, the first African-American writer to receive this honor.

Words & Expressions

quest/kwest/*n.* 追求,探索
fantastic/fæn'tæstik/*adj.* 幻想的,异想天开的
Manhattan/mæn'hætən/*n.* 曼哈顿岛(纽约市中心)
myth-hero 神话英雄
espionage/'espiəniʤ/*n.* 间谍活动
woodsman/'wudsmən/*n.* 护林人
forerunner/'fɔːˌrʌnə/*n.* 先驱者
transcendentalist/ˌtrænsen'dentəlist/*n.* 超验主义者
authoritarian/ɔːˌθɔri'tɛəriən/*adj.* 权力主义者,命令主义的
imagery/'imiʤəri/*n.* 意象,形象
Transcendence/træn'sendəns/*n.* 超越
symbolism/'simbəlizəm/*n.* 象征的表现,象征主义
romance/rə'mæns/*n.* 爱情故事
exotic/ig'zɔtik/*adj.* 异国的
allegory/'æligəri/*n.* 比喻,寓言
prototype/'prəutətaip/*n.* 原型,典型
optimism/'ɔptimizəm/*n.* 乐观主义
regionalism/'riːʤənəlizəm/*n.* 地方主义
printer's shop 印刷所
Midwest 中西部
outrageous/aut'reiʤəs/*adj.* 令人反感的
tall tale *n.* 夸张的,令人难以相信的故事
prose style 散文体
metaphor/'metəfə/*n.* 隐喻
deterministic/diˌtəːmi'nistik/*adj.* 宿命论的
impressionistic/imˌperʃə'nistik/*adj.* 印象派的
insightful/'inˌsaitful/*adj.* 具有洞察力的
in the wake of 紧跟
sketch/sketʃ/*n.* 速写,短篇小说
crudeness /kruːdnis/*n.* 天然,粗糙
caricature/ˌkærikə'tjuə/*n.* 漫画
satirize/sætəraiz/*v.* 讽刺

imagism/ˈimədʒizəm/*n.* 意象主义

pessimistic/ˌpesiˈinistik/*adj.* 悲观的

anarchistic/ˌænəˈkistik/*adj.* 无政府主义的，混乱的

disillusionment/ˌdisiˈluːʒənmənt/*n.* 幻灭

poignantly /ˈpɔinəntli/*adv.* 尖锐地，辛辣地

exquisite/ˈekskwizit/*adj.* 精致的，细腻的

melancholy/ˈmelənkəli/*adj.* 忧郁的，令人伤感的

nostalgic/nsəˈtælʤik/*adj.* 怀旧的

chic/ʃiːk，ʃik/*adj.* 时髦的

blues 黑人"布鲁斯"音乐，"蓝调"

undercurrent/ˈʌndəˌkʌrənt/*n.* 潜流，暗流

escapism/isˈkeipizəm/*n.* 逃避现实，逃避现实的文学

depict/diˈpikt/*v.* 刻画，描写

mysticism/ˈmistisizəm/*n.* 神秘主义

ecstasy/ˈekstəsi/*n.* 狂喜，入迷

anthology/æn·θɔləʤi/*n.* 选集

Notes

1. in search of the lost continent of Atlantis：寻找失去的大西岛。古希腊传说在大西洋中有一个理想之国大西岛。柏拉图在他的著作中谈到该岛被摧毁前曾是高度发达的文明社会的情况。这个传说一直在欧洲流传。美洲大陆被认为是古代失去的大西岛。

2. They came looking for... Coronado's imagination：他们到这里来寻找科罗纳多想象中的满地黄金的塞波拉金城。传说在今天的新墨西哥州内塞波拉有 7 个金城。科罗纳多朝思暮想要找到这些金城。科罗纳多是 16 世纪西班牙探险者。他的美洲探险一无所获，传说却流传很广。

3. They searched for the fabled Northwest Passage to the Orient：他们寻找传说中一条通往东方的西北航道。14～15 世纪的许多欧洲人相信，从欧洲大西洋向西航行就可到达富庶的东方，即中国及印度等国。哥伦布就是寻找这条航道的航海家之一，并因此发现了新大陆。

4. a New Canaan：迦南是《圣经》中赐给人类祖先亚伯罕的地方，后比喻为希望之乡。清教徒把新大陆赐给他们的新的希望之乡。

5. The Mormons... by a similar vision：18 世纪 40 年代，摩门教徒在同样的理想鼓舞下，经过艰苦的长途跋涉，穿过美国中西部大平原，到达现在是摩门教中心的犹他州。

6. Washington Irving：华盛顿·欧文(1789～1859)。美国革命战争后第一个重要的文学家，主要作品有《纽约外史》、《哥伦布传》、《攻克格拉纳达》、《草原漫游记》以及《瑞普·凡·温克尔》和《睡谷的传说》。

7. of his history... Spain：以及他的历史传奇故事集《阿尔罕伯拉》，阿尔罕伯拉是摩尔人统治西班牙的格拉纳达时期建造的华丽宫殿。

8. James Fenimor Cooper：费尼莫·库珀(1789～1851)。第一个采用民族题材的美国作家，出版近 50 部作品，包括长篇小说、旅行札记、政论、讽刺小品、传奇等。主要作品有《间谍》以及《皮袜子故事集》，由 5 部小说组成：《拓荒者》、《最后的莫希干人》、《大草原》、《探路人》和《杀鹿者》。小说的主人公是穿皮袜子的猎人纳蒂·班波。

9. Ralph Waldo Emerson：拉尔夫·沃尔多·爱默生。他的超验主义(transcendentalism)是清教主义、欧洲浪漫主义思想以及康德先验哲学相结合的产物。超验主义认为，真理超

越人的有限感觉之外,不能通过理性认识,而要以直觉来领悟普遍真理。爱默生推崇自然,认为大自然本身是一种象征,人们可以从中看到上帝的存在。他的基本思想包括在他最重要的著作《论自然》、《论美国学者》等之中。

10. In this volume, Emerson... without formal religion:在这一著作中,爱默生宣称,通过学习自然,与自然沟通,个人能够达到一个更高的精神境界,而不必借助正式的宗教。

11. thanks to a growing popular lecture circuit... the country:这归功于一个日益受欢迎的巡回演讲团将一些有争议的演讲者带到全国各地的小城镇。circuit 是指以爱默生为中心的"超验主义俱乐部",一个经常讨论超验主义等问题的聚会。

12. Henry David Thoreau:亨利·大卫·梭罗。是超验主义的另一个代表。他在超验主义影响下形成自己的思想。他把自然界看做人类进行活动的舞台,认为人要回到大自然中寻找生活的意义。其代表作有《在梅里马克河的一周》、《论公民的不服从》。《沃尔登,或林中生活》记述了他在林中独自一人度过的边劳作边学习的生活。

13. that the dictates of... of society:个人良心的支配应该高于社会的要求。take precedence over:优先于…地位在…之上

14. Edgar Ellen Poe:埃德加·爱伦·坡。美国小说家、诗人、批评家,著有怪诞恐怖小说、侦探推理小说,其中著名的有短篇故事《被盗的事件》、《厄舍尔厦的倒塌》、《红死病的假面舞会》以及诗歌《乌鸦》。

15. explored the realms... were recognized:早在人们了解认识科幻与神秘小说这些文学类型之前,他就探索了这些领域。

16. Nathaniel Hawthorne:纳撒尼尔·霍桑。19 世纪美国文学史上最有影响的浪漫主义小说家,其作品着重心理分析。主要作品有短篇故事集《重述的故事》以及长篇小说《红字》。《红字》描写在清教主义统治下的新英格兰发生的通奸案,揭示宗教对人们心理的影响。

17. Herman Melville:赫尔曼·梅尔维尔。美国小说家,主要作品有根据他的航海经历写成的《泰皮》和《欧穆》两本游记。他的长篇小说《白鲸》被公认为美国文学杰作之一。

18. had worked... sea voyages:干过许多工作,后业于 1839 年到一艘海轮上当差,开始了一系列的海上航行。

19. Ironically, the very books... today:具有讽刺意味的是,他在世时那些不被人接受的书正是今天最被人们推崇的作品。

20. Walt Whitman:瓦尔特·惠特曼。美国 19 世纪杰出的诗人。他的成名作《草叶集》包括《自我之歌》等 12 首诗歌。《草叶集》在美国文学史上有划时代的意义。

21. Whitman ventured... American spirit:惠特曼大胆突破了传统的形式,以便有更大的空间来表现美国精神。

22. He celebrated... the democracy:他称颂了美国风景的广阔画面,用近于神秘的手法歌颂了使这一民主国家中的公民团结一致的生活节奏。

23. Harriet Beecher Stowe:哈里叶特·比彻·斯托。所著长篇小说《汤姆叔叔的小屋》是揭露南方奴隶制的文学代表作,它的出版推动了当时的废奴运动。

24. Sentimental and melodramatic... Simon Legree:该书具有伤感和情节剧的特点,把黑人奴隶描绘成遭受苦难的值得同情的人物,并把西蒙·拉格瑞刻画成一个残酷的奴隶主形

象。

25. William Dean Howells:威廉·狄思·豪威尔斯。美国小说家、评论家,曾任具有影响力的《大西洋月刊》的主编。他反对浪漫主义小说,是美国现实主义文学奠基人。他的主要作品为《现代婚姻》和《赛拉斯·拉帕姆的发迹》。

26. Mark Twain:马克·吐温。是美国著名现实主义小说家塞缪尔·朗赫思·克莱门斯的笔名,著有自传成分的《艰苦岁月》、《密西西比河上》等,旅行札记如《傻瓜出国记》;社会讽刺批判作品如《竞选州长》、《败坏哈德莱堡的人》等。他的最受读者喜爱的作品是讲述儿童故事的《汤姆·索耶历险记》和《哈克贝利·费恩历险记》。

27. the entire spectrum of humanity:各种各样的人。spectrum:光谱;范围,幅度,系列,如 a wide spectrum of opinion:各种不同的意见。

28. Emily Dickinson:爱米莉·狄更生。美国女诗人,被誉为抒情短诗的大师。她的诗表现出对人生、死亡、宗教、自然等重要主题的理解。

29. She was also more than... death:她对死亡这一主题颇感兴趣。

30. Henry James:亨利·詹姆斯。美国著名小说家、文学评论家。代表作品有《黛西·密勒)、《女士的画像》、《波士顿人》、《一个美国人》等。他被视为心理现实主义的创始人之一。

31. Emile Zola:左拉(1840~1902)。法国自然主义文学奠基人,著有长篇连续小说《鲁贡玛卡家族》,其中重要的有《娜娜》、《萌芽》、《金钱》、《崩溃》等。之后写了长篇小说三部曲《三城市》,并著有论文《实验小说论》。

32. Stephen Crane:斯蒂芬·克莱恩。美国小说家和诗人,其小说《街头女郎玛吉》和《红色英勇勋章》的自然主义色彩十分浓厚。

33. Theodore Dreiser:西奥多·辛克莱(1878~1916)。以揭露社会弊端而闻名的美国小说家,被称为"资本主义的叛逆者",其主作品有《铁蹄》、自传体小说《马丁·伊登》等。

34. Upton Sinclair:厄普顿·辛克莱(1878~1968)。美国自然主义小说家,所著小说《屠场》是本世纪初一部揭露资本主义制度的重要小说。

35. that primitive urges... of animals:原始的冲动是一切生命的基础,它甚至使人类降低到动物的水平。

37. but this focused... were feeling:但这将注意力从情节和背景转移开,集中到人物的感情上。

38. Edith Wharton:伊迪丝·华顿(1862~1937)。美国女作家,著有《欢乐之家》、《纯真年代》、《伊坦·费洛美》等小说。

39. Kate Chopin:凯特·肖邦(1851~1904)。美国小说家,最主要的作品《沉醒》描写了女性的意识。

40. Willa Cather:薇拉·凯瑟(1873~1947)。美国女作家,其作品《啊!拓荒者》、《我的安东妮亚》等描写了移民们在边疆生活中表现出的坚韧不拔的开创精神。

41. W. E. B. DuBois:威·爱·伯·杜波依斯。美国黑人作家和政治活动家。他积极投身于黑人运动中,是全国性组织"有色人种协进会"的创始人之一,也是泛非运动的领导者。他著有小说、诗歌、散文和学术著作,主要作品有散文集《黑人的灵魂》和传记《约翰·布朗》。

42. Sherwood Anderson：舍伍德·安德森(1876～1941)。美国小说家，代表作《俄州的瓦恩斯堡》包括22个短篇，描写中西部小镇生活，揭示小镇的传统道德对人们的精神束缚。

43. Sinclair Lewis：辛克莱·路易斯(1885～1951)。美国小说家，代表作《大街》揭露了中西部小镇的陋习。其他主要作品有《巴比特》和《艾罗史密西》，前者因塑造了一个典型的美国商人形象而使Babbit成为一切对文化价值不感兴趣，只为自己的金钱和名誉的成功而自鸣得意的人代名词。

44. Gopher Prairie：格费草原。路易斯小说中的中西部小镇地名。

45. Ezra Pound：埃兹拉·庞德(1885～1972)。美国意象派诗人，后定居伦敦，与欧洲的意象派有密切联系。主要作品有《诗章》，第一首意象诗题为《在地铁站内》。庞德因在第二次大战中采取了亲法西斯的立场面成为一个有争议的诗人。

46. T. S. Eliot：托·斯·艾略特(1888～1965)。诗人、戏剧家、文学评化家。生于美国，后定居英国并加入英国籍。他的最重要的作品长诗《荒原》是西方现代诗歌的一个里程碑。该诗长400多行，运用了大量文学和其他艺术形象的典故，插入了6种外语，诗中通过象征手法描写了战后西方社会的精神危机。

47. Eliot dominated... in poetry：艾略特主宰了被称之为诗歌的现代派运动，现代派打破了传统的文学形式和表现手法，运用象征、意象、意识流等创新手段。

48. E. E. Cummings：爱德华·埃斯特林·肯明斯(1894～1940)。美国现代派诗人，著有诗集《郁金香与烟囱》。他的诗分行、排列、空格、标点符号均不合常规，诗中一般不用大写，连自己的名字也用小写。

49. "the Lost Generation"："迷惘的一代"。指20世纪20年代出现的一代年轻作家，他们中有的参加过第一次世界大战，对战争感到厌恶，对战后社会的幻想破灭，具有相似的迷惘、失望和悲观情绪。

50. F. Scott Fitzgerald：弗·司各特·菲兹杰拉德(1896～1940)。美国小说家，代表作为小说《了不起的盖茨比》、《夜色温柔》以及短篇小说集《爵士乐时代的故事》。这些作品描绘了20年代，即"爵士乐时代"的美国社会生活。

51. in three novels... motion pictures：在《美国》三部曲中，约翰·多斯·帕索斯将许多故事情节、人物和背景交织在一起，既有虚构的也有非虚构的，时间上前后跳动，风格上类似电影这一当时新兴的大众化艺术形式。

52. Ernest Hemingway：厄内斯特·海明威(1899～1961)。美国小说家，主要作品包括《太阳照样升起》、《永别了，武器》、《丧钟为谁而鸣》等小说。海明威在文体风格上独树一帜，在文学界产生了重要影响。

53. William Faulkner：威廉·福克纳(1897～1962)。美国文学家，被誉为现代派小说大师之一。他著有19部长篇小说和70篇短篇小说，其中大部分故事以他虚构的密西西比州的一个小县为背景。他的代表作包括《喧哗与骚动》、《八月之光》等长篇小说。

54. To show the relationship... her consciousness：为了表现过去与现在的关系，他有时颠倒故事情节的时间顺序，为了揭示一个人物的本能冲动或社会偏见，他真实地不加编辑地记录该人物意识的自由流动。

55. The Harlem Renaissance：哈莱姆文艺复兴。哈莱姆区位于纽约市内，是美国城市中最大的黑人聚居区，集中了美国最优秀的黑人艺术家和文学家，20年代以哈莱姆为中心开展了黑人文艺复兴运动,或称“新黑人运动”。

56. Eugene O'Neill:尤金·奥尼尔(1888~1953)。美国现代戏剧的最重要代表,1916年普罗温斯顿剧团首次上演了他的作品。他的主要作品包括《榆树下的欲望》、《悲悼》、《卖冰的人来了》、《长夜漫漫路迢迢》等。

57. John Steinbeck:约翰·斯坦贝克(1902~1968)。美国小说家,经济大萧条时期最重要的作家。代表作长篇小说《愤怒的葡萄》描写了雇农乔德一家在萧条时期不得不背井离乡外出谋生的故事。

58. Joseph Heller:约瑟夫·海勒(1923~)。美国文学家,代表作《第22条军规》开60年代所谓“黑色幽默”文学的先河。该书中的第22条军规作为一个固定名词进入词典,意思是法规中的自相矛盾之处使执行者进退两难。

59. Richard Wright:理查德·赖特(1908~1960)。美国黑人作家,其小说《土生子》成为黑人抗议小说的代表作。

60. Ralph Ellison:拉尔夫·埃利森(1914~1944)。美国黑人作家,他的长篇小说《看不到的人》被视为美国20世纪最重要的小说之一。

61. James Baldwin:詹姆斯·鲍德温(1924~1987)。美国黑人作家,著有《向苍天呼吁》、《下一次将是烈火》等作品。

62. Saul Bellow:索尔·贝娄(1915~)。美国小说家,其成名作是《奥吉·玛琪历险记》,其他重要小说有《只争朝夕》、《赛姆勒先生的行》、《洪堡的礼物》等。

63. Isaac Bashevis Singer:艾萨克·巴什维斯·辛格(1904~)。美国作家,著有30多部作品,包括小说、剧本、回忆录等,全部用犹太人使用的意第绪文写成,其中以短篇见长。

64. Tennessee Williams:田纳西·威廉斯(1911~1983)。美国戏剧家,主要作品有《玻璃动物园》和《欲望号街车》。

65. the “Beat Generation”:“垮掉的一代”。其代表人物诗人艾伦·金斯堡的诗歌《嚎叫》代表年轻一代向社会发出愤怒的抗议嚎叫,倡导无拘无束的生活追求,无视一切社会道德与行为准则。

Exercise

Ⅰ. Explain the following

1. The Letherstocking Tales
2. Transcendentalists
3. Leaves of Grass
4. the naturalists
5. the “Lost Generation”
6. the Harlem Renaissance
7. the “Beat Generation”

Ⅱ. Fill in the blanks

1. ______________ and ______________ are the two major writers of the post-Revolutionary period.

2. "The Masque of the Red Death" and "The Fall of the House of Usher" were stories wiritten by ___________.

3. In 1852, a New England woman named Harriet Beecher Stowe wrote novel titled ___________, which intensified the political debate on slavery.

4. Mark Twain's ___________ is considered the greatest novel in American literature.

5. Hery James' major works include ___________ and ___________. His works often described Americans living in ___________.

6. Upton Sinclair's novel ___________ exposed the horrible lives of meat-packing factory workers.

7. Ezra Pound's poetry is famous for ___________, the use of strong, concrete images.

8. T. S. Eliot's long poem ___________ revealed a pessimistic view of post-World War I society. He dominated the so-called ___________ movement in poetry.

9. After World War I, many novelists produced literary works of disillusionment, Some of them lived abroad and were known as the "___________."

10. F. Scott Fitzgerald's novel ___________ was about youth's golden dream turning to disappointment.

11. Name three novels written by Ernest Hemingway: ___________, ___________ and ___________.

12. The Sound and the Fury was written by ___________, whose prose style was experimental.

13. Name two plays written by Eugene O'Neill: ___________ and ___________,

14. John Steinbeck's The Grapes of Wrath was a portrait of a poor family during the period of ___________.

15. Richard Wright wrote the novel ___________, and Ralph Ellison wrote the novel ___________. Both were ___________ writers.

16. The representative work of the "Beat Generation" was Alan Ginsberg's poem ___________.

17. ___________ won the Nobel Prize for Literature in 1993, the first Afro-American writer to receive this honor. Two of her best novels are ___________ and ___________.

Ⅲ. Choose the correct answer in each of the following

1. Which of the following was a writer of the post-Revolutionary period?

   A. Edgar Allan Poe.

   B. Natty Bumppo.

   C. Washington Irving.

   D. Rip Van Winkle.

2. Which of the following is considered an American masterpiece?

   A. The Last of the Mohicans.

   B. The Legend of the Sleepy Hollow.

C. The Masque of the Red Death.

D. Moby Dick.

3. Which of the following was written by Thoreau?

A. Nature.

B. Walden.

C. The Scarlet Letter.

D. The Fall of the House of Usher.

4. Whitman's poetry has the following characteristics except ________.

A. fragmented haunting images

B. long irregular lines

C. celebrating the American spirit

D. free-flowing structure

5. Mark Twain's works are characterized by the following except ________.

A. sense of humor

B. egotism

C. jokes

D. tall tales

6. Three of the following are characteristics of Emily Dickinson's poems. Which one is not?

A. Her poems mix gaiety and gloom.

B. Her verses are filled with the names of faraway, exotic places.

C. Her poems are very long and powerful.

D. Her poems show that she was fascinated by both life and death.

7. ________ was mainly interested in writing about Americans living Europe.

A. Henry James

B. Mark Twain

C. William Dean Howells

D. Stephen Crane

8. ________ is NOT included in the group of naturalists.

A. Sherwood Anderson

B. Stephen Crane

C. Jack London

D. Theodore Dreiser

9. Which one is not a Nobel Prize winner?

A. Ernest Hemingway.

B. Eugene O'Neill.

C. William Faulkner.

D. F. Scott Fitzgerald.

10. ________ does NOT belong to the "Lost Generation".

A. John Dos Passos

B. Ernest Hemingway

C. F. Scott Fitzgerald

D. John Steinbeck

11. ________ was NOT written by Hemingway.

A. Light in August

B. The Sun Also Rises

C. A Farewell to Arms

D. For Whom the Bell Tolls

12. Which of the following is NOT a black author?

A. Richard Wright.

B. Alan Ginsberg.

C. James Baldwin.

D. Ralph Ellison.

13. The following authors were women writers who wrote novels in the late 19th and early 20th century with the exception of ________.

A. Emily Dickinson

B. Edith Wharton

C. Willa Cather

D. Kate Chopin

14. The following writers represent new American voices except ________.

A. Toni Morrison

B. Alice Walker

C. T. S. Eliot

D. Maxine Long Kingston

Ⅳ. Answer the following questions briefly

1. What is the main theme is American literature according to the author?
2. What theories does Ralph Emerson explain in his essays? Why are they so influential?
3. Why is Walt Whitman considered one of the most important poets in America?
4. Why did Mark Twain win so many readers both at home and abroad?
5. What are some of the major themes in novels written by the "Lost Generation"?

Chapter 15 Religion and Beliefs

Religious Liberty

By the middle of the 18th century. many different kinds of Protestants lived in America. Lutherans[2] had come to America from Germany. The Dutch Reformed Church flourished in new York and new Jersey[3]. Presbyterians[4] came from Scotland and Huguenots[5] from France. Congregationalists[6], as the Puritans came to be called, still dominated in Massachusetts and the neighboring colonies, and area which came to be known as new England.

Although the Church of England was an established church in several colonies, Protestants lived side by side in relative harmony[7]. Already they had begun to influence each other. The Great Awakening of the 1740s, a "revival" movement which sought to breathe new feeling and strength into religion, cut across the lines of Protestant religious groups, or denominations[8].

At the same time the works of John Locke were becoming known in America. *John Locke* reasoned that the right to govern comes from an agreement or "social contract" voluntarily entered into by free people. The Puritan experience in forming congregations made this idea seem natural to many Americans. Taking it out of therealm of social theory, they made it a reality and formed a nation.

It was politics and not religion that most occupied Americans' minds during the War of Independence and for years afterward. A few Americans were so influenced by the new science and new ideas of the Enlightenment in Europe[9] that they became deists[10], believing that reason teaches that God exists but leaves man free to settle his own affairs.

Many traditional Protestants and deists could agree, however, that, as the Declaration of Independence states. "all men are created equal, that they are endowedby their creator with certain unalienable rights," and that "the laws of Nature and Nature's God"[11] entitle them to form a new nation. Among the rights that the new nation guaranteed, as a political necessity in a religiously diverse society, was freedom of religion.

The First Amendment to the constitution of the United States forbade the new federal government to give special favors to any religion or to hinder the free practice, or exercise, of religion. The Unites States would have no state-supported religion. In this way, those men who formulated the principal tenets of the newly established political system hoped to insure that diversity of religious belief would never become the source of social or political injustice or disaffection. But Protestant churches kept a privileged position in a few of the states[12]. Not until 1833 did Massachusetts cut the last ties between church and state[13].

The First Amendment insured that American government would not meddle in religious affairs or require any religious beliefs of the citizens. But did it mean that the American government would have nothing at all to do with religion? Or did it mean that government would be religiously neutral, treating all religions alike?

In some ways, the government supports all religions. Religious groups do not pay taxes in the United States. The armed forces pay chaplains of all faiths[14]. Presidents and other political leaders often call on God to bless the American nation and people. Those whose religion forbids them to fight can perform other services instead of becoming soldiers[15].

But government does not pay ministers' salaries or require any belief—not even a belief in God—as a condition of holding public office. Oaths are administered, but those who, like Quakers, object to them, can make a solemn affirmation, or Declaration, instead[16].

The truth is that for some purposes government ignores religion and for other purposes it treats all religions alike—at least as far as is practical. When disputes about the relationship between government and religion arise. American courts must settle them.

American courts have become more sensitive in recent years to the rights of people who do not believe in any God or religion. But in many ways what Supreme Court Justice william O. Douglas[17] wrote in 1952 is still true. "We are a religious people," he declared, "whose institutions presuppose a supreme Being."[18]

In the early years of the American nation, Americans were confident that God supported their experiment in republican government. They had just defeated Great Britain-probably the most powerful nation in the world at that time. Protestant religion and republican forms of government, they felt went hand in hand[19].

Protestants in the United States

Today, the majority of Americans belong to the Protestant church. Over 60% of Americans are said to be Protestant believers. The Baptists are the largest Protestant group. They believe in adult baptism by immersion, symbolizing a mature and responsible conversion experience[20]. Form a beginning in 17th century England, the Baptists have continued on a small scale in England where they are about 1% of the population. But in the Unites States, they have their main strength, with over 25 million members(19. 4% of the population), divided among more than 20 branches and concentrated particularly in the Southern Bible Belt[21]. Some white Baptists have liberal attitudes toward the blacks and stand up courageously in difficult circumstances for their belief in the equality of all human beings before God, whatever their color. But the great majority seem to have no difficulty in reconciling their Christian belief and practice with their racial prejudice[22]. Meanwhile, most of the blacks are Baptists too, but they got to different churches from the white. In southern communities the blacks find their main social center in their Baptist churches and sometimes a base from which to organize group action.

Next to the Baptists, the most numerous Protestants are the Methodists[23], adherents of the group which grew up in 18th century England following the lead of John Wesley[24]. Most Methodists are united in the Methodist Church, which has a form of service based on that of the Church of England.

Thus the main Protestant groups with the origins in Britain are flourishing, and seem to have taken on a distinctively American character, including a tendency to form subgroups. But this is not the whole story of Protestantism. Smaller sects from Europe have taken root, and new sects have formed within America, some of them around individual leaders.

There are more than 100 other Protestant sects, many of them hardly known to anyone except their own members, but with a combined membership of more than 20 million. They express variety, rather than doctrinal schism[25]. Some of them are of recent foundation, and the dominant trend is fundamentalist[26]. Four of thee smaller sects are really quite large, with 2 million or more members. These are thee Latter Day Saints, the Churches of Christ, the United Church of Christ and the International Convention of Disciples of Christ[27]. Some of the small sects are extremely intolerant, and depend on a highly emotional and even hysterical approach. Some have shown themselves particularly ready to be pragmatic in adapting themselves to what they imagine to be the ideas of modern society. And new prophets and movements of religion are appearing all the time.

Catholics

Although the largest church is of the Protestant faith, the largest single religious group is that of Roman Catholics. More than one-quarter of all Americans are now of the Roman Catholic faith. According to a survey done in the early 1990s. Roman Catholics represent 26. 2% of the U. S. population(the 4 large Protestant groups, the Baptists. Methodists. Presbyterians. Episcopalians[28] represent 31. 9% of the population). The majority of the Catholics are descendants of immigrants from Ireland. Italy and Poland. Most of the early Catholics stayed near the east coast. They were concentrated especially in New York and Massachusetts, and are still a very important element of the population in those two states. By the Civil War, over a million Irish Catholics, many driven by hunger, had come to the United States. Most were working people. Anti-Catholic prejudice was so strong that. on a few occasions, it broke out in mob violence. In 1844, two Catholic churches were burnt and 13 people died in rioting that swept through the city of Philadelphia, Pennsylvania. More often prejudice took the form of discrimination, particularly at the polls. By 1960, however, John F. Kennedy's presidential election victory put to rest the catholic religion as an issue in national politics. Kennedy was Roman Catholic. Catholics were not shut out of public schools and hospitals but they wanted their own schools, colleges and hospitals. Catholics believed that these institutions were needed to preserve their faith. Many Catholics now attend public schools and secular colleges. But Catholic institutions, especially in large cities, still serve large numbers of Catholics and a growing number of non-Catholics, who are attracted by the discipline and education offered in these schools. By the 1950s, many Catholics had risen to positions of leadership, not only in labor unions, but in business and politics as well. As Catholics grew more confident about their place in American life, they began to challenge, not the basic idea of separation of Church and State, but the way American courts interpreted it. The costs of modern education had made their schools very expensive to maintain. Catholics began to seek some way in which they could obtain public funds to help meet these expenses. Other private schools, not necessarily religious in origin or concern, also sought this help.

The lawmaking bodies of many states were sympathetic to these demands. But most attempts to provide help for religious schools were ruled unconstitutional (declared to violate the Constitution) by the Supreme Court of the United States. Giving public money to a religious school was held to violate the clause, or part, of the First Amendment which prohibits the establishment of religion. Public money for religious schools remains an issue in American politics in the 1990s.

If Catholics feel that government should support the non-religious aspects of private education, other American groups call for even less government connection to religion. Sunday closing laws were a real hardship to Jews and Seventh Day Adventists[29]. In effect, they were forced to observe two Sabbaths, or days of rest—their own and the majority Christian one as well. Nonbelievers, and some religious people as well, objected to prayer and Bible reading in public schools. They thought that a modern government in a free society should be basically secular.

Three Faiths

Like Catholics, Jews were a small minority in the first years of the American republic. Until the late 19th century, most Jews in America were of German origin. Many of them belonged to the Reform movement, a liberal branch of Judaism[30] which had made many adjustments to modern life. Anti-Semitism, or anti Jewish prejudice, was not a big problem before the Civil War. But when Jews began coming to America in great numbers, anti-Semitism appeared.

Usually, Jewish children attended public schools. The children of the immigrants moved rapidly into the professions and into American universities, where many became intellectual leaders. Many remained religiously observant. Others, while they continued to think of themselves as ethnically Jewish, adopted a secular, nonreligious outlook.

When faced with prejudice and discrimination, Jews responded by forming organizations to combat prejudice. The Anti-defamation League[31] played a major role in educating Americans about the injustice of prejudice and making them aware of the rights, not only of Jews, but of all minorities.

By the 1950s, a kind of "three faiths" model of the United States had developed. Americans were considered to come in three basic varieties: Protestant, Catholic and Jewish, the order reflecting the strength in numbers of each group. But an increasing number of Americans did not fit into any of these categories. And some who could be considered Protestant had styles of life and beliefs that did not fit into "Mainstream" America.

Religious Diversity

The United States has always been a fertile ground for the growth of new religious movements. Frontier America provided plenty of room to set up a new church or found a new community. For example, the ancestors of the Amish[32], very strict Protestants who live in rural areas and scorn modern life, came from Germany in the 18th century to escape persecution.

Many religious communities and secular utopias, or experiments in new forms of social living, were founded in 18th and 19th century America[33]. Most did not last long. But some prospered for a while and a few are still in existence. 20th century Americans who follow the impulse to withdraw from society and "join a commune" are following in an old American tradition[34].

Small sects and "cults" do have certain tendencies in common. Often they regard the larger society as hopelessly corrupt. Prohibition of alcohol, tobacco and caffeine are common. Sometimes dramatic expectations about the future—predictions of the end of the world or the dawning of a new age—form the main tenets, or doctrines, of the group. Often the founder is a charismatic person, dynamic personality who claims some special revelation or relationship with God. Some groups never win a large following. Others grow smaller or disappear when the founder dies or his prophecies fail to come true. Still others prosper, win large followings and "graduate" into the ranks of the "respectable" denominations.

Some groups, like the Amish of Pennsylvania, simply want to be left alone in their rural communities. They wish to keep their children out of high school so they will not be affected by modern society.

A few prefer faith healing to modern medicine or object to certain medical practices[35]. What should society do when a Jehovah's Witness[36] refused a blood transfusion for himself or his child?

Questions like these often come before the courts in the United States. They are generally settled according to a principle the Supreme Court established when it ruled that the Mormons, a large and prosperous Christian sect which settled the state of Utah, could not marry more than one wife. Individuals may believe anything they please in America, but they may not do anything they want, even if the action is based on a religious belief. Such questions do not usually cause great controversy, because they do not reflect basic divisions in American society. The Mormons[37], for example, continue to flourish, and are one of the fastest growing church groups in the United States.

But other questions reflect continuing conflicts in American life. When a 1973 Supreme Court decision made abortion legal in America, many Catholics were shocked[38]. Many evangelical Protestants and Orthodox Jews also objected. Yet more liberal Protestant and Jewish clergymen joined non-believers in maintaining that abortion is a basic right in a pluralistic, or religiously varied, society.

Other world religions are increasing their numbers and influence in America. Over 2 million members of the Islamic religion live in America. Some are immigrants or the children of immigrants; others are Americans, including some black Americans who have converted to Islam.

Buddhism is a growing faith in America. Recent immigration from Asia has raised the number of Buddhists in America to several hundred thousand—no one seems quite sure how many. Several hundred thousand Hindus have also come to America. In recent years, young native-born Americans have shown great interest in these and other Eastern religions and philosophies.

American pastors are as varied as the flocks they serve. Some of them are women. The Protestant Episcopal Church now ordains women as priests, although the Catholic Church continues to have an all-male clergy. The United Methodist Church has appointed women as bishops. Women can also be ordained as rabbis among some Jewish congregations. Catholic nuns teach and manage large hospitals. Chaplains of all faiths visit the sick in hospitals and nursing homes.

American pastors of churches are expected to be active in the civic affairs of their communities. Often they have psychological training and spend part of their time counseling people with personal problems. They preach to congregations assembled in small chapels and huge city cathedrals, in modem synagogues, and even sometimes in drive-in churches where people can worship without leaving their cars! Some evangelical preachers reach a television audience of millions.

How do Americans of so many different religions manage to live together under common laws and pursue common goals? The answers can be found in the American character of religion.

American Character of Religion

Some phenomena in American religion are uniquely American. First of all, Americans with different religions live together under the same law. The Bill of Rights in the U. S. Constitution insists that there should be no state religion. The freedom of religion and the separation of state and church guaranteed in the Constitution is believed to be the basic principles against religious persecution. Due to this tradition and the basic law about religion, various religious groups in America have coexisted more harmoniously than the Old World.

Secondly, the religious beliefs of Americans continue to be strong with social progress. Every Sunday morning, all over America, people pour into the churches.

Half of American Protestants are active church members, and there are few who habitually stay away. Not only the Catholic churches, but the Protestant ones too, are flourishing, and new church buildings, some with interesting architecture, keep pace with the ever-growing suburbs. Yet in England, leaving aside the Catholics, four-fifths of the people go to church less than once a month, and in Sweden the vast majority hardly ever go to church at all. In America, through all the social and economic changes religion has remained a constant factor. In Europe, scientific and economic advance and rising material prosperity have accompanied by a decline in religious observance, but in the United States this has not happened.

Thirdly, in the United States every church is a completely independent organization, and concerned with its own finance and its own building. There has been little concentration on doctrine or religious argument such as in European history. If one goes to a Protestant church he or she will hear morality preached, but not a word of doctrine[39]. Anglicans do not pay much attention to 39 articles on which the belief of the Anglican Church is based[40]. Churches and religious sects are expressions of group solidarity rather than of rigid adherence to doctrine. Baptist ministers are invited to preach in Methodist churches. Exchange of pulpits has been common for many years. A Protestant family moving to a new place will probably try out several of the nearby churches before deciding on the one that suits them best, not for doctrinal reasons, but that is where they find their friends.

Several explanations may be offered. In American history, religion has not been identified with an oppressive of dominant social class or set of political institutions[41]. The Pilgrim Fathers, and many of those who followed them, left Europe to be free to worship in their own way, not as the established authorities told them to. Although some religious groups were also persecuted in early America and Catholics were prejudiced against, generally speaking. Americans have enjoyed greater religious freedom than Europeans. Paradoxically, the original basis of freedom creates a social pressure in favor of religion[42]. Most people want to identify themselves with dominant values, and going freely to the church of one' s choice is a way of doing so, and of gaining acceptance in the face of a subtle demand for conformity[43]. And the church is a place where people can meet others with whom they would like to make friends. Religion, for most people, is important mainly as a means of getting together with others in a context which is so little defined that its values, expressing merely generally good will, can be easily shared[44]. People go to church and it helps them feel that they have a place in a community.

Words & Expressions

Lutheran/ˈljuːθərən/*n.* 路德派教徒

Presbyterian/ˌpresbiˈtiəriən/*n.* 长老会教友

Huguenot/ˈhjuːgənɔt/*n.* 胡格诺派教徒

Congregationalist/ˌkɔŋgriˈgeiʃənəlist/*n.* 公理会教友

enlightenment/inˈlaitənmənt/*n.* 启蒙运动

deist/ˈdiːizt/*n.* 自然神论者

adherent/ədˈhiərənt/*adj.* 追随者

schism/ˈsizəm/*n.* 分派

fundamentalist/ˌfʌndəˈmentəlist/*adj.* 原教旨主义的

Episcopalian /iˌpiskəˈpeiljən/*n.* 圣公会教徒

secular/ˈsekjuːlə/*adj.* 世俗的

Judaism/ˈdʒuːdeiizəm/*n.* 犹太教

anti-Semitism/ˈæntiˈsemitizəm/*n.* 反犹太主义

Amish/ˈeimiʃ/*n.* 阿门教派

utopia/juːˈtəupiə/*n.* 乌托邦,空想主义

Mormon/ˈmɔːmən/*n.* 摩门教徒

evangelical/ˌiːvænˈdʒelikəl/*n.* 新教福音派教会的

Islam/izˈlaːm/*n.* 伊斯兰教

Buddhism/ˈbudizəm/*n.* 佛教

Hindus/ˌhinˈduː/*n.* 印度教派

flock/flɔk/*n.* 教徒群

rabbi/ˈræbai/*n.* 犹太教教士

psychological/ˌsaikəˈlɔdʒikəl/*adj.* 心理的

counsel/ˈkaunsl/*v.* 劝告

preach/priːtʃ/*v.* 布道

chapel/ˈtʃæpəl/*n.* 教堂(小型)

cathedral/kəˈθiːdrəl/*n.* 大教堂

synagogue/ˈsinəgɔg/*n.* 犹太教堂

drive-in church 露天教堂(教徒可不下汽车进行宗教仪式)

Anglican/ˈæŋglikən/*n.* 圣公会教徒

pulpit/ˈpulpit/*n.* 教士,牧师(集合词)

Notes

1. "WASP" culture:盎格鲁·撒克逊白人新教文化。WASP 是 white Anglo-Saxon Protestant 的缩写。

2. Lutherans:路德派教徒。追随宗教改革家马丁·路德的新教教徒。

3. The Dutch Reformed Church... New Jersey 在纽约及新泽西州兴旺的荷兰改革派教徒。他们也是新教徒。纽约地区原被荷兰开发,后被英国人侵吞。

4. Presbyterians 长老会教徒。该教起源于苏格兰,信奉加尔文教义的新教教派。

5. Huguenots:胡格诺派教徒。16 世纪及 17 世纪在法国出现的加尔文派教徒。

6. Congregationalists:公理会教友。由新英格兰地区的清教演变而来。

7. Although the Church of England... in relative harmony:英国国教虽然在几个殖民地是官立教会,但新教各派都能和平相处。英国国教也是新教各派中的一派,它在南方几个殖民地虽属官方教会,但美国革命后,特别是美国宪法制订后,这种官立地位就不再存在。

8. The Great Awakening of the 1740s... or denominations:18 世纪 40 年代的宗教大复兴运动力图把新的感觉和新的力量注入北美各殖民地人民的宗教信仰中去。这次"复兴"运动打破了新教各派的界限。随着欧洲各国移民的源源不断到来,北美定居者不断向西部荒

野地区挺进,许多人宗教观念开始淡薄起来。这种情况引起宗教界的恐慌。一些宗教狂热分子从南向北发起向群众布道运动,以增强大家的宗教信仰。这次复兴运动虽然没有达到预想的全部目的,却唤醒了北美人民的民族意识,促进了美国革命的爆发。

9. the Enlightenment in Europe:欧洲的启蒙运动。这是 17~18 世纪欧洲思想界兴起的思想运动,研究上帝、理性、自然、人类之间的相互关系,强调理性、科学和人道主义思想,主张改革和革命。主要的启蒙运动思想家有法国的伏尔泰、孟德斯鸠,英国的洛克等。

10. deists:自然神论者。自然神论学说起源于 17~18 世纪的欧洲。他们从理性主义出发,认为上帝是存在的,他创造了世界及其自然规律,但以后再参与共事,人类自己去发现世界的奥妙,解决自己的问题。

11. the laws of Nature and Nature's God:自然规律及自然的上帝。这就是自然神论者的观点。他们认为,在上帝创造的自然中人人享有自然权利,这是上帝赋予的权利,任何人都不能剥夺。

12. But Protestant Churches kept a privileged position in a few of the states:新教在一些州享有特殊的地位。比如在新英格兰各州,由于历史的原因,清教信仰在很长时间里一直处于支配地位。

13. Not until 1833 did Massachusetts cut the last ties between Church and State:直到 1833 年,马萨诸塞州才彻底割断州政府与教会的关系。

14. The armed forces pay chaplains of all faiths:军队对所有不同信仰的随军教士都发放军饷,以示一视同仁。

15. Those who... instead of becoming soldiers:那些因宗教信仰禁止他们上前线打仗的人,可以不去参军,而以其他服务来代替。比如贵格派教友是和平主义者,认为一切战争都是有罪的。

16. Oaths are administered... or declaration, instead:在进行宣誓时,那些反对这样做的人,如贵格派,可以不宣誓而代之以庄严的承诺或宣告。

17. William O. Douglas:威廉·道格拉斯。曾任美国最高法院大法官(1939~1975)。

18. whose institutions presuppose a Supreme Being:我们的社会风俗习惯都是以上帝存在为前提的。

19. Protestant religion... went hand in hand:美国人认为新教与共和制政府是一致的。共和体制的基本是不要国王一人独裁,而要求民选政府,即政府的权力必须得到人民的同意,而新教强调个人信仰上帝,不需教皇或教会的干涉,这一点和共和制有相似之处。

20. They believe in adult baptism... conversion experience:浸礼教徒主张成人全身浸水以表示成熟负责任的皈依经历。他们相信这种用"圣水"浸礼的人就获得了新生。

21. the Southern Bible Belt:指南部信仰原教旨主义的地区。美国建国前后,许多人从弗吉尼亚一带,即原来的南部地区带着《圣经》移居今天美国的最南部地区,如田纳西州周围各州,因此,这里有"南部《圣经》地带"之称。

22. But the great majority... with their racial prejudice:但浸礼会的大多数教徒却很容易地把他们虔诚的宗教信仰同种族歧视一致起来。他们从《圣经》中找出依据,说白人高于有色人种是上帝的意志。

23. the Methodists:卫理公会派教徒。该派属新教,起源于 18 世纪英国的牛津大学。

24. John Wesley:约翰·韦斯利(1703~1791)。卫理公会派的创始人。

25. They express variety, rather than doctrinal schism:他们反映的只是教派的不同,而并不是教义的分歧。

26. fundamentalist:原教旨主义的。原教结果主义者基督教徒坚信《圣经》中所说的一切都是准确无误的,不能有新的解释。他们强烈反对进化论思想。

27. These are the Later Day Saints... the International Convention of disciples of Christ:这些教派是现代基督教圣徒派、耶稣教、联合耶稣教及国际耶稣信徒会等,都是原教旨派,是新教中的小教派。

28. Episcopalians:新教圣公会教徒。美国的这个教派由英国国教演变而来。

29. Sunday closing laws... Seventh Day Adventists:星期日关门不营业不娱乐法对犹太教徒和周六安息日派造成极大困难。基督教徒把周日定为安息日,犹太教等的安息日是周六。

30. Judaism:犹太教。以《圣经》中的"旧约"为教义。

31. The Anti-Defamation League:反诽谤协会。

32. the ancestors of the Amish:阿门教派的祖先。阿门教派是17世纪德国阿门创立的教派,它教规严格,属于新教的一个支派。居住在宾洲的阿门教徒是18世纪从德国移居美国的。他们至今仍保持着德国中世纪的农业社会的生活方式,拒绝使用电、机器等现代设备。

33. Many religious communities... in 18th and 19th-century America:18、19世纪,有许多宗教团体和世俗的"乌托邦"组织或试验新的社会生活方式的团体在美国成立。最著名的有宣扬独身主义的新教派"震教派"(the Shakers);英国空想社会主义者罗伯特·欧文(1771~1858)建立的新协和模范工业城等。

34. 20th century Americans... in an old American tradition:20世纪要求"离开社会"加入公社的那些美国人的冲动继承了美国这种历史传统。最明显的例子是60年代美国出现的反主流文化中的嬉皮士派,还有如今天渴望"回归自然"的许多美国人的思想。

35. A few prefer faith healing to modern medicine or object to certain medical practices:一些教派相信信仰疗法,而不相信现代医学,或反对某些医疗方法。基督教科学派就是其中之一,他们生病后不去求医,而相信上帝会治好他们的疾病。

36. Jehovah's Witness:耶和华见证派。他们反对输血等现代医疗手段。耶和华即是上帝。

37. the Mormons:摩门教。属新教派,其中心在美国的犹他州,曾实行过一夫多妻制,现已放弃。

38. When a 1973 Supreme Court... many Catholics were shocked:1973年,美国最高法院宣布堕胎合法,许多天主教徒对此裁决感到震惊。天主教、新教中的原教旨主义派以及正统犹太教都反对堕胎。他们说婴儿是上帝送来的,他们也是生命,因此,堕胎违背上帝的旨意,是谋杀生命。

39. If one goes to a Protestant church... but not a word of doctrine:进入新教的教堂,你听到的只是道德方面的宣讲,却听不到任何有关教义方面的布道。

40. Anglicans do not pay much attention... is based:圣公会教派不大注意圣公会教派的

基础“39 条款”教义的布道。英国国教（在美国称“圣公会”）于 1571 年通过“39 条款”，从教义上批判了罗马天主教的某些教规和宗教仪式。这个条款被称为英国圣公会的“新教声明”，使英国国教成为真正的新教派。

41. In American history... set of political institutions：美国的宗教从来没有和社会上的压迫阶级或统治级联系在一起，和政治机构也没有关系。这句话不确切。在美国历史上，清教就和当时的新英格兰统治阶级有着紧密的联系，就是今天的美国社会也不能说宗教和统治阶级没有关系。

42. Paradoxically... in favor of religion：矛盾的是，宗教自由的历史基础反而产生了一种使人信仰宗教的社会压力。

43. Most people want to identify themselves... for conformity：大多数人希望自己和社会的主流价值观保持一致，自觉自愿地选择去一个教堂就是达到这一目的的方式之一，也是面对社会上无形压力要求大家保持一致而得到别人承认的方法。

44. Religion, for most people... can be easily shared：对大多数人来说，宗教主要是和大家交往的手段。对于处在不稳定的环境中的人来说，主要是表达善意的宗教价值观是很容易被大家所共享的。in a context which is so little defined：指北美环境原始荒凉，生活很不稳定。

Exercises

Ⅰ. Explain the following

1. "WASP" culture
2. religious liberty in the U. S.
3. Three Faiths in the U. S.
4. religious diversity

Ⅱ. Fill in the blanks

1. "WASP" stands for ________________.
2. The Great Awakening of the 1740s tried to breathe new feeling and strength into religion, and cut across the lines of ________________.
3. According to John Locke, the right to govern comes from an agreement or ____________ voluntarily entered into by free people.
4. ____________ believes that reason teaches that God exists but leaves man free to settle his own affairs.
5. The majority of the Catholics in the U. S. are descendants of immigrants from ________, ________ and Poland.
6. Prayer and Bible reading in public schools in the U. S. are ________.
7. The Three Faiths in the U. S. refer to ________, ________ and ________.
8. According to the text, in England, ________________ percent of the people except Catholics go to church less than once a month; in Sweden ________________ go to church at all. Yet ________________ of American Protestants are active church

members.

9. Freedom of religious belief or non-belief is provided in the __________ in the U. S. Constitution.

10. The fist Catholic president in the U. S. was __________.

Ⅲ. Choose the correct answer in each of the following

1. Which of the following was NOT a Protestant denomination?
   A. The Baptists.
   B. The Catholics.
   C. The Methodists.
   D. The Presbyterians.
2. Which of the following is unconstitutional in the United States?
   A. Catholics can build their own schools and hospitals.
   B. Non-Catholics can go to Catholic-run schools.
   C. Public money is provided to support religious schools.
   D. Women have the right to abortion.
3. Which of the following is NOT regarded as one of the three basic religious beliefs?
   A. Protestant.
   B. Catholic.
   C. Islamic.
   D. Judaism.
4. Which of the following is true?
   A. Many Catholics are not opposed to abortion.
   B. Many evangelical Protestants do not object to abortion.
   C. Orthodox Jews are for abortion.
   D. Liberal Protestants and Jews join non-believers in maintaining that abortionis a basic right for women.
5. Which of the following continues to have an all-male clergy?
   A. The Catholic Church.
   B. The Protestant Episcopal Church.
   C. The United Methodist Church.
   D. Jewish Congregations.
6. The following are distinctively American features of religion except __________.
   A. Various religious groups have coexisted in the U. S. more harmoniously than Europe
   B. Scientific and economic advance and material prosperity have not been accompanied by a decline in religious faith
   C. There has been little concentration on doctrine or religion argument in the US.
   D. There has been very much concentration on doctrine or religious argument in the U. S.
7. In the United States, people go to church mainly for the following reasons except __________.

A. for finding a job in society

B. for having a place in a community

C. for identifying themselves with dominant values

D. for getting together with friends

8. Which of the following statements is NOT correct according to the author?

A. American mainstream culture is based on Protestantism.

B. Protestant Church is an established church by law in the U. S.

C. The Catholic Church is the largest single religious group in the U. S.

D. The largest church is of the Protestant faith in the U. S.

Ⅳ. Answer the following questions briefly

1. What made religious freedom a historical necessity in the United States?
2. What is the relationship between government and religion in America?
3. What promotes the diversity in American religion?
4. What are some of the features in religion that are particularly American? What are some of the major differences between American religion and religion in Europe?

Chapter 16 American Character

The United States is a huge nation, the fourth largest in the world. Within its Borders, there are vast regional differences in climate, geography, and historical experience. Each section of the United states is often thought to have its own customs and attitudes, and stereotypes have developed about the people of each region. For example, the New Englander is described as stern and self-reliant, the Southerner as gracious and leisurely, and the Westerner as casual and friendly.

Most regional distinctions, however, have been erased by modern transportation, communication, and mass production. From coast to coast, we find the same kinds of shopping centers, supermarkets, motels, suburban houses, and urban apartments. National advertising has created national tastes in consumer goods. Home furnishing, cars, and clothing look much the same throughout the nation.

Though some regional differences remain, most notably in cooking styles and speech patterns, the attitudes and values that Americans share are of far greater signifcance, The pioneering spirit of the immigrant is still an important part of the American character. Except for the slaves brought from Africa, immigrants came to America voluntarily, eagerly, in search of greater prosperity and freedom.

In the mid-nineteenth century, the pioneering spirit led American settlers to travel westward by the thousands in search of land and gold. This westward movement has never ceased. Today, Northerners and Midwesterners are attracted to the West because of good business opportunities and a mild climate. From 1950 to 1970, Los Angeles (the nation's third largest city) grew 43 percent in population, while Tucson and phoenix (Arizona's two major cities) grew more than 400 percent!

The desire to start a new life in a new place is noticeable throughout the nation. About 40 million Americans change residences every year. The average American moves fourteen times in his lifetime, compared to five moves for the average Japanese. Because so many people move often, even those who stay put have a steady supply of new neighbors[1]. In the United states, one cannot go home to find one's past. The old neighborhood revisited usually looks completely different, with high-rise buildings on the old softball sandlots. Childhood friends have long since moved away.

Much of this residential shifting is local and primarily related to the need for bigger or smaller living quarters as family size changes[2]. Some local moving is alo related to neighborhood changes. When families move into nicer residential areas, leaving the older, deteriorating neighborhood to poorer people. long distance moves are often related to job opportunities. Some workers move from a city where there is little chance of employment to another city where industry is expanding. Some workers, employed by large corporations, move from one city to another because job promotion within the company requires such changes. In addition, about half of the nation's young single adults live away from their home towns because they are attending college, serving in the armed forces, or just seeking new and independent lives.

What does all this moving about do to attitudes and values? Vance Packard, one of the nation's well-known nonfiction writers, discusses the problem in his popular book *A Nation of strangers*. He believes that the highly mobile American society leaves individuals with feelings of footlessness, isolation, indifference to community welfare, and shallow personal relationships. He urges that efforts be made to stabilize our shifting population so that Americans can "rediscover the natural human community"[3].

Americans who do not change residence are also on the move — traveling by air or auto to see their own country and to visit others. The need to explore a new frontier is basic to the American character. Now that most of the nation's wilderness is settled, the frontier of outer space has become the latest challenge[4].

The courage to try something new has been American characteristic since colonial times, when the nation's founding fathers started one of the greatest experiments of all times — the creation of American democracy. The citizens of the United states, through their elected representatives, establish the nation's laws and determine its foreign policy. Those who disapprove of the laws and policies established by their representatives may openly express their disapproval and try to elect new representatives to carry out their wishes.

American democracy means majority rule, but it also means protection of minority rights. There are certain freedoms which the United states promises to all its citizens, and members of minority groups cannot be denied these rights by a vote of the majority. The basic rights of every citizen, outlined in the first ten amendments to the Constitution, are known as the Bill of Rights. These rights include freedom of speech, freedom of religion, and freedom from unreasonable search and arrest.

In the United States, democracy is not only a form of government; it is a way of life. The belief that those who must live by the rules should help make the rules basic to nearly all American institutions and organizations[5]. American children are introduced to the democratic concepts of majority rule and representative government at a very early age. Many families hold weekly meetings to determine household rules and activities. Most schools have a student council with elected representatives so that students can voice their opinions about school regulations and activities. Social, civic, labor, and charitable groups elect their officers and vote on issues. In business, stockholders elect the directors they feel are best qualified to control the company. Local and state governments are also based upon democratic principles.

"All men are created equal," says the Declaration of Independence. This statement does not mean that all human beings are equal in ability or ambition. It means, instead, that all people should be treated equally before the law and given equal privileges and opportunities, insofar as government can control these. In practice, this ideal often does not work perfectly. These have always been those who would deny the rights of others for their own self-interest. There are times when the American people need to be reminded that any denial of basic rights is a weakening of the total system. However, equal treatment and equal opportunity for all are ideals toward which American society is moving ever closer.

The American belief in equality of opportunity is illustrated by the Horatio Alger myth. Horatio Alger was a nineteenth-century American novelist who wrote stores about poor boys who became successful. His books told about the little newsboy or bootblack who, because he was hardworking. honest, and lucky, grew up to become rich and respected. These popular "rags-to-riches" stories exemplified thee American Dream—the belief that any individual, no matter how poor, can achieve wealth and fame through diligence and virtue.

For many immigrant Americans, this dream became reality. Most of them, particularly those who came to the United states during the nineteenth century, were peasants and laborers in their native lands. Within a generation or two, nearly all these immigrant families rose on the social and economic scales. Financial success was often the result of taking a risk, of quitting a salaried position and starting a new business. Becoming an entrepreneur is still an open, though sometimes rugged, pathway to prosperity[6].

Social mobility-movement from class to class—has always been characteristic of the United States. However, although sociologists talk of the country's class structure, most Americans do not think in these terms. They do not see themselves as struggling to move from the lower middle class to the upper middle class. Instead they think in terms of higher income to the pay for a bigger house, a trip to Europe, summer camp for their children, or more retirement insurance.

Prior to the mid-1960s, American initiative to experiment was encouraged by a generally optimistic outlook. The typical American believed in trying something new in an attempt to make life better. He had firm faith in the possibility, even the probability, of progress. This attitude was based upon his own and his family's past experiences. Older people often told their children about how hard life had been before the invention of countless work-saving devices and ready-made products. Parents could remember the days when orange juice had to be squeezed from oranges by hand rather than poured from a can and diluted. Grandpa described thee old fashioned washer and feeding the clothes into the wringer, piece by piece. Great-grandma showed the blisters on her hands from churning butter and cranking the ice-cream maker. Great-grandpa talked about walking five miles to school before the days of public transportation and car pools.

Because life was getting easier, people assumed that it was getting better. The prevailing American attitude was one invented by a French pharmacist who , in treating his patients by hypnosis, instructed them to say, "Every day in every way I am getting better and better." Until the mid-1960s, the typical American had this kind of faith in automatic improvement. But by the end of the decade, this national optimism, which set the United states apart from all other nations, was gone.

Before the mid-1960s, Americans shared another happy attitude—a naive patriotism that said the United states was the best of all possible places; that American policy was determined by ethics, not expediency; that we had never fought an unjust war; that we were always on the side of right and by noble motives.

Then came the 1960s, a period when Americans realized if conditions could change for the better, they could also change for the worse. Even more frightening, people began to notice that the quality of life in the United states was already changing for the worse and that the trend if serious and immediate efforts were not made to stop the trend, life would soon be unlivable in this best of all possible places. Americans also realized that their government, big business, and other major institutions were not always ethical and could not always be trusted to do what would be best for the nation and the world.

What killed American optimism? First and perhaps most important, there was

Viet Nam War. During the 1960s, American involvement kept growing, and the bloodshed entered the American living room via TV. The horrors of our twelve years there—46 000 American dead and many more Vietnamese—formed only one part of the violence which characterized the decade. Several assassinations of public figures[7] and a continued rise in the violence crime rate led to a great demand for gun control legislation[8]. There were race riots in many cities. student rise on many campuses, policemen with tear gas and guns to quiet the rioters, and TV cameramen to bring it all home to the American public.

Public protests (both violent and nonviolent) left their mark upon the American Character[9]. Noisy demonstration occurred as various groups pointed out that they always been discriminated against in this country. Women, blacks, Indians, and Spanish-speaking citizens all gave their versions of American history and destroyed any remaining illusions that this nation has offered freedom, justice, and equality to all[10]. White Americans began to feel guilty about their aggressive destruction of nonwhite cultures. American men were warned that the exploited, subservient American house wife was a dying breed[11]. Women's Liberation groups deplored the "packaged" woman whose major interest was in maintaining an attractive facade in order to win and hold a husband. This type of woman was depicted as a victim of and a traitor to her sex.

In the 1960s still another exploited American made himself heard—the consumer. Choosing daily from a vast array of goods, the American shopper often found that the products he brought home were not what he assumed they were, not what they claimed to be, and sometimes not even safe to use. The idea of consumer protection received a big boost in 1962 when President Kennedy delivered a special message listing four basic consumer rights: the right to safety, the right to be informed, the right to choose, and the right to be heard. Then, in 1965, a young lawyer named Ralph Nader published a shocking book telling the American public that their automobiles were unnecessarily dangerous. As a result of his efforts, the huge automobile industry was forced to produce a safer product. Seat belts became standard equipment, designs were changed to reduce injuries from collisions, and automobiles with faulty mechanisms were recalled for repair.

Nader came upon the scene at a time when big business was giving the public a great many shoddy goods and services[12]. His success in dealing with the auto industry inspired others to campaign for better products. Today more than a thousand consumer programs are operated by the federal government. The majority of state governments have consumer fraud units[13], and more than fifty cities have agencies to protect the consumer. Legislation has done much toward accomplishing the concerned consumer's two major goals—product safety and truth in advertising. Labeling on packaged foods is more explicit than ever before. Manufactures of dangerous articles (such as cigarettes and toxic substances) must label the products with appropriate warnings. In 1973, the labeling of ingredients in cosmetic products became mandatory.

Today the American shopper is better protected against fraud and danger than ever before. In addition, people are learning to purchase more intelligently and economically. All across the country, consumer cooperatives[14] are developing, enabling members to buy goods at wholesale prices. Also, schools, unions, supermarket chains, and many other organizations are helping to educate buyers so theat they will get the most and the best for their money.

Of all the protest groups competing for public attention during the 1960s, the most alarming were those that spoke out against pollution. Americans learned that their air, water, land, and food were being polluted in a variety of ways. This pollution was reaching a dangerous level which could in the near future become a threat to human, plant, and animal life. Air pollution was coming primarily from automobile exhaust fumes and industrial smokestacks. Water pollution was due to industrial waste, garbage, detergents, and other sources. The land and its animal and plant life were being polluted by a variety of man-made chemicals, especially insecticides and herbicides. Disposable but indestructible products of plastic and metal were cluttering the land. Consumers were asked to buy only products that could be recycled. Americans were encouraged to bring these products to the recycling centers rather then discard them with other garbage.

Advertisers appeal to the American desire to look youthful and be physically attractive. Commercials attempt to sell many products—shampoo, toothpaste, deodorant, and soap, for example—by implying that their particular brand will help its user be more appealing.

But Americans also make many purchases for practical reasons. They buy labor-saving devices to do routine household chores more quickly and easily. Every housewife wants a vacuum cleaner, and electric mixer, a steam iron, an automatic clothes washer and dryer, and a dishwasher. Nearly every homeowning husband would like a power lawn mower, a snow-blower, and an electric drill.

Americans also buy things because they like to do things. Equipment for hobbies and books about "do-it-yourself" projects are very popular. Americans want to know how to cook with a "continental" flair while refinishing the bedroom furniture and making a million dollars in the stock market[15]. The American love of activity is part of a generally pragmatic outlook on life, a belief that thee value of knowledge is related to its usefulness.

Because of their tremendous expenditures for goods and services, Americans are often accused of being materialistic, of valuing above all else money and the comforts and pleasures that money buy. However, Americans are, on the whole, quite idealistic. They ask much more of life than just day-to-day enjoyment and financial security. They ask that life be meaningful. In choosing careers, Americans consider the significance of their work just as important as the income the job will bring. Also, most Americans are still under the influence of the Protestant ethic, which considers a life of pleasure sinful activity. In fact, many cannot enjoy their expanding number of leisure hours unless most of their "free" time is spent doing something constructive—such as working on the lawn or cleaning out the garage.

True, Americans enjoy money and the things it can buy. But in defense of the so-called materialistic American, one expert in American culture points out. "... however eager we are to make money, we are just as eager to give it away. Any world disaster finds Americans writing checks to relieve distress. Since the war we have seen the spectacle of the United States sending billions and billions of dollars' worth of goods to countries less fortunate than we. Write some of it off, if you will, to a desire to buy political sympathy; there is still an overplus of good will strictly and uniquely American[16]. Generosity and materialism run side by side."

The average American is also accused of being "rough around the edges"[17]—that is, of lacking sophistication in manners and understanding of things cultural. He tries hard to polish those edges through education and travel[18]. But no matter how much he learns and sees, his interests are less with the past than with the present and future, less with the decorative than with the functional. He maybe bored by medieval art but fascinated by modern engineering. Foreigners will find him always ready to compare cultures, though he may conclude that American methods are more efficient and therefore better. In expressing his views, he may be blunt to the point of rudeness. He admires efficiency and financial success. Eager to get as much as possible for his time and money, he is sometimes impatient, tense, and demanding. Often, he is in a hurry and unable to relax, His intensely competitive, outlook is probably his greatest fault. But one must give him credit for his virtues: he is friendly, spontaneous, adaptable, efficient, energetic, and kindhearted. All things considered, he is a likable guy.

Words & Expressions

stern / stəːn / *a.* 严肃的

gracious / ˈgreiʃəs / *a.* 温雅有礼的

leisurely / ˈleʒəli / *a.* 从容不迫的

casual / ˈkæʒjuel / *a.* 随和的

pioneering / ˌpaiəˈniəiŋ / *n.* 开拓性的

soft ball 垒球

sandlot / ˈsændlɔt / *n.* 沙地

bracket / ˈbrækit / *n.* 等级，阶层

deteriorating / diˈtiəriəreitiŋ / *a.* 衰落的

charitable / ˈtʃæritəbl / *a.* 慈善的

stockholder / ˈstɔkhəuldə / *n.* 股东

bootblack / ˈbuːtblæk / *n.* 以擦皮鞋为生的人

initiative / iˈniʃiətiv / *n.* 首创精神

dilute / daiˈljuːt / *vt.* 冲淡

pool / puːl / *n.* 几个家庭组织起来轮流送孩子上学

mandatory / ˈmændətəri / *a.* 强制性的

materialistic / məˌtiəriəˈlistik / *a.* 物质至上的

idealistic / aiˌdiəˈlistik / *a.* 理想主义的

Notes

1. even those who stay put... new neighbors：就是那些住在原地没有搬过家的人也不断有新的邻居搬进。

2. Much of this residential shifting... as family size changes：这种住宅变化大多是在当地附近发生的，主要是和因为家庭大小变化而需要调整住房有关。

3. "rediscover the natural human community"："寻回那种充满人情味的社会集体"。

4. Now that ... the latest challenge：美国的荒野地区大多已有人居住，向外空发展因而成了最新的挑战。

5. The belief... and organizations：谁想要按规章制度生活谁就应该自己制订这些规章制度。这差不多是美国所有机构和组织的基本信念。

6. Becoming an entrepreneur... to prosperity：成为企业家是兴旺发达的开阔大道，虽然有时也是一条崎岖不平的道路。

7. several assassinations of public figures：60 年代几次对著名人物的暗杀事件是指对肯尼迪总统、黑人民权运动领袖马丁·路德·金等人的暗杀.

8. led to a great demand for gun control legislation：根据美国《宪法权利法案》第二条，美国人民有权保存和持有枪支。60 年代的几次暗杀事件和枪杀犯罪率的上升促使一些人要求国会通过控制拥有武器的法案。但因遭到反对，有关法案未获通过。

9. Public protest... the American character：各种群众性的抗议活动(激烈的与和平的)对美国人的性格有着深刻的影响。

10. women... equality to all：妇女、黑人、印第安人，还有讲西班牙语的公民，对美国历史都有不同的解释。他们摒弃了所谓美国能为所有人赋予自由、公正和平等的幻想。

11. American men... a dying breed：美国的男人被告知，被剥削的处于从属地位的家庭妇女型的妻子正在消失。

12. Nader came upon the scene... services：内达正是在大公司为社会提供次品和劣质服务的时候出版他的书的。come upon the scene 原意是"出现"的意思。

13. consumer fraud units：消费者反欺诈组织。

14. consumer cooperatives：消费者合作社是由消费者参加管理，为消费者提供市场行情，负责其成员购买或批发商品的组织。

15. Americans want... in the stock market：美国人既要把卧室布置得漂漂亮亮，在股票市场挣上百万美元，也想知道怎样做一手"高级的法国风味菜"。

16. Write some of it off ... uniquely American：（第二次世界大战后，美国给一些国家提供大量经济援助。）即使承认美国人要收买政治支持，但是主要还是反映了独特的美国式的善意。write off 勾销，除去。

17. "rough around the edges"："思想简单，文化意识不强"。

18. He tries hard to ... travel：美国人努力通过加强教育和外出旅行来提高自己的文化修养。

Exercises

Ⅰ. Explain the following

1. the pioneering spirit
2. the residential shifting in America
3. equality in American society
4. Horatio Alger myth
5. the American Dream
6. social mobility
7. materialistic outlook of Americans
8. idealistic outlook

Ⅱ. Fill in the blanks

1. The New English is often described as ________ and ________; the Southerner as ________ and ________; the westerner as ________ and ________.
2. Some regional differences still remain, most notably in ________ and ________.
3. "All men are created equal" is from the document ________.
4. According to the author, equality means ________ and ________.
5. the four basic consumer rights listed by President Kennedy were. ________, ________, ________ and ________.
6. The consumer is concerned about accomplishing two goals: ________ and ________.
7. The American, according to the author, has these virtues: he is ________, ________,

________, ________, ________ and ________.

Ⅲ. Choose the correct answer in each of the following

1. In the United States, one cannot go home to find one's past because of the following reasons except ________.

A. Americans hate the past

B. their old neighborhood no longer exists

C. their childhood friends have moved away

D. high-rise buildings are on the old softball sandlots

2. Shifting population in the U. S. tends to affect Americans in three of the following ways. Which is the exception?

A. Americans become rootless.

B. Americans become more and more isolated.

C. Personal relationships become shallow.

D. Community welfare becomes more and more interesting to Americans.

3. "Every day in every way I am getting better and better." which of the following American attitudes does not reflect the value represented by the statement?

A. Americans' naive patriotism.

B. Faith in automatic improvement.

C. American optimism.

D. The American dream.

4. In the 1960s, Americans came to realize three of the following. Which is the exception?

A. There was no automatic improvement.

B. The quality of life was changing for the worse.

C. Life was no longer livable in the U. S. .

D. The government, big business and other major institutions were not always ethical and trustful.

5. Which of the following did not take place in the 1960s?

A. The Anti-Viet Nam War Movement.

B. The Anti-drug Movement.

C. Women's liberation Movement.

D. Public protests by blacks and other minority groups.

6. The consumer in the 1960s felt that he was exploited because of three of the following except that ________.

A. many products were shoddy goods

B. some products were dangerous to use

C. there were a lot of frauds in advertisements

D. there were too many cooperatives

Ⅳ. Answer the following questions briefly

1. Why does the author think that the pioneering spirit is still an important part of the

American character?

2. Why do so many Americans move about every year? How does this mobility affect American attitudes and values?
3. What, according to the author, was one of the greatest experiments of all times started by the founding fathers of the American nation?
4. Why does the author say that equality is just an ideal in American society?
5. What is the Americans' naive patriotism? Why is it naive?
6. What changes took place in the 1960s concerning American consumers?
7. What was the situation of pollution in the 1960s?
8. Are Americans materialistic or idealistic?

Chapter 17 American Education

The Academic Levels

Education is "like a big window opening", according to the English novelist Mary Webb. Americans are proud of the fact that the window of knowledge is never slammed shut for any of the nation's citizens. All American children are offered twelve years of free public education, and most good students can get financial help to continue their studies for many more years. Adults who wish to attend school also find many opportunities. In this nation of rapid change, there can be no age limit on learning; everyone must study—in classrooms or independently—to keep in touch with the changing life around him.

Early Childhood Education

In most areas, free public school education begins with kindergarten classes for five-year-olds. Through these half-day sessions (usually two to three hours long), the child becomes accustomed to being separated from Mommy, playing and sharing with other children, and following the directions of a teacher. He is also introduced to skills and information that will help him later with academic work. For example, he learns the colors and the alphabet, how to write his name, to count to ten, to work with art supplies, and to enjoy books. Early childhood education is considered so beneficial that some public school systems also offer pre-kindergarten programs for four-year-olds, though some tuition is usually charged.

Nearly three million American children attend kindergarten each year. For many, kindergarten is their first school experience. But some are introduced to the classroom situation at a much younger age, either through nursery schools or day care centers.

Nursery schools accept children from three to five years old for half-day sessions ranging from twice a week to five days a week. The typical nursery school classroom is equipped much like a kindergarten, with dolls, toy furniture, building blocks, books, puzzles, and art supplies. Most nursery schools (like school for older children) have an outdoor playground. A youngster who has no playmates his age living nearby may benefit greatly from attending nursery school. Nursery school usually charge tuition, though some are subsidized and some offer scholarships.

Day care centers provide care for pre-school children of working mothers who need a place to leave their children all day, five days a week. Some day care centers accept pre-scholars from infancy on. The children have lunch and snacks at the center and spend the entire day there. Day care has been maligned by those who believe that children belong with their mothers and that "a woman's place is in the home." But more and more women are coming to believe that motherhood should not be their sole occupation. The Women's Liberation Movement[1], which became extremely prominent in the 1960s, has widely publicized the idea that free, high-quality day care is essential if women are to participate fully in society.

At the present time, the need for more day care centers is acute. For the six million pre-school children whose mothers are working, there are only 625 000 openings in certified day care centers. Many working mothers pay a large percentage of their earnings to babysitters; many take turns with other mothers to provide day care for small groups of children in their homes; some, in desperation, leave their pre-schoolers alone all day.

Existing day care centers are operated and funded by many different organizations. Some are profit-making facilities supported by tuition fees. Others are non-profit centers run by philanthropic, religious, governmental, or industrial sponsors. These are subsidized by the sponsoring agency and charge a graduated fee according to income[2]. Organizations that employ a large number of women (hospitals, federal agencies, and several large corporations) have become involved in the establishment of day care centers as have many universities and a few unions. Also, some communities have pre-and post-school programs[3] for school-age children whose mothers leave for work before school begins and come home after school lets out.

About 30 percent of mothers with children under age six are now in the labor force. Government statistics predict that between 1975 and 1985 there will be a 32 percent increase in the number of working mothers with pre-school children. So, although the federal government is already spending more than a billion dollars a year on day care, there will certainly be continued pressure for increased public support.

Grammar School and High school

In the United States, classes of students are divided into twelve academic levels called *grades*. Generally, one academic year (from September through June) is required to completed each grade. Academic work — learning to read, write, and do arithmetic — begins when the child enters first grade, at about age six.

The first academic institution that a child attends is called *grammar school or elementary school*. In some school systems, elementary school includes grades one through eight. The next four years are called *high school*. In other school systems, there are three divisions: *elementary school* (grades one through six), *junior high school* (grades seven through nine), and *senior high school* (grades ten through twelve).

The typical elementary school day starts at 9:00 A. M. and ends about 3:30 P. M. Junior high and high school students usually attend classes from 8:30 A. M. until 3:30 P. M. for all levels, schools are in session five days a week, Monday through Friday. Traditional vacation periods of one to two weeks are scheduled at Christmas and in the spring, and the schools also close for certain holidays. Most students do not go to school during July of August, unless they enroll in summer sessions.

Grammar schools teach reading, arithmetic, and language arts such as creative writing, spelling, and handwriting. Social studies, science, music, art, and physical education (athletics) are also part of the program. In high school, subject matter becomes more specialized. English classes stress grammar and literature. Social studies is split into separate courses in American history, American government, and European history. Algebra, geometry, and trigonometry are offered. High school students usually take a one-year general science course, then more detailed courses in biology, chemistry, and physics. Most high school students study a foreign language-usually Latin, French, Spanish, or German. Courses in music, art, and physical education are often required. Some high schools specialize in vocational education and train students for various technical careers.

During the elementary years, students are grouped into classes, and each group stays together for the entire school day and the entire school year. Generally, the class has the same teacher for most subjects, although art, music, and physical education are usually taught by teachers who specialize in these areas. In most high school, students meet with a different teacher and a different group of students for each subject. The high school student's day may be divided into nine periods: five for academic subjects, one session for physical education, a lunch period, and two study periods. The study periods may by used for visiting the library of participating in an extracurricular activity such as the school orchestra, newspaper staff, or math club.

Colleges and Universities

When a student graduated from high school, he may attend college if his high school record and test scores are good enough to gain him admittance. American education on the college level (sometimes called *higher education*) is provided by more than 3 000 institutions. They range in size from very small schools serving only a few hundred students to huge state universities with student bodies exceeding 40 000. Some are supported privately and some by local and /or state governments. Some admit only men and some only women, but most are coeducational. Some are called colleges, which means that they offer only undergraduate courses. Others are called universities, which means that they have undergraduate, graduate, and professional schools. Recently, more and more junior colleges (offering the first two years of college only) have been established.

Since World War II, one of the most dramatic developments in higher education has been the enormous increase in the number of students. In 1939, about 1.5 million men and women were enrolled in the nation's colleges and universities. By 1970, the number had grown to 8.5 million; estimates for 1980 run to 11 million. To meet this demand, colleges and universities have expanded tremendously. Between 1945 and 1967, 300 university branches were established. In addition, many new school have been built. This huge expansion reflects the nation's population explosion as well as a trend toward democratizing higher education. Today, a college education is seen as the right of any capable student rather than as a privilege reserved for the wealthy.

Colleges and universities offer a vast array of subjects. The student can sample different fields of knowledge, but he usually concentrates (majors) in one field during his last two years of college. If he wishes, he may obtain professional training agricultural experts and engineers. For those who wish to prepare for military careers, the United Stated government maintains four special academies.

At the college level, the academic year is about nine months long (usually from-mid-September until early June or from late August until May). After completing four academic years with acceptable grades in an approved course of study[4], the student earns a bachelor's degree. some students complete college in less than four years by attending summer sessions. At most colleges, the academic year is divided into either two or three semesters, excluding the summer session. College grades, from highest to lowest, run *A*, *B*, *C*, *D*, *F*[5]. An *F* is a failing grade; if a student receives an *F* in a particular course, he does not get credit for having taken the course. College students must maintain at least a low *C* average in order to remain in school.

American universities offer three main categories of graduate degrees. In most fields of specialization, a master's degree can be earned by one or two academic years of study beyond the bachelor's degree. A Ph. D. degree (doctor of philosophy) usually takes at least three years beyond the master's. To earn a Ph. D. in almost any field, the student must generally pass oral and written examinations in his specialty, produce a long research paper which makes an original contribution to his field of study, and pass reading examinations in one or two foreign languages. There are also graduate professional schools in medicine, dentistry, and law, among other fields.

A college community is an interesting and lively place. Students become involved in many different activities-extracurricular, religious, social, and athletic. Among the extracurricular activities are college newspapers, musical organizations, dramatic clubs, and political groups. Some of these have faculty advisers. Many religious groups have their own meeting places where services and social activities can be held. Student groups run parties of all types-from formal dances to picnics. Most colleges have a student union where students can get together for lunch, study sessions, club meetings, and socializing.

At many schools, campus life revolves around fraternities (social and, in some cases, residential clubs for men) and sororities (similar clubs for women)[6]. These organizations exist on more than 500 campuses. The best known are national groups with many *chapters* at schools throughout the country. Their names are Greek letters such as Alpha Delta Phi. These groups have been much criticized for being cruel and prejudiced because membership is limited and selective. A student must be invited to join. There is often great competition among freshmen and sophomores who want to join. Those who seek membership must go through *rush* (a period when prospective members visit different *houses* to meet and be evaluated by current members.) The whole experience can by very painful if a student goes through *rush* and then is not asked to *pledge* (become a trial member of) any of the houses he or she has visited. Sororities and fraternities also tend to limit membership to one particular racial and religious group, thereby depriving its members of the wonderful opportunity that college offers for broadening social contacts. However, these groups do help students find friends of similar backgrounds; thus, they help combat loneliness for those away from home.

Athletics is an important phase of life on most campuses. In addition to required physical education courses, voluntary programs are provided for health, recreation, and the development of teams for intercollegiate competition. Most coeducational and men's schools belong to an athletic league. The teams within the league play against each other, aiming for the league championship. Football is the college sport which stirs up the most national interest[7]. At large schools, promoting football, developing a team, and playing before huge crowds have become a big business. Season tickets are sold for substantial prices. Games, complete with student marching bands and entertainment, are major productions. Other sports—particularly basketball, swimming, and track—are also pursued with enthusiasm. Some schools have competitive tennis, skiing, sailing, wrestling, soccer, and baseball.

College campuses are attracting students from all social classes despite the rapidly rising cost of higher education. The cost of a college education has doubled within the last fifteen years and tripled within the last thirty. A typical college now charges about $3 000 a year for room, board, and tuition. The student attending a private Eastern college spends at least $3 500 and probably closer to $5 000 a year, including tuition, housing, food, books, and personal expenses. At the other end of the scale, a student attending a state college in a rural area may get by on $1 500 a year. State colleges and universities have rather low tuition fees (ranging from about $60 to about $450) for state residents. In some communities, low-cost public education is available at city colleges or junior colleges[8].

Fortunately for students with limited funds, financial help is available from many sources. Every year college students receive more than $300 million in monetary assistance, including scholarships, loans, and part-time jobs. More than 200 000 scholarships are offered by industries, alumni groups, individual donors, the federal government, and college and universities. The "G. I. Bill"[9], passed in 1944, was the first in a series off laws giving financial help to armed forces veterans. A student may cut costs by living at home, attending a state of community school, or combining part-time work with a part-time college program. Many college students use their summer earnings to help finance their education. Some students pursue undergraduate or graduate degrees in night school while working full time during the day. Some college courses are offered on television, and these are inexpensive.

Many young people from poor families struggle along on limited budgets in order to stay in school because they know that a college degree brings higher income, greater job security, more prestige, and a more significant career. "Every son must rise above his father"[10] is a major aspect of the American Dream — and one that is most often realized through higher education.

Words & Expressions

tuition / tju(ː)ˈiʃən / *n.* 学费

malign / məˈlain / *vt.* 攻击,批评

opening / ˈəupəniŋ / *n.* 机会,空额

babysitter / ˈbeibiˌsitə / *n.* 为人临时照看孩子者

philanthropic / ˌfilənˈθrɔpik / *a.* 慈善事业的

graduated / ˈgrædjueitid / *a.* 分等级的

academy / əˈkædəmi / *n.* 学院;科学院

faculty / ˈfækəlti / *n.* 教员

fraternity / frəˈtəːniti / *n.* 男生联谊会

sorority / səˈrɔriti / *n.* 女生联谊会

chapter / ˈtʃæptə / *n.* 分部,分会

geometry / dʒiˈɔmitri / *n.* 几何学

trigonometry / ˌtrigəˈnɔmitri / *n.* 三角

biology / baiˈɔlədʒi / *n.* 生物学

chemistry / ˈkemistri / *n.* 化学

physics / ˈfiziks / *n.* 物理学

vocational / vəuˈkeiʃənl / *a.* 职业的

extracurricular / ˈekstrəkəˈrikjulə / *a.* 课外的

orchestra / ˈɔːkistrə / *n.* 管弦乐队

staff / staːf / *n.* 编辑部

phase / feis / *n.* 方面

intercollegiate / ˈintə(ː)kəˈliːdʒiit / *a.* 院校之间的

league / liːg / *n.* 联赛

alumni / əˈlʌmnai / *n.* （单数）

alumnus / əˈlʌmnəs / (复数)校友

Notes

1. the Women's Liberation Movement:在美国,妇女解放运动起源于19世纪中期。妇女中的激进分子要求在政治、经济、社会和教育上与男人享有平等的权利。20世纪60年代前,这个运动一般称为“争取女权运动”(feminism)。60年代,妇女解放运动掀起新高潮。1966年,美国成立了“全美妇女组织会”,要求改革有关人工流产法律,要求联邦政府资助成立儿童日托中心、同工同酬以及取消其他一切有损妇女权利的法律和措施。

2. charge a graduated fee according to income 采取按收入而分级收费的办法。即收入越高,付的托儿费就越多。

3. pre-and post-school programs:成立学前和放学后的托儿班。

4. with acceptable grades in an approved course of study:读完学校规定的课程,成绩合格。

5. A, B, C, D, F:相当于中国的5,4,3,2,1制的记分法。D是刚及格。为了计算平均分的方便,还有一个折合计分方法,A——4,A-——3.7;B+——3.4,B——3,B-——2.7;C+——2.4,C——2,依次类推。一般大学要求平均成绩在2以上才能保留学籍,平均分数

在3.4以上才能有资格申请奖学金。

6. fraternities and sororities:美国大学里的男女生联谊会。这些组织和学生会不一样。联谊会对一年级要求入会的人要经过严格的挑选。在争取入会的考验期(rush)内,这些申请者必须做各种服务工作,经考验合格者方可入会。入会后,有的住在同一栋楼,但不得泄露该会的秘密,如每个联谊会的拉丁字名称的含义等。

7. Football is the college sport which stirs up the most national interest:大学生的美式足球(也称"橄榄球")是最能引起全国普遍兴趣的运动。

8. city colleges or junior colleges:(学费低、教育质量差、学生入学水平低的)城市学院或属于社区组织的大专学校。

9. the"G. I. Bill":"G. I." 是"government issue"的缩写,是指政府发给士兵的装备、衣服,后来就把美国兵称为G. I.。"美国兵法案"是第二次世界大战结束前(1944年)为防止战后大批复员士兵出现的生活困难而制订的预防性措施。根据这个法案,美国兵复员后可以申请资助费用,用来上学,进行职业培训,用于医疗失业保险,或可以借款买房或经营企业等。

10. "Every son must rise above his father":"青出于蓝胜于蓝"。这所以成为"美国梦"的一个重要组成部分,是因为早期到美国的移民大多是穷苦人,第二代、第三代就超过他们的父辈, 因此形成了这个概念。

Exercises

Ⅰ. Explain the following

1. grammar school
2. G. I. Bill
3. fraternity
4. sorority

Ⅱ. Fill in the blanks

1. All American children are offered ________ years of free public education ________.
2. There is no ________ limit on learning.
3. Public school education begins with ________.
4. The first academic institution that a child attends is called ________.
5. The huge expansion of colleges and universities since World War Ⅱ reflects ________ as well as ________
6. The law giving financial help to armed forces veterans is called ________.
7. ________ is the college sport that often stirs up the most national interest.

Ⅲ. Choose the correct answer in each of the following

1. In the United States of America, children are offered ________ years of free public education

   A. 6 B. 9 C. 12 D. 15

2. In the United States school systems, which of the following divisions is true?

A. Elementary school, grammar school.

B. Elementary school, junior high school.

C. Elementary school, secondary school.

D. Junior high school, senior high school.

3. Which of the following is NOT mentioned in American higher education?

A. Universities and colleges.

B. Research institutions.

C. Technical institutions.

D. Undergraduate institutions.

4. How many categories of degrees are offered by American universities?

A. 3. B. 4. C. 5. D. 6.

5. The rapid growth of American high education is mostly the result of ________.

A. the national economic increase

B. the government policy

C. the population growth

D. the trend toward democratizing higher education

Ⅳ. **Answer the following questions briefly**

1. How do the young people of poor families deal with their financial problem at school?

2. What is campus life like in American universities?

Chapter 18 American Family Life

In the United States, the family is still very much alive, despite its many ailments[1]. The vast majority of Americans live with people to whom they are related by blood or marriage[2]. There are about 53 million American families (including married couples that do not have children living with them). Most American couples have two or three children, though larger families are not unusual.

Typically, the family group that occupies one household consists of parents and their unmarried children. Middle-aged and elderly people generally do not live with their married children. However, parents usually keep in close contact with their gown children and take great interest in their grandchildren. On holidays, members of the larger family group—grandparents, aunts, uncles, and cousins—often dine together.

About three-fourths of American families live in areas classified as urban, though this label includes many different styles of living. Less than five percent of Americans live on farms, but small town living is still widespread. About 50 million Americans live in communities smaller than twenty-five hundred. The United States has more than a thousand cities with populations between ten and twenty-five thousand. However, more than two-thirds of Americans live in or near cities of fifty thousand or more. A greater number of Americans live in suburbs (about 37 percent of the population) than in cities (about 31 percent).

Each type of community has its virtues and its limitations. Intimate, slow-paced rural and small town living often seems dull and stifling, especially to young, single people. Suburbs offer the advantages of small town living with the facilities of the big city nearby. But suburban living is often criticized for its sameness because the people of suburbia are predominantly white, middle-class, and under fifty years of age. Big city life is varied, exciting, and culturally stimulating. However, the nation's big cities are also overcrowded, crime-ridden, overcast with air pollution, short on public recreational facilities[3], and lacking in neighborhood spirit. The city dweller is often an anonymous figure unknown to the person living next door.

Although the majority of families live in homes, many live in apartment buildings. These range in size from walk-ups containing from two to six apartments to high-rise elevator buildings[4] that may have more than 100 apartments. Some high-rise apartments are very expensive and elegant, but many are built for moderate or even low-income families.

More than 7 million Americans live in *mobile homes* (once called *house trailers*). Mobile homes are living quarters built with wheels. They can be moved, but generally they are brought to a site that is intended to be more or less permanent. Then the wheels are removed, and the home is fastened to the ground. Because they cost much less than conventional homes, mobile homes are especially popular among young couples and elderly retired couples. Usually, the mobile home itself is paid for in installments, and the site is rented. Some experts predict that by 1983 about 20 million Americans will be living in mobile homes.

Of the nation's 71 million dwelling units, 64 percent are occupied by their owners. Though most homes are owned by their residents, some are rented. Apartments are usually rented; but in recent years increasing numbers of apartment buildings have become cooperatives, meaning that each resident owns his own apartment.

About 87 percent of American families are headed by a married couple. We like to think of the typical American household as being closer to a democracy than to a dictatorship. Ideally, Mother and Father have an equal voice in decision-making, and, on certain matters, the children, too, have a vote (perhaps at weekly family council meetings). That is the ideal, but obviously not all households are run this way. many families still live by the old principle that Father's work is law. In many others, Father is rarely home when the children are awake, and, as far as the children are concerned, Mother is the dominant personality and major decision-maker.

Then, there are about 3 million households (with about 8 million children) in which one parent is absent as a result of separation, divorce, or desertion. Almost 90 percent of these households are headed by women whose children spend relatively little time with their fathers. In these families, Mother is boss.

In many other households, the children seem to be in charge. Some parents are reluctant and perhaps even afraid to say "no" to their children for fear of stifling their personalities or losing their love. As a result, the children and their possessions take over most of the house, and the youngsters make excessive demands upon their parents' time and money. In these families, the adults often suffer in silence, believing that they are doing "the right thing" for their children. The children suffer, too, lacking the security of strong, decisive parents who set appropriate limits and provide intelligent guidance.

For better or worse, Americans are devoted and permissive parents-so much so, in fact, that they are often accused of creating a child-centered culture[5]. The ambitions of American parents are more often related to their children's lives than to their own[6]. For this reason, parents often turn to the writings of experts-pediatricians, psychiatrists, and psychologists—for advice on child-rearing.

Because they believe that knowledge leads to a meaningful life, American parents try to give their youngsters many opportunities to develop skills and worthwhile interests. The typical middle-class child has a large assortment of educational toys and athletic equipment. He may also receive instruction in sports and music. To help him do well is school, he may be given his own room and desk, a set of encyclopedia, and, if necessary, private tutoring.

When school lets out for the summer, parents try to give their children other kinds of learning experiences through camping or travel. Family automobile trips to places of historical interest, national parks, and resort areas are commonplace. Summer day camps and residential camps[7] are popular with American youngsters. They provide supervised group play, nature study, and instruction in crafts and athletics.

Parental roles have altered somewhat since the advent of the working mother. Today, about 10 million American mothers with children under eighteen years of age have jobs. In some families, the working mother is a necessity because the father is unable to find employment or cannot earn enough for all the family's basic needs. In other households, the mother may work to supplement the father's income so the family can enjoy a higher standard of living. Then, too, some women want to work even if the family does not need extra income. Once their children are attending school, many women find it boring to stay home alone all day. Being a homemaker is no longer a full-time job for women who have access to modern household appliances and prepared foods. many working mothers employ a cleaning woman one or more days a week to help with housework and child care, but few have live-in servants.

When a working mother has no household help, her husband often takes a more active part in housekeeping and child-rearing. But even in families where the mother does not have an outside job, the father typically spends a significant amount of his leisure time with his children. he will often take a special interest in teaching his youngsters athletic skills. On weekends, especially, the family is likely to spend time together-attending church, visiting relatives, watching a ball game, going bike-riding, touring the zoo, or just playing "catch" in the backyard while the hamburgers are barbecuing[8]. On weekends, Dad may try hard to be a pal to his children. However, during the week his children may see him very little. he may leave home early in the morning and come back when it's almost bedtime for the youngsters.

The various tensions, arguments, and hostilities which exist within the family are reflected in the well-known expression: "God gives us our relatives; thank God we can choose our friends"[9]. Conflicts between husband and wife and conflicts between different generations develop for many different reasons. One of the most common causes of quarrels is insufficient family income. Foreigners may think that Americans have more money than they know what to do with, but most Americans feel that they do not have enough. The median family income in the United States is about $11 000 a year. This is not a lot of money when one realizes the tremendous number of American needs. Products that most people did not even dream of thirty-five years ago (such as home air-conditioners, TVs, and electric dishwashers) are now desired by nearly everyone. In most families, there is a shortage of money to supple all the things that family members consider essential for enjoyable, comfortable modern living.

In addition to the need for possessions, there are a great many costly services which most parents want to give their children, such as good medical and dental care, religious training, music lessons, and a college education. Parents may quarrel between themselves or with their children about priorities; and when there isn't enough to go around, the wife may secretly resent her husband for being an inadequate provider. More often, she decides to go to work. Teenage children, too, often work part time after school, perhaps babysitting, selling, waiting on tables, mowing lawns, or delivering newspapers. Clearly, the need for many material things strongly influences the way American families live.

Concerning money or anything else, conflicts between husband and wife usually reflect a power struggle. Conflicts between parent and child often center around the same issue. As children enter adolescence, they begin to demand greater freedom to go where they please, do what they please, and make decisions without parental interference. Many American parents do not know how to deal with their teen-agers and seek advice from books, lectures, and parent-training courses. Parents want to maintain a friendly relationship with their teen-agers and also want to guide them so that their behavior will be whatever the parents consider proper and constructive. But in a society of rapidly changing social and moral values, parents and children often disagree about what is important and what is right. Arguments may concern such unimportant matters as styles of dress or hairdos. But quarrels may also concern school work, after-school jobs, decisions about how the teen-ager spends his money, career decisions, use of the family car, dating, and sexual behavior. Some families have serious problems with teen-agers who drop out of school, run away from home, or use illegal drugs. Because so much publicity is given to the problem teen-ager, one gets the impression that all teen-agers are troublemakers. Actually, relatively few adolescents do anything outrageously wrong, and nearly all grow up into "solid citizens" who fulfill most of their parents' expectations. In fact, recent studies show that the "generation gap" is narrowing. The vast majority of teen-agers share most of their parents' values and ideas. Many parents of teen-agers feel that they get along with their adolescents quite well.

The "Generation gap" also causes problems between married children and their parents. The mother-in-law is the butt of many jokes. Seemingly, no one can get along with her because (according to the stereotype) she is an interfering busybody always criticizing what the younger generation is doing and sure that she knows a better way. Because of the stereotype, many mothers-in-law are afraid to make any suggestions at all to their married children. But many do interfere simply because they have little else to do. Women who have devoted their adult years exclusively to child-rearing may find it difficult to be left with an "empty nest"[10]. In addition, many middle-aged and elderly women are widows, since most American wives outlive their husbands by several years. The mother-in-law who cannot occupy herself with a job, volunteer work, hobbies, or social activities may become a too-frequent and sometimes unwelcome visitor in the homes of her children.

Middle age is a problem for some Americans, but for many others it is a pleasurable period of life, a time when they enjoy the fruits of their earlier labors—a comfortable income, a nice family, professional accomplishment. Most of the leadership in all areas of American life comes from middle-aged people.

For the elderly, however, life is often quite trying. In addition to the medical problems that inevitably come with old age, there are great economic and social problems. The difficulties of older Americans have been getting more attention in recent years as the elderly have increased in number. There are now 21 million Americans sixty-five years or older.

In many stable societies, older people are highly respected because of their experience and wisdom. But in a rapidly changing industrial society, the skills and knowledge of the elderly often become obsolete. The elderly American, commonly forced to retire from his job at age sixty-five, is left with too much leisure time and too little money. About 40 percent of the nation's elderly live in poverty or near-poverty. Many struggle along on the meager monthly income they get from the government by living in rundown hotels and eating mostly soup, potatoes, and bread. There are several government programs to supply free food and necessary services to the elderly. However, these programs do not reach anything close to the number of people who need help. As a result, there are probably millions of elderly Americans who live in isolation and misery.

The news media, in describing the plight of the elderly poor, sometimes create the false impression that Americans are heartless people who discard their aged parents and leave them to struggle alone in illness and poverty. Most old people are not dumped into nursing homes and mental institutions and forgotten. More than half of the elderly in the United States live in their own homes, with one of their children, or with friends. many who live alone do so by choice. Some live in special buildings or small communities established for the elderly. These communities usually have many kinds of recreational facilities and a doctor or nurse on duty at all times.

Despite the euphemisms which refer to "senior citizens" enjoying their "golden years", one finds that in this society which worships youth, the elderly are sometimes ignored or even avoided. American society provides a monthly income and free medical car to the aged, but it often deprives them of important psychological forms of support—a feeling of being respected, wanted, and needed.

Many older people find more satisfactory social relationships among other "senior citizens" than among members of their own family. However, within the family, one often sees strong bonds between grandparents and grandchildren. American family life has been much enriched by medical advances which have prolonged life. An American boy born in 1970 can be expected to live to age sixty-seven, a girl to age seventy-five. Most of today's children have living grandparents and many have living great-grandparents.

Another problem facing the nuclear family (mother, father, and dependent children) is the fact that it is expected to do too much. Years ago, families settled down in a particular residence and stayed there for many years. Often, other relatives (grandparents, aunts, uncles, cousins) lived nearby and were part of the daily scene. Close bonds with neighbors developed, providing lifelong friendships. Today, Americans are extremely mobile. Every year about 40 million Americans change residences. That statistic suggests that everyone moves every five or six years! Young people from farms and small towns come to the big cities for excitement and job opportunities. Couples with young children move from cities to suburbs to provide a safer, more spacious environment for their children and a better school system. Southern blacks and Appalachian whites move to northern industrial areas like Chicago and Detroit in search of full-time employment and higher wages. All this shifting around puts a great burden upon family members sharing one household. They must supply the psychological support that was once provided by a much larger group, and many families cannot do it.

In some ways, the family as an institution fails its members[11]. However, there are certainly a great many happy families; and, although people complain about and quarrel with members of their family, when trouble arises, close relatives are usually the first to step in and help. Americans frequently say, "Blood is thicker than water"[12].

Words & Expressions

ailment /ˈeilmənt /n. 失调,问题
overcast /ˈəuvəkaːst /a. 阴暗的
stifling /ˈstaifliŋ /a. 沉闷的
recreational /ˌrekriˈeiʃənl /a. 娱乐的
stimulating /ˈstimjuleitiŋ /a. 振奋人心的,有刺激性的
suburbia /səˈbəːbiə /n. 大都市郊区
crime-ridden *a.* 犯罪活动猖獗的
anonymous /əˈnɔniməs /a. 无名的,不知名的
mobile home 活动房屋
installment /imˈstɔːlmənt /n. 分期付款
homemaker /ˈhəumˌmeikə /n. 家庭主妇
cooperative /kəuˈɔpərətiv /n. 合作团体(每家拥有自己的房间,共同管理全楼)
appliance /əˈplaiəns /n. 器械,用器
barbecue /ˈbaːbikjuː /vi. vt. 烤烧
solid citizen 可靠的居民
desertion /diˈzəːʃən /n. 遗弃
possession /pəˈzeʃən /n. 财物
butt /bʌt /n. 对象,目标
busybody /ˈbizibɔdi /n. 爱管闲事的人
trying /ˈtraiiŋ /a. 艰难的
obsolete /ˈɔbsəliːt /a. 过时的
psychiatrist /saiˈkaiətrist /n. 精神病专家
meager /ˈmiːgə /a. 微薄的
plight /plait /n. 困境
psychologist /saiˈkɔlədʒist /n. 心理学专家
dump /dʌmp /vt. 抛弃
euphemism /ˈjuːfimizəm /n. 委婉语

Notes

1. the family is very much alive, despite its many ailments：美国家庭仍然生气勃勃地存在着，尽管它面临着许多问题。

2. by blood or marriage：因为血缘或婚姻关系。

3. short on public recreational facilities：缺乏公共娱乐设施。

4. These range ... buildings：这些套间楼房（或公寓楼）大小不等，从没有电梯的只有2到6套房间的公寓到拥有电梯的高层公寓都有。walk-up：没有电梯的楼房。

5. Americans are ... a child-centered culture：美国父母对他们的孩子都非常宠爱、非常放任，因此，有人说他们是一种以孩了为中心的文化。

6. The ambitions ... to their own：美国父母的抱负总和他们孩子的生活联系在一起，对孩子的关心经常胜过考虑自己的生活。

8. playing "catch" ... barbecuing：有组织的住在一起的野营活动。在后院烤汉堡包时，和孩子练习"接球"。

9. "God gives us our relatives; thank God we can choose our friends"："上帝注定我们有什么样的亲人；谢天谢地，我们可以自由选择自己的朋友。"

10. Women who have ... with an "empty nest"：一直专心致志扶养孩子的妇女很难适应孩子离家以后的"空窝"。

11. In some ways ... its members：在有些方面，作为社会机构的家庭使它的成员感到失望。

12. "Blood is thicker than water"："血浓于水"。"亲人总比外人亲"。

Exercises

Ⅰ. Explain the following

1. mobile home
2. nuclear family
3. a child-centered culture
4. the working mother
5. the generation gap

Ⅱ. Fill in the blanks

1. The communities can be roughly divided into three types, ____________________, ____________________ and ____________.
2. In recent years increasing numbers of apartment buildings have become cooperatives, meaning that ____________________.
3. American society worships __________ and often deprives the aged of important psychological forms of support ____________________.
4. Walk-ups refer to ____.

Ⅲ. Answer the follwing questions briefly

1. What is the impact of the working mother on the family?
2. What is the major problem facing the young?
3. What is the general situation of the aged in the U. S. ? What factors have contributed to this situation?
4. What are some of the problems caused by the mobility of the population?

Chapter 19 Thanksgiving and Christmas

Thanksgiving

In the United States the fourth Thursday in November is called Thanksgiving Day. On this day Americans give thanks for the blessings they have enjoyed during the year. Thanksgiving is usually a family day, celebrated with big dinners and happy reunions.

The first American Thanksgiving was held in Plymouth. Massachusetts in 1621. The people of Plymouth had come to America from England in 1620. In their native land they had been called puritans because they wished to "purify" the Church of England. Before 1600, some of them decided that they could not reform the Church from within, so they broke away and formed their own churches. When English officials began to persecute them, they fled to Holland.

Several years passed. The Puritans living in Holland were threatened by religious suppression and war and were saddened to see their children growing up Dutch instead of English. They wanted to keep their native language and traditions and to be free from religious persecution. Once again, they thought of moving. This time they considered America. In an unsettled land they would finally be free to live as they chose; and the idea of bringing the word of Christ to remote parts of thee world appealed to them immensely[2]. Some English merchants agreed to finance their journey in return for a share of the profits produced by the new colony. So, after traveling from Holland back to England, a small group of Puritans, together with some other passengers, set sail for the New World. The Puritans began to call themselves *Pilgrims because* of their wanderings in search of religious freedom.

It was September of 1620 when their ship, called the Mayflower, left port with 102 men, women, and children on board. This was the worst season of the year for an ocean crossing, and the trip was very rough. Yet, during the voyage, the travelers suffered only one death. Since there was also a birth aboard ship, the Mayflower was still carrying 102 passengers when, after sixty-five days at sea, she landed in Provincetown Harbor, inside the tip of Cape Cod, Massachusetts. The party had planned to land further south, nearer to the only other English colony in America, which was in Jamestown. Virginia. But errors in navigation and adverse winds brought the Mayflower to New England.

The Pilgrim leaders knew that they were in unsettled territory which had no governing body[3]. They also knew that, in order to survive, every society needs a means of establishing and enforcing proper rules of conduct. Partly to protect themselves from rebels within their own ranks, forty-one men aboard the *Mayflower* held a meeting to choose their first governor and sign the historic Mayflower Compact, the first formal agreement for self-government in America.

For about a month longer, the Pilgrims lived aboard ship and sent out scouting parties to explore the coastline of Cape Cod Bay. At Plymouth, the scouts found a harbor with excellent fishing, some cleared land, cornfields, little rippling brooks with pure, fresh water, and a high hill that could be fortified. The site had once been an Indian village, but a smallpox epidemic a few years earlier has killed the entire Indian population. The scouts steered their small boat back to the *Mayflower* and reported their discovery. A few days later, the *Mayflower* sailed across Cape Cod Bay and anchored in Plymouth Harbor. Coming ashore in their small boat, the Pilgrims landed (according to tradition) on a large rock later named Plymouth Rock. This was the beginning of the second permanent English settlement in America.

The Pilgrims were poorly trained and poorly equipped to cope with life in the wilderness. During their first winter in the new land, they suffered tremendously. Poor food, hard work, infectious diseases, and bitterly cold weather killed about half of them. By the end of this terrible first winter, only about fifty Plymouth colonists remained alive.

One spring morning in 1621, an Indian walked into the little village of Plymouth and introduced himself in a friendly way. Later, he brought the Indian chief, Massasoit, who gave gifts to the Pilgrims and offered assistance. The Indians of Massasoit's tribe taught the Pilgrims how to hunt, fish, and grow food. They taught the Pilgrims to use fish for fertilizer in planting corn, pumpkins, and beans. Because of this help from the Indians, the Pilgrims had a good harvest.

Governor William Bradford[4] was following an ancient tradition when, in the fall of 1621. he issued a proclamation establishing a day of thanksgiving to God. The Governor also decided to use this religious occasion to strengthen the bond of friendship between the Pilgrims and their Indian neighbors. So he invited Chief Massasoit and his braves to share the Thanksgiving feast.

The Indians gladly accepted and sent five deer ahead. The pilgrim men went hunting and returned with turkey and other wild game. The women of Plymouth prepared delicious dishes from corn, cranberries, squash, and pumpkins.

The first Thanksgiving dinner was cooked and served out-of-doors. Although it was late autumn, huge fires kept the hosts and guests warm. Massasoit and ninety Indians joined the Pilgrims for the first Thanksgiving feast. The celebration lasted three days! On the first day, the Indians spent most of the time eating. On the second and third days, they wrestled, ran races, sang, and danced with the young people in Plymouth Colony. The holiday was a great success[5].

Many of the traditions of the modern American Thanksgiving cone from that first Thanksgiving celebration more than 350 years ago. The modern Thanksgiving turkey is much like the ones that were hunted in the forests around Plymouth. Squash and corn, which were also harvested by the early Pilgrims, appear on the Thanksgiving table. Pumpkin pie and Indian pudding (a custard made from corn) are traditional Thanksgiving desserts.

The first Thanksgiving lasted three days. Today, for many Americans, it is a four-day holiday. Schools are closed on Thanksgiving Day and the day after. Many adults have both Thursday and Friday off from work. Relatives from other cities, students who have been away at school, and many other Americans travel long distances to spend the holiday at home.

Going home for Thanksgiving is a national custom, but every Thanksgiving about 10,000 Americans take a sentimental journey into early American history by visiting Plymouth[6], a modern city that reveres its past. In Plymouth Harbor, sightseers tour Mayflower II, a recently constructed ship similar to the original *Mayflower*. They see (but are not allowed to touch) the famous Plymouth Rock. Then they spend a few hours walking through a faithful reproduction of the original Pilgrim village as it looked in 1627. They enter the homes of famous colonists like Miles Standish and John Alden[7], and talk to the "residents" dressed in Pilgrim garb. The primitive living conditions reveal how very little the Pilgrims possessed in the way of material comforts[8]. Modern Americans take great pride in these courageous forefathers who had so little by today's standards, but who were deeply thankful to God for giving them the things they valued most—a good harvest and the freedom to live and worship as they pleased. The half-million tourists who come to Plymouth every year find here a uniquely moving and inspiring experience.

Christmas

Christmas season is the most festive time of the year in the United States.

Students from grammar school through college have one to two weeks' vacation, beginning shortly before Christmas and ending soon after New Year's. Many families go away for the holidays, perhaps to ski in Colorado or to swim and sunbathe in Florida. Those who stay home have fun, too. There are numerous parties to celebrate the birth of Christ and the arrival of the new year.

Although no one knows exactly when Jesus was born. Christians throughout the world celebrate His birthday on December 25. This date was selected in the fourth century so that Christmas would replace the pagan celebration of the winter solstice. Ancient peoples believed that daylight hours began to lengthen when the sun god started his journey back to earth. They celebrated the beginning of his journey on December 25.

In the United States, the spirit of Christmas arrives about a month before the holiday itself. Late in November, street lights and store windows are decorated with the traditional Christmas colors of red and green. Snowmen. Santa Claus, shepherds, angels, and Nativity scenes appear in countless shop windows. Fir trees, holly wreaths, and mistletoe are familiar sights. Families decorate their homes, inside and out, with colored lights and evergreens.

The manufacture and distribution of Christmas items is big business. Stores depend upon Christmas shoppers for about one-fourth of their annual sales. Smart shoppers buy their gifts in November or early December, before the "Christmas rush" makes shopping a chore. Christmas is expensive. To earn extra money for gifts, thousands of Americans get part-time jobs during December delivering mail or selling gifts, trees, ornaments, or greeting cards. Many people make monthly bank deposits in special Christmas accounts so that they will have enough money to provide a nice Christmas for their families.

Although Americans enjoy the commercial gaiety of Christmas, the most beautiful and meaningful aspects of the holiday occur at home and in church. Many families go to church on Christmas Eve and Christmas morning. After services, they gather around the tree and open their gifts. Then they sit down to enjoy a traditional Christmas dinner-turkey or ham, sweet potatoes, vegetables, cranberry sauce, and nuts. For dessert, there is usually fruit cake, plum pudding, or mince pie.

Most of the Christmas customs which Americans enjoy today are variations of traditions brought here by European immigrants. These are some of the most popular customs:

Exchanging Gifts. The first Christmas gifts were those that the three Wise Men brought to the infant Jesus[9]. The custom of giving gifts to family members and close friends is extremely popular in the United States today. Both children and adults get Christmas presents, although children usually get many more.

Receiving Toys from Santa Claus. Many American children believe that on Christmas Eve Santa Claus, a fat, jolly man who wears a red suit, red hat, and long white beard, slides down their chimney to bring them gifts. According to the story, Santa Claus travels in a sleigh pulled by eight reindeer. Children tall Santa Claus what toys they want by writing him a letter or visiting him in a local department store. On Christmas Eve many youngsters lie awake listening for Santa and his sleigh. Some children even leave him a snack of milk and cookies.

Santa Claus is the American name for St. Nicholas, a generous fourth-century bishop who lived in what is now Turkey. It was his custom to go out at night and bring gifts to the needy. After his death, his fame spread throughout Europe. During the Middle Ages, he became the patron saint of schoolboys. His feast day (December 6) was once celebrated in many European countries and is still celebrated in some. Dutch immigrants brought the concept of St. Nicholas (whom they called *Sinter Klaas*) to America, where the name was mispronounced and finally changed to *Santa Claus*. Nineteenth-century American artists and authors altered St. Nick's appearance and created the roly-poly man in red that we see today. Santa's sleigh and reindeer were derived from an old Norse legend.

The American version of Santa Claus as a person who brings gifts and goodwill at Christmas time has also become popular in Canada, England, and Australia.

Hanging a Stocking near the Chimney. As in Great Britain, American children hang stockings by the fireplace, hoping that Santa will fill them with candy and toys.

Decorating the Home with Evergreens. The winter custom of decorating homes and churches with evergreens began in ancient times. Branches of fir or spruce were thought to bring good luck and guarantee the return of spring. The early Germans believed, for example, that in winter evil spirits killed the plants and trees and caused green leaves and flowers to disappear. They felt that bringing evergreens into their homes would protect them from the spirit of death.

Germans of the sixteenth century probably originated the custom of decorating trees. In the nineteenth century, the idea spread throughout Europe and the United States. Now, at Christmas time decorated trees stand in about two-thirds of American homes. The modern American tree is usually covered with colored balls and strings of colored lights. The star on top represents the star in the East which guided the three

Wise Men to Bethlehem[10].

In ancient times, a branch of mistletoe was hung over doorways for good luck. Today the custom continues, but now it is for fun. A man may kiss any girl he catches standing under the mistletoe.

The poinsettia plant is another familiar Christmas decoration. Its star-shaped red leaves are an ideal symbol of the holiday. This plant is native to Central America and Mexico. In the nineteenth century it was adapted to cultivation in the United States by Dr. Poinsett of South Carolina. It is a distinctly modern and American Christmas tradition.

Singing Christmas Carols. In the early days of the Christian Church, the bishops sang carols on Christmas Day. Now everybody sings them. Soloists and choirs on the radio, on TV, in church, and in school all help fill the winter air with beautiful music. Copying an old English custom, many Americans join with friends and walk from house to house singing the traditional carols of Christmas.

Sending Christmas Cards. The custom of sending Christmas cards began in London in 1843 and came to the United States in 1875. Today, most Americans (Christians and non-Christians) send dozens of Christmas cards or "season's greetings" to relatives, friends, and business associates.

Words & Expressions

anchor/ˈæŋkə/*vi.* 抛锚
blessing/ˈblesiŋ/*n.* 上帝的赐福
Plymouth/ˈpliməθ/*n.* 普利茅斯
pumpkin/ˈpʌmpkin/*n.* 南瓜
flee/fliː/*vi.* 逃跑
bean/biːn/*n.* 豆
scout/skaut/*vi. vt. n.* 侦察;童子军
pagan/peigən/*a.* 非基督教的
smallpox/ˈsmɔːlpɔks/*n.* 天花
Nativity/nəˈtiviti/*n.* 耶稣诞生
Norse/nɔːs/*n.* 斯堪的纳维亚人,北欧人

Notes

1. . . . were saddened. . . instead of English:他们伤心地看到,他们的孩子成长为荷兰人而不是英国人了。

2. the idea. . . appealed to them immensely:把耶稣的声音带到这个世界遥远地方的想法对他们有极大的吸引力。the word of Christ:耶稣的教导,或《圣经》。

3. they were in unsettled territory which bad no governing body:他们到达了一块没有任何政府机构的荒无人烟的地方。

4. William Bradford:布拉德福是新英格兰第一个殖民地选举产生的总督。著有《普利茅

斯殖民地历史》一书。

5. The holiday was a great success:感恩晚会很成功,但不久,白人忘了前恩,侵犯印第安人的土地,破坏印第安人的文化,因此双方冲突迭起,互相残杀,许多印第安人部族被摧毁,不少被驱往他乡。所以,今天的印第安人从来不庆祝感恩节。

6. take a sentimental journey into early American history by visiting Plymouth:(今天,每当感恩节来临,上万美国人)抱着怀古的感情,到普利茅斯城参观旅行。

7. Miles Standish and John Alden:斯坦迪什和奥尔登都是第一批来到普利茅斯的殖民先驱。据说两人是好朋友,爱上同一位妇女,斯坦迪什因害羞不敢向那位妇人求爱,因此请他的朋友奥尔登代他求爱。但那位妇女爱上的却是奥尔登。两位朋友因此决裂,最后又和好如初。这个浪漫故事流传至今,这三个人也因此出名。

8. The primitive living conditions... material comforts:如果从物质享受的方面来衡量,这些移民先驱的生活条件非常原始,有的财产也很少。

9. the three Wise Men brought to the infant Jesus:《圣经》故事说,三位智者找到婴儿耶稣后就下跪祷告,并向他敬献礼物。圣诞节互赠礼物的习俗即由此传说而来。

10. Bethlehem:传说是耶稣的出生地,位于约旦西部。

Exercises

Ⅰ. Explain the following

1. Pilgrims
2. the Mayflower Compact

Ⅱ. Fill in the blanks

1. Thanksgiving Day falls on ________________, on which Americans give thanks for ______________.
2. The Puritans, who later became Pilgrims, fled to ________________ first because of ________________ in England.
3. Some English merchants agreed to finance the journey of those Puritans who wanted to emigrate to the New World in return for ________________.
4. Christmas is on ________________ ,which is celebrated for ______________.
5. The traditional Christmas colors are ________________ and ______________.

Ⅲ. Choose the correct answer in each of the following

1. The first American Thanksgiving was hosted by ________.

   A. the Indians

   B. the Pilgrims

   C. the Spanish settlers

   D. the French settlers

2. The first group of English Puritans to land in America called themselves "Pilgrims" because ________.

   A. it was the name of their church

B. they had been persecuted

C. they had wandered for a great distance in search of freedom

D. they came from Holland

3. The Pilgrims were able to survive in America because ________.

A. they received help from the Indians

B. the were supported by rich companies

C. many ships brought them food from England

D. they had signed the Mayflower Compact

4. Which of the following traditions came from Germany?

A. the Christmas tree.

B. Exchanging gifts.

C. Santa Claus.

D. Sending Christmas cards.

5. Which of the following Christmas traditions came from England?

A. The Christmas tree.

B. The poinsettia.

C. Christmas cards.

D. Exchanging gifts.

6. Which of the following traditions began in America?

A. Singing Christmas Carols.

B. Mistletoe.

C. Hanging stockings.

D. The poinsettia plant.

Ⅳ. Answer the following questions briefly

1. How did the Pilgrim Fathers set up the first English Colony in Plymouth?
2. What are some of the traditions of the modern American Thanksgiving that come from that first Thanksgiving celebration?
3. How do Americans celebrate Christmas? What are some of the customs associated with Christmas?

Chapter 20 Social Problems

The Racial Problem

Unlike most other peoples, Americans are primarily a nation of immigrants. The citizens or their ancestors immigrated from many parts of the globe—some as refugees from religious and political persecution, some as adventurers from the Old World seeking a better life, some as captives brought to our shores against their will to be sold into slavery. Though all share a common American culture, the nation contains many racial and ethnic subcultures with their own distinctive characteristics. These differences might seem trivial or irrelevant to outside observers, but they have contributed to intergroup conflicts that have been a persistent social problem to American society.

The United States was explicitly founded on the principle of human equality, but in practice the nation has fallen far short of that ideal. American society is a stratified one, in which power, wealth, and prestige are unequally distributed among the population. This inequality is not simply a matter of distinctions between social classes: it tends to follow racial and ethnic lines as well, with the result that class divisions often parallel racial divisions. The first settlers from "Anglo-Saxon" northern Europe quickly took control of economic assets and political power in the United States, and they have maintained this control, to a greater degree ever since. Successive waves of immigrants from other parts of Europe and elsewhere in the world have had to struggle long and hard to become assimilated into the mainstream of American life. Some have succeeded and have shared in the "American dream"; others—notably those whose ethnic or racial characteristics differ most markedly from those of the dominant group—have been excluded by formal and informal barriers from full participation in American life. The result of this discrimination has been a severe and continuing racial tension in the United States that has periodically erupted into outright violence. Particularly since the civil rights demonstrations, ghetto riots, and other unrest in the 1960s, race and ethnic relations have been a major preoccupation of social scientists, politicians, and the general public.

Poverty

By many standards the United States is the most fabulously wealthy society in history. Yet over 24 million people, more than 1 American in 10, are living at or below the official poverty line[1], on incomes that the federal government considers insufficient to meet basic requirement of food, clothing, and shelter. These people are not the only poor in the United States, there are millions more, living slightly above the poverty line, whose plight is not much better. Despite our celebrated affluence, social services in the United States compare unfavorably with those in most industrialized societies. Furthermore, the affluent majority sometimes seems indifferent to the problems of the poorest section of the population.

Poverty in the United States does not simply mean that the poor do not live quite as well as other citizens. It means many old people eating dog and cat food to supplement their diets. It means malnutrition and deprivation for hundreds of thousands of children It means greater susceptibility to disease, to alcoholism, to victimization by criminals, and to mental disorders. It often means unstable marriages, slum housing, illiteracy, ignorance, inadequate medical facilities, and shortened life expectancy. Poverty can mean low self-esteem, despair, and stunting of human potential.

The problem of poverty in the United States is aggravated because it occurs in a society in which the overall distribution of wealth (property and other capital) and income (wages, salaries, and other earnings) is very unequal. Like all but the most simple societies, the United States is characterized by social stratification that is, it is divided into social classes that have varying degrees of access to the rewards the society offers[2]. It was estimated in the 1970s that if the wealth in the United States were evenly distributed, every adult would have a net worth of around \$ 25 000. But the distribution of wealth is highly unequal. The poor workers run as high as 50%, or about 8 times the rate for the American work force as a whole. This "underclass" could continue to persist, even in the absence of racial discrimination, in much the same way as other pockets of poverty persist—that is, for reasons of social-class inequality. In any event, such progress as has been made in the past decade has brought no benefit whatever to the black "underclass", who are living in an environment of poverty, decay, crime, drug addiction, joblessness, and hopelessness. Most of this wealth has not been accumulated through the hard work or imaginative skills of those who now enjoy it[3]. It has been inherited. Just as the children of the poor are born into poverty and tend to remain there, so the children of the rich tend to enjoy a lifetime of affluence.

The distribution of income in the United States follows a similar pattern. The richest one fifth of American families receives over 40% of the national income, whereas the poorest fifth receives only 5.2%. This pattern has remained virtually unchanged at least since World War II. About 3 000 families receive, in addition to whatever wealth they may possess, an annual income of over $1 million, most of it from investments. The highest executives of major corporations enjoy staggering salaries. A 1979 Industrial Conference Board report showed that the heads of the nation's major manufacturing corporations earned an average of $ 241 000 a year. Corporate executives enjoy many other tax-free benefits from their companies, such as the use of cars and private jets, expense accounts[4], medical care, and vacations disguised as business trips. These untaxed benefits can easily represent the equivalent of hundreds or even thousands of dollars of income every month. It was found that 80% of the checks at the most expensive restaurants and over a third of Broadway theater tickets were covered by expense accounts.

The continued existence of poverty in a generally affluent American society raises serious moral questions[5] and inevitably creates fierce conflicts of interest and many political controversies.

Drug Abuse

Drug abuse in the United States has come to be regarded as one of the most challenging social problems facing the nation. Indeed, the very word "drug" excites strong emotions, and opinion polls since the late 1960s have shown that the "drug problem" is perceived by most Americans as a major threat to our society, particularly to its younger members.

Drug abuse in the United States is a social problem because it has a wide range of social costs, or dysfunctions—some obvious and measurable, some hidden and difficult to quantify.

Crime. There is a strong association between some forms of drug use and crime. The use of alcohol, for example, is highly correlated with violent crime; more than half of those committing murder and other violent assaults have consumed alcohol immediately before the crime. Heroin addiction, too, is related to crime, although not so directly to violence. Heroin addicts may need as $ 100 a day to support their habit, and most addicts find that they must steal in order to raise these sums. In addition, users of illegal drugs have to rely directly or indirectly on criminal networks that manufacture, smuggle, and distribute these drugs. The profits from this illicit commerce are vast and the Malta and other criminal syndicates[6] have become deeply involved in the supply of heroin and, more recently, of cocaine.

Automobile accidents. Alcohol use is directly responsible for tens of thousands of highway accidents and injuries; the drug is blamed for half of the annual total of road traffic fatalities. Some 60% of all drivers fatally injured in auto accidents have a blood-alcohol concentration of over. 0.05%[7], a level that the National Safety Council considers sufficient to impair driving ability, and over 35% have a concentration of over 0.15%, a level high enough to cause intoxication. Thee cost of property damage and medical expenses due to alcohol-related automobile accidents totals about $ 1 billion each year.

Effects on individuals. Drug dependence takes a significant toll in terms of personal health and safety[8]. The heavy user of drugs is much more likely than a member of the general population to be killed or to commit suicide, either deliberately or accidentally. Alcoholics, for example, have a death rate nearly three times higher than that of the general population; they represent a third of all suicides and are seven times more likely than non-alcoholics to suffer fatal accidents. Use of heroin increases one's chances of premature death through overdose, infectious disease such as hepatitis and Aids or suicide. Many drugs have severe and sometimes irreversible effects on mental as well as physical health. Drug dependence, too, may affect other areas of the individual's life, ranging from the home to the work place to personal relationships with friends.

Economic losses. The cost of alcohol abuse alone totals over $43 billion a year in accidents, medical bill, lost production, and so on. It is difficult, however, to estimate the total economic costs of drug use. One reason is that there are many indirect costs society must pay to support drug-dependent persons. Treatment and control of drug abuse constitute a major drain on law-enforcement and other public resources. Chronic drug abusers, for example, may become unemployable and end up on the welfare rolls[9]. By the mid-1970s, federal and state governments were spending over $1 billion per year on the treatment of various drug abusers. Another half billion dollars annually goes into processing drug users through the criminal justice system[10].

Crime

Crime is one of the most serious social problems facing the nation. Former

President Nixon[11] remarked on several occasions that crime is the "number one enemy" and that "we must declare war against it" (Ironically, President Nixon and many of his top administrative officials later faced criminal charges—with some being imprisoned—in connection with the Watergate affair).

It is generally agreed that serious, violent crime has reached alarming proportions in the United States. A survey by the Law Enforcement Assistance Administration (LEAA)[12] found that 61% of all women feel unsafe in their own neighborhoods at night; that 45% of the population is afraid to walk alone at night near their own homes; and that 47% own guns, largely for self-protection.

Those arrested for crimes are disproportionately likely to be male, young, a member of a racial minority, and a city resident. Males are arrested about four times as often as females. Only in juvenile runaway cases and prostitution are females arrested more often than males. There are two major reasons why males are more often arrested. One is the sex role stereotyping which encourages males to be more aggressive and daring, while females are encouraged to be more passive and conforming to rules and norms. The second reason is the tendency of police officers and the courts to deal more leniently with female offenders. However, it should be noted, in the past decade, crime among females has been increasing at much faster rate than among males, a negative side effect which has been attributed to women challenging the traditional sex roles of passivity and conformity.

Young people appear to commit far more than their share of crime[13], including the crimes that are classified by the FBI[14] as most serious—rape, murder, robbery, arson, burglary, aggravated assault, auto theft, and larceny. In 1985, 31% of all arrests were of persons under the age of 21, and 50% of all arrests were of persons under 25. A partial explanation of the high arrest rate among juveniles and young adults is that they may be less skillful than older adults in avoiding being arrested. Another reason is that they tend to commit crimes, such as auto theft, which are highly visible to the police. Even when all these factors are taken into account, it is still the case that the young commit more crimes than the old.

Members of racial minority groups have a disproportionately higher rate of arrests. The arrest rate for the black population is three times higher than for whites. One reason for this higher rate is that a higher proportion of the black population is poor or unemployed; and there are high correlation's between poverty (and unemployment) and the types of crime classified by the FBI as most serious. An additional reason for the higher arrest rates among minority groups may be racial prejudice. A number of studies have shown that the probability of arrest, prosecution, conviction, and incarceration for an offense that is committed decreases as thee social status of the offender increases[15]. In one study, 36 judges were given fact sheets on a hypothetical case and asked to recommend an appropriate sentence. The fact sheets contained the following information:

"Joe Cut", 27, pleaded guilty to battery. He slashed his common-law wife on thee arms with a switchblade. His record showed conviction for disturbing the peace, drunkenness, and hit-run driving. He told a probation officer that he acted in self-defense after his wife attacked him with a broom handle. The prosecutor recommended not more than 5 days in jail or a $100 fine.

Half the fact sheets identified "Joe Cut" as white, and the other half identified him as black. The judges who thought he was white recommended a sentence of 3to 10 days, while those who thought he was black recommended a sentence from 5 to 30days.

It must be noted that the Serious Crime Index of UCR[16] focuses on crimes which are more apt to be committed by persons of lower social and economic status. It does not contain the types of crimes typically committed by higher income groups; fraud, false advertising, corporate price fixing, bribery, embezzlement, industrial pollution, tax evasion, and so on. If white-collar crimes were included in the Crime Index, and if authorities were more vigorous in their enforcement, the profile of a typical criminal would be very likely older, wealthier, whiter, and more suburban than suggested by the Crime Index.

In summary, the Serious Crime Index of the FBI provides an indication of the rates and trends of certain crimes in the United States. Yet these statistics that overlook white-collar crimes are affected by police reporting practices and have to be viewed against the fact that many crimes are unreported. It further appears that the poor, the undereducated, and minorities have been the victims not only of selective law enforcement, but also of misleading statistics on crime[17]. Some sociologists have contended that, since higher-income classes are far more involved in white-collar crime (which is often ignored by law enforcement agencies), the higher classes may actually have a higher rate of crime than the lower classes.

The Abuse of Power by Government and Corporations

A crucial problem of government and corporations concerns power—and the abuse of it. American lives are dominated by large public and private organizations.

The public organizations, primarily government agencies, affect almost every area of their experience. They register births, provide education and social services, record our marriages, regulate many of the conditions of employment, collect taxes, influence countless aspects of lives through thousands of laws, and finally register deaths. The private organizations, primarily business corporations, provide jobs for the bulk of the population and supply most of consumer needs, from banking and television services to clothing and gasoline. American lives and their entire complex civilization are largely dependent on big organizations. Yet these organizations, originally established to satisfy needs and improve the quality of lives, are often experienced as oppressive, unresponsive, impersonal, inefficient, arrogant, and even corrupt. Particularly since the Watergate scandal of the early 1970s, it has been apparent that the major organizations in American society sometimes work in concert to advance their own interests rather than those of the people. The lack of public answer ability of these large organizations has become a major social problem.

Government and corporations are widely distrusted in the United States. The presidencies of Lyndon Johnson and Richard Nixon were marked by a well-founded public belief that their administrations were deliberately and systematically lying to the people[18]. Distrust of government reached its height during the Watergate affair, when the discovery of the abuse of power drove a president from office. Although Nixon himself was pardoned by his successor and escaped accountability for his acts in office, the Watergate affair led to the trials and convictions of many high public officials on such charges as extortion, perjury, conspiracy, subverting the course of justice[19], misuse of campaign funds, bribery, illegal wiretapping, and tax fraud.

The scandal provoked congressional investigations of the FBI and the CIA[20] that turned up literally thousands of illegal acts in the executive branch of government. The FBI, for example, was responsible for hundreds of burglaries of presumed critics of the administration, and was guilty of widespread illegal wiretapping[21]. It had also deliberately attempted to sabotage the civil rights movement in the 1960s. The CIA, whose charter specifically prohibits it from surveillance over the domestic population, had infiltrated the civil rights and antiwar movements, compiled dossiers on tens of thousands of Americans, and intercepted and read hundreds of thousands of private letters and telegrams[22]. It had also, without any authorization from Congress, plotted the assassination of foreign heads of state, including Fidel Castro of Cuba. The agency had also tested a variety of drugs, including LSD, on many people who were unaware that they were being used as guinea pigs, and had caused several deaths in the process[23].

As for corporations, they are widely believed to be more concerned with their own profits than with social responsibility, and the quality or price of their products, or the truth of their advertising. To further their interests, large corporations maintain professional lobbyists in Washington. D. C. to influence public officials behind the scenes. They argue for legislation to serve their own ends, influence the appointment of officials, block reforms they consider undesirable, and seem to have more say in the councils of government than the ordinary voters. There are now more than 15 000 professional lobbyists in Washington, representing a variety of economic and other special-interest groups. One poll showed that three out of five college students believe that "big business has taken the reins of government away from Congress and the Administration"[24], and a national opinion poll found that nearly 60% of Americans think that "government is run by a few big interest groups looking after themselves".

Words & Expressions

intergroup 种族之间
stratified/ˈstrætifaid/*adj.* 有等级的
assimilate/əˈsimileit/*v.* 同化,融化
ghetto/ˈgetəu/*n.* (少数民族或穷人)聚居区
riot/ˈraiət/*n.* 暴乱,骚动
inferiority/in, fiəriˈɔriti/*n.* 低劣,劣种
promiscuity/prəmiˈskjuːiti/*n.* 乱交
assiduously/əˈsidjuəsli/*adv.* 反复不断地
propagate/ˈprɔpəgeit/*v.* 宣传
segregation/segriˈgeiʃən/*n.* 隔离
disclaim/disˈkleim/*v.* 放弃
integration/intiˈgreiʃən/*n.* 融合
elimination/ilimiˈneiʃən/*n.* 消除
hierarchy/ˈhaiəraːki/*n.* 等级
bloc/blɔk/*n.* 群体,集团
divergence/daiˈvəːdʒəns/*n.* 分歧
plight/plait/*n.* 困难处境
affluence/ˈæfluəns/*n.* 富裕
indifferent/inˈdifərənt/*adj.* 漠不关心
deprivation/ˌdepriˈveiʃən/*n.* 剥夺
susceptibility/səˌseptəˈbiliti/*n.* 易感性
victimization/ˌviktimaiˈzeiʃən/*n.* 受害
slum/slʌm/*n.* 贫民窟
illiteracy/iˈlitərəsi/*n.* 文盲
life expectancy 寿命
self-esteem 自尊
accumulate/əˈkjuːmjuleit/*v.* 积累
Broadway/ˈbrɔːdwei/*n.* 百老汇街(纽约市中心的一条大街)
poll/pəul/*n.* 民意测验
dysfunction/disˈfʌŋkʃən/*n.* 不正常行为
addiction/əˈdikʃən/*n.* 吸毒成瘾
smuggle/ˈsmʌgəl/*v.* 走私,私运
illicit/iˈlisit/*adj.* 非法的
cocaine/kəˈkein/*n.* 可卡因
fatality/fəˈtæliti/*n.* 灾难,死亡
concentration/ˌkɔksiˈkeiʃən/*n.* 浓度
intoxication/inˌtɔksiˈkeiʃən/*n.* 酒醉,麻醉
toll/təul/*n.* 死亡
suicide/ˈsuːisaid/*n.* 自杀

overdose/ˈəuvədəus/n. 过量
infectious/inˈfekʃəs/adj. 传染的
hepatitis/ˌhepəˈtaitis/n. 肝炎
prostitution/ˈprɔstitjuːʃən/n. 卖淫
stereotype/ˈsteriətaip/n. v. 陈规,老套
incarceration/inˌkaːsəreiʃən/n. 监禁
hypothetical/ˌhaipəˈθetikəl/adj. 假设的
common-law wife 同居的配偶
switchblade 弹簧刀
hit-run 闯祸后逃跑
probation/prəˈbeiʃən/n. 缓刑
prosecutor/ˈprɔsikjuːtə/n. 起诉人,检察员
corporate price fixing 控制市场价格
bribery/ˈbraibəri/n. 贿赂
embezzlement/imˈbezə/mənt/n. 盗用,挪用(公款)
evasion/iˈveiʒən/n. 偷漏(税)
white-collar 白领阶层
pardon/ˈpaːdn/v. 赦免,宽恕
extortion/iˈkstɔːʃən/n. 敲诈,勒索
perjury/ˈpəːdʒəri/n. 伪证
conspiracy/kənˈspirəsi/n. 阴谋
subvert/səbˈvəːt/v. 破坏,颠覆
wiretapping 窃听
sabotage/ˈsæbətaːʒ/v. 破坏
infiltrate/inˈfiltreit/v. 渗透
dossier/ˈdɔsiei/n. 全套档案
intercept/ˌintəˈsept/ 截取

Notes

1. the official poverty line：官方规定的贫困线。美国政府定期公布各项统计数字,其中包括国民收入状况,据此确定当年贫困线标准以及生活在贫困线以下的户数及其在全国总户数中所占的百分比。

2. it is divided... the society offers：美国是分为各个不同阶层的国家,每个阶层获得社会提供的回报的程度是很不相同的。有些阶层的人的地位和报酬很高,而另一些则很低。

3. Most of this wealth... who now enjoy it：这种财富的大部分自然不是靠其享受者的辛勤或通过他们的创造性的技术而积累起来的。

4. expense accounts：公费帐。即使用公司或国家的公款办事。许多人使用这种办法为个人享受服务,因为这种帐所付的款项不是个人收入,而且免交所得税。

5. The continued existence... moral questions：在富裕的美国社会里长期存在着贫困现象,反映出了严重的道德问题。作者认为,美国有能力解决贫困问题,但许多人却漠不关心,使贫困问题长期得不到解决,这就构成了道德问题。

6. the Mafia and other criminate syndicates：黑手党及其他犯罪集团。黑手党源起19世纪意大利西西里岛的犯罪集团,后泛指一切从事贩毒、赌博、卖淫等犯罪活动的黑社会组织。

7. a blood alcohol concentration of over. 0.05%：司机的血液里酒精浓度如超过0.05%个单位就被认为是酒后开车。

8. Drug dependence... and safety：吸毒成瘾会给个人健康与安全带来极大危害。

9. Chronic drug abusers... on the welfare rolls：长期吸毒者可能无法被雇佣,只能靠福利金过日子。

10. Another half billion dollars... through the criminal justice system：每年还有5亿美元用在司法机关处理吸毒者刑事犯罪上。

11. Former President Nixon：前总统尼克松。他因水门丑闻被迫辞职。这在美国历史上还是第一次。水门丑闻是指 1972 年美国大选时尼克松总统下属人员潜入民主党总部水门大楼窃取情报而被查获的事件。

12. the Law Enforcement Assistance Administration：美国政府的执法辅助局。

13. Young people appear to commit far more than their share of crimes：青少年犯罪比例要比其他年龄组犯罪比例高得多。

14. the FBI：美国联邦调查局，美国国内的安全警察总部，它是英文"Federal Bureau of Investigation"的缩写。

15. the probability of arrest... increases：犯罪者的社会地位越高，他被捕、被起诉、被定罪、被监禁的可能性就越小。

16. The Serious Crime Index of UCR：美国联邦调查局的犯罪报告一览表（Uniform Crime Report）中的"严重犯罪报表"。这里提及的报表是联邦调查局于 1986 年发表的。

17. the poor, the undereducated... on crime：穷人、没有文化的人以及少数民族的成员，不仅是执法偏见的受害者，而且也是误导人的犯罪统计表的受害者。

18. The presidencies of Lyndon Johnson and Richard Nixon... lying to the people：公众有充分的证据说明：约翰逊和尼克松总统是故意地、有计划地对人民说谎。作者的意思是，约翰逊总统在越战问题上、尼克松总统在水门事件上都没有向人民讲真话。

19. subverting the course of justice：暗中破坏法律程序。如水门事件中牵连的官员制造伪证等。

20. the CIA：美国中央情报局。是美国对外的间谍和反间谍机构，它是英文"Central Intelligence Agency\"的缩写。

21. The FBI... illegal wiretapping：比如，美国联邦调查局数千次地非法窃入被认为是批评政府的人员的家中，广泛地非法使用窃听器。

22. The CIA... private letters and telegrams：美国中央情报局渗透到民权和反战运动中，给数以千计的美国人私立档案，窃截和非法阅读成千上万封私人信件和电报。按照法律，美国中央情报局对国内人进行侦查是违法的。

23. The agency... caused several deaths in the process：中央情报局还在许多人身上进行各种实验，包括实验可使脑神经紊乱的麻醉药 LSD，被试验的人自己完全不知道他们被当成试验品。在实验过程中发生了几次死亡事件。guinea pigs：任何被用来作为试验的动物、人或物。

24. "big business... the Administration"："大企业已经从国会和总统手中篡夺了政府领导权"。

Exercise

Ⅰ. Explain the following

1. the black "underclass"
2. socially stratified American society
3. drug abuse

4. white-collar crimes
5. the abuse of power by government
6. the abuse of power by corporations

Ⅱ. Fill in the blanks

1. Former President ________ said that crime is America's number one enemy."
2. Name two of the illegal acts by the FBI: ________ and ________.
3. Name two of the illegal acts by the CIA: ________ and ________.
4. The dominant group in American society that has taken control of economic assets and political power from the beginning of the nation is ________.
5. American slavery was finally abolished by, ________, ________ and ________.
6. After the abolition of slavery, many states ________ to keep the races apart in schools, housing, restaurants and public facilities, and ________ kept blacks in the lowest-paid jobs.
7. Those arrested for crimes are disproportionately likely to be ________, ________, ________ and a city resident, if white-collar crimes were included in the Crime Index, and if authorities were more vigorous in their enforcement of law, the profile of a typical criminal would very likely be ________, ________, ________ and more suburban than the above suggested by the Crime Index of the FBI.
8. ________ had tested variety of drugs, including LSD, on many people who were unaware that they were being used as ________ and had caused several deaths in the process.

Ⅲ. Choose the correct answer in each of the following

1. Three of the following factors contribute the higher arrest rates among minority groups. Which is the exception?
   A. The aggressive nature of these groups.
   B. Racial prejudice against them.
   C. Low social status of these groups.
   D. Poverty and unemployment among minority groups.
2. Which of the following does NOT belong to the white-collar crime?
   A. bribery.
   B. Tax evasion.
   C. False advertising.
   D. Robbery.
3. Which of the following statements is NOT true?
   A. The Northern states had outlawed slavery by 1830.
   B. Slavery was finally abolished in the South in 1865.
   C. The Northern states did not have racial discrimination.
   D. Segregation laws continued to be enforced in Southern states until the 1950s.
7. Drug abuse in the United States is a social problem because it has a wide range of social

costs. Which of the following is NOT a dysfunction caused by drug abuse?

A. There is a strong association between drug use and crime.

B. Drug dependence takes a significant toll in terms of personal health and safety.

C. Drug abuse is a major cause of unemployment.

D. There are great economic losses because of drug abuse.

5. If white-collar crimes were included in the Crime Index and if authorities were more vigorous in their enforcement of law, the profile of a typical criminal in the United States would be ________.

A. older

B. wealthier

C. whiter

D. living near city centers

6. Which of the following used human beings as guinea pigs to test drugs including LSD?

A. The FBI.

B. The CIA.

C. Congress.

D. Richard Nixon.

Ⅳ. Answer the following questions briefly

1. What does poverty mean in the United States? Why is poverty a social problem in America?

2. Why does the drug issue always excite the strong emotion among Americans?

3. Why is crime "the number one enemy" in the United States?

4. What is the cause of racial problem in America?

Part Ⅲ

Language and Culture

Section 1 The Importance of the English Language

Ⅰ. English is becoming global

There are thousands of languages in the world. Each language seems to be the most important to those who speak it as their native language. This is not strange at all, seeing that it is the language they learned at their mothers' knees and may be the only language they will ever know all their lives.

There are many things for a language to exist for human communication. The first is the number of native speakers that a language happens to have. The second is how widely the native speakers are distributed over the world. Next comes the cultural, economic and political influence of those who speak it as their mother tongue and who write in it.

There can be no doubt now that English is one of the world's most widely used languages. People use a language in one of the three ways: as a native language, as a second language, or as a foreign language. English is spoken as a native language by nearly 300 million people in the United States, Britain, Australia, New Zealand, Canada, some Caribbean countries and South Africa. As a second language, English is often necessary for official business, education, information and other activities in a great many countries such as India, Pakistan, Nigeria, Singapore, and the Philippines. It is one of the few working languages of the United Nations and is more frequently used than the others.

It is said that English has become the language of the international trade, communication and cooperation in science and technology. More than 60 percent of the world's radio broadcasts and 70 percent of the world's mail are in English. The most advanced results in space, nuclear and computer research are published in it. Scientists and scholars who speak and write English are in closer touch with the scientists in other countries than those who don't.

It is true that someone has invented a world language named Esperanto. As it has no stable population of speakers, nor cultural heritage which is necessary for any national language to exist, it is only used as a game. But here it is the real world language—English. All students are thus encouraged to learn it and learn it well.

Historically, the English Language has undergone three periods of development. Descended from the language of the Germanic people who invaded Britain in the 5th century, the Anglo-Saxons, it had, then, a complicated system of grammar, with many inflections (changes in word forms). Several dialects of Old English were spoken; the West Saxon dialect, which was used by the King, became the leading literary language. After the Norman Conquest of 1066, and because of contact with Danes in England, the English language became simpler and took in many words from Norman-French and from Danish. Middle English took shape by about 1150. Largely through the influence of the poet Chaucer, the dialect of London became the most-used literary language, and developed into Modern English by about 1450. All through its history the English language has borrowed words from other languages, so that it now has a very large vocabulary, in which the Latin element is as important as the Anglo-Saxon. At the same time English grammar has changed, becoming simpler than that of any other European language. English spelling was not fixed until the mid-17th century. Although written English has become more or less standardized, many dialects remained in Britain, and new forms of English were developed in the U. S. A., Australia, Africa, and India. English has a rich literature, and is now spoken most widely all over the world.

Ⅱ. The growth of American English

Earlier in the seventeenth century, the language taken by Captain John Smith to

Virginia and by the Pilgrims to Massachusetts was Elizabethan English. Ben Jonson, for example, was then at the height of his career and Shakespeare was still writing when Jamestown was settled. Plymouth Colony was founded before the publication of Shakespeare's First Folio and less than a decade after the completion of the Authorized Version of the Bible.

Elizabethan English sounded somewhat different from its contemporary counterpart. For instance, in Shakespeare's time, both the /iː/ and the /ei/ sounds could be heard in such words as *meat*, *teach*, *sea*, *tea*, *lean* and *beard*. Shakespeare was capable of rhyming *please* with either *knees* or *grace*. The same fluctuation could be noticed in the words pronounced with the vowels of /əː/ and /aː/. Shakespeare rhymed *convert* with *art*, *serve* with *carve*, *heard* with *regard*. This shows that the pronunciation of many of these words had not yet become standardized in Elizabethan English.

In addition, seventeenth century English differed from present-day English in spelling. For instance, the word *guest* assumed different forms (*gest*, *geste*, *ghest*, *gheste*). *Publicly* and *publikely*, *straight*, and *strayt*, *limbs* and *limus*, *yield* and *yielde* were used interchangeably.

The difference between Elizabethan English and contemporary English can also be found in other aspects of speech. The best way of acquiring a feel for these differences is to observe with some care a selection of one of the earliest examples of what might be called American English. The following selection from William Bradford's History of Plimmoth Plantation will serve the purpose:

> In these hard and difficulte beginnings they found some discontents and murmurings arise amongst some, and mutinous speeches and carriages in other; but they were soone quelled and overcome by the wisdome, patience, and just and equall carrage of things by the Bov(erno)r and better part, which clave faithfully togeather in the main. But that which was most sadd and lamentable was, that in 2 or 3 months time halfe of their company dyed, espetialy in Jan: and February, being the depth of winter, and wanting houses and other comforts; being infected with the scurvie and other diseases, which this long voiage and their inacomodate condition had brought upon them; so as ther dyed some times 2 or 3 or a day, in the aforesaid time; that of 100 and odd persons, scarce 50 remained. And of these in...

Most noticeable, perhaps, in the passage just quoted is the usage of some words. The word *inacomodate*, for example, rarely occurs in current English. Other words have come to be used in contexts quite unlike those in which they appear in this passage. For instance, *carriages* no longer signifies behavior in the abstract sense; *offices* and is used here in the sense of *services* and this usage now survives only in the set phrase *by (through) the good offices of sb.*

Likewise, certain changes in the forms of words have taken place. Almost at the beginning of the passage, *other* was used as a plural pronoun, although the modern form *others* appears later on. *Scarce*, in an adverbial use, indicates that the fetish of the *ly* ending was somewhat less strong at that time than it is at present. As might be expected, the most pronounced differences are in the verb forms, where *clave* appears as past tense it should be replaced by *cleaved* or *cleft* in current English.

Differences in syntax are even more numerous. The plural form of the abstractions discontents and murmurings would be unlikely to appear in presen-tday usage. Closely connected with this same problem of number is the lack of agreement between subject and verb in "There was but 6 or 7 sound persons." The word *as* in the construction "so as ther dyed" would today be replaced by *that*.

Even more striking than any of these features is the sentence structure. In general, the sentences lack unity and are replete with dangling phrases and clauses. The first sentence in the selection contains fifty-three words and the second eighty-three. These are all long according to modern standards. In the second sentence the parallelism of the phrases introduced by *being* and *wanting* is faulty. The majority of the sentences are without coherence and direction in the present sense of these terms.

The victory of the War of Independence marks the end of the colonial period. With political independence there arose a tendency to develop an American brand of English. In his dissertation on the English Language, Noah Webster, the most intelligent and vocal of the early champions of the American language, wrote that "The reasons for American English being different from English are simple: As an independent nation, our honor requires us to have a system of our own, in language as well as in government. Great Britain, whose children we are, and whose language we speak, should no longer be our standard..."

In 1780, the word *American* was first used to refer to the language of the newly independent nation. In 1802 the term *the American Language* was first recorded in the U. S. Congress; and in 1806 Noah Webster coined the more precise term

American English.

As might be expected, the development of American English was not plain sailing. At first the English rejected it as "barbarous", "corrupt" and "sacrilegious". When Dr. Johnson used the term *American dialect*, he meant it as an insult. The English found merely colorful or quaint such American terms as *ground hog*, *lightning rod* and such borrowings as *boss* (*Dutch*) and *ranch* (Spanish). But they sneered at and condemned as unnecessary or illiterate hundreds of American terms and usages. It wasn't only the words that the English disliked, but the pronunciation and grammar as well.

The earliest American attitudes towards American English split between those who deplored its deviation from the parent language and those who recognized the need to develop American English as a separate unit. Some American writers developed a sense of inferiority, overshadowed by a culture superior to their own. Fillmore Cooper, for example, concealed his national identity and claimed to be an Englishman when he published his Precaution in 1820. At the other extreme of the scale, some writers developed a sense of "linguistic nationalism". Mark Twain, for example, responded to British pretension to linguistic superiority by saying that "The King's English is not the King"s. It's a joint stock company, and Americans own most of the shares." A few other American writers emphasized the separateness of the American language, as well as of American literature.

In the twentieth century some people in Britain maintained their negative attitudes towards American English. In 1930, Sir Alfred Knox, a Conservative Member of Parliament, called in the House of Commons for a limit on the importation of American films, explaining: "The words and accent are perfectly disgusting, and there can be no doubt that such films are an evil influence on our language."

Today there is no such pattern of attack and justification. There is, in Britain, little pretension to linguistic superiority, and a wide acceptance on both sides that the language is a shared property and heritage. Britain is neither chauvinistic nor culturally isolationist. In fact, it is now chic to use American terms in a way that in another age, it was chic to use French terms, so that they appear often in voguishly sophisticated publications. A women's page columnist in The Observer once wrote about a man "laying his wife", a Sunday Times column referred to a "New York hooker", and the New Statesman headed a book review simply "Chutzpah."

As vehicles of communication, both British English and American English are serving remarkably well the needs of the British and American peoples. There is no point in speaking disparagingly of one in favor of the other. "What matters is the matter, but not the form."

Ⅲ. Characteristics of American English

1. CONSERVATIVENESS AND CREATIVENESS IN USAGE

American English contains archaic features of the language which have disappeared in England itself. Some words now obsolete in England are familiar and in common use in America. The word *loan*, for example, when used as a transitive verb, is labeled an Americanism in most dictionaries. British usage prefers *lend*. Verbal *loan* originated in England, perhaps as early as 1200. There is no question about the authenticity of *longing* as it appears in the state papers of Henry VIII, and two seventeenth century citations recorded by the Oxford English Dictionary are equally unmistakable. *Loan* occurred in a verbal function in American writings as early as 1729. For the nineteenth and twentieth centuries, American writers continue to furnish the bulk of evidence for its use.

Another convenient sketch of the same tendency can be found in the usage of the verb *to progress*. The word was in common use in England from 1590 to 1670. It fell into disuse in England in the eighteenth century, but was apparently retained in America, where it became very common toward the end of the century. It found its way back into England after 1800, but was described there as an Americanism, and it is still much more used in America.

Conservativeness in usage constitutes one aspect of American English; there is another aspect to it. American English is characterized by "Yankee Ingenuity and the Frontier Spirit", to use Albert H. Marckwardt's words.

Functional change may serve as the first illustration of the creativeness in usage in American English. The conversion of one part of speech to another is not exclusively American. However, in a good many instances it has occurred in American English but not in British or some time has elapsed before the word appeared in its changed function in England. Moreover, function change is sometimes accompanied by the addition of a new meaning to a word after its conversion. For instance, the word *mainstream*, when used as a verb, means "draw (handicapped children) into the mainstream of life," as in "Some educators warn that markedly handicapped children can profit more from segregated or individual education than from being mainstreamed into classrooms with other youngsters."

American English has demonstrated a fondness for compound formations. Many compounds are created in response to the local situations. Farming, carried on under totally different conditions, both physical and economic, developed such combinations as *log cabin*, *hog ranch*, *corn belt* and *hired help*. *Baseball*, in its present form a distinctively American game, has produced a large number of compound terms: *pinch hit*, *bush league*, *double header*, *grandstand play*, *college try* and *rain check*. *Basketball* is just as full of compounds, as is the somewhat more sedentary poker, with its *full house*, *straight flush*, *jack pot* and *seven card stud*.

Frequently the American compound is elliptical rather than self-explanatory. *Soap opera* is not immediately clear to the uninitiated. It refers to a daytime radio or television serial drama of a highly melodramatic, sentimental nature based on romances of the boy-meets-girl type or stories of supposedly American family life. It is so called since many original sponsors were manufacturers of toilet and laundry soaps. Another example is the word *wetback*, which refers to a Mexican laborer who enters the United States by swimming or wading across the Rio Grande, thereby avoiding quota restrictions and immigration formalities in general.

Metaphor is another feature of an American compound. A *disc jockey* has nothing to do with *horses*; he is an employee of a radio station and conducts a program of recorded music. *Rat race*, *captive mine*, *ghost town*, *and double talk* all employ one of their elements figuratively.

Many new words have been created by American English through other devices of word formation.

2. VERBOSITY AND BREVITY OF EXPRESSION

The most prevalent defect in writing as seen in present-day American English is a tendency to convey an idea in as complicated a way as possible. Instead of being simple, terse and direct, the style is stilted, longwinded and circumlocutory; instead of choosing the simple and direct word, it prefers the quaint and the picturesque. This tendency is known as verbosity or verbiage (which means "an excess of words beyond those needed to express concisely what is meant").

Stefan Kanfer wrote two articles for Time in 1978 and 1979, dealing with the state of language in those two years. Most of the examples he provided were taken from American English. As evidence of verbosity, a departmental rejection slip was offered: "The involved document, though clothed in diplomatic costume, is more than a transmittal note and is, thus, of no decisional significance." This is typical of the pompous style of the official documents. "Transmittal note" is some kind of bureaucratic jargon, referring to an interoffice memo conveying the results of a decision. The phrase "of no decisional significance" probably means "not legally binding". Another sample of the same nature was taken from the U. S. Labor Department: "No lost time injuries that do not result in a medical expense should not be reported to the OWCP (short for Office of Workman's Compensation Payment)." This is a badly constructed sentence, presumably meaning "Injuries that do not result in a loss of working hours or involve payment of medical expenses should not be reported to the OWCP."

At the end of the article published in 1979, Stefan Kanfer pointed out that "Certainly our language has been besieged by vulgarities. But it has also been enriched by vigorous phrases and terms. To those who speak and write with care, those words are the unmistakable beats of life."

The article ends on a promising note. It is true that there is another aspect to American English. As opposed to verbosity, brevity is one of the salient features of the language. In American English there can be found no lack of prose or fiction marked by a simple, terse and direct style. For examples of this kind, turn to the text proper.

3. THE HETEROGENEOUS NATURE OF AMERICAN VOCABULARY

A. The melting pot

At the turn of the twentieth century, Israel Zangwill used the term the melting pot to refer to America. Long before this, Hector St. John Crevecoeur had recognized that "here individuals of all nations are melted into a new race of men." In the field of language, it can be said that American English is a linguistic melting pot in miniature.

American English has supplemented its word stock by adoptions from more foreign words than British English. For one thing, new physical conditions in a new continent call for new words. For another, Americans were in contact with foreign languages more than their British cousins during the period of colonization and wholesale immigration.

The migration of the English to North America resulted in the adoption of many loan words from the various Indian languages of the continent, e. g. *persimmon*, *tamarack*.

Besides the various Indian influences, American English reflects the other non-

English cultures which the colonists and frontiersmen met in their conquest of the continent. In the westward expansion of their territory, the English-speaking colonists came into contact with the French, the Dutch and the Spanish. The loan words adopted from these sources are: *portage*, *rapids* (French); *cole slaw*, *waffle* (Dutch); and *mustang*, *alfalfa* (Spanish).

The German element in the vocabulary of American English stems from an immigrant people, not a colonial rival. The words of German origin which have found their way into American English are: *hamburger*, *noodle*, *hoodlum*, *ecology*, etc.

In addition, as widely varied Swedish, Italian, Yiddish and Chinese have all made some contributions to the American vocabulary.

B. Slang, jargon and cant

The American vocabulary abounds with varieties of substandard language such as slang, jargon and cant. Slang is the body of words and expressions frequently used by or intelligible to a rather large portion of the general public, but not accepted as good, formal usage by the majority. This definition distinguishes slang from dialect, which is a local speech form; from jargon, which is the language of a certain calling or class; and from cant, which is specifically the language of the underworld. There is another term argot, which is something of a cross between cant and jargon; it refers to either the secret language of the underworld or any specialized occupational vocabulary, *the argot of the racetrack*, for example. The boundaries between these levels of vocabulary are often vague, and there is a large measure of interchange among slang, dialect, cant and jargon. Moreover, not only social and ethnic groups, but even agegroups (teenagers, for example) and sexes have their own terminologies.

American slang tries for a quick, easy, personal mode of speech. It is mostly derived from cant, jargon and argot words and expressions whose popularity has increased until a considerable part of the general public uses or understands them. Much of this slang retains a basic character of its origin: it is intelligible only to the initiates.

American slang is characterized by fluidity in usage. Some slang phrases have penetrated standard speech to such an extent that they can hardly be called slang any more, e.g. *to have had it*, *let's face it* or *on a slightly lower plane*, *get with it.* These phrases have acquired the status of colloquialisms. Some expressions like *eager beaver*, *bigwig*, *hit the road*, *bats in the belfry* are on the borderline between slang and colloquialisms.

Other slang expressions are short-lived; they flourish for a time with varying popularity and then are forgotten. Consider, for example, *the fate of scram*, *nuts*, *stacked*, *Howling Horance* (for sirens).

The jargons of the various occupations are as numerous and varied as the occupations themselves. Some, by reason of contact with the outside world, or constant representation in fiction and the press, have risen in status and become part of standard speech, e. g. *confrontation*, *conventional*, *overkill*, *nuclear umbrella* (military jargons); *play ball*, *straight from the shoulder* (sports jargons); *deadpan*, *double task* (jargons of the theatrical world).

Some jargons remain at a lower level of usage. They are simply used by the restricted few. For example, *a girl* is *a hat* and *star dusting* means *going steady*; *shoes* may go by the name of *kicks*, *bottoms* or *ends* and *a car* may be known as *go it all*, *rubber*, *short or wheels.*

Cant is the sublanguage of the underworld. Each branch of the underworld has its own specific lingo. Automobile thieves, for instance, speak of *lookers* (browsers in used car lots), *ups* (prospective customers for stolen cars), *tramps* or *junkers* or *crates* (broken down cars) and *cream puffs* (good cars). Illegal gamblers know their occupation under the various names of *clearing house*, *butter and eggs*, *the bug.* A *drop* is the store where you place your bet; a *runner* is the man who takes it. Dope peddlers speak of *junk* (dope in general), and *junkie*, *hophead*, *coke* or *snowbird* (addict). From the pickpockets' lingo come *moll buzzing* (stealing from a woman), *softy* (victim), *breech bridge* (side pocket), *hole* (subway).

Ⅳ. Differences between British English and American English

1. DIFFERENCES IN PRONUNCIATION

The most marked difference between British English and American English lies in the pronunciation of the vowels of *dance*, *fast*, *grass* and *half.* Americans pronounce these words with a sound /æ/ as in *cat*, whereas their British cousins pronounce them with a sound /ɔː/ a broad /a/. Another noticeable difference can be found in the pronunciation of words like *for*, *door*, *farm* and *lord.* In America these words are pronounced with *r* sounded as a fricative, whereas in England it is silent except in expressions like *far away* and *the door opens* where a linking *r* is naturally inserted. In addition, Americans pronounce words like *dock*, *fog*, *hot* and *rod* with a slow back sound /a/ like the vowel sound in *car* and *father* shortened.

They pronounce words like *dew*, *duke*, *new* and *steward* with the /juː/ sound reduced to /uː/ so that *dew* and *duke* sound like /duː/ and /duːk/.

Furthermore, it may be noted that both word-stress and sentence-stress are weaker in American than in British English, and intonation is more level. Consequently, American speech is more monotonous, but at the same time it is generally more distinct. Unstressed syllables are pronounced with more measured detachment and therefore with greater clarity. In words like *temporary* and *extraordinary*, for example, Americans invariably give prominence to the unstressed syllables and consequently, great audibility. In words like *dormitory* and *necessary*, they habitually place a secondary stress upon the penult or last syllable but one. Some words Americans stress differently from the English. The former stress aristocratic and primarily on the second syllable whereas the latter stress them on the first. Conversely, Americans stress address and inquiry on the first syllable whereas the English stress them on the second. Other words, like *advertisement* and *financier* are stressed on the second syllable in England but on the third syllable in America.

2. DIFFERENCES IN SPELLING

In dealing with the spelling of the American vocabulary, people usually turn to Webster's New International Dictionary as an official guide. It sanctions such spellings as *or* for *our* in *honor* and *favor* for British English *honour* and *favour*; *er* for *re* in *center* and *meter* for British English *centre* and *metre*; one consonant for two in *traveler* and *wagon* for British English *traveller* and *waggon*; *s* for *ce* in the substantives *defense* and *offense* for British English *defence* and *offence*; various simplifications such as *ax*, *catalog*, *check*, *jail*, *mask* and *program* for British English *axe*, *catalogue*, *cheque*, *goal*, *masque* and *programme*. Hundreds of American spellings have won acceptance in English, not only *public* for *publick*, *jail* for *gaol*, *cider* for *cyder*, *asphalt* for *asphalte*, and the like, but also the *or* spellings for all agent substantives *author*, *censor*, *donor*, *tailor*, *tutor*, and *visitor*, all, in fact, except *paviour* and *saviour*.

3. DIFFERENCES IN VOCABULARY

If an American junior executor goes to London, to work in the British branch of his firm, he finds that in a few respects business speaks a different language over there. He must learn to call bonds "debentures" and payroll a "salary sheet". He doesn't get a raise in salary, but a "rise". Here the New York Times follows British usage. He finds that he has, not a white collar job, but a "blackcoat" position. A soft snap is a "cushy job". A sitdown strike becomes a "stayin" strike. A realtor is a "house and estate agent". A check stub is dignified as a "cheque counterfoil." And in the advertising field, a billboard becomes "hoarding."

There are novel words for items of ordinary living. The American must look not for an apartment but for a "service flat." He goes up not in an elevator, but in a "lift". If he looks around for a lunch counter, he'll find it under the sign of a "snack bar" (this term is now coming into use in America). If he forgets the key to his "flat," it would do no good to try to climb in through "transom," for in British nomenclature (terminology) that means the horizontal bars across a door or windowtop; what Americans call a transom is a "fanlight". An American porch climber or second story man is a "cat burglar." You ring not for the janitor, but for the "caretaker", to make repairs to the "tap" (American English water faucet). Groceries come up in the "kitchen lift", not a dumbwaiter. For dinner, you have a "sweet", the masquerade for dessert; the biscuits served at tea time are neither hot nor are they in the American sense; they are what we call cookies. You get a "cut from the joint" rather than a slice off the roast.

The preceding two passages are taken from How to Double Your Vocabulary by S. Stephenson Smith. Now we will quote a passage from Our Language by Simeon Potter to show how an Englishman is made aware of differences in vocabulary when he arrives in the United States.

... he (an Englishman) decides to continue his journey by rail, that is, by railroad. He does not register his luggage but he checks his baggage, which is then placed, not in the luggage van, but in the baggage car, perhaps he must first rescue it from the left luggage office, which, he discovers, is called the checkroom. A goods train is referred to as a freight train and a brake van becomes a caboose. He looks for the inquiry office in order to corroborate details and he finds that it is called the information bureau; or he may decide to consult a bulletin board, in England a timetable, on his own account. He is surprised to learn that a season ticket is a commutation ticket and that a season ticket holder is a plain commuter. The driver of his train is the engineer and the guard is the conductor. He hears someone refer to a switch, which turns out to be a point, and he soon discovers that a grade crossing is merely a level crossing. When he reaches his destination he finds an automobile waiting for him at the railroad depot. He cannot help noticing that the windscreen is called the windshield, the bonnet the hood, and that petrol is alluded to as gasoline or plain gas. That explains why the filling station is named the gas station and why accelerating is described as stepping on the gas...

In spite of all the above differences between British English and American English it should be noted that the unifying factors outweigh splitting factors and that there are potent forces at work bringing the two main streams of English closely together. American and British scholars are stepping up their cooperation in the writing of composite books addressed to the English-speaking countries and the councils of learned societies have taken steps to standardize technical terminology. The ubiquity of radio and television, the interchange of films, novels, journals, plays and the presence of communication satellites all serve to make the divergence narrower and narrower.

Ⅴ. Language Variety and Language Variation

It s generally acknowledged that members of a language community cannot be expected to speak exactly the same language in exactly the same way. Thus the question of variety arises. Let us compare the following two sentences:

a. Please keep quiet, others have gone to sleep.

b. Quietness is requested for the benefit of those who have retired.

We can see that while the meaning is the same, it is expressed quite differently in both cases: the first is informal and the second is very formal. They are both "English", but in this sense "English" is a mere generalization of many different types of the same language. Some linguists say that the concept of a "whole language" is so vast that it is hardly useful for any linguistic purpose. We need a framework of categories to describe the varieties of a language. When varieties are classified in terms of user, they are called dialects. When they are classified in terms of use, they are called styles or registers.

1. DIALECTS

The term "dialect" is a very wide concept. It involves all variations arising from differences among users, such as the geographical location, period of history and social position.

The form of a given language used in a certain geographical space is called geographical or regional dialect, such as Cockney dialect and Yorkshire dialect in Britain, or North Midland dialect and South Midland dialect in the United States.

Serious investigation of regional dialects has been carried on for many years. Now many maps have been published showing the prevalence of particular speech forms in particular areas.

The kind of language we use is also determined by the time we live in, and this kind of variety is usually referred to as temporal dialect. There are two major temporal dialects in Chinese—classical Chinese and modern Chinese, with finer differences in between. In English, there are marked differences between Old English and Modern English. We can study the temporal dialect of one historical period, which belongs to synchronic linguistics. We can also approach these dialects from the point of view of their historical development. This is part of diachronic linguistics.

Dialects which identify where a person is placed on the social scale are called social dialects. Since members of a community bind themselves together in groups for gain, security, amusement, or solidarity, for example, they tend to use the same kind of language which is highly stratified in terms of social division, such as class, professional status, age and sex. Although the differences are not so fundamental in Modern English, we can still find some usages in vocabulary, grammar and pronunciation which are influenced by these social factors. Take sex for example. It has been suggested that there is a great deal of extra politeness in female speech which makes use of the following devices:

a. Frequent use of expressions like "I'm afraid that...", "I'm not sure but...", "I may be wrong but..."
b. Abundant use of tag questions as in "The lecture is terribly interesting, isn't it?"
c. Greater use of qualifiers and intensifiers than men: "awfully", "lovely", "terribly", and "fascinating", for example.
d. Preference for use of the standard form of language on many occasions when men would not.

2. STYLES

The study of varieties is complicated by the fact that speakers can adopt different styles of speaking. One can speak very formally or very informally and choice of words may be governed by circumstances. Ceremonial occasions almost always require very formal speech; public lectures are somewhat less formal. Casual conversations are quite informal; exchanges between intimate friends on matters of little importance can be extremely informal. We can relate the level of formality to many factors: the kind of occasion; the social, age and other differences among the participants; the particular task that is involved; the channel of communication (writing, speaking, or telephoning); the emotional involvement of one or more of the participants. It may be difficult to characterize clear levels of formality, but it is fairly easy to show that native speakers control a range of styles. It is also possible to predict the kind of style that a native speaker tends to use on certain occasions.

3. REGISTER

In M. A. K Halliday's linguistics register is a special term, referring to an instance of language-in-action. It is the form of language used resulting from the configuration of several contextual features: the topic focus of the interaction, the medium of communication and the relationship between the participants. Each of these contextual features determines to some extent the kind of language to be used. The language used for talking about horse-racing will be different from the language of cooking. The topics are clearly different. The kind of language appropriate for a given topic will be further shaped by the medium of communication. Suppose the topic remains the same, say horse-racing, the language used will be different when the communicating is done in speech from that when it is carried out in writing. Sometimes a speech is spontaneous, without preparations; sometimes a speech is prepared to some extent; there are times when a speech has been written out but delivered orally. The relationship between the speaker and hearer, writer and reader, is also relevant; friends or enemy, close friends or casual acquaintances,—that is, whether the communication is designed to provide information, or to explain and to teach, or to persuade or convince, to amuse or entertain. Clearly, a story, for example, which is written to teach, will be different linguistically from one written to entertain. When all these contextual features are fixed, the kind of language is more or less determined. Register then is a variety embedded in situations.

As can be induced, language variety results from the fact that language is subject to change and is in constant change. Language variation refers to the process of changing in the development of a specific language or individual qualities of any kind of change. Universally, all languages are in their constant change. So variation is one of the universals of language. The 19th century historical linguistics is especially interested in language changes, and research in this field has brought out some interesting discoveries. Two aspects concerning language variation have been generally accepted.

a. the universality of language change—All living languages, without exception, are subject to change, just like a living being in natural world.

b. the continuity of language change—The process of language change, ever since its beginning, is going on all the time without stop.

Influenced by Darwin's view of evolution in biology and Hegel's dialectic philosophy, the study of language in the 19th century got well-developed, especially in classification of languages. Linguists paid more attention to vernacular languages rather than to the ancient written literary languages—Latin, for instance, which had long been the exclusive object of linguistic study ever since the ancient times. Both European and non-European languages were investigated. The result seemed to be exciting. For many languages were found to bear genetic relationship. Terms such as "family of languages, branches, parent languages, descendent languages" were borrowed from biology in describing and classifying world languages.

According to their genetic relationship, languages can be grouped into families by virtue of their common descent from an earlier parent-language or ancestral language.

The Causes of Language Change—internal factors and external factors, and sometimes the overlap of the two. Sound changes, grammatical changes, and lexical changes can be either the result of internal reconstruction or external reconstruction. Changes that take place exactly within the modulation of language itself, for instance, the hypercorrection (between you and I), the gradual sound drift, and analogy in grammar and vocabulary, are classified as internal changes. External changes refer to social and cultural factors that are responsible for the internal changes of language. When people of different language communities meet, it is very likely that their respective languages will be used with some kind of adaptation or modulation, in sound, grammar, and vocabulary. Bilingualism, pidginization and creolization are the result of such socio-cultural mixture. As has been mentioned above, conquest, wars and colonization also bring about language change.

Section 2 Introduction to Language and Culture

Ⅰ. Concept of Culture

The concept of culture is extremely difficult to define due to its broad and complex nature. In an attempt to reduce that nature, the theorists have employed different strategies to define culture. Some writers have specified the connotation of culture by presenting lists of items; whereas others have simply abandoned the attempt to define it by avoiding precise definition. Hammerly, on the other hand, has suggested a simple and useful "threefold classification", which lends itself to the incorporation of culture into second/foreign language teaching. As Stern puts it, "the three-fold distinction is useful in that it brings together humanistic and anthropological concepts and introduces a helpful division into a number of categories which are particularly well adjusted to the needs of the second language classroom." This is therefore the main meaning of the concept of culture throughout this paper.

Hammerly has defined the three major areas that are to be covered by culture as: (a) information (or factual) culture, (b) behavioural culture, and (c) achievement (or accomplishment) culture.

Information (or factual) culture. "This refers to the information or facts that the average educated native knows about his society, the geography and history of his country, its heroes and villains, and so on". "The second language learner who wants to communicate with native speakers must somehow get a sense of the world view native speakers have of themselves and their own country".

Behavioural Culture. This is a different version of way-of-life culture by Hammerly. He defined it as typical "actual behaviour plus attitudes, values, etc." This kind of culture, Hammerly reckons as the most important for second language learning: "Behavioural culture—especially conversational formulas and kinesics is the form of culture most important to successful communication".

Achievement (or accomplishment) culture. This is the humanistic aspect of culture, i.e. "artistic and literary accomplishments" (ibid), which Hammerly does not attach so great importance as to Behavioural culture for second / foreign language learning.

However, all the three aforesaid aspects will be covered by the concept of culture in this paper. Next the relationship between culture and language will be reviewed for the purpose of exploring why culture teaching should be integrated with second/foreign language teaching.

Ⅱ. Relationship between Culture and Language

Culture and language are inseparable, which is strongly advocated by Byram et al, who have contended that cultural learning and language learning cannot take place independent of each other. This appears to ring true, as we shall see later.

On the one hand, culture is an integral part of language. Many theorists have expressed this point of view from various perspectives. For example Kramsch has made the point that the purpose for learning a foreign language is "a way of making cultural statement" as well as "learning a new way of making communication". While other theorists have attached great importance to culture for language understanding. For instance, Byram et al have argued that only when the cultural context is understood can the language rooted in the context be thoroughly comprehensible. This point has found an echo with Brown:

Misunderstandings are... likely to occur between members of different cultures; ... differences are real and we must learn to deal with them in any situation in which two cultures come into contact.

Among the theorists, Malinowski might have made the most powerful argument that an understanding of the language was impossible without constantly relating it to the culture in which it was operative.

Language, on the other hand, is an inseparable part of culture as well. Byram has elaborated this idea in one of his books "*Cultural Studies in Foreign Language Education*" as "... language pre-eminently embodies the values and meanings of a culture, refers to cultural artifacts and signals people's cultural identity." Other theorists have defined culture in such a way that language is put at the centre of an account of a particular culture. Geertz, for example, defines culture as "a historically transmitted pattern of meanings embodied in symbols, a system of inherited conceptions expressed in symbolic form by means of which men communicate, perpetuate and develop their knowledge about and attitudes towards life". Brown has provided another such definition in which he describes language as

" the most visible and available expression of a particular culture."

In sum, culture is an inseparable part of language and vice versa. Culture would be difficult to be transmitted from place to place and from generation to generation if there were no language—the principal carrier of values and meanings of a culture, etc. On the other hand, language would be impossible to be understood without constant reference to the cultural context which has produced it. It may, therefore, be argued that culture and language cannot be treated exclusive of each other in second/foreign language teaching programs. In other words, it is necessary and more proper to teach both language and culture in an integrated way. It is worthy of note here that one of the basic practices of integrating the two is to use the target language as the medium of instruction in culture teaching. In the next part, the extent to which culture should be part of second/foreign language teaching programs will be considered.

Ⅲ. Culture and the Individual

Between culture and the individual the relationship is, and always has been, strangely ambivalent. We are at once the beneficiaries of our culture and its victims. Without culture, and without that precondition of all culture, language, man would be no more than another species of baboon. It is to language and culture that we owe our humanity. And "What a piece of work is a man!" says Hamlet: "How noble in reason! how infinite in faculties! . . . in action how like an angel! in apprehension, how like a god!" But, alas, in the intervals of being noble, rational and potentially infinite,

man, proud man,

Dressed in a little brief authority,
Most ignorant of what he is most assured,
His glassy essence, like an angry ape,
Plays such fantastic tricks before high heaven,
As make the angels weep.

Genius and angry ape, player of fantastic tricks and godlike reasoner in all these roles individuals are the products of a language and a culture. Working on the twelve or thirteen billion neurons of a human brain, language and culture have given us law, science, ethics, and philosophy; have made possible all the achievements of talent and of sanctity. They have also given us fanaticism, superstition and dogmatic bumptiousness; nationalistic idolatry and mass murder in the name of God; rabble-rousing propaganda and organized lying. And, along with the salt of the earth, they have given us, generation after generation, countless millions of hypnotized conformists, the predestined victims of power-hungry rulers who are themselves the victims of all that is most senseless and inhumane in their cultural tradition.

Thanks to language and culture, human behavior can be incomparably more intelligent, more original, creative and flexible than the behavior of animals, whose brains are too small to accommodate the number of neurons necessary for the invention of language and the transmission of accumulated knowledge. But, thanks again to language and culture, human beings often behave with a stupidity, a lack of realism, a total inappropriateness, of which animals are incapable.

Each of us is born into some culture and passes his life within its confines. Between every human consciousness and the rest of the world stands an invisible fence, a network of traditional thinking-and-feeling patterns, of secondhand notions that have turned into axioms, of ancient slogans revered as divine revelations. What we see through the meshes of this net is never, of course, the unknowable "thing in itself." It is not even, in most cases, the thing as it impinges upon our senses and as our organism spontaneously reacts to it. What we ordinarily take in and respond to is a curious mixture of immediate experience with culturally conditioned symbol, of sense impressions with preconceived ideas about the nature of things. And by most people the symbolic elements in this cocktail of awareness are felt to be more important than the elements contributed by immediate experience. Inevitably so, for, to those who accept their culture totally and uncritically, words in the familiar language do not stand (however inadequately) for things. On the contrary, things stand for familiar words. Each unique event of their ongoing life is instantly and automatically classified as yet another concrete illustration of one of the verbalized, culture-hallowed abstractions drummed into their heads by childhood conditioning.

It goes without saying that many of the ideas handed down to us by the transmitters of culture are eminently sensible and realistic. (If they were not, the human species would now be extinct.) But, along with these useful concepts, every culture hands down a stock of unrealistic notions, some of which never made any sense, while others may once have possessed survival value, but have now, in the changed and changing circumstances of ongoing history, become completely irrelevant. Since human beings respond to symbols as promptly and unequivocally as they respond to the stimuli of unmediated experience, and since most of them naively believe that culture-hallowed words about things are as real as, or even more real than their perceptions of the things themselves, these outdated or intrinsically nonsensical notions do enormous harm. Thanks to the realistic ideas handed down by culture, mankind has survived and, in certain fields, progresses. But thanks to the pernicious nonsense drummed into every individual in the course of his acculturation, mankind, though surviving and progressing, has always been in trouble. History is the record, among other things, of the fantastic and generally fiendish tricks played upon itself by culture-maddened humanity.

What can, and what should, the individual do to improve his ironically equivocal relationship with the culture in which he finds himself embedded? How can he continue to enjoy the benefits of culture without, at the same time, being stupefied or frenziedly intoxicated by its poisons? How can he become discriminatingly acculturated, rejecting what is silly or downright evil in his conditioning, and holding fast to that which makes for humane and intelligent behavior?

A culture cannot be discriminatingly accepted, much less be modified, except by persons who have seen through it by persons who have cut holes in the confining stockade of verbalized symbols and so are able to look at the world and, by reflection, at themselves in a new and relatively unprejudiced way. Such persons are not merely born; they must also be made. But how?

In the field of formal education, what the would-be hole cutter needs is knowledge: knowledge of the past and present history of cultures in all their fantastic variety, and knowledge about the nature and limitations, the uses and abuses, of language. A man who knows that there have been many cultures, and that each culture claims to be the best and truest of all, will find it hard to take too seriously the boastings and dogmatizings of his own tradition. Similarly, a man who knows how symbols are related to experience, and who practices the kind of linguistic self-control taught by the exponents of General Semantics, is unlikely to take too seriously the absurd or dangerous nonsense that, within every culture, passes for philosophy, practical wisdom and political argument. As a preparation for hole cutting, this kind of intellectual education is certainly valuable, but no less certainly insufficient. Training on the verbal level needs to be supplemented by training in wordless experiencing. We must learn how to be mentally silent, must cultivate the art of pure receptivity.

In the exploration of the vast and mysterious world of human potentialities the great artists, visionaries and mystics have been trailblazing pioneers. But where they have been, others can follow. Potentially, all of us are "infinite in faculties and like gods in apprehension." Modes of consciousness different from normal waking consciousness are within the reach of anyone who knows how to apply the necessary stimuli. The universe in which a human being lives can be transfigured into a new creation.

Within our current systems of education, training on the nonverbal level is meager in quantity and poor in quality. Moreover, its purpose, which is simply to help its recipients to be more "like gods in apprehension" is neither clearly stated nor consistently pursued. We could and, most emphatically, we should do better in this very important field than we are doing now. The practical wisdom of earlier civilizations and the findings of adventurous spirits within our own tradition and in our own time are freely available. With their aid a curriculum and a methodology of nonverbal training could be worked out without much difficulty.

From the nonverbal world of culturally uncontaminated consciousness we pass to the subverbal world of physiology and biochemistry. A human being is a temperament and a product of cultural conditioning; he is also, and primarily, an extremely complex and delicate biochemical system, whose inwardness, as the system changes from one state of equilibrium to another, is changing consciousness.

Unprecedentedly rapid technological and demographic changes are steadily increasing the dangers by which we are surrounded, and at the same time are steadily diminishing the relevance of the traditional feeling-and-behavior-patterns imposed upon all individuals, rulers and ruled alike, by their culture. Always desirable, widespread training in the art of cutting holes in cultural fences is now the most urgent of necessities. Can such a training be speeded up and made more effective by a judicious use of the physically harmless psychedelics now available? On the basis of personal experience and the published evidence, I believe that it can. In my utopian fantasy, Island, I speculated in fictional terms about the ways in which a substance akin to psilocybin could be used to potentiate the nonverbal education of adolescents and to remind adults that the real world is very different from the misshapen universe they have created for themselves by means of their culture-conditioned prejudices. "Having Fun with Fungi" that was how one waggish reviewer dismissed the matter. But which is better: to have Fun with Fungi or to have Idiocy with Ideology, to have Wars because of Words, to have Tomorrow's Misdeeds out of Yesterday's Miscreeds?

How should the psychedelics be administered? Under what circumstances, with what kind of preparation and follow-up? These are questions that must be answered empirically, by large-scale experiment. Man's collective mind has a high degree of viscosity and flows from one position to another with the reluctant deliberation of an ebbing tide of sludge. But in a world of explosive population increase, of headlong technological advance and of militant nationalism, the time at our disposal is strictly limited. We must discover, and discover very soon, new energy sources for overcoming our society's psychological inertia, better solvents for liquefying the sludgy stickiness of an anachronistic state of mind. On the verbal level an education in the nature and limitations, the uses and abuses of language; on the wordless level an education in mental silence and pure receptivity; and finally, through the use of harmless psychedelics, a course of chemically triggered conversion experiences or ecstasies these, I believe, will provide all the sources of mental energy, all the solvents of conceptual sludge, that an individual requires. With their aid, he should be able to adapt himself selectively to his culture, rejecting its evils, stupidities and irrelevances, gratefully accepting all its treasures of accumulated knowledge, of rationality, human-heartedness and practical wisdom. If the number of such individuals is sufficiently great, if their quality is sufficiently high, they may be able to pass from discriminating acceptance of their culture to discriminating change and reform. Is this a hopefully utopian dream? Experiment can give us the answer, for the dream is pragmatic; the utopian hypotheses can be tested empirically. And in these oppressive times a little hope is surely no unwelcome visitant.

Ⅳ. Questions to ask about Culture

This is not meant to be a definitive list of questions, but an indication of what general areas of culture might contain significant information for the teacher in a bilingual education program, together with illustrations of what kinds of specific questions might need answers and what their significance might be. The various aspects of culture do not have the same relative importance to people in different groups, but that is among the questions for which we need answers.

- 1. General
- 2. Family
- 3. The Life Cycle
- 4. Roles
- 11. Dress and Personal Appearance
- 12. History and Traditions
- 13. Holidays and Celebrations
- 14. Education

- 5. Interpersonal Relationships
- 6. Communication
- 7. Decorum and Discipline
- 8. Religion
- 9. Health and Hygiene
- 10. Food
- 15. Work and Play
- 16. Time and Space
- 17. Natural Phenomena
- 18. Pets and Other Animals
- 19. Art and Music
- 20. Expectations and Aspirations

1. GENERAL

a. What are the major stereotypes which you and others have about each cultural group? To what extent are these accepted by the group being typed?

b. To what extent and in what areas has the traditional culture of each minority group changed in contact with the dominant American culture? In what areas has it been maintained?

c. To what extent do individuals possess knowledge of or exhibit characteristics of traditional groups?

These general questions must be kept in mind when asking questions about "traditional" or "typical" cultural beliefs or behaviors in all of the areas of culture which follow. While there are systematic differences between groups of people which we need to recognize and understand, we need to critically analyze all information for the effects of stereotyping, recognize the facts of acculturation, and be sensitive to individual differences. Otherwise there is a danger of merely adding to the stereotypes, of incorrectly identifying minority groups in the United States with ancestral groups in the country of origin, or generalizing what is "typical" to all.

2. FAMILY

a. Who is in a "family"? Who among these (or others) live in one house?

b. What is the hierarchy of authority in the family?

c. What are the rights and responsibilities of each family member? Do children have an obligation to work to help the family?

d. What are the functions and obligations of the family in the larger social unit? To the school? To its individual members?

e. What is the relative importance of an individual family member vs. the family as a whole? What is the degree of solidarity or cohesiveness in the family?

The family is the initial and often the primary socialization unit for the child, and many of the individual's most basic social perceptions and values are formed in that context. An understanding of the family structure and system of expected responsibilities, values, and behaviors is essential to the teacher, not only so that these may be realistically portrayed and reflected in the classroom, but also to provide a source of guidance in dealing with the child or the child's parents or guardians. Such knowledge can be helpful in anticipating and interpreting the behaviors or attitudes of the child or other family members in particular situations. In addition, it may serve as a point of departure or contrast in presenting information about family patterns in the majority culture. Teachers at all levels should be aware of the often very subtle presuppositions about family structure and responsibilities which pervade literary and even nonfictional writing, and can lead to misunderstandings or self-depreciation on the part of the student. Since family structure is so variable, particularly under circumstances of immigration and acculturation, individual differences (including those associated with social class) should be carefully determined. At the same time, differences between expressions of group "norms" or "ideals" and individual reality should be appropriately recognized.

3. THE LIFE CYCLE

a. What are criteria for the definition of stages, periods, or transitions in life?

b. What are attitudes, expectations, and behaviors toward individuals at different stages in the life cycle? What stage of life is most valued? What stage of life is most "difficult"?

c. What behaviors are appropriate or unacceptable for children of various ages? How might these connect with behaviors taught or encouraged in the school?

d. How is language related to the life cycle?

e. How is the age of children computed? What commemoration is made of the child's birth (if any) and when?

The stages in the life cycle, while to some extent biologically determined, are like all aspects of human existence, basically culturally defined. When one ceases to be a child, when and by what criteria one becomes an adult, how one is treated at different stages by members of other age groups, what one's privileges and responsibilities are at different stages, are quite different in different societies. It is not "natural", for example, for children to be uninhibited and noisy—this is a product of socialization in a particular society. In many societies (e.g., Samoan), children already have significant economic responsibilities by the time they are seven. Stages recognized in one culture, e.g., teenage, may be absent in others.

Adulthood may be defined by something other than age, such as marriage or becoming a parent. Attitudes and values regarding stages differ widely; in some cultures, sixty is the age of wisdom, in others of retirement. Passage from one stage to another may be totally unmarked in one society, and a major traumatic event in another. Stages may also differ by socioeconomic class, as may also the attention given to occasions of passage. Of particular significance for educational (and sometimes mental health) concerns is the fact that for groups undergoing rapid acculturation, such as Koreans or Arabs, there may be wrenching changes taking place in the traditional roles, relationships, and responsibilities of different stages in the life cycle, making them individually variable and causing great psychological stresses and strains.

4. ROLES

a. What roles within the group are available to whom, and how are they acquired? Is education relevant to this acquisition?

b. What is the knowledge of and perception by the child, the parents, and the community toward these roles, their availability, and possible or appropriate means of access to them?

c. Is language use important in the definition or social marking of roles?

d. Are there class differences in the expectations about child role attainment? Are these realistic?

e. Do particular roles have positive or malevolent characteristics?

In addition to many other aspects of culture, the early socialization of children involves learning a role. Initial role acquisition includes learning what behaviors are appropriate (and expected) when relating to different members within the family, and then when relating to different classes of individuals within the wider social group. Most children find the new roles they assume when beginning school a fairly natural extension of their earlier socialization experiences, but for some, patterns of social interaction, which they have learned at home are not of value in the school context, and these children must acquire entirely new roles. Since the child's life aspirations are often based on roles recognized by the group, it is important for the teacher to know how these differ from or match roles which may be explicitly or implicitly taught in school. In addition, since children (and parents) from minority cultures often have limited experience with and understanding of majority culture roles and how to acquire them, the child's knowledge and perception of these matters should be examined also.

5. INTERPERSONAL RELATIONSHIPS

a. Is language competence a requirement or qualification for group membership?

b. How do people greet each other? What forms of address are used between people in various roles?

c. Do girls work and interact with boys? Is it proper?

d. How is deference shown?

e. How are insults expressed?

f. Who may disagree with whom? Under what circumstances?

g. Are mitigating forms used?

Mitigation techniques are different within different groups, and students may encounter many problems in our schools when they come from cultures that do not use the same ones that are accepted there. A middle-class child from the dominant culture has learned to avoid unpleasant tasks with such indirect excuses as "I'm tired. Can't I do that later?", "Can I finish this first?", or by dawdling or day dreaming until the time is up. While these techniques are often unsuccessful, the attempt brings no serious reproof. If a student has not learned these cultural strategies and says "No, I don't, or just "No"—which have essentially the same meaning—he may be considered belligerent or rude, and threatened with the principal's office. Teachers must be perceptive as to how they themselves (as culturally conditioned beings) interpret and respond to violations of sociolinguistic expectations and recognize that such "violations" may simply reflect cross-cultural differences in interactional rules and norms, not occasions for punishment.

6. COMMUNICATION

a. What languages, and varieties of each language, are used in the community? By whom? When? Where? For what purposes?

b. Which varieties are written, and how widespread is knowledge of written forms?

c. What are the characteristics of "speaking well", and how do these relate to age, sex, context, or other social factors? What are the criteria for "correctness"?

d. What roles, attitudes, or personality traits are associated with particular ways of speaking?

e. What range is considered "normal" speech behavior? What is considered a speech defect?

f. Is learning language a source of pride? Is developing bilingual competence considered an advantage or a handicap?

g. What is the functionality of the native language in the work-place or larger environment?

h. What gestures or postures have special significance or may be considered objectionable? What meaning is attached to direct eye contact? To eye avoidance?

i. Who may talk to whom? When? Where? About what?

There is no complete inventory of different social rules for language usage or of different attitudes toward language which may be consulted, but we must still consider both to be very important components of bilingual education; all aspects of culture involve communication. One very general difference concerns who should talk and when. The school supports the convention of talking one at a time (after raising a hand and being called on) and not interrupting; other cultures would consider that rude, a sure sign that no one was interested in what the primary speaker was saying. Some cultures feel it is inappropriate for children to talk at all in the presence of adults, and others that it is inappropriate to respond immediately to a question. The uses of silence differ, as do the contexts for the uses of different languages. Code-switching between English and the native language—actually a very complex linguistic skill—may be highly valued socially. No teacher in a bilingual program can afford not to have a thorough understanding of the status and uses of languages in the local community.

7. DECORUM AND DISCIPLINE

a. What is decorum? How important is it for the individual and for the group?

b. What is discipline? What counts as discipline in terms of the culture, and what doesn't? What is its importance and value?

c. What behaviors are considered socially unacceptable for students of different age and sex?

d. Who or what is considered responsible if a child misbehaves? The child? Parents? Older siblings? School? Society? The environment? Or is no blame ascribed?

e. Who has authority over whom? To what extent can one person's will be imposed on another? By what means?

f. How is the behavior of children traditionally controlled, to what extent, and in what domains?

g. Do means of social control vary with recognized states in the life cycle, membership in various social categories, or according to setting or offense?

h. What is the role of language in social control? What is the significance of using the first vs. the second language?

The choice of a language for controls and directions is important in a bilingual program, with English often perceived by students as milder than their home language; at the same time, students from other backgrounds may interpret the normal classroom projection level of English as a signal of anger, even when none is intended. Attempts by teachers to get parents to force children to do their homework or attend school may prove futile if the concept of coercion conflicts with basic cultural values. The desired ends may be achieved, not by imposing the will of the teacher or the school on the parent or child, but by cooperating with other effective mechanisms employed in the child's culture.

8. RELIGION

a. What is considered sacred and what secular?

b. What religious roles and authority are recognized in the community?

c. What is the role of children in religious practices? What are they supposed to know or not to know about the religion?

d. What should an outsider not know, or not acknowledge knowing?

e. What taboos are there? What should not be discussed in school; what questions should not be asked; what student behaviors should not be required?

f. Are there any external signs of participation in religious rituals (e.g., ashes, dress, marking)?

g. Are dietary restrictions to be observed, including fasting, on particular occasions?

h. Are there any prescribed religious procedures or forms of participation if there is a death in the family? What taboos are associated with death and the dead?

Violations of beliefs and practices in this area of culture probably result in the most serious conflicts which occur between home and school. Forcing a child to wash "dirt" off his face (when it had ritual significance), bringing human bones to class for a science lesson, and insisting that children eat lunch during a period of a prescribed religious fast are all examples of very real mistakes made by teachers who did not understand the religion of their students.

9. HEALTH AND HYGIENE

a. Who or what is believed to cause illness or death (e. g., the "germ theory" vs. supernatural or other causes)?

b. Who or what is responsible for curing?

c. How are specific illnesses treated? To what extent do individuals utilize or accept "modern" medical practices by doctors and other health professionals?

d. What beliefs, taboos, and practices are associated with menstruation and the onset of puberty?

e. What are beliefs regarding conception and childbirth?

f. What beliefs or practices are there with regard to bodily hygiene (e. g., bathing frequency and purpose)?

g. If a student were involved in an accident at school, would any of the common first aid practices be unacceptable?

Most cultures have traditional concepts regarding the body, health, illness, and curing which are based in part on the accumulation of practical experience and in part on often profound philosophical and religious beliefs. The cooperation and support of the local community in a bilingual program may depend upon the evidence of respect and acceptance of these beliefs and practices, many of which are in fact demonstrably efficacious. At the same time, lack of understanding by parents of the cause and spread of certain diseases creates a need for culturally sensitive communication to ensure appropriate treatment (including quarantine for infectious diseases, regular administration of prescribed medication, etc.). In addition, an adequate understanding of traditional concepts may be necessary for the adequate diagnosis of illness.

10. FOOD

a. What is eaten? In what order? How often?

b. What foods are favorites? What taboo? What "typical"?

c. What rules are observed during meals regarding age and sex roles within the family, the order of serving, seating, utensils used, and appropriate verbal formulas (e. g., bow, and if, one may request, refuse, or thank)?

d. What social obligations are there with regard to food giving, preparation, reciprocity, and honoring people?

e. What relation does food have to health? What medicinal uses are made of food, or categories of food?

f. What are the taboos or prescriptions associated with the handling, offering, or discarding of food?

Food—including the very definition of what does and what does not constitute food—is of enormous social, symbolic, and economic importance in all cultures. The exchange of food and conditions on its exchange form a central theme in some cultures, and major social values are built around it in others. In many cultures it even has religious significance, often as expressed in taboos on consumption or prescribed use in ceremonies. The rules for the eating of food may significantly reflect and provide a means of maintaining the social order. The growing realization that some of the nutritional concepts of the majority culture (such as drinking milk) may be deleterious to certain groups or individuals underscores the cultural basis of nutritional science. Textbooks should be examined for ways in which their portrayal of food may conflict with community values.

11. DRESS AND PERSONAL APPEARANCE

a. What clothing is "typical"? What is worn for special occasions? What seasonal differences are considered appropriate?

b. What significance does dress have for group identity?

c. How does dress differ for age, sex, and social class?

d. What restrictions are imposed for "modesty" (e. g., can girls wear shorts, or shower in the gym)?

e. What is the concept of beauty, or attractiveness? How important is physical appearance in the culture? What characteristics are most valued?

f. What constitutes a "compliment", and what form should it take (e. g., in traditional Latin American culture, telling a woman she is getting fat is a compliment)?

g. Does the color of dress have symbolic significance (e. g., black vs. white for mourning)?

Since dress and personal appearance are for the most part readily observable, most of the questions raised are fairly easy to answer. Despite this fact, however, probably more cross-cultural communication "misfires" take place in this area than any other. In part this is because the values underlying dress and appearance are not as easily discovered, leaving the superficial aspects highly susceptible to misinterpretation and stereotyping, and in part because no other aspect of a person's behavior (except perhaps speech) is so strongly tied to self image and group identity. The significance of this area makes it one which teachers and administrators need to thoroughly understand. At the same time, it is an area for which textbooks need to be examined for implicit cultural bias.

12. HISTORY AND TRADITIONS

a. What individuals and events in history are a source of pride for the group?

b. To what extent is knowledge of the group's history preserved?

c. In what forms and in what ways is it passed on?

d. To what extent is there a literate tradition of the history of the group (i. e., written history, and knowledge of written history within the group itself)?

e. To what extent are traditions and historical events reflected in aphorisms and proverbs?

f. Do any ceremonies or festive occasions reenact historical events?

g. How and to what extent does the group's knowledge of history coincide with or depart from "scientific" theories of creation, evolution, and historical development?

h. To what extent does the group in the United States identify with the history and traditions of their country of origin?

i. What changes have taken place in the country of origin since the group or individuals emigrated?

j. For what reasons and under what circumstances did the group or individuals come to the United States (or did the United States come to them)?

Prior to the spread of mass public education in this century, the majority of people in most countries were totally or largely illiterate, and possessed little knowledge of the history or cultural achievements of their country or ethnic group. Among native groups on this continent and elsewhere who lacked a means of graphically representing their languages, knowledge of historical events rarely extended back more than a few generations and, beyond that point, merged into myth. Even with compulsory public education and a highly literate population in the U. S. today, actual knowledge of history on the part of most people is minimal and of literature and art even less. Viewed against such a background, it should not be surprising that many members of minority groups in the U. S., drawn as they have been primarily from uneducated peasant stock, possess little knowledge of the history of their country of origin, or of its literary and artistic monuments. Immigrant farm workers from Mexico do not revel in the glory of 16th century Spanish literature any more than Anglo farm workers in the Midwest take rapturous delight in Shakespeare. These realities must be kept carefully in mind if the absurdities of the "romantic fallacy" are to be avoided. Many bilingual education curricula commit the error of introducing historical and literary-artistic content of questionable relevance from a group's country of origin, and totally ignore the history and achievements of the group within the U. S. The effect of the romantic fallacy is to produce a curriculum which is irrelevant to the actual background and experiences of the students in the program. The questions above are designed to provide a more realistic basis for the treatment of this area in the curriculum.

13. HOLIDAYS AND CELEBRATIONS

a. What holidays and celebrations are observed by the group and individuals?
b. What is their purpose (e. g., political, seasonal, religious, didactic)?
c. Which are especially important for children and why?
d. What cultural values do they intend to inculcate?
e. What aspects of socialization/enculturation do they further?
f. Do parents and students know and understand school holidays and behavior appropriate for them (including appropriate non-attendance)?

Holidays and celebrations are among the most obvious aspects of a culture, and for that reason are readily adopted by schools attempting to be "bicultural". However, often only the most superficial aspects of the celebrations are imported into the school context, and there is great danger that they may be distorted in the process, or that the incorporation of the activities in the curriculum may be taken to satisfy the need for minority cultural content, and so prevent the inclusion of much more basic and important aspects of culture. Worse yet, the observance of celebrations may reinforce the stereotypic misconception that this is all there is to the other culture. Hence great care should be taken to learn the true significance of such events, and their function within the context of the student's own culture and community (not just that of some foreign country). Some aspects of some celebrations, including songs, belong to the home or other locale and should not be brought into the school. Among Native American groups, certain songs or dances are of a sacred nature and should never be performed by the wrong persons or at the wrong time of year. Conversely, parents may not understand the meaning of American holidays, and especially why school may be closed, so these matters must be carefully taught, and communicated to the parents as well as the students.

14. EDUCATION

a. What is the purpose of education?
b. What kinds of learning are favored (e. g., rote, inductive)?
c. What methods for teaching and learning are used at home (e. g., modeling and imitation, didactic stories and proverbs, direct verbal instruction)?
d. Do methods of teaching and learning vary with recognized stages in the life cycle? With the setting? According to what is being taught or learned?
e. What is the role of language in learning and teaching?
f. Is it appropriate for students to ask questions or volunteer information? If so, what behaviors signal this? If not, what negative attitudes does it engender?
g. What constitutes a "positive response" by a teacher to a student? By a student to a teacher?
h. How many years is it considered "normal" for children to go to school?
i. Are there different expectations by parents, teachers, and students with respect to different groups? In different subjects? For boys vs. girls?

Although our educational system most closely represents the culture of our mainstream middle-class population, it has developed some attitudes, values, and expectations in its own right which set it apart as a subculture within our society in these respects. Successful advancement in the system quite naturally requires adoption of or adaptation to these concepts. Educators must be seen from this perspective as successfully acculturated (since they must have adapted themselves to the subculture in order to complete the years of training for certification); they are transmitters of these attitudes, values, and expectations to the next generation so that it, too, may "achieve" in school. It is a self-perpetuating cycle.

Educators must therefore learn about their own system of learning and realize that education does not have the same ends and means for members of different social groups. Stereotypes result if we assume that other systems of education are less advanced, or the students who don't succeed in our particular system are "deficient" in some respect. Since students learn how to learn from their families in early childhood, cultural differences are very well established by kindergarten or first grade.

15. WORK AND PLAY

a. What range of behaviors are considered "work" and what "play"?

b. What kinds of work are prestigious and why?

c. Why is work valued (e. g., financial gain, group welfare, individual satisfaction, promotion of group cohesiveness, fulfillment or creation of obligations to/from others, position in the community)?

d. Are there stereotypes about what a particular group will do?

e. What is the purpose of play (e. g., to practice social roles, skills training, muscle development and coordination)?

Play is often not valued positively in our culture, but is counterpoised to the serious business of life, which we call work. Nevertheless, as anthropologists have shown, what is thought of as play may have a strong educational function aimed at developing certain patterns of socialization. In addition, what may superficially appear to an outside observer to be play may have a serious religious purpose. The system of rewards associated with the attainment of particular roles or the fulfillment of various kinds of activities may differ considerably between cultural groups or even between social classes, and are subject to change over time or under conditions of acculturation. The teacher should be familiar with these factors, particularly in implementing a career education program, to minimize cross-cultural conflict and maximize effective learning.

16. TIME AND SPACE

a. What beliefs or values are associated with concepts of time? How important is "punctuality"? Speed of performance when taking a test?

b. Is control or prescriptive organization of children's time required (e. g., must homework be done before watching TV, is "bedtime" a scheduled event)?

c. Are particular behavioral prescriptions or taboos associated with the seasons (e. g. , not singing certain songs in the summertime or a snake will bite, not eating oysters when there is an R in the month)?

d. Is there a seasonal organization of work or other activities?

e. What is acceptable presence or grouping of individuals (e. g. , do children stay with adults and listen or go outside)?

f. How do individuals organize themselves spatially in groups (e. g. , in rows, circles, around tables, on the floor, in the middle of the room, around its circumference)?

g. What is the spatial organization of the home (e. g. , areas allotted to children or open to children, appropriate activities in various areas of the home)?

h. What geo-spatial concepts, understandings, and beliefs exist in the group or are known to individuals?

i. What is the knowledge and significance of cardinal directions (North, South, East, West)? At what age are these concepts acquired?

j. What significance is associated with different directions or places (e. g. , heaven is up, people are buried facing West)?

The organization of time and space is of enormous significance in most cultures, and one of the most frequent areas for cross-cultural conflict or misunderstanding, in large part because it is so often unconscious. Edward T. Hall has even referred to it as "the silent language" in the title of his book by that name. In particular, the teacher cannot assume that many of the concepts and attitudes regarding time and space (including personal space) held by the majority culture can be taken for granted, but must be explicitly taught. At the same time, a knowledge of the concepts and attitudes of the minority group regarding time and space is important, since it must form a point of departure in teaching, and is essential if the teacher is to recognize when students (or their parents) are following the rules of their own culture for appropriate behavior, so as to avoid penalizing them for apparent infraction of rules they do not know.

17. NATURAL PHENOMENA

a. What beliefs and practices are associated with the sun and moon (including eclipses and phases of the moon), comets, and stars?

b. Who or what is responsible for rain, lightning, thunder, earthquakes, droughts, floods, and hurricanes?

c. Are particular behavioral prescriptions or taboos associated with natural phenomena? What sanctions are there against individuals violating restrictions or prescriptions?

d. What means are there for obviating the negative effects of natural phenomena?

e. How and to what extent does the group's beliefs about these phenomena coincide with or depart from "scientific" theories?

f. To what extent are traditional group beliefs still held by individuals within the community?

Science is sometimes considered a culturally neutral area of the curriculum, but many of the topics taught under that label are loaded with culture-specific beliefs, values, and behavioral rules. While many students succeed in keeping the theories learned at home and school compartmentalized so they may "believe" both concurrently, with one or the other called to consciousness depending on the context and even the language being used, many others find this area of the curriculum a source of cultural conflict and confrontation. Whenever such conflict can be anticipated, or when students question a scientific theory on the basis of teachings from home and community, the teacher should not hesitate to say that while the school theories are believed by many, there are also many who disagree (which is quite true). Above all, the teacher should not convey the impression that there is only one explanation for natural phenomena, or that people who hold differing views are stupid or superstitious. Even scientists today are increasingly becoming aware of the extent to which culture affects their concepts and perceptions. Science, as a cultural phenomenon itself, can never be entirely culture-free.

18. PETS AND OTHER ANIMALS

a. Which animals are valued, and for what reasons?

b. Which animals are considered appropriate as pets; which are inappropriate, and why?

c. Are particular behavioral prescriptions or taboos associated with particular animals?

d. Are any animals of religious significance? Of historical importance?

e. Are there seasonal restrictions on talking about or depicting certain animals

(e. g. , except when hibernating, during hunting season)?

f. What attitudes are held toward other individuals or groups which have different beliefs and behaviors with respect to animals?

g. Which animals may be kept in the classroom? Which may not, and why?

The typical social studies unit on pets begins with the ethnocentric assumption that everyone considers the same species of animals to be appropriate for this category. The most serious cultural violations occur in cases where particular animals have religious significance, and where even talking or reading about them is restricted or prohibited. Less serious, though unpleasant, are the negative attitudes which may be directed toward the teacher who expresses fondness for cats or dogs, for instance, which are considered "unclean" in some other cultures. Again, information on cultural differences is essential.

19. ART AND MUSIC

a. What forms of art and music are most highly valued?

b. What media and instruments are traditionally used?

c. What conventions are of particular significance? How do artistic conventions differ from those used or taught in school (e. g. , the musical scale, two-dimensional representation of distance or depth)?

d. Is the creation of art and music limited to specialists, or within the competence of a wide range of individuals in the community?

e. What forms of art and music are considered appropriate for children to perform or appreciate?

f. Are there any behavioral prescriptions or taboos related to art and music (e. g. , can both men and women sing, does cutting faces in pumpkins or other fruits and vegetables violate religious concepts)?

g. How and to what extent may approval or disapproval be expressed?

Most serious conflicts occur when religious restrictions are violated. These range from depiction of the human form to the "desecration" of living things (as in cutting jack-o-lantern faces or stringing berries). Artistic conventions are very important for the interpretation of any tests which make use of pictures, adding to their potential for cultural bias. Each culture has prescribed conventions for both art and music, and no experience which is outside the bounds of those conventions will be recognized or appreciated as "art". Receptive appreciation of culturally different conventions may be cultivated, but truly satisfying aesthetic experience is probably limited to the range of conventions which has been internalized as part of socialization. Of course, in art as in all else, it is essential to avoid stereotyping the individual, particularly in minority groups undergoing rapid acculturation.

20. EXPECTATIONS AND ASPIRATIONS

a. What defines the concepts of "disadvantaged" and "successful"?

b. To what extent is it possible or proper for an individual to express future goals (e.g., is it appropriate to ask, "What do you want to be when you grow up?")?

c. What beliefs are held regarding "luck" and "fate"?

d. What significance does adherence to the traditional culture of the group have for the individual's potential achievement (from both the viewpoint of the minority and dominant cultures)?

e. What significance does the acquisition of the majority culture and the English language have (from both minority and dominant cultural perceptions)?

f. What potential roles are available within the native community which can provide individual fulfillment and satisfaction?

g. Do parents expect and desire assimilation of children to the dominant culture as a result of education and the acquisition of English?

h. Are the attitudes of community members and individuals the same as or different from those of community spokesmen?

One of the primary rationales for bilingual / ESL education is the enhancement of the students' self-image, but little attention is given to the cultural relativity of that concept. Adopting dominant values for personal "success" and "fulfillment" is usually a late stage in the process of acculturation; dominant-culture expectations and aspirations should never be assumed of children who are still primarily under the enculturation influences of the home, and they should never be imposed on individuals who choose to find their own fulfillment and satisfaction within the native community. More members today are seeking to find fulfillment within their traditional communities, and the expectation that success is to be measured in the context of the larger society—which is implicit or subtly present in much school text materials, tests, and teacher attitudes or behaviors—can have the strong and dysfunctional effect of contributing to a sense of anomie or failure on the part of the student.

To reiterate, education is not just formal schooling, but includes all of the formal and informal procedures for transmitting the knowledge and values of a group from one generation to another, whether in the form of telling stories and proverbs in the family or holding organized classes to teach factual or technical information. Similarly, preferred styles of learning may be present among certain groups or in particular contexts. Trial and error learning, the cornerstone of our educational methodology (including the use of tests), may be antithetical to students" cultural values and have dysfunctional results because it causes embarrassment by forcing students to demonstrate knowledge or skill mastery before they are ready. Traditional education in some cultures may be primarily religious in orientation, or may have the important function of supporting the maintenance of social structures or values which are at variance with those taught in the majority-culture secular public school. The potential conflicts which may arise in bicultural situations clearly need to be recognized if the students" educational experience is to be positive, and consonant with the expectations and desires of the parents and the community.

V. The Nature and Scope of Culture

The concept of culture represents differing ranges of human behaviors, products, and institutions to people with differing academic and experiential backgrounds. The most common range included in the definition is the narrowest, encompassing only "the arts", or perhaps admitting the uniquely identifiable behavior of "cultured" individuals, such as extending the little finger at an appropriate angle when holding a tea cup, or pronouncing tomato with the "proper" sound for a. Educators have generally recognized a broader scope of phenomena: evidence of "culture" in a classroom includes such things as travel posters hanging from the wall, art projects ranging from making maracas out of gourds to constructing kites for Chinese holidays, and cooking-and-tasting sessions with tortillas, fry bread, or rice boats. Meetings and in-service workshops for teachers often feature "cultural events", defined as singing and/or dancing typical of "folk" in another country.

This may be good; this is certainly fun; but this is also an entirely inadequate perspective on "culture" for the nature and goals of bilingual / ESL education.

To the anthropologist, the ethnographer who describes and explains the life-ways of diverse groups of people, culture includes all of the rules for appropriate behavior which are learned by people as a result of being members of the same group or community, and also the values and beliefs which underlie overt behaviors and are themselves shared products of group membership. It is this scope of "culture" which I believe must be understood, accepted, and accounted for in bilingual education.

Formal education (including the American educational system) is itself a cultural invention. In the United States, it is a system which serves primarily to prepare middle-class children to participate in their own culture. Students who come into the system from other cultures, including the lower social classes, have generally been considered "disadvantaged" or "deficient" to the degree that their own cultural experiences differ from the mainstream, middle class "norms". (Programs in compensatory education in the United States have been based primarily on this rationale, and serve to provide middle-class cultural experiences to children who have been "deprived" of them.) Our educational system cannot be blamed for attempting to teach the dominant American culture to all of its students, since such enculturation (or socialization) is the essential purpose of education in all cultures. We can blame our traditional educational system for inadequate provision or respect for students culturally diverse backgrounds, however, and such criticism has constituted one of the basic motivations for the implementation of bilingual /ESL programs.

Culture is not an optional component of bilingual education, whether or not we add the term bicultural to the title of our programs. Nor is it an optional component of the programs which train bilingual teachers. Whether consciously recognized or not, culture is a central force in all education.

Use of the hyphenated label "Bilingual-Bicultural Education" is meant to stress the view that more than language learning is involved in bilingual programs. Such a usage implies that formal recognition is given to aspects of the student"s traditional culture within the instructional program, both to ensure that the student has the opportunity to learn about it, and to enhance the student's feelings of acceptance within the school context. The relation of second language learning to the development of biculturalism, however, is a question that so far has received little attention.

To what extent is learning a second culture necessarily related to learning a second language? Historically, the pragmatic answer to this question has been somewhat imperialistic in nature, and often also in intent. It has been considered axiomatic that because language is an integral component of culture, only the culture of the speech community from which the language derives is appropriate content for its expression, and that teachers must transmit that content to those who are learning the language.

Similarly, when the focus is explicitly on inculcating a second culture, teaching the language that goes along with it has been considered a primary and necessary means to that end. This has been shown clearly in American history by the language and educational policies adopted toward Native Americans. In the 1880's, for instance, the Commissioner of Indian Affairs reported:

> The first step to be taken toward civilization, toward teaching the Indian the mischief and folly of continuing in their barbarous practices, is to teach him the English language we must remove the stumbling-blocks of hereditary customs and manners, and of those language is ore of the most important.

Even today, it is probably fair to say that most of the foreign language teaching efforts of such official agencies as the ICA (International Communication Agency), the British Council, the Goethe Institute, and the Alliance Francaise are much more concerned with spreading the influence of their respective cultures than with teaching their languages in and of themselves.

This same belief in the intrinsic relation between a language and the culture of the speech community from which it historically derives forms the basis for one of the principal arguments raised against bilingual education in the United States: the language of the United States is English; to speak anything else is considered somehow un-American, and to teach another language is viewed as culturally divisive, and contrary to the goals of national unity.

There is no intrinsic reason that the structures and vocabulary of one language cannot be used by many diverse speech communities to express their respective cultures, and in ways in keeping with their rules of appropriate behavior. Thus, although language is unquestionably an integral part of culture, the supposedly necessary relation between learning a language and learning the traditional culture associated with that language is not automatic. The relationship between a language and the culture in which it is used depends on the social context for learning and teaching the language, and the social functions which it assumes.

In the learning of a native language, that language is both part of the native culture being acquired in the process of children's enculturation, or socialization, and a primary medium for the transmission of other aspects of that culture from one generation to the next, such as values, beliefs, and rules for social behavior. If speakers remain in contact with their native culture, their native language proficiency, expands to include expression of the new concepts they develop, the new domains in which they function, and the new role-relationships in which they participate. This intrinsic relationship of language to culture is so "natural" as to operate at an unconscious level for most native speakers, furthered by informal means more than by formal education, and by family and peers more than by professional educators.

When English is learned as a second language in countries such as the United States where it is the language of the dominant culture, and where proficiency in English is essential for full educational, political, and economic participation in the larger society, acquiring the language involves much more than merely learning English phonology, syntax. and vocabulary, for it must be able to serve most of the same functions that English does for the native speaker: medium of instruction, expression of concepts and feelings, participation in expanding social domains and role-relationships. Thus, second language speakers must be able to function according to the rules of the English-dominant American culture. While the native of a culture acquires these rules quite naturally and unconsciously in the process of *enculturation*, the process for students acquiring a second culture is *acculturation*, the addition of a second set of rules for behavior which may coexist beside the first, replace them, or modify them. One possible result of this acculturation process is loss of the native culture or the merger of cultures until they are indistinguishable, called *assimilation*, and the resulting society a "melting pot". Perhaps one of the most important contributions of the movement for bilingual education in the United States has been the valuation of another possible result of acculturation: the selective maintenance and use of both cultural systems, or *biculturalism*.

The nature and extent of students' *cultural competence* is thus just as important as their linguistic competence for determining appropriate level and content for instruction in bilingual-bicultural education. It is now beginning to be recognized that students who enroll in bilingual programs in the United States have varying degrees of proficiency in the two languages of instruction. Cultural competence will also vary. There is no reason to assume, for instance, that Spanish-dominant students have acquired the culture of such Spanish-speaking countries as Cuba, Mexico, or Spain in the process of acquiring Spanish as their native language. They indeed have acquired a culture, but it might well be the beliefs, values, and rules for appropriate behavior common to the dominant American society; in this case, being "bicultural" would involve learning about their ancestral cultural heritage, which is analogous in many respects to learning about the culture associated with a foreign language.

Most probably, except for students who have immigrated directly from Spanish-dominant countries, Spanish-speaking students in the United States will have been enculturated into the minority subculture of a bilingual community. It is important that bilingual educators recognize the validity of these students' culture; comments have been made that students who have not acquired the culture of the dominant American society or the culture of the dominant society of a Spanish-speaking country have no culture at all. These comments are often from the same people who feel that students who do not speak a standard variety of English or Spanish, or who code-switch between them, are "alingual". These views are based on ignorance and misunderstanding of the nature of language and culture, and are potentially as damaging to students' self-concepts and identity as those which forbid the use of their native language at school.

While I have been making my point with specific reference to Spanish-speaking students because these constitute the largest target group for bilingual education, the same is also true for most other language groups in the United States: French speakers may or may not have learned the culture of France; Chinese speakers may have acquired the culture of a Chinese American community in San Francisco, New York, or Seattle or of the dominant American society rather than the culture of Taiwan or Hong Kong; Polish speakers in New England or Texas might well feel like (and be considered) cultural aliens if they returned to Poland.

The relevance of these observations for teaching culture in a bilingual classroom is in recognizing the range of cultural backgrounds which may be "native" even to speakers of the same language. Bicultural education assumes there are only two: the culture of the student's home and that of the dominant society; but the result is often the teaching of two foreign cultures without recognizing or providing for the student's native culture at all in the process.

While recognizing and accepting the culture which students bring to school is important, however, the fact remains that the same reasons exist for learning the dominant American culture as for learning English: it is necessary for full participation in the larger society. Teaching an ancestral culture, such as that of Spain or Mexico for Spanish-speaking students, or of the Philippines for Tagalog-speaking students, may be of considerable value for developing and understanding of traditions and for developing "roots" for ethnic identity, but the objectives for developing positive self-concepts through bicultural education will be negated if the actual culture of home and community is ignored or disparaged.

Ⅵ. Language and Thought

No one would disagree with the claim that language and thought interact in many significant ways. There is great disagreement, however, about the proposition that each specific language has its own influence on the thought and action of its speakers. On the one hand, anyone who has learned more than one language is struck by the many ways in which languages differ from one another. But on the other hand, we expect human beings everywhere to have similar ways of experiencing the world.

Comparisons of different languages can lead one to pay attention to "universals"—the ways in which all languages are similar, and to "particulars"—the ways in which each individual language, or type of language, is special, even unique. Linguists and other social scientists interested in universals have formulated theories to describe and explain human language and human language behavior in general terms as species-specific capacities of human beings. However, the idea that different languages may influence thinking in different ways has been present in many cultures and has given rise to many philosophical treatises. Because it is so difficult to pin down effects of a particular language on a particular thought pattern, this issue remains unresolved. It comes in and out of fashion and often evokes considerable energy in efforts to support or refute it.

Relativity and Determinism

There are two problems to confront in this arena: linguistic relativity and linguistic determinism. Relativity is easy to demonstrate. In order to speak any language, you have to pay attention to the meanings that are grammatically marked in that language. For example, in English it is necessary to mark the verb to indicate the time of occurrence of an event you are speaking about: It's raining; It rained; and so forth. In Turkish, however, it is impossible to simply say, "It rained last night". This language, like many American Indian languages, has more than one past tense, depending on one's source of knowledge of the event. In Turkish, there are two past tenses—one to report direct experience and the other to report events that you know about only by inference or hearsay. Thus, if you were out in the rain last night, you will say, "It rained last night" using the past-tense form that indicates that you were a witness to the rain; but if you wake up in the morning and see the wet street and garden, you are obliged to use the other past-tense form—the one that indicates that you were not a witness to the rain itself.

Differences of this sort have fascinated linguists and anthropologists for centuries. They have reported hundreds of facts about "exotic" languages, such as verbs that are marked or chosen according to the shape of an object that is being handled (Navajo) or for the relative ages of speaker and hearer (Korean). Such facts are grist for the mill of linguistic relativity. And, indeed, they can be found quite readily in "non-exotic" languages as well. To cite a fact about English that is well known to linguists: It is not appropriate to say Richard Nixon has worked in Washington, but it is perfectly OK to say Gerald Ford has worked in Washington. Why? English restricts the present perfect tense ("has worked") to assertions about people who are alive. Exotic!

Proponents of linguistic determinism argue that such differences between languages influence the ways people think—perhaps the ways in which whole cultures are organized. Among the strongest statements of this position are those by Benjamin Lee Whorf and his teacher, Edward Sapir, in the first half of this century—hence the label, "The Sapir-Whorf Hypothesis", for the theory of linguistic relativity and determinism. Whorf proposed: "We cut nature up, organize it into concepts, and ascribe significances as we do, largely because we are parties to an agreement to organize it in this way—an agreement that holds throughout our speech community and is codified in the patterns of our language". And, in the words of Sapir: "Human beings... are very much at the mercy of the particular language which has become the medium of expression for their society ... The fact of the matter is that the 'real world' is to a large extent unconsciously built up on the language habits of the group".

Investigating Language and Thought

How can such bold claims be substantiated beyond examination of individual languages themselves? If one takes the hypothesis seriously, it should be possible to show that Turks are more sensitive to evidence than are Americans, but that Americans are more aware of death than Turks. Clearly, the hypothesis cannot be supported on so grand a level. Rather, experimental psychologists and cognitive anthropologists have sought to find small differences, on controlled tasks, between speakers of various languages. Maybe Navajos are somewhat more sensitive to shapes of objects, for example.

The results have been mixed. In most cases, human thought and action are over-determined by an array of causes, so the structure of language may not play a central causal role. Linguistic determinism can best be demonstrated in situations in which language is the principal means of drawing people's attention to a particular aspect of experience. For example, if you regularly speak a language in which you must pick a form of second-person address (you) that marks your social relationship to your interlocutor—such as Spanish tu ("you" for friends and family and for those socially subordinate) vs. usted ("you" for those socially above in status or for those with whom you have no close connection) or French tu versus vous—you must categorize every person you talk to in terms of the relevant social dimensions. (As a thought experiment of linguistic determinism, think of the categorizations of social relationships that would have to be made if Spanish became the common language of the United States.)

Going beyond thought experiments, some of the most convincing research demonstrating some degree of linguistic determinism is being conducted under the direction of Stephen C. Levinson at the Max Planck Institute for Psycholinguistics in Nijmegen, The Netherlands. Levinson and his collaborators distinguish between languages that describe spatial relations in terms of the body (like English "right/left", "front/back") and those that orient to fixed points in the environment (like "north/south/east/west" in some aboriginal Australian languages). In a language of the second type one would refer, for example, to "your north shoulder" or "the bottle at the west end of the table"; in narrating a past event, one would have to remember how the actions related to the compass points. Thus, in order to speak this type of language, you always have to know where you are with respect to the compass points, whether you are speaking or not. And Levinson's group have shown, in extensive cross-linguistic and cross-cultural studies, that this is, in fact, the case.

Much more research needs to be done, but it is not likely that the Sapir-Whorf hypothesis will be supported in the strong form quoted above. For one, language is only one factor that influences cognition and behavior. For another, if the Sapir-Whorf hypothesis were really true, second language learning and translation would be far harder than they are. However, because language is so pervasive—and because we must always make cognitive decisions while speaking—weaker versions of the hypothesis will continue to attract scientific attention.

Section 3 Cultural Elements in Language Communication

Ethnolinguistics is concerned with how culture (cultural categories) is reflected in language. The exact nature of the relationship between language and culture is an interesting one. Culture is what a person must know in order to function in a particular society so that "one is able to operate in a manner acceptable to its members", Thus, culture is "socially acquired knowledge". The necessary behaviors are learned and do not come from any genetic endowment.

Clark and Clark (1977) define knowledge thus as being composed of three types:

a) cultural knowledge which is learned from other people

b) shared non-cultural knowledge which is shared by people within the same community or the world over, but is not learned from each otherI

c) non-shared non-cultural knowledge which is unique to the individual

Most language is cultural knowledge which is learned from other individuals and some is shared non-cultural knowledge.

1. LANGUAGE AND COGNITION

One of the long claims concerning the relationship between language and culture is that the structure of a language determines the way in which speakers of that language view the world. The Sapir-Whorf hypothesis acknowledges the close relationship between language and culture, maintaining that they are inextricably related so that you could not understand or appreciate the one without a knowledge of the other.

Sapir (1929b) says in his book that: "Human beings do not live in the objective world alone, nor alone in the world of social activity as ordinarily understood, but are very much at the mercy of the particular language which has become the medium of expression for their society... The fact of the matter is that the "real world" is to a large extent unconsciously built up on the language habits of the group... We see and hear and otherwise experience very largely as we do because the language habits of our community predispose certain choices of interpretation."

The strong form of the Sapir-Whorf hypotheses is generally labelled as *linguistic determinism*. This claims that people from different cultures think differently because of differences in their language. A native speaker of Hopi, Whorf claimed, perceives reality differently from a native speaker of English because she uses a different language. Few sociolinguists would accept such a strong claim but most accept the weaker claim of linguistic relativity that language influences perceptions, thought and at least potentially, behaviour.

The Chinese word for eleven *shi-yi* is literally "ten-one" and for twenty the Chinese word is *er-shi* which is literally "two-ten". Consequently, learning to count beyond ten is easier for Chinese-seeking children than for English-speaking children. More recently, it has been suggested that Chinese, Japanese and Korean children understand number concepts earlier than English and French children because of the ways their respective languages code numbers above 10. If true, this is interesting support for the idea that language facilitates particular kinds of thinking. This suggests that the categories provided by a language may favor certain ways of perceiving "reality" or "the world" and make certain behaviors easier.

It must be noted that the claim that it is impossible to describe certain things in a particular language because that language lacks the necessary resources is only partially valid. This is because *it is quite possible to talk about anything in any language provided a speaker is willing to use some degree of circumlocution. Some concepts may be more "codable" than others and easier to express in some languages than in others.* Every natural language not only provides its speakers with a language for talking about every other language, that is, a metalanguage, but also provides them with an adequate system for making any kinds of observations that they need to make about the world.

2. EXPLORING THE RELATIONSHIP BETWEEN DIFFERENT LANGUAGES AND CULTURES

A. Kinship systems

One interesting way in which people use language in daily living is to refer to various kinds of kin. Kinship systems are a universal feature of languages because kinship is so important in social organisation. Some systems are much "richer" than others, but all make use of such factors such as sex, age, generation, and marriage in their organisation. Kinship terminology is one basic way of showing systems of classification in language and society.

B. Color terminology

Color terminology has also been used to explore the relationship between different languages and cultures. All languages make use of basic color terms. A basic color term must be a single word, e. g. blue or yellow, not some combination of words e. g. light blue or pale yellow. Nor must it be the obvious sub-division of some higher-order term like scarlet or crimson which come from red. A basic color term must also have quite a general use and must not be applied only to a very narrow range of objects e. g. Blond can only be used in English exclusively for hair colour and wood. The term must not be highly restricted in the sense that it is used by only a specific sub-set of speakers such as interior decorators or fashion writers.

According to Berlin and Kay, an analysis of the colour terms found in a wide variety of languages reveals certain very interesting patterns. If a language has only two terms, they are for equivalents to *black and white or dark and light.* If a third is added, it is usually *red.* The fourth and fifth terms will be yellow and green, the sixth and seventh terms are blue and brown. And then, as in English, come terms like grey, pink, orange and purple but not in any particular order.

There is some reason to believe that communities that show little technological development employ the fewest colour terms. For example, some tribes in New Guinea only have words corresponding to dark and light alone. On the other hand, technologically advanced societies have terms corresponding to all eleven colours mentioned above.

C. Prototype Theory

Rosch (1976) proposes that concepts are best viewed as "prototypes". A bird is classified as a bird not because of a set of features that refer to such e. g. feathers, wings, etc but by reference to a typical instance like a robin. Experiments have shown that individuals classify quite consistently objects of various kinds according to what they regard as being typical instances; for example furniture. So a chair is a typical item of furniture but an ashtray is not. For clothing, shirts and trousers are typical items but not purses or wallets. Hudson (1980) believes that prototype theory allows us to understand how people learn to use language, particularly linguistic concepts from kinds of instances they come across. He says that:

"a prototype-based concept can be learned on the basis of a very small number of instances—perhaps a single one—and without any kind of formal definition, whereas a feature-based definition would be much harder to learn since a much larger number of cases, plus a number of non-cases would be needed before the learner could work out which features were necessary and which were not..."

Hudson suggests that prototype theory may be applied to the social situations in which speech occurs. When people hear a new linguistic item, they associate with it who seems to use it and what apparently is the typical occasion of its use. We are also able to judge our social competence in the use of language. We judge circumstances as being typically this or typically that and we place people in the same way. we then tailor our language to fit, making it appropriate to the situation and the participans as we view these.

D. Taboo and Euphemism

While language can be used to express cultural meaning, it can also be used to avoid saying certain things as well as to express them. Certain things are not said, not because they cannot be, but because people don't talk about these things (taboo) or if those things are talked about, they are talked about in a very roundabout way (euphemism).

Tabooed subjects can vary widely: from sex to death to bodily functions to religious matters. What is tabooed and what is not is determined by standards and norms of a particular society. Sometimes language taboos can also arise from bilingual situations. For example, Thai students who learn English might avoid certain Thai words which have phonetic resemblance to certain taboo words in English.

Euphemisms are more obvious than taboo words and expressions in society. Euphemistic words and expressions allow us to talk about unpleasant things and "neutralise" the unpleasantness e,g, the subjects of death and dying, employment, etc. They also allow us to give labels to unpleasant tasks and jobs in an attempt to make them sound almost attractive e. g. housewife-domestic engineer, stupid-mentally challenged.

Each social group is different from each other in how it constrains linguistic behaviovr in one way. Perhaps one linguistic universal is that no social group uses language quite uninhibitedly. When we speak, we must constantly make choices of many different kinds: what we want to say, how we want to say it, and the specific sentence types, words and sounds that best unite the what with the how. In fact, the content and the form are quite inseparable. One way of looking at this inseparable relationship is to examine a few specific aspects in communication: e. g. solidarity, politeness and address forms. However, before we delve into the discussion of these aspects, we need to bear in mind that there are many functions of speech (to request, to command, to apologise) and one of them is to express solidarity and empathy.

E. Phatic Communication

Conversation serves both an affective (or social) function and a referential (or informative function). Initial greetings and comments on the weather serve a social function; they establish contact between the two participants. The exchange then moves on to become more information-oriented or referential in function. When utterances are used to express solidarity and empathy with others, they are called phatic utterances (e.g. Hi, how are you, lovely day, isn't it?). Such expressions convey information not only about social relationships but are part of politeness strategies.

Example:

Boss: Good morning Sue. Lovely day.

Secretary: Yes, it's beautiful. Makes you wonder what we're doing here doesn't it?

Boss: Mm, that's right. Look I wonder if you could possibly sort this lot out by ten. I need them for a meeting.

Secretary: Yes sure. No problem.

Boss: Thanks, that's great.

Politeness

Being polite is a complicated business in any language. It is difficult to learn because it involves understanding not just the language, but also the social and cultural values of the community.

Example:

Israeli passenger and driver on an inter-city bus

Passenger: Turn the light on, please.

Driver : What?

Passenger: Turn the light on, please.

Driver : It disturbs me.

Passenger: I wanted to read.

We often don't appreciate just how complicated it is, because we tend to think of politeness simply as a matter of saying please and thank you in the right places. In fact, politeness involves a great deal more than the superficial politeness routines that parents explicitly teach their children.

Take for example the word please. Children are told to say please whenever they are making requests, as a way of expressing themselves politely. However, please can also have the effect of making a request or command sound less polite.

Example:

a. Could you take my bags up?

b. Could you take my bags up, please.

c. Answer the phone Jo.

d. Please answer the phone Jo.

As always, a great deal depends on intonation and tone of voice, but please does not necessarily increase the politeness of these requests and commands.

The example above raises the question of what we mean by politeness. Generally speaking, politeness involves taking account of the feelings of others. A polite person makes others feel comfortable. Being linguistically polite involves speaking to people appropriately in the light of their relationship to you. Inappropriate linguistic choices may be considered rude. Using an imperative such as stop talking or shut the door to a superior at work is likely to earn the junior worker a reprimand.

Making decisions about what is or is not considered polite in any community therefore involves assessing social relationships along the dimensions of social distance or solidarity, and relative power or status. We also need to understand the social values of a society in order to speak politely.

Positive politeness

Positive politeness is solidarity oriented. It emphasizes shared attitudes and values. When the boss suggests that a subordinate should use first name (FN) to her, this is a positive politeness move, expressing solidarity and minimizing status differences. A shift to a more informal style, using slang and swear words will function similarly as an expression of positive politeness.

Negative politeness

Negative politeness pays people respect and avoids intruding on them. Indirect requests or commands express negative politeness.

Example

Could you stay a bit later tonight, do you think, and finish the job?

That job's taking longer than we predicted. I don't know what we'll do if it isn't ready for tomorrow.

Negative politeness also involves expressing oneself appropriately in terms of social distance and respecting status differences. Using title + last names (TLN) to your superiors and to older people that you don't know well, are further examples of the expression of negative politeness.

Social Factors involved

"Marked setting" refers to formal settings such as Parliament and law courts where people act in role and where the speech is governed by relatively explicit discourse rules. Forms of address are derived from identity in the context, e. g. Your Honour, Prime Minister.

"Higher rank" refers to social superiors or people of higher status in a hierarchy.

"Ascending generation" is the generation above the speaker e. g. parents and parents' sisters, brothers and cousins.

"Dispensation" refers to the fact that a superior may absolve the speaker from the obligation of using TLN and permit them to use FN, e. g. Dr Worth is far too formal. Please call me Helen.

"Profession title" refers to occupational or courtesy titles e. g. Doctor, Professor, Sister for a nun, Father for a priest, etc.

Examples of dimensions which differ from community to community are:

The line between adult and child

Kin

Well-acquainted

Higher rank

Conflict in terms of address

We can cause offence by treating someone too familiarly or by treating them too distantly. Being polite means getting the linguistic expression of social distance right as far as your addressee is concerned. This is very variable from one community to another. For example, in the north of England, many newspaper vendors, bus conductors and people selling railway tickets call everyone love regardless of how well they know them, and often regardless of gender. By contrast, mutual TLN (Mr Hoc, Ms Ha) is usual between upper-working class neighbours who live close to each other but who are not friends and do not see each other socially. In some English speaking cultures, mutual FN is used with people you work with, regardless of how little or much you like them. In other English speaking cultures, mutual FN is considered too familiar.

In earlier centuries, the norms of address were simpler. Status was the major consideration. In general, people used TLN upwards to superiors and FN downwards to subordinates no matter how well they knew them. Solidarity became relevant only between equals. Today, however, the interaction between social status and social distance in many Western societies is more complicated. This results in a conflict of norms in two situations:

a. high status with high solidarity

b. low status with low solidarity

For example, if your addressee is of lower status and you know them well, then either way you use FN to them. But what form do they use to you?

There is no problem when you do not know someone well and they are your superior. Both factors predict that you will use TLN. But when someone is your subordinate and you don't know them well, what do you use? This is a tricky area but in general the solidarity dimension tends to win out: the degree of solidarity is what counts.

Example:

Interviewer: How do you address the custodian of your building?

Professor: We have a young college boy now, so I call him by his FN. Now our housekeeper, I call her Mrs and she calls me Miss. Once in a great while I call her by her FN. But I want the students to know that I respect her, so in public, I call her Mrs. And she's not in the category of a cleaning lady. She wears a uniform and makes a vital contribution to the department.

Cross-cultural differences in the rules of politeness

We have talked about how dimensions like age, gender, kinship relationships, social status, occupation, education and formality of the context are all relevant. Though these relevant dimensions may be universal, people from different speech communities often unwittingly offend each other. The way the dimensions are expressed and interactive rules may be the source of misunderstandings.

Example:

Tino, a young Samoan boy who had recently arrived in New Zealand, was summoned to the office of the school principal for being repeatedly late for school.

He knocked on the door of the principal's office. When he was told to come in, he walked in with hunched shoulders, scuttled over to a chair and sat down without being asked to do so by the principal. In response to the principal's questions he either said nothing or he muttered I don't know. He looked down at the floor throughout the interview and never met the principal's eyes. What impression do you think he gave?

Non-verbal messages are particularly powerful but also particularly vulnerable to misinterpretation. A hunched gesture may be seen as an uncooperative stance, possibly expressing resentment. It is polite to wait till asked to sit down in the office of a superior. Avoiding the questioner's eyes is likely to be interpreted as evasive behavior. However, these non-verbal communicative patterns are culturally appropriate ways of expressing respect to a superior in Samoan culture. A bowed posture is respectful, since one must attempt to keep oneself at a lower level than the superior. This accounts for Tino's sitting down quickly. Keeping one's eyes lowered is similarly a signal of respect. Finally, it is not appropriate in Samoan culture for Tino to "answer back". He should hear the principal's reprimand in silence.

Learning another language usually involves a great deal more than learning the literal meaning of the words, how to put them together and how to pronounce them. We need to know what they mean in the cultural context in which they are normally used and that involves some understanding of the cultural and social norms of the users.

A. Polite acceptance and refusal

There are sociolinguistic rules for polite acceptance and refusal which differ cross-culturally. For example, refusing an invitation appropriately in Western culture usually involves a mandatory excuse (I'm busy tonight I'm afraid) because in many Western communities, people expect to be provided with a more specific reason for a refusal. Where solidarity is the dominant social dimension, privacy is reduced and vagueness about one's activities is seen as evasive. However is this true of Asian cultures?

How do you accept food when it is first offered?

Which seat do you take when you go for a meeting? Do you wait for your host to offer you a seat?

Does yes really mean no?

The sociolinguistic norms used in such a situation reflect very much the cultural norms of the society.

B. Silence

When silence contrasts with speech, it can be very communicative. In different cultures and contexts, silence may convey different meanings: respect, consent, disagreement, attention, disapproval, anger or boredom.

For each of the contexts below, there are some cultures where silence is the appropriate response and others where talk is the appropriate response. Is silence or speech more appropriate in these contexts in your culture? If speech is appropriate, then what message does silence convey?

a) On first meeting someone.

b) When someone has put forward a proposal at a meeting.

c) At the dinner table

d) When you are accused of wrongdoing.

e) While listening to someone talk.

Section 4 Culture and Foreign Language Learning/Teaching

Ⅰ. Socio-cultural Influences on Learning and Teaching

To understand and facilitate learning in any area of the curriculum, teachers should know not only what it is that is being acquired, but how it relates to what has already been learned. The learning of culture, like the learning of language, begins with a child's first experiences with the family into which he is born, the community to which he belongs, and the environment in which he lives. By the time children begin their formal education at the age of five or six, they have already internalized many of the basic values and beliefs of their native culture, learned the rules of behavior which are considered appropriate for their role in the community, and established the procedures for continued socialization; they have learned how to learn.

Different child-rearing practices are preferred in different cultures, and these will have a significant effect on later learning. They range from very lenient when compared to dominant group standards, with little physical restraint or coercion employed, to very strict control of early behaviors. For example, although few pronouncements can be made about "Indian children" as a group, since the many tribes maintaining their identity in the United States are very heterogeneous with regard to language, culture, and even physical (racial) traits, there are a few social values and practices that are quite wide-spread among the various Native American communities. In general, little or no physical punishment is used, for instance, with children commonly disciplined by teasing, ridicule, or fear, or by indirect example through folklore. Their learning of physical tasks is often more through observation than verbal instruction, but many social and religious lessons are also taught through story-telling. A number of studies suggest that the visual perception and visual memory of Native American children raised in these groups are much higher than that of their Anglo age-mates.

Another example of the effect of traditional child-rearing practices is the Puerto Rican differentiation of sex roles from a very early age; these make a significant difference in educational attitudes and performance. For one thing, Puerto Rican girls show a higher anxiety pattern than boys when they are in a situation where they are threatened with failure, as when taking a test. The boys' lower anxiety is probably a function of the cultural attitude toward their admission of anxiety.

Other behaviors of three and four year old Anglo and Puerto Rican children have been observed and compared while they were responding to a "demanding cognitive task". The differences were not believed to be due to differences in socio-economic level (although this was evidently not controlled), but in home experiences: focus on social interaction rather than tasks; age at which independence is expected; and regarding toys as entertainment rather than education. Such differences should be related to questions about cultural differences in values, stages in the life cycle and acquisition of roles, and perceptions of the nature of work and play.

It is obvious that children who learn to learn in one culture and then must learn in the modes of another must experience some confusion and dislocation in the process. They are unfamiliar with the school structure, the expectations of the teacher, and the classroom procedure. They may encounter very different values which are being considered essential for learning (i. e., cleanliness, attendance, and punctuality). They may find behaviors which they have been taught to follow suddenly and inexplicably penalized or rejected (e. g., not asking questions, not attempting to do what you are not sure of being able to do successfully, being very concerned for correctness even on a timed test). All of this is in addition to the communication problems they may be facing when their language is other than English and the social stress and culture shock they may be experiencing if, as with many Koreans or Southeast Asian or Pacific Island students, they have only recently immigrated to this country.

Many research projects have been designed to show what differences in cognitive styles are systematically related to particular social group membership and cultural practices. The visual modality has been shown to be a relatively stronger learning style for Chinese and Native American students than for Puerto Ricans and Anglos, and there is considerable evidence that Mexican American students may be more field dependent (i. e., make more use of the overall context in, learning and processing information) than are Anglo students, who may be more field independent.

There are cultural differences in teaching styles as well, although the acquisition of specific teaching skills during professional training is part of the socialization of educators to the subculture of the school. It is not at all certain that teachers from a similar cultural background to the students' will teach them more effectively, although research in this area is still far too sketchy to draw definite conclusions. It does seem clear, however, that all teachers would profit from greater understanding of differences in learning styles, and greater tolerance of differences. Particularly inappropriate for bicultural education are categorical claims about the best way to learn or teach *anything* (which are all too common in teacher training); the claim that "children learn best by doing", for instance, is not true for all children. Cultural sensitivity and respect requires *relativism* and *flexibility* in teaching styles. Such eclecticism is nothing new as an option in pedagogy, but it is necessary, not optional, when teaching students from diverse socio-cultural backgrounds.

Also clearly affecting learning are the attitudes and motivation of students and their parents, many of which are culture-specific. Cultural attitudes and values most assuredly affect teaching as well, since educators acquire these as members of their own cultural group, learn and generally adopt those of the dominant group where it is different, and have different attitudes and expectations toward students from different minority cultures.

Our educational goals are not limited to instructional objectives, but include the enculturation or socialization of children to values and expectations as well. This involves a weighty responsibility and requires careful thought, because, for good or ill, we often succeed. For example, accepting the goal "success in school" often requires alienation from home, family, friends, and cultural heritage, and this is a terrible price to ask students to pay. We must learn to understand both the medium and the content of what we are teaching, and learn to be sensitive to the differences between what we are teaching and what the student brings to the classroom, so that our teaching becomes an aid and not a hindrance to the full realization of the student's potential as a human being.

Ⅱ. Cultural Identity

People are categorized by themselves and by others along a variety of dimensions: according to race primarily by skin color and other physical characteristics; according to social class by the amount of money they earn and where they live and work; and according to ethnicit by their national origin or ancestry, and their own feelings of group membership.

The dimension of race is in part biologically determined and in part socially defined, and social class is at least partly determined by environmental factors and partly by the constraints and opportunities which our social system permits. It is along the dimension of ethnicity that we in the United States are most clearly categorized according to cultural knowledge, behaviors, and identity.

Both adults and children have diverse attitudes about their cultural categorization, as perceived by them or by others. Most value their own group membership. Some reject their own group and wish to change. This is always a possibility in our society, using such means as education, marriage, or emigration (including just moving across town). Many may wish or need to function as members of more than one group and be "bicultural".

These diverse attitudes can all be viewed as positive forces, and all can be compatible with learning a second language and with other school achievement, but they are often viewed in a negative light. Those who value their own group membership and don't wish to acculturate to the dominant group may be treated as not "well adjusted" to our society. Those who reject their own group and wish to change may be viewed as "traitors" to family and old friends.

Those who wish to belong to more than one group may be mistrusted by both, and seen as 'spies". Whatever choice is made regarding group membership, language is often a key signal of identification, and this fact is critical in bilingual education. I am quite sure that students will have a better chance to reach their intellectual potential if early cognitive development continues in the native language, where the expanding reasoning processes can be most fully expressed and understood, but students must want to continue identification with their native culture if such native language development is to succeed. Students who want to change cultural identities generally also want to change their linguistic identification badge; such a shift before a critical level of first language competence has been achieved may result in "semi-lingualism" —full competence in no language.

Students must learn English as a second language if they are to participate fully in the dominant society, but negative attitudes toward features of the dominant culture might well inhibit learning. Above all, this culture should not be perceived as threatening by students if their participation is really desired.

While dominant group membership should be an available option, it cannot be imposed. The task is to teach about the second culture, and how to operate within it effectively—without requiring changes in students' cultural identity and loyalty—and to develop positive feelings about both cultures.

Recent research supports these claims:

Psycholinguistic research... although only, now getting underway, indicates that the hyphenated American can perhaps most easily become fully and comfortably American if the Spanish, Polish, the Navajo or the French prefix is given unlimited opportunity to flourish.

Full biculturalism is probably a rare phenomenon, if by "full biculturalism" we mean cultural knowledge, values, skills, and rules for appropriate conduct in all of the domains of two distinct cultures. A more reasonable goal for bicultural education may be the creation of a cultural state in students analogous to linguistic *diglossia*. The minority culture first learned by many limited English speakers in the United States is comparable to the "Low" (L) variety of a language as it is described by Ferguson, and the dominant American culture to the "High" (H) variety of a national language. Just as with Ferguson's L and H language varieties, the minority cultures are generally learned by children at home, the dominant one at school; the dominant culture has more prestige in the society than the minority ones; and most importantly for educational applications, there is a specialization of function for H and L language, for dominant and minority cultures. I have proposed that this relationship and distribution be called dinomia as it relates to varieties of culture.

This concept has importance for teacher training and curriculum development because it recognizes the nature and viability of students' native culture, while at the same time providing for identification of the aspects of the dominant culture which need to be acquired for appropriate situations, and prediction of potential areas of cultural interference where there are conflicts or overlap between the two. All instruction which relates to developing and reinforcing positive feelings of individual and group identity should be based on such recognition and understanding.

A major hazard in teaching a second culture is that students may reject parts of their native culture without knowing or accepting comparable parts of the second, or that they will find themselves repeatedly facing cultural interference as the rules or values of one conflict with the other in a single situation or domain. When this happens, either one culture "wins", or students must deal with emotional and cognitive stress.

As a target for bicultural education, dinomia emphasizes the acquisition of the dominant culture for minority group students in only those domains in which it is in minimal conflict with the minority culture, or in which is essential for "success" in the dominant society: education and communication to be sure, and perhaps business/economics and politics as well. Values, beliefs, and behaviors of the dominant culture in such domains as religion and family life only need to be learned for passive recognition and understanding, but not necessarily adopted for active use. (The converse would be true for majority group students in a bilingual-bicultural program.) Dinomia requires the productive acquisition of only those elements of the second culture which could coexist in complementary distribution with those elements of the first culture which must be maintained by their students who choose to retain native cultural identity.

Bicultural education should be an enriching experience for all students, not a limiting or compensatory one; it should broaden the range of choice for cultural identity which students may one day make, but it should not make such choices for them, nor force unnecessary or premature decisions.

Ⅲ. Culture Traits and Generations

Many of us are uncomfortable when referring to or being identified as members of any special social group because of the stereotyping so frequently associated with such identification, and the pejorative connotations group labels may engender—including the label "Anglo". On the surface, at least, this discomfort with categorization is somewhat at odds with our positive views about "cultural identity" in a more abstract sense. Identification with which culture(s)? With what beliefs, values, and behaviors (culture traits)? The fact that these traits operate primarily at an unconscious level—coupled with our hesitancy to make generalizations about cultural differences—probably explains the typical limitation of the cultural content of bilingual education to such superficial and relatively trivial phenomena as rice boats, and folk dancing.

Our hesitancy to make cultural generalizations is justified. For example, the following list of characteristics of "disadvantaged" or other "culturally different" children:

a. Their parents are less likely to belong to or attend church.

b. They do not share the principle of cleanliness. "Water costs money or effort if it must be carried from an outdoor pump."

c. They do not. understand the principles of saving.

d. They cannot put reason before emotion.

e. They are freer and more social in their expressions of sex.

f. They have not learned that doing one's duty and living up to the expectations of others pays off.

g. They believe the future is non-existent.

h. They believe education is an obstacle course to be surmounted until they can go to work.

This exemplifies generalizations of a type which have no place at all in teacher training and classroom practices, except as examples of stereotyping. They are not culture traits at all, but negative statements of the values held by the stereotyper: attending church, cleanliness, thrift, sexual repression, future orientation, and the Golden Rule. These *positive* values might well be included in a list of traits for our dominant culture, but their expression in negative form says nothing about others. It does, however, say a great deal about the attitudes of the stereotyper toward the minority culture.

Even some "traits" which are supposed to be soundly based on educational research must be questioned for cultural bias. We are told, for instance, that American Indians have a low self concept. The Coleman report indicates that the pupil attitude factor has a stronger relation to achievement than all the "school" factors together, and that Indian pupils in the twelfth grade have the lowest self concept of all minority groups tested. These data and similar interpretations of the Havighurst study have been widely accepted, but the low self concept is inferred largely from students' feelings that they have little or no control over their environment. However, many Indian cultures do not believe that actively controlling natural forces is desirable, or even reasonable. This research does not seem to take into account *Indian* perception of what constitutes a positive self concept, but rather evaluates the Indian self concept in terms of the values of the dominant culture.

Other conclusions about students' "negative self image" may be equally ethnocentric when based on such "evidence" as not knowing their birthdays. Children from some groups don't know their precise birth date because they have never celebrated it: it is not culturally important. Other dates may be emphasized instead. Vietnamese children, for instance, traditionally add a year to their age at Tet, and many children from a Latin American heritage traditionally celebrate their saint's day instead.

A trait often attributed to Mexican American culture is non-competitiveness. "They lead a peaceful rural existence and do not care to join the urban rat race. Nor is much attention paid to such competitive aspects of school as test scores and grades."

A study of the cooperative vs. competitive behavior of Anglo, Black, Mexican American, and Mexican elementary school students shows the Anglos and Blacks most competitive, with Mexican Americans somewhat less but still much more so than the Mexicans. This may well be an urban/rural difference instead of an ethnic one, however, since the Mexican group was rural and only about twenty percent of the Mexican Americans in the Southwest still live in rural areas. It may also be a social class difference, since Wasserman reports more cooperative behavior among "blue-collar children"—whether Mexican American, Black, or Anglo. Another study by Kagan and Madsen included four and five year old children and showed no differences at all at that age. Only three percent of the moves of each group in the test rated "competitive", and no group behavioral differences appeared along this dimension until age seven to nine. Yet another study finds that Mexican American children score higher on competitive values than do Anglos.

I am also suspicious of the "active-passive" distinction reported in educational research. A number of years ago I heard a well known Mexican psychologist report on his cross-cultural studies during a meeting at the National University in Mexico City. At the very time he was presenting his statistically impressive evidence that Mexicans are passive, the University was just beginning to recover from a full-scale student riot. His conclusions were drawn from the responses to such multiple-choice questions as, "What would you do in case of an earthquake?" Texas Anglo students included in the study were judged "active" for responding that they would run outside, while Mexicans were judged "passive" for responding that they would stay inside. These responses prove only that Mexicans know more about earthquakes than do Texans. Californians, too, stay inside in doorways during an earthquake if they are in an area of tall buildings, and it usually takes only one such experience for children to learn such "passivity".

Yet another probable example of cultural bias in the interpretation of data results from the use of "interaction analysis" (such as in the classroom observations reported by the Commission on Civil Rights 1973, which contrasted teacher "positive responses" to Anglo vs. Mexican American students, and by Anglo vs. Mexican American teachers). Such studies are often questionable because they fail to recognize that assumptions as to what behavior constitutes a "positive response" by a teacher to a student are themselves culture-bound and will not be the same for members of diverse cultural groups. Direct eye contact with the student may be positive, but it may be interpreted as aggressive or humiliating; smiling may be positive, but it may be derisive; touching may be positive, but it may be embarrassing or repugnant. Singling a student out for attention of any kind would not be considered a positive teacher response by a number of minority groups in the United States.

The kinds of cultural information which seem crucial for us to have, therefore, include answers to such questions as what constitutes a positive self image, and what behaviors will be interpreted as a positive teacher response. Because there are no "canned" lists of culture traits which can be accepted out of band, teacher competencies for bicultural education must include first knowing the significant questions to ask about cultures and then knowing how to get the answers, as well as knowing how to use the cultural information for instructional purposes.

IV. Getting the Answers: Suggestions for Teacher Training

The most important steps in getting answers to the kinds of questions about culture which may yield significant information for the bilingual classroom are 1) recognizing that the beliefs, values, and behaviors which are questioned are part of culture, 2) being sensitive to the probability that there will be diverse responses whenever such questions are asked of people from different linguistic and cultural backgrounds, and 3) accepting the fact that there are no "right" or "wrong" answers—just differences. Securing information about one's own or another culture requires some degree of objectivity and openness; anyone who does not accept the reality and validity of cultural differences as a general concept is not ready for experiences in cultural data collection and interpretation. A strongly ethnocentric or culturally insensitive person might well offend those from whom data are to be collected and thus hinder, rather than further, the goals of bilingual education.

The basic data collection skills which should be developed are ***introspection***, ***interviewing***, ***observation***, and ***participant observation.*** Selection among procedures will be dependent on the teacher's relation to the group in question, the cultural topic, and the situation or context within which the information is being collected.

Introspection is a means for data collection only about one's own culture, but it is an important skill to develop for that purpose. This is important not only for data collection per se, but for establishing the fact that everyone has a culture, and that questions about various aspects of culture require answers from the perspectives of the teacher's own culture (and that of the school) as well as the culture(s) of the students. Teachers who are themselves bicultural need to differentiate between beliefs, values, and behaviors which were part of their enculturation (first culture learning) and acculturation (second culture learning or adaptation). This exercise in itself will provide valuable information and insights on the group and on individuals.

The most productive means for developing this skill in a training program is to ask individuals to formulate very specific answers from their own experience to various questions about culture. A second step is to recognize the significance of differences between answers which reflect cultural "ideals" or norms, and the "real", or what actually occurs. This distinction between the "ideal" and the "real"—long familiar to anthropologists—is not a matter of truth versus falsehood, and should not be put in a negative light. Rather it is a recognition of the differences between abstract normative rules and specific behaviors. A useful analogy may be drawn with the question of what drivers do when they encounter a stop sign: the "ideal" answer is that they always stop; the "real" specific behaviors show that slowing (but not completely stopping) is a common response. Distinguishing between "ideal" and "real" behaviors is an important stage in viewing culture objectively. Responses to questions about culture will usually be in "ideal" terms, and learning the "ideal" answers is an important part of the formal education of group members. "Real" behaviors are more often acquired by informal modeling, and are more likely to occur at an unconscious level where they may be difficult for individuals to consciously recognize.

Group discussion is the next stage in teacher training, with members of the same cultural groups comparing answers, and members of different groups contrasting them and trying to identify potential areas of interference for students who might come from similar cultural backgrounds to their own. Again, it is critical to remember that there are no "right" or "wrong" answers to questions about culture, since individual perceptions, conceptions, and behaviors may always be expected to differ to some extent.

Interviewing is the next skill to be developed, beginning with the questions about culture which are to be discussed by the group of teachers in training. It includes developing a sensitivity to signs that a question is making someone uncomfortable in some way. Such questions should never be pursued directly when the interviewing context advances to asking questions of students, parents, or other community members; interviewing a friend and colleague under such circumstances may allow an opportunity to discover sensitive cultural information, but questions should not be pushed when there is any sign of discomfort, even with someone who is quite close. One of the most valuable contributions which teachers can make to each other in the intra-group training stage of interviewing is an overt statement of such discomfort, as "That's too personal", or "I'd rather not answer that kind of question".

Interviewing of students or parents should first be conducted as limited and closely supervised activities. Answers to specific and non-threatening, non-personal questions should be elicited and compared in the group. Tape recorders should generally not be used during interviews about culture unless the interviewer has already established trustworthiness and credibility, and a recorder should *never* be used without the knowledge and consent of the person or group being questioned.

Questions that might be asked of students at this stage are:

a. Who is in your family?

b. Who lives in your house?

c. What language do you usually use with ____? (Repeat for each person in the house.)

d. What is your favorite food?

e. What do you usually eat for breakfast? For dinner?

f. What holiday do you think is most important? Why?

It is important to be sensitive even when asking such questions as these; no questions about culture are guaranteed to be "neutral". Family membership and house occupants may be considered sensitive topics if dominant marriage customs are not being followed, and very threatening if undocumented aliens are present in the home. Questions on food may be very sensitive if students have already been taught at school what they *should* be eating at home. Many minority group members report having had strong feelings of guilt or shame as students when their family meals differed greatly from what was on the charts used for Health lessons in school. In any case, "ideal" answers should always be accepted without challenge, even when they seem to be unrealistic. This is a clue that an area of cultural or individual sensitivity may have been broached.

Parents might be asked:

a. What do you think is most important for your child to learn at school? Why?

b. What else is it important for him to know?

c. What holidays or celebrations are most important? Why?

d. Has your child ever been sick? What are you supposed to do when someone has ____? (Repeat for any illnesses mentioned.)

Many other questions may best be answered by interviewing, but the selection of informants is very important when you begin to touch on potentially more sensitive questions. Someone well known to the interviewer, fully accepted by the community, and well informed about traditional beliefs and practices is ideal. Interviewing a small group rather than a single individual may yield more reliable information, although an interviewer who is not a member of that cultural group may find it more difficult to elicit sensitive information from a group than from an individual. In any case, any information which is given confidentially must be kept in confidence. Part of what must be determined by individual teachers is what cultural content should not be included in the curriculum or shared with others.

Observation is a primary method of data collection used by anthropologists, and ultimately of great value to teachers as well. The first steps in developing the skill require reporting observable behaviors without imposing value judgments or drawing conclusions, but more advanced steps involve making inferences about such unseeable aspects of culture as beliefs and values from the behaviors or things which are observed. The key to successful observation and inference is freeing oneself as much as humanly possible from the filter of one's own cultural experience (remembering that the possibilities for self-delusion are great). This requires cultural relativism, knowledge about cultural differences, and sensitivity and objectivity in perceiving others. Observation is often aided in educational training by check lists, including scales for "interaction analysis", but most of these begin with a cultural bias by having observers rate occurrences of "positive response", etc., without first determining what, positive response would be in the culture being observed. These should not be used in multicultural contexts without critical analysis for cultural bias.

When observing in classrooms, it is often useful to note differential behavior of students from dominant and minority groups, or of a student considered "well adjusted" by the teacher versus one with "problems". While the quantification of observational data may be useful for some purposes, the basic tasks to be emphasized here are *description* and *contrastive analysis*.

Observational exercises for teachers developing this skill might take the following form:

a. What question is to be answered? (e.g., *How do individuals organize themselves spatially in groups*? In the case of this question, behaviors are often best recorded in the form of a diagram indicating the location and/or pattern of movement of those being observed in relation to others in the same setting.)

b. Who is being observed? (List one or more individuals or groups, identifying by age, sex, role, and group membership.)

c. Where? (e.g., Setting: classroom, playground, home.)

d. In what situation and event? (e.g., In the classroom: reading lesson, committee project, or "free" activity.)

e. What is being done/not done? (By whom, to whom, in what manner, for what purpose, in what relation to other events?)

One observer answering this question in a bilingual kindergarten classroom noted that all of the Anglo children in the class were seated around tables during unstructured art activities, while all but one of the Latino children seated themselves in small groups on the floor, in close proximity. In one junior high social studies class I observed in which seating was student-selected, all and only Chinese students were in the two rows on the left side of the room, all and only Blacks were in the back of the middle and right two rows, and all and only Anglos were in the front of the middle and right rows. Much can reasonably be inferred about interaction patterns from such observational data, and more integrative classroom procedures suggested and evaluated on such bases—if integration is an educational goal.

Other questions which lend themselves to analysis from observational data are:

a. How do people greet each other? What forms of address are used between people in various roles?

b. Do girls interact with boys?

c. How is deference shown?

d. How are insults expressed?

e. Who may talk to whom? When? Where? About what?

f. How does dress differ for age, sex, and social class?

g. What methods for teaching and learning are used at home?

Still other questions may be answered on the basis of observational data, but require an additional level of inference and interpretation. These include:

a. What is the hierarchy of authority in the family?

b. Who has authority over whom? To what extent can one person's will be imposed on another? By what means?

c. What is the role of language in social control?

d. What constitutes a "positive response" by a teacher to a student? By a student to a teacher?

In these cases, observation should be combined with interviews of group members before interpretations can be considered at all reliable; hasty generalizations only add to the already abundant store of stereotypes.

Observation of student and teacher behaviors in the classroom or on the playground is easy to effect, but great care and tact should be exercised when behaviors are to be observed or interviews conducted in students" homes or elsewhere in the community. Willingness on the part of teachers to visit students" homes does not insure they will be welcome there, and the presence of an outsider in any case is likely to influence behaviors to a degree that makes observation of natural conditions very difficult. Prolonged contact with the community is generally necessary before observations in that context may be considered reliable.

With the involvement and consent of community members, however, cultural training should include guided information-gathering trips into the students' home area to observe, ask questions, test interaction techniques and reactions, and participate in community activities relating to the students. Other cultural training activities at this level might include preparation of behavioral profiles of culturally diverse students observed in demonstration classes or on video tape, objectively describing their language use, their non-linguistic interaction techniques, and their styles of coping and learning. This exercise should be followed by discussion and comparison of observations and interpretations among the teachers, with a leader who is trained and experienced in cross-cultural observation, and with one or more members of the other cultural group(s) being observed who have seen the same demonstration class or tape. Also useful is role-playing in assuming the role of parents or students in different cultural groups under different (staged) circumstances, again followed by supervised discussion of the interpretations.

Participant-observation skills must be developed by teachers in order to collect data in situations in which they are themselves taking part, including data on their own behaviors in relation to others. In these cases the use of a tape recorder can be an aid in reconstructing the event for description, as can videotaping when available. Also very valuable is team observation, where teachers take turns visiting each other's classes and comparing observations.

Teachers should also make a conscious effort to practice participant-observation skills within their own cultural group, whether dominant or subordinate in the larger society, and in the subculture of the school. Answers to the questions about culture which were arrived at in the earliest stages of training through introspection should be tested and expanded by teachers observing behaviors in themselves, family, and friends.

Contrastive analysis may simply involve a comparison of responses to questions about culture, and a search for systematic and consistent differences between cultural groups. Robert Lado suggests a model for contrasting aspects of culture which is quite relevant to educational purposes. He suggests that aspects of culture (as language) which are entirely different are less likely to cause interference and cultural misunderstanding than those which are similar on the surface but differ significantly in other ways. Three types of cultural difference which might predictably cause problems are:

a. Same form, different meaning.

Very similar (even the same) overt behaviors may have very different meanings in different cultures. Hissing, for example, means disapproval in the United States, but asks for group silence in Spanish-speaking countries; in Turkey, it may be a means of calling a cat. Silence, or lack of verbal response, in a conversation may mean agreement, disagreement, anger, insult, politeness, or deference, depending on the cultural context.

b. Same meaning, different form.

Depending on the culture, the meaning of "positive acceptance of a student by a teacher" might take the form of singling that student out for praise, of teasing, or of paying no apparent attention to the student at all. Students from different cultures requesting a teacher's attention might raise their hand, snap their fingers, or merely wait with an expectant posture.

c. Same form, same meaning, different distribution.

The same behaviors expressing the same meaning, such as cooperation on school assignments, may have culturally different contexts in which they are appropriate or inappropriate. The same "cooperative" behavior, for example, may be considered "cheating" on some occasions. Another type of problem in this category relates to social distribution, when the same form and meaning may hold for an aspect of culture across groups, but only for a restricted segment of one or both of the populations.

Different cultural groups often behave toward each other in accordance with the stereotypes they hold. To return to the general questions about culture which should pervade all data collection and analysis, we need to critically analyze all information for the effects of stereotyping, recognize the facts of acculturation, and be sensitive to individual differences.

The methods for getting answers which I have been discussing should be developed primarily through field-based training, but formal training in classes, workshops, and seminars can contribute to an understanding of cultural relativity as well, primarily by illustrating the great variety of beliefs, values, and behaviors which can and do occur in diverse cultures of the world. While no sets of culture traits described may be assumed to exactly fit any particular group of students, an awareness of the range of possibilities can help teachers think more flexibly about alternative life-ways, and thus ultimately be better prepared to recognize and accept the cultural diversity they encounter among their students. Course activities should include learning about the possible range of responses which might be given to questions such as those given earlier. The training program should include many specific examples from written sources or the experiences of the course instructor, participating teachers or teacher-trainees, and invited guests.

While printed lists of cultural traits cannot be accepted without question, the guided and critical analysis of such lists in group contexts may be useful in developing skills for recognizing stereotypes and cultural bias. Lists of dominant American culture traits, such as those prepared for the training of foreign service personnel, should be included for discussion.

Some programs include "cultural sensitivity" sessions of one kind or another, but these should be approached critically, and with great caution, inasmuch as they have the potential for doing more harm than good, or for creating a very superficial sense of understanding. The concept is a very important one, since having awareness, sensitivity, and knowledge about culture also entails being able to recognize cultural influences on oneself and others. All of us know that we have culture, but seldom do we recognize that this culture determines much of our own thinking and behavior. It is precisely because our culture is so much a part of us that it controls us at a subconscious level, unless we are trained to be conscious of its influence.

The potential hazard of "cultural sensitivity training" is that it may be limited to the "I'm O. K., you're O. K." variety, which may merely serve to reinforce naive ethnocentrism. True cultural sensitivity training means learning to observe cultural patterns and learning how to respond to them appropriately; it does not deal just with attitudes, but involves training in ethnographic, observational techniques and changes in unconscious micro-behaviors. It is an active process which has relevance for curriculum development, classroom practices, and testing.

Part Ⅳ

Key tO the Exercises

（客观题部分）

Part Ⅰ The United Kingdom of Great Britain and Northern Ireland

Chapter 1

Ⅱ. 1. four; Scotland; Wales; Northern Ireland

2. the Roman Empire; Vikings; the Normans

3. the 5th

4. London; government; economy; culture

5. overrule the parliament

6. Glasgow; Edinburgh

7. Scotland

8. 72; 38

9. Edinburgh; beauty

10. British; investment; America

Ⅲ. 1. C. 2. D. 3. A. 4. C. 5. A. 6. B. 7. B. 8. C. 9. D. 10. D.

Chapter 2

Ⅱ. 1. The Crusades

2. Columbus; Vasco da Gama

3. the Hundred Years' War

4. the parliament; the Crown
5. Charles Darwin
6. Great Depression
7. the League of Nations; the United Nations Organization

III. 1. D. 2. D. 3. A. 4. A. 5. D.

Chapter 3

II. 1. AD 587; 1066
2. Latin; Germanic
3. French
4. Anglo-Saxon; Latin; French
5. Middle English; Modern English
6. 1500
7. the educated southern upper classes

III. 1. D. 2. A. 3. C. 4. C.

Chapter 4

II. 1. King Egbert
2. the sovereign derived his authority from God, not from his subjects
3. roundheads; cavaliers
4. John, Magna Carta
5. the Great Council
6. the Bill of Rights
7. the Prime Minister
8. the Queen; the House of Commons
9. statute laws; the common laws; conventions
10. pass laws
11. the Queen; the House of Lords; the House of Commons
12. Windsor Castle; Buckingham Palace
13. the Prime Minister; the sovereign
14. male / patrilineal
15. Choose the correct answer in each of the following

III. 1. A. 2. C. 3. B. 4. C. 5. B. 6. A. 7. D. 8. A. 9. C. 10. A.

Chapter 5

II. 1. India; material

2. domestic industrial investment; overseas investment

3. a relative; an absolute

4. the International Monetary Fund

5. Margaret Thatcher; privatization

6. international direct investment

7. primary; tertiary / service

8. BSE disease

9. North Sea

10. drug; ICI

11. The London Stock Exchange

12. jet engine.

III. 1. C. 2. D. 3. D. 4. A. 5. B. 6. C. 7. B. 8. A. 9. B. 10. B. 11. A

Chapter 6

II. 1. Beowulf

2. The Canterbury Tales

3. tragedies; comedies; historical plays

4. Hamlet; Romeo and Juliet

5. Jane Eyre; Wuthering Heights

6. novelists; critics

7. Walter Scott; Robert L. Stevenson; Oliver Twister

8. Modernism; Postmodernism

9. 20th; female; the stream of consciousness

10. Joseph Conrad; John Fowles; George Orwell

11. The French Lieutenant's Woman

12. John Le Carre.

III. 1. A. 2. C. 3. C. 4. D. 5. B. 6. D. 7. A. 8. C. 9. B. 10. A

Chapter 7

II. 1. Roman Catholic Church; nonconformist Churches

2. Old Testament; New Testament

3. The Queen; the Primate of All England of the Archbishop of Canterbury

4. Jesus; Holy Spirit

5. Presbyterian
6. the Pope
7. the Church of England; the Methodist Church; the Congregational Church; Baptist Church; the Presbyterian.
8. lower species

Chapter 8

II. 1. ill-bred
2. modesty; self-praise
3. a sense of humor
4. sportsmanship as an English ideal

Chapter 9

II. 1. Oxford; Cambridge.
2. Eton; Winchester.
3. five; sixteen.
4. five; eleven; primary.
5. secondary; nineteen.
6. state; private.
7. private; education.
8. general; academic; practical.
9. St. Andrews; Glasgow.
10. Open university.
11. General Certificate of Secondary Education.
12. General Certificate of Education-Advanced.
13. General National Vocational Qualifications.

III. 1. C. 2. B. 3. A. 4. D. 5. D. 6. C. 7. A. 8. B. 9. D. 10. A

Chapter 10

II. 1. "White" territories; "Non-white" territories; Mixed territories
2. "Indians"; Eskimos; Aborigines; Maoris
3. Canada; Australia; New Zealand; English
4. India; Pakistan; Sri Lanka; Malaya
5. foreign; Color
6. the Queen

Part II The United States of America

Chapter 11

II. 1. 13,35, Hawaii, Alaska
2. Alaska, Virginia
3. Eastern, Central, Mountainous, Pacific
4. Maine, New Hampshire, Vermont, Connecticut, Massachusetts, Rhode Island
5. Pennsylvania, New Jersey, Maryland, New York, Delaware, West Virginia
6. Potomac, Washington
7. Appalachian, Vermont, Canada
8. Appalachian, Rocky
9. California, Oregon, Washington
10. Northeast, Mid-Atlantic, South, Mid-West, Pacific States, Western Part

III. 1. C 2. A 3. D 4. D 5. C 6. A

Chapter 12

II. 1. Letters from An American Farmer
2. Asia, Europe, Africa
3. Aztecs, Incas, Mayas
4. 1492
5. John Cabot
6. Martin Luther, John Calvin
7. Virginia, 1607
8. tobacco
9. Maryland, Catholic
10. Puritans, William Penn, Quaker
11. the spirit of liberty & equality, separation of state and church
12. The American Revolution

13. stamp tax, tea tax

14. the Second Continental Congress

III. 1. A 2. D 3. B 4. C 5. A 6. A 7. C 8. D 9. A 10. D

Chapter 13

II. 1. Congress, Articles of Confederation

2. Philadelphia

3. 1787, George Washington

4. a strong central government

5. power, central authority, its constituent parts

6. the executive, legislative, judicial

7. House of Representatives, 435, tbe Senate, 100

8. lobbies

10. judicial review

11. 26

12. Democratic, Republican, conservative

III. 1. D 2. B 3. B 4. A 5. B 6. C 7. C 8. B 9. D 10. A

Chapter 14

II. 1. Irving, Cooper

2. Edgar Allan Poe

3. Uncle Tom's Cabin

4. Huckleberry Finn

5. The American, Golden Bowl, Europe

6. Jungle

7. imagism

8. Wasteland, modern

9. Lost Generation

10. Great Gatsby

11. Old Man and Sea, A Farewell to Arms, The Sun also Rises

12. William Faulkner

13. Desire under the Elms, Long Day's Journey into Night

14. the Depression

15. The Native Son, Invisible Man, black

16. Howl

17. Toni Morrison, Song of Solomon, Be Loved

III. 1. C 2. D 3. B 4. A 5. B 6. C 7. A
8. A 9. D 10. D 11. A 12. B 13. A 14. D

Chapter 15

II. 1. White Anglo-Saxon Protestant
2. Protestant Religious groups
3. social contract
4. Deist
5. Ireland, Italy
6. unconstitutional
7. Protestant, Catholic, Jewish
8. 80%, vast majority hardly, half
9. First Amendment
10. John F. Kennedy

III. 1. B 2. C 3. C 4. D 5. A 6. D 7. A 8. B

Chapter 16

II. 1. stem, self-reliant, gracious, leisurely, casual, friendly
2. cooking styles, speech patterns
3. Declaration of Independence
4. equal treatment, equal opportunity
5. right to safety, right to be informed, right to choose, right to be heard
6. product safety, truth in advertisement
7. friendly, spontaneous, adaptable, efficient, energetic, kind-hearted

III. 1. A 2. D 3. D 4. C 5. B 6. D

Chapter 17

II. 1. 12, and most good students can get financial help to continue their study
2. age
3. kindergarten classes for 5-year-olds
4. grammar/elementary school
5. population explosion, popularization of higher education
6. G. I. Bill
7. Football

III. 1. C 2. D 3. C 4. A 5. D

Chapter 18

II. 1. rural & small town, urban, suburban

2. each resident owns his own apartment

3. youth, a feeling of being respected, wanted and needed

4. apartment buildings containing 2 to 6 apartments

Chapter 19

II. 1. 4th Thursday in November, blessings they enjoy

2. Ireland, persecution

3. a share of the profits from the new colony

4. Dec. 25th, the birth of Jesus Christ

5. red and green

III. 1. B 2. C 3. A 4. A 5. C 6. D

Chapter 20

II. 1. Nixon

2. many burglaries of wire-tapping

3. compiling dossiers on many Americans, infiltration into the civil rights and Anti-war movements

4. Anglo-Saxon

5. Civil War, Lincoln's emancipation of slaves in 1863, 13th Amendment to the Constitution in 1865

6. passed segregation laws, institutionalized discrimination

7. male, young, a member of a racial minority group, older, wealthier, whiter

8. CIA

III. 1. A 2. D 3. C 4. C 5. D 6. B